THE O

BL
PRICE GUIDE OF UNITED STATES COINS

TWENTY-NINTH EDITION

BY MARC HUDGEONS, N.L.G.

HOUSE OF COLLECTIBLES • NEW YORK

Important Notice. All of the information, including valuations, in this book has been compiled from the most reliable sources, and every effort has been made to eliminate errors and questionable data. Nevertheless, the possibility of error, in a work of such immense scope, always exists. The publisher will not be held responsible for losses which may occur in the purchase, sale, or other transaction of items because of information contained herein. Readers who feel they have discovered errors are invited to *write* and inform us, so they may be corrected in subsequent editions. Those seeking further information on the topics covered in this book are advised to refer to the complete line of *Official Price Guides* published by the House of Collectibles.

This is a registered trademark of Random House, Inc.

Cover: 1804 Dexter Silver Dollar. The most valuable U.S. coin ever sold at auction, it was jointly purchased by Blanchard and The American Rare Coin Fund on July 7, 1989, for the total price of $990,000. *Courtesy of Stack's, New York. Cover photo by George Kerrigan.*

Published by: The House of Collectibles
201 East 50th Street
New York, New York 10022

Distributed by Ballantine Books, a division of Random House, Inc., New York, and simultaneously in Canada by Random House of Canada Limited, Toronto.

Manufactured in the United States of America

Library of Congress Catalog Card Number: 79-643730

ISBN: 0-876-37823-8

Twenty-Ninth Edition: July 1990

10 9 8 7 6 5 4 3 2 1

TABLE OF CONTENTS

The publisher also wishes to express special thanks to the American Numismatic Association for their continuing support and assistance. Certain photographs are courtesy of the Bowers and Merena Galleries, Inc., Wolfboro, NH 03894.

PUBLISHER'S NOTE

This book is presented as a guide to the values of U.S. coins, as an aid for the beginner, advanced collector, and dealer. We are not dealers. We do not buy or sell coins. Prices listed are intended as a guide only and are not warranted for accuracy.

MARKET REVIEW

As we enter a new decade, we look back on the 1980s as a very interesting and exciting time of growth for coin collectors. Many new issues of coins have appeared, such as gold coins, bullion coins, and many commemorative issues which contributed to the excitement during the last decade. Experienced and new collectors alike realize that these relatively new issues could be the serious collectible of tomorrow. The continuance of these issues and many new issues should ensure the stability of the field of numismatics in the future. Nineteen eighty-nine had its ups and downs, but it also produced one of the strongest periods of growth in coin collecting history. Record prices were paid for many rare or scarce dates. The number of auctions has increased as well as produced record sales. Quality slab, certified, graded coins have become the word of the day as far as finer grade coins are concerned; watch for this trend to continue to grow. Growth can be measured by strength in the market. During the middle of 1989, a forty million dollar limited partnership was formed for the purpose of investing in a wide variety of numismatic material. If growth can be measured by the dollar strength in the market, this indicates an even stronger decade to come for collectors.

Knowledgeable collectors are aware of the truly limited number of high quality, scarce coins that remain in existence. It is a very limited supply from which to draw. At the present time, the demand to purchase this type of material is growing. However, more and more investors and collectors will realize that there is an extremely limited supply and any slight increase in demand will, without question, dramatically increase the price on any specific rare coin. As an example, look at the astronomical prices being paid for one-of-a-kind art and, if you examine this further, you will see the same huge increases for lesser artists. These prices have increased because collectors believe that one day all major pieces of art will fall into the hands of individuals who can afford to keep them and, therefore, will almost never be sold or, if sold, will be so expensive that even the largest museums could not afford the price. Another example is the classic car market. Millions of dollars are now being paid for cars that only a few years ago sold for a few thousand dollars, because there is a very limited supply of these collectibles. As this knowledge is applied to the coin market, it will only be a matter of time before a similar cycle will be experienced in the coin market.

While this kind of activity is good for the hobby in general, it is still important to be cautious. We must continue to study and learn as much as possible about the hobby of coin collecting.

1990s

Many new and exciting things are on the horizon for the 1990s. Discussions as to the possible changing of coin design have all been forgotten, yet some say the idea is not dead and those who remain interested in these changes are waiting for the right moment to try again. There is still talk about phasing out the common one-cent piece as we know it. Interesting, but will it happen? The latest good news is the possibility of restoring .90 fine silver coins in proof sets starting in 1990. Many other rumors are flying. While some will remain as rumors, many will become a reality.

Several areas of coin collecting have been fairly constant throughout the last several years, with recent gains on a steady upward trend.

All better-grade type coins have probably had the highest increases in any category, along with most high-grade and key-date gold coins. These two areas should be watched for continued growth.

Proof and mint sets are steady with increases in several early and specific dates. Watch for a bigger and better decade. All Large cents and Small cents ranging from early Large cents, Flying Eagle cents, Indian Head cents, and finally including Lincoln cents have had very little growth. Demand is almost nonexistent. The only pieces that have increased at all are several scarce or key dates. These prices have increased slightly. It is difficult to figure out why. We see many dates that could be bargains and should be picked up.

Early Shield nickels, Buffalo nickels, and Jefferson nickels have all suffered the same fate as cents. Again, there have been occasional and moderate increases on key or rare dates but, overall, very soft demand. There is no specific reason. Just keep looking for future growth and hope. Early Barber dimes, Mercury dimes, and Roosevelt dimes fared slightly better than cents and nickels, but not much. There is spotty action on key pieces and BU rolls. Early Barber material should begin to move upward.

Put dimes in a plus situation. Quarters and half dollars have had firm movement. Prices are higher on several dates. Overall, silver dollars have moved ahead, with many key dates and better grades showing most of the increases. Look for this series to move forward in the near future.

Older issue commemoratives have shown increases mostly in MS-60 condition. Recent issues have been pretty steady. In and of themselves, these new issues will be important as having another issue to collect. But more importantly, it gives the hobby something to talk about; the publicity these kinds of things promote is an important part of numismatics that newspapers write about. TV and radio news releases will report them and books will be written about them. The more material that is created and disbursed to the public, the more collectors will become involved and the more investors and collectors will be created.

One recent area of collecting that has had great impact on the hobby is the slab certified grading system of coins. While this concept has produced many supporters, it has developed some problems. Slab coins and their grading systems are good and afford great stability to the hobby. In fact, in years to come, most coins will be bought and sold in this fashion. The problems that this system may have created will be worked out by those involved in the trading of this material. It may take a little time, but it will be resolved.

Reflecting back on the 1980s, it certainly had its ups and downs. For the most part, it was very quiet but also a period of great changes and adjustments. In our opinion, all were changes for the better. The 1990s will still be a period of changes and adjustments and, in addition, it will be a great decade for the numismatic's positive healthy growth and stability.

COIN CERTIFICATION

By Robert W. Cornely, Sr.

More than a decade ago, the American Numismatic Association began certifying U.S. coins. The original intent of the ANA effort was to provide expert, unbiased opinions on the authenticity of rare coins. The opinion supplied was whether or not the coin was genuine. Certification evolved, by public demand, to include an opinion on the grade of the coin.

A fee was charged for the service and the ANA earned a tidy sum over the years, certifying coins for anyone who would send a coin with the proper fee. Problems occurred when the marketplace began discounting the price for ANA certified coins that had older papers, as the American Numismatic Association Certification Service periodically changed or refined the grading criteria it employed. Thus, a coin certified as an MS-65 in 1980 often could only meet the requirement to be graded MS-63 if submitted for certification in 1983. This created more problems and the marketplace demanded solutions.

ENTER THE PRIVATE CERTIFICATION SERVICE

By the mid 1980s, the Numismatic Certification Institute introduced a guaranteed certification service that became an immediate hit. Their fees were reasonable, their processing time was prompt, and their packaging and marketing propelled NCI to the forefront.

THE SLAB

It did not take long for the competition to announce "a better mousetrap." The Professional Coin Grading Service eliminated the necessity of photographing coins in the certification process by sonically sealing each coin along with a slip of the coin description, serial number, and grade in an inert, hard plastic container. PCGS also created a nationwide dealer network that would buy and sell PCGS certified coins on a sight-unseen basis. This provided liquidity to the coin marketplace.

PCGS grades uncirculated U.S. coins in one-point increments from MS-60 through MS-70. No other grading entity had attempted this complex task on a mass basis before. The grading criteria for the one-point incremental system has not been made public, and the criteria used by PCGS is unique to them.

The Numismatic Guarantee Corporation was quick to follow PCGS with a hard, plastic slab and the eleven grades of uncirculated coins (MS-60, 61, 62, 63, 64, 65, 66, 67, 68, 69, and 70). NGC also has a dealer network and enjoys widespread acceptance in the marketplace. The grading criteria is unique to NGC.

SUBMITTING COINS FOR CERTIFICATION

Coins must be submitted to PCGS and NGC by coin dealers who are affiliated with these associations, otherwise they will not be accepted for certification.

Coins may be submitted to ANACS or NCI directly. ANA will certify coins with a photographic certificate or in a slab. The grading criteria used by each grading entity is not the same as that used by any other.

COIN GRADING: AN EVOLUTIONARY PROCESS

There has never been a comprehensive grading criteria for U.S. coins that has been uniformly interpreted and accepted by the marketplace. There has been talk of electronic laser grading technology that is currently being developed; some hope that will solve the problem. Beauty will always be in the eyes of the beholder but, for right now, certification by one of the leading services seems to offer the coin owner a means of realizing better prices if he wishes to sell in the marketplace today.

PEOPLE PAY MORE FOR COINS THEY LIKE

The idea that a coin certified in a slab is a guarantee of realizing prices in current sheets is pure fiction. It is as it always has been: dealers pay more for the coin they like the looks of, as they have done since coin collecting began.

This article was prepared by:

Robert W. Cornely, Sr.
Numismatic Consultant
Member ANA since 1959
4665 Lower Roswell Road
Marietta, Georgia 30068

Any comments or questions related to this article can be sent to Mr. Cornely directly.

SPECIAL REPORT: ERRORS AND VARIETIES

Error and variety collecting has become one of the most popular facets of numismatics. Some coins of this nature have traditionally been listed in the *Blackbook,* while space limitations have prevented inclusion of numerous others. This special report is designed to acquaint *Blackbook* readers with the various types of error and variety coins.

As with any product manufactured in large numbers, variations can occur in the striking of coins. Almost everyone has noticed, in ordinary pocket change, coins displaying some abnormality. While the majority of such "odd" coins found in common circulation are not true errors or varieties, some do, indeed, reach circulation. These, of course, are few in number compared to the quantities created over the years and available on the numismatic market. Ever since establishment of the U.S. Mint, nearly 200 years ago, coins that can be classified as errors and varieties have been produced. Some of these coins are so bizarre and exotic that they can be spotted at first glance by anyone. In others, the variation from strict normality is slight, requiring numismatic knowledge and, usually, the aid of a magnifying glass to distinguish the variation.

In learning about error and variety coins it is important, initially, to realize that the two terms are used to mean two distinctly different things. While a numismatist often collects both error and variety coins, these are separate groups unto themselves. The term *variety* is applied to any coin that differs in any respect from the standard issue of that year and type. The difference or variation may be intentional, and in most cases is. But whether intentional or not, the variety coin is nearly always manufactured from a die (or dies) which impart its variation. Hence this variation—which could be an overdate, a doubling, a re-engraving, etc.—is likely to appear on a rather substantial number of coins. An error coin, on the other hand, is manufactured from normal dies. Its abnormality results from a malfunction of the coin-striking machinery, or any one of the other various processes leading up to a finished coin. The error may be in the alloying of metal, long before the planchet or blank rides down into the machinery for striking: in other words, its fate as an error coin is sealed even if the striking is accomplished without incident. By and large, it is these coins, the victims of mechanical malfunction, that have the more obvious appearance of being "different."

In the collecting of error and variety coins, a number of factors contribute to the desirability of any given specimen and thereby aid in establishing a market value. On the whole, it is more difficult to state precise market values for error coins than for variety coins, owing to the fact that each error coin tends to be slightly different than any others. With variety coins, this difficulty is not normally encountered, as any defect or variation in the die will produce numerous identical coins. Because of this, situations sometimes occur in which the variety is no scarcer than the ordinary standard coin of that year and type; or, if it is scarcer, its greater scarcity is not sufficient to exercise any influence on demand or market value. The early Half Dollar series offers a number of examples of this phenomenon. The 1807 Capped Bust includes a Small Stars, Large Stars, and "Fifty over Twenty" variety out of a total mintage in the neighborhood of three quarters of a million. It is not known which of the three had the smallest mintage, and the only tangible evidence—the quantities of each passing through the rare coin market—fails to provide a strong clue. Roughly the same circumstance prevails with the 1811 Half Dollar, where one finds a Small 8, a Large 8 and the so-called *Punctuated Date.* Though the Punctuated Date is the most unusual of the 1811 varieties, and might be suspected on that account to be the rarest, this is not an established fact. If three dies were being used and one had a Punctuated Date, all three varieties were probably turned out in similar numbers. The same is true if six dies were used and two had Punctuated Dates, and so on. The Mint itself has no records of any of this, so it remains within the province of numismatists to speculate upon.

Another important point to be kept in mind, for the beginner just entering into error and variety coinage, is that *varieties* are more plentiful on the very old coins, while *errors* are far more common on modern coins. This is due to the methods used in minting. The pioneer techniques of minting were slow and deliberate, basically involving hand work. This made for a low proportion of errors while, at the same time, the limited output of coins enabled each specimen to be examined before distribution. Even if the early Mint did make many errors, which is doubtful, its error coins were almost always detected and not permitted to enter circulation. Today there is *absolutely no* examination of coins after production, except for proofs going into the Mint's proof sets. The business strike coins designed for general use are not even subject to a passing glance before being bagged and trucked to Federal Reserve Banks. *Varieties* are more plentiful on the old coins because the dies were not machine-made and were not, like present-day coin dies, duplicates of each other. The dates, for example, were individually punched or sunk into the dies by hand, as were some of the other coin design elements such as stars beside the Liberty Head portrait. Thus, there was the opportunity for considerable variation from one die to another, even if no actual error was involved in their preparation.

Phantoms. This category comprises coins which appear to be errors or varieties but which, upon analysis, fall into other groups. While many phantoms could be confusing to an inexperienced collector, they are weeded out from the coin market with no great difficulty. Phantoms include coins whose abnormalities result from post-striking damage, intentional and accidental, and coins doctored into novelties for sale to the general public.

Post-Striking Damage. An absolute and unbending rule of the hobby is that any abnormalities of a coin must have occurred during the manufacturing process to render the coin collectible. If the abnormality has resulted subsequent to manufacture, the coin is worthless as a collector's item, regardless of the extent or oddity of its abnormality. Most freak coins seen in everyday change fall into this category. They left the Mint in quite ordinary condition and became "different" at some point thereafter. From a numismatic point of view, "subsequent to manufacture" means anything that happens after the actual striking itself, which is the final phase of operation in coin production. Even if a coin is damaged at the Mint, before or while being bagged, it cannot qualify as an error if this damage occurred after striking. Once having entered circulation, coins can understandably fall victim to damage of various descriptions. Even purely accidental damage can, in some instances, impart a most unusual appearance to a coin, while intentional damage—which is common—knows no bounds. The most frequent sort of accidental damage involves the coin contacting some heavy or sharp object, with the result that it becomes warped, dented, bent, or otherwise disfigured. Coins that have been dropped on the ground and lost, remaining outdoors for months or possibly years, may acquire a corrosive surface which can be mistaken for an alloying deficiency. This is most likely to happen when the coin is in contact with an acidic soil or sand. By the same token, a coin may turn black or some other color in the same way. Black copper pennies, which are quite common and of absolutely no premium value, have in most cases been victims of excess acidity over a long period of time. It would be easy to create such coins artificially, by bathing them in citric acid, but as they have no sales value this is not done.

Intentional damage is often, though far from exclusively, the result of a fraudulent effort to sell an ordinary coin as an error. Some of the defects found on genuine error coins can be imitated by doctoring ordinary ones, while others are very difficult or impossible to imitate. One of the simplest for the faker is the clipped planchet coin, in which a portion of the planchet is missing. In a genuine specimen this occurred before striking, and the portion of design intended for the missing portion is naturally absent. Using a vise and power tools, the faker can break or saw off a portion of a coin. The fake thus created, though unconvincing to an expert, may possibly fool some collectors and earn a small profit for the faker. If such errors commanded high prices, it is quite probable that faking would become widespread.

There are other ways in which phantoms can be fraudulently created. So-called *brockage strikes* are among the favorites of fakers as they can be counterfeited with relatively little in the way of equipment or labor. These coins have a reverse image of the same coin atop their design, either on one or both sides, but most often on only one. When a brockage strike is created at the Mint, it is the fault of a coin failing to eject from the collar or holder during the striking process. Another planchet is fed in before the previous one is ejected, with the result that the fresh planchet does not contact the die but rather contacts the previously struck coin. This error is counterfeited by placing two coins of the same type together, possibly heating them a bit, and using pressure to transfer the impression of one coin to the other. The pressure is supplied with a vise, by pounding with a sledgehammer, by a hydraulic press, or in various other ways.

The more sophisticated fakers have created an array of other fakes, sometimes including errors which have no real counterpart among authentic error coins. Space does not permit a detailed discussion of this subject, but one or two random examples may help to illustrate the point. The faker may file the designs away from an ordinary coin, which is quite easy to do using mechanical files such as those employed by geologists and gem cutters. At this point he has what appears to be a blank, shiny planchet that escaped the Mint without being struck. Depending on his wishes and the degree of trouble to which he cares to subject himself, he can attempt to sell the item as an unstruck planchet or he can use it in fabricating another type of error coin. Unstruck, blank planchets are collectible when genuine, though their price is modest. An unstruck Lincoln Cent planchet sells for only about $1, so this is definitely not the road to riches for a faker, unless he can turn them out by the hundreds per day. Furthermore, he might well encounter difficulty in attempting to sell such a fabrication, unless the intended victim had little numismatic knowledge. A blank planchet created in this manner, by filing down the design from an authentic coin, will have a weight of considerably less than that within the Mint's established tolerance ranges. A good deal of metal is lost in the filing process, so the coin becomes thinner and consequently lighter in weight. If the coin is clad, it may even begin to show the core material.

Should the faker decide that the low monetary return plus the risk of detection renders the sale of his "blank planchet" inadvisable, he can continue to operate upon it until he has succeeded in achieving something more salable. This will usually be accomplished by creating a very dramatic 70%–80% off-center strike, using a genuine coin or coins from which to obtain the design impressions plus the aforementioned vise, hydraulic press, or other equipment. The faker now has something which might sell for a good deal more than the $1 or so potential of his faked blank planchet. It could have a possible sales value of $100, $200, or even more. But there is a slight problem: if such a coin were genuine, it would be difficult to explain why the design is reversed in mirror image. Often the faker is bold enough to look upon this kind of circumstance as an advantage to himself, rather than a disadvantage. He has created an error specimen so different, so unusual, so bizarre that (in his view at least) it cannot fail to be appealing to devotees of the unique. Often he is correct.

Novelty Coins. Very prevalent among the phantoms are novelty coins, with which almost everyone is familiar. These are not classified as fakes, as they are not manufactured with the intent of selling them as genuine errors to numismatists. Rather, their potential audience is the general public, and they tend to be channeled along in the market with all other types of novelties such as magic tricks, exploding cigars, fake dice, and the like. They are widely sold by mail order, but this is not their only means of distribution. Included among the novelties are coins with two heads or two tails; Lincoln Cents with Lincoln smoking a pipe; Kennedy and Lincoln on the same coin; coins that have been dipped or washed to resemble a different metal ("gold pennies"), and numerous others. It is safe, perhaps, to state that the majority are of such an obviously impossible nature that they could not be mistaken by anyone as genuine error or variety coins. The chief exception to this statement is the double-sided coin or "gambler's coin," having two heads or (less frequently) two tails. Some persons who are not familiar with coin collecting or the study of error coins truly believe, or can be talked into believing, that such coins could be authentic Mint errors. Of course it is impossible under any minting process, old or new, for a coin to strike heads on both sides or tails on both sides. This is one of the "phantoms" that simply cannot exist. As these coins are made strictly as novelties, no great pains are taken to hide the evidence of doctoring, as would normally be the case in fakes designed for possible sale to collectors at high prices. In manufacturing a coin with two heads or two tails, two coins are used. Each is split down the core, and the two appropriate halves are joined together, usually with a common metal bonding glue. Sometimes the overflow of glue is noticeable on the edge. Even when this is not the case, it is very obvious that two halves of coins were joined together, as the coin has a seam running around its circumference. In the case of a fake designed for the numismatic market, an effort would be made to file down or otherwise conceal the seam. Some numismatic fakes are indeed made by cutting two coins in half and joining together the desired halves. This is not done too frequently but it happens, such as in the case of a coin which is rarer with one type of reverse than another.

Novelty coins, it should be noted, have a very long and even (surprisingly) a somewhat distinguished history. While coin collectors are definitely not interested in the novelty coins now being produced, a market does exist for older novelties. These are frequently sold by dealers and offered in coin auctions. Novelty coins have been made for well over 200 years, initially in Europe and later in the United States. One of the most popular types is the so-called pill box coin. These were made by taking a very large, thick coin such as the British twopence "cartwheel" of George III and slicing it into two halves. The halves, each of which was thicker than a U.S. Silver Dollar, were hollowed out and then rejoined with a hinge at the side. The coin thus became a small box which could be carried in a gentleman's pocket or lady's purse as a container for pills, snuff, tobacco, or any small articles. This type of novelty coin is worth a good deal more than the ordinary coin from which it was produced, if it can be shown to be an early product rather than something of recent vintage. In the case of a pill box made from a British twopence cartwheel, the ordinary coin in average circulated condition is worth only about $20, while the box made from it will sell for $100 to $150. Another coin used in the manufacture of pill boxes was the ten kopecks copper of Russia dating from the reign of Catherine the Great. This immense coin is larger in diameter than the British cartwheel but is not quite as thick. It is also a much rarer and more valuable coin, and it is *not* more valuable when made into a box. There has never been a U.S. coin thick enough to be suitable for a pill box, so you will not find this novelty among our coins. However, there were many other novelties made from our earlier coins. Among the most prevalent, and very highly collectible, is the advertising coin. These are mainly Silver Dollars and Half Dollars of the period from about 1870 to 1900, though occasionally one finds a Quarter of that era that was utilized as an advertising coin. In most instances the coin, itself, was not tampered with in manufacturing an advertising coin. It was simply fitted into a collar, usually of copper or nickel but sometimes silver, and the advertising message was imprinted on the collar. Advertising coins may also be found with celluloid collars that have colored printing, but the metallic collars are more numerous. Less often, advertising coins were made by filing down one of the sides, removing its design, and imprinting it with the advertising slogan, message, and/or illustration. While there was no law against doing this, the practice was less frequent because it entailed greater labor and expense, and the resulting product was not as eye-catching as the collared advertising coin. These early advertising coins are collected and valued according to the company whose advertising they carry. Some are extremely rare, only one or two examples being recorded, while others rank as relatively common.

Another type of early U.S. novelty coin, which is extremely popular as a collector's item, is the *love token.* This was made by taking a silver coin, usually a Quarter or Dime, and removing the design from the reverse side. The design was replaced by an engraving of a heart, or sometimes an elaborate engraving with cupids and cherubs, coupled with initials and a presentation inscription. Of course the really elaborate work had to be done on a coin larger than a Dime. Sometimes one finds love tokens made from Silver Dollars but these are quite out of the ordinary. Those made from Dimes and Quarters exist in the multi-thousands and are stocked by quite a few coin dealers, as well as dealers in antique jewelry. After completion of the artwork they were fixed with a loop, or simply punched with a hole near the top, to be strung on a thin chain and worn as a pendant. There was a nationwide craze for these love tokens, beginning around 1880 and extending into the 1890s. At that time they were in such demand that all commercial jewelers made them. Each one was made to order as far as the engraving was concerned, but the jewelers kept scraped coins on hand so they could fill a customer's order while he waited. In most cases, love tokens are worth more than the coin would have been worth if left alone.

The 1943 Copper Cent. This is undoubtedly the most celebrated of all error and variety coins. It is very rare, very expensive, and highly controversial. The *Blackbook* does not list this coin insofar as the opinion of experts is divided on whether it can be regarded as a true Mint issue. Some experts consider it perfectly legitimate. Apparently this view is not only widely held but gaining ground, as the coin could not otherwise command the sort of prices at which it sells (in the $10,000–$20,000 range). Much of the suspicion and doubt surrounding the 1943 copper Cent is not really the fault of the coin itself, but of fakes that have surfaced over the years. During the late 1940s and early 1950s, when it was worth a few hundred dollars, scores of bogus specimens were turning up, made by dipping the standard 1943 steel Cent into copper or bronze wash. Some dealers saw so many of these fakes that they gradually began doubting the existence of any actual 1943 copper Cents. They simply said, "no, thank you" whenever one was offered to them, without even examining it. As this practice of refusing to handle 1943 copper Cents became widespread in the trade, it naturally brought a stigma on the coin, the remnants of which still persist after thirty or more years. Then there were the dealers (and collectors, too, as the collecting community was by no means universally convinced of their authenticity) who would give a standard reply to all inquiries about the coin: "It cannot exist because the Mint claims it does not exist." It is entirely correct that official Mint records indicate the production of no copper Cents dated 1943, and accepting that testimony as conclusive, one would have a difficult time nurturing any trust in the 1943 copper Cent. We know for a fact, however, that official Mint reports are not infallible evidence of the existence, or lack of existence, of any particular coins. A number of coins that are not in official Mint records are very much in physical existence, and their authenticity as actual Mint products has been accepted. By the same token, some coins said to have been struck by the Mint cannot be found, even in a single solitary specimen. This is not an indication that the Mint records are in actual error, however. It is a matter of interpretation of the word "official," as applied to "officially produced." There is every likelihood that some coins have been struck at the Mint, by parties unknown, which were not authorized and not accounted for in official tabulations. This may be the explanation for the 1943 copper Cent: a coin collector or prankster at the Mint who fed a number of copper planchets in with the millions upon millions of steel planchets. There could, however, be other explanations. A small quantity of copper planchets used in striking the 1942 Cent might have remained in one of the storage tubs after it was presumed to be empty. Considering the immense size of these tubs, a few dozen small planchets could easily have escaped attention, especially if they blended in with the tub's natural color.

Even if a prankster was not responsible for the 1943 copper Cent, one was almost certainly to blame—or credit, depending on your convictions—for the 1913 Liberty Nickel. This coin is rarer than the 1943 copper Cent but is not technically an error or variety: it is just a highly mysterious coin. Only five specimens are known to exist and once again this is a coin that the Mint denies having produced. All Nickels for 1913 were supposed to carry the Buffalo/Indian Head design, and these are the only Nickels included in the Mint's report for that year. The circumstances surrounding discovery of the five known 1913 Liberty Nickels were suspicious, to put things mildly. All five turned up in the possession of the same person, a noted coin and stamp collector of that era named Colonel Edward Howland Robinson Green. Colonel Green was the son of Hetty Green, the so-called female wizard of Wall Street. At an early age he lost a leg and spent the remainder of his life dabbling in various hobbies, on which he reputedly spent several million dollars. There is no evidence to suggest that Colonel Green was responsible for manufacturing, or causing to be manufactured, the five 1913 Liberty Nickels. However, it is entirely possible that he was indirectly responsible. Quite possibly some worker at the Mint, knowing of the Colonel's reputation as a buyer of odd and curious collectors' items, manufactured these coins with the intent of selling them to him. This would, of course, not be so simple a matter as slipping a few copper planchets into a storage bin; it would require a Liberty die with a 1913 date, which the Mint professes was not available. The Mint employee intent on this deception, if indeed such an individual existed, could not have fashioned such a die single-handedly. This fact seems to refute the "prankster" theory. But suppose such a die already existed, having been made by the Mint sometime during 1912 for potential use the following year in the event of a continuation of the Liberty design and then stored away and forgotten. If the existence of this die escaped being recorded in Mint records, an opportunity would certainly have been presented to create a coin about which the Mint knew nothing. This is really the only logical explanation for the existence of the 1913 Liberty Nickel. Had a 1913 die with Liberty design been inadvertently placed in use on one of the Mint's striking machines, it would have produced a good deal more than five coins before being noticed.

Another Odd Nickel: Josh Tatum's "Gold Five." One of the most celebrated of all phantom coins, and the one which caused the most embarrassment to the Mint, was the "gold" Nickel of 1883. Prior to 1883, and, in fact, for several months during that year, the U.S. 5¢ piece carried a shield design on one side and the number five on the other, with the word CENTS beneath it. In 1883 a switch was made in design, placing a Liberty head on the obverse and changing the Arabic "five" on the reverse to a Roman five, represented by the letter V. This would have worked smoothly but for one apparently insignificant detail. In an effort to achieve a design of classical symmetry and appeal, it was decided to omit the word CENTS, in the presumption that the letter V was a sufficient identification of the coin's face value. In 1883 Roman numbers were known by every school child, so there was, supposedly, no danger of confusion. Also, the coin's size was different than that of any other U.S. coin. Its size most closely approximated that of the Quarter, but there was certainly enough difference to easily distinguish them.

Just as the Mint had anticipated, there was no objection from the general public to this new "no cents" Nickel. But another problem, which the Mint had not even considered, soon occurred. An ingenious tramp named Josh Tatum, who became immortalized in history for this one devilish act, struck upon a method of earning a $4.95 profit from every one of the new nickels. He bought a bottle of gold varnish from the hardware store and dipped the Nickels, turning them a bright golden color. Now that they were "gold," that V on the back could not possibly indicate just 5¢. It had to mean $5. Josh knew how to pass and promote the coins. He pushed them on shopkeepers whom he knew to be nearsighted, and on foreigners unfamiliar with our coinage. He spoke of how this country "sure makes funny gold coins." Sometimes his "gold fives" were refused. But surprisingly, more often than not he was successful. His favorite approach was to buy a 5¢ cigar and receive $4.95 change. The change would, of course, include at least one nickel, and if it was a new "no cents" variety Josh promptly dipped it and made himself another $4.95. Josh tried this a little too often, and was finally apprehended, after he had apparently collected several hundred dollars on the scheme. But the court, which found the whole case rather hilarious, acquitted him on all counts. Josh Tatum's defense was that he was just joking, and a new phrase—"just Joshing"—found its way into the language.

Needless to say, the Mint quickly changed the design and installed the word CENTS beneath the V symbol, but this was not done until five and a half million of the "no cents" Nickels reached circulation. Josh Tatum probably varnished close to a hundred of those, and possibly a few imitators of his were responsible for some too. Sad to say, it is virtually impossible to distinguish an authentic Josh Tatum "gold Nickel." After all the publicity surrounding Josh, many promoters began selling souvenir Nickels that had been treated in similar fashion. Even many years afterward, people were dipping the 1883 "no cents" Nickels in gold varnish, selling them as "Josh Tatum Nickels." But the uncoated 1883 "no cents" Nickels are available on the numismatic market and rank as a desirable collector's item. This is a major variety which has always been regarded as such and has always had its listing in the *Blackbook*.

Early Varieties. The early formative years of the U.S. Mint witnessed an excessive number of varieties, occurring on almost every denomination during each year of manufacture, sometimes to the extent of 20, 30, or more varieties for a single coin. Of course, these were not all in the category of *major varieties*. Most of them are in the nature of die breaks or cracks, which, as a rule, are not regarded as major varieties. In fact, until fairly recently many of these die-break coins were totally overlooked except by the most advanced specialists. When sold, they were not identified as varieties at all. It will probably be years before die-break varieties are assigned listings in a publication such as the *Blackbook,* but their absence from listings does not reflect upon their legitimacy. They *are* genuine varieties, and to some collectors, especially numismatists of a scholarly turn of mind, are of far greater interest than other types of varieties. One of the intriguing features of die-break varieties is that they sometimes show the gradual breaking or splitting of the die, in stages from minor to serious. A tiny die crack on one coin can often be identified as the beginning of a very large die crack on another coin of the same year. This shows that both coins were struck from the same die and that the specimen exhibiting the smaller crack was struck earlier. Pinpointing die cracks and their contours is a source of satisfaction to the advanced collector. Affording them can be a problem. Most of the coins involved are over 150 years old and quite expensive. Furthermore, to observe the crack clearly it is necessary to have a specimen in uncirculated or AU condition, as any slight surface wear will have obliterated evidence of the die crack.

The abundance of die-crack varieties throughout our early coins bears testimony to the Mint's poverty at that time. Workers were instructed to keep dies in service so long as the die was capable of producing a coin of respectable appearance. Die cracks, unless extremely severe, were not considered sufficiently detrimental to call for scrapping the die. The economic considerations went beyond the mere cost of producing fresh dies. Unless a large batch of dies was kept on hand—which might never be used—it would then be necessary to interrupt production or at least slow it down while replacement dies were being manufactured. This cost would have been greater than the mere expense of making the dies themselves. So the Mint made do. Most dies were kept in use until they literally fell apart, or until the cracks became so wide that some of the coin's design no longer struck the planchet.

The methods by which coins were manufactured by the U.S. Mint in its early years were essentially responsible for the majority of varieties. While some *striking* varieties can be found, 99% of our early coin varieties were accounted for by variations in the dies. They are *die varieties.* Those are the two major categories of varieties among all coins as a whole: die varieties and striking varieties.

The large number of overdates among our early coins comprises an interesting group of varieties. Of course, overdates per se are by no means confined to early coins; they have occurred on coins of the 20th century, but most of them belong to the era before 1830. Their explanation is the same as that for die-crack varieties: economy. When the production year had come to an end, a review was made of all the dies then in use. Those with noticeable cracks were set aside, as it was considered less than worthwhile to repunch them only to have them break after a few weeks of renewed use. The better preserved dies were punched with the new date in cases where this could be done without much difficulty. Making a change from 1799 to 1800 was a major undertaking, as it involved three digits. Most changes involved only one digit, and if they were roughly similar in shape, such as 8 and 9, this was considered ideal. There were several possible approaches to actually doing this. The new digit or digits had to be stamped in with a punch, but before doing this it might be necessary to do some work on the die.

If the die was still quite fresh—which few of them were by December 31—punching a new digit over a preexisting one would make a muddled appearance. The old digit would show through almost as plainly as the new one, and it might, in fact, be difficult to determine what the intended date of the coin really was. In these circumstances, the preexisting digit or digits had to be filed down on the die, prior to repunching. If they were already fairly worn they were, apparently, repunched without formality. It is not clear who made the decisions on these matters, but many overdate coins bear clear evidence of a not-too-strict adherence to Mint policy. The new dates were punched over very fresh old dates, creating a digit that looks like nothing but a blur until closely examined. It is interesting to note that in some instances the Mint went back and resurrected dies that had been used two and three years earlier for the purpose of repunching and reusing them. This was undoubtedly planned in advance. When the digits in a date could not easily be changed to digits for the following year, they were probably shelved until a more accommodating year arrived, for example storing a die for a year ending in "5" until three years later when a year ending in "8" rolled around.

Variations in Numbers of Stars. The early Liberty Head designs on our silver and gold coins (though not on the Cent and Half Cent) frequently featured a crescent of stars on either side of the portrait. Opinion on the significance of these stars is far from uniform. Some believe they served a purely artistic function, while others maintain that the original intention was to use 13 stars as standard procedure, to signify the 13 original colonies. The majority of coins bearing these decorative stars do, in fact, contain 13, but whether or not this may be simply coincidental is difficult to state. If there was any firm resolution on the Mint's part to maintain the number of stars at a fixed 13, it failed miserably: some coins have 14, 15, 16, or 17 stars. Just like the date, the stars were punched into each die utilizing a small punch that made one star at a time. Thirteen stars meant thirteen separate punchings. It is not difficult to see where the discrepancies crept in. One man might start punching in his stars from the top, another from the bottom. One might do all the left side stars first, then start on the right side; another might do one right side star, then one left, alternating. One man might start punching his stars further up on the die than another. It was easy to lose count, if anyone was really seriously counting in the first place (which seems unlikely). If one worker placed his stars more closely together than another, he could fit seven in a space occupied by six of the other die-puncher's star. Or maybe he could even fit eight or nine; apparently he could, as there are die-variety specimens showing just such variations. Thus a situation arose in which *not only* did the number of stars per coin differ from one die to the next, so did the numbers on one side of the Liberty portrait vs. those on the opposite side. This resulted in the familiar varieties—all of them listed in this book, as they are all major recognized varieties—of "seven stars left, six right; eight stars right, seven left; six stars left, seven right," and so on.

Varieties of this type might seem classifiable as errors, as it was a mistake of the Mint workers not to get together and make certain everyone was following the same procedure. However, in the strict numismatic definition of error, they are not error coins. They are *die varieties.*

Misspelling. Quite a few of our early coins, such as one variety of the 1796 Large Cent ("Li*h*erty" Cent), appear to contain misspellings. On this coin, the name of Liberty is spelled with an "h" instead of a "b." These are almost always classified as major varieties though, like other major varieties, they do not automatically carry a premium value (see the listings in this book for specific price information). Since the spellings on early coins were applied in the same manner as the aforementioned dates and stars, by punching in the letters individually with hand punches, the obvious conclusion is that a worker would occasionally misspell a word by accident or ignorance. This, however, was not in fact the explanation for misspellings on our coins. The words were apparently spelled correctly at the time of preparing the die, but, as the result of wear or injury to the die, certain small delicate portions of letters were destroyed, giving them the appearance of other letters. In the case of the Liherty Large Cent, this coin was struck from a die in which the spelling of Liberty was correct at first, but from which the bottom lobe of the "b" became broken at some point along the way. Without the bottom lobe, the "b" turned into an "h" and transformed Liberty into Liherty. Nevertheless, even though their true explanation is perhaps not so endearing as the thought of illiterate Mint workers, these coins are still considered prime curiosities and are avidly sought.

Head of One Year, Tails of Another. This is likewise a group of varieties which occurs on our very early issues. These coins are described as having "head of 1799, tails of 1800," or "head of 1806, tails of 1805." They resulted from a change being made in one or more dies used to strike one side of the coin, without a corresponding change in the opposite die. If this change took place in midyear, as it usually did, a considerable batch of coins was produced in each of the two distinct varieties (in some instances there were more than two varieties). Let us say that a particular coin was being struck with standard designs for obverse and reverse, and that these designs had been in use for several years or longer. We will call these Type A obverse and Type A reverse. If an alteration was made in the Type A reverse during the course of any given year, coins would exist from that year with Type A obverse and Type A reverse, as well as others with Type A obverse and Type B reverse. The numismatists always refer to these different types by the year in which they were introduced. As with most varieties, the specific cash value is largely a matter of quantities produced and quantities preserved over the years.

Errors, Freaks and Other Mint Blunders. As previously stated, coins that can be classified as true errors—rather than varieties—are far more plentiful among those of the modern era. The entire 19th century saw fewer error coins released from the Mint than are released in a single modern decade. This was partly the result of fewer error coins being produced and partly due to the spot-checking safeguards in use during the 19th century. Today's coin-striking machinery operates at intense speed and the operation is almost wholly mechanical, with little in the way of human supervision. Everything is calculated and measured down to the fraction of an inch and fraction of a second. As soon as a finished coin is ejected from the striking collar, a fresh planchet is in place, with a speed so rapid that the eye can scarcely follow it. Just one tiny accident or malfunction in this highly sophisticated process, such as a planchet not feeding correctly or not ejecting correctly, inevitably results in a misstruck or error coin; it may, in fact, produce more than one, depending on the nature of the accident or malfunction. If the malfunction is not sufficiently serious to cause stoppage of the machinery, which it very rarely is except in the case of a major electrical voltage failure, there will be no indication to Mint personnel that anything has gone wrong and that the bin or tub contains misstruck coins. The coins thus struck will simply be mixed with tens of thousands of others, totally camouflaged. There is no hand-sorting of coins at any point along the line, and absolutely no opportunity to detect and confiscate misstrikes. Of course, this is an excellent circumstance for the collector. It virtually assures that all error coins will reach circulation, and reaching circulation invariably means reaching collectors sooner or later.

Misstrikes, while possibly the most familiar of error coins, are not the only types. Errors can occur in the metal mix or alloy and in the use of wrong planchets, such as a Quarter struck on a planchet intended for a Nickel. The so-called clipped planchet varieties, in which a portion of the coin is actually missing, are not striking errors, as these defective planchets were already defective when struck.

Lamination Freak or Error. This is essentially a modern species of error coin and is probably better described as a freak or oddity than a real error. In 1965 the U.S. Mint introduced layered coins, in which a coin's composition begins with a central copper core bonded to outer layers of a different metal. At the intense temperatures and pressures under which the planchet layers are bonded, there is, of course, a very secure bond created in nearly all specimens. Yet, as if seeming to prove the rule that anything which may happen *will* happen occasionally, a coin is sometimes encountered from which one or both of the outer layers have begun to peel away from the central core. This is referred to as a lamination freak, as the outer layers are called (by collectors at any rate) "lamination." The peeling may be so slight that it can be noticed only when the coin is viewed from its edge, or so severe that one or both layers appears ready to depart the coin. To be entirely candid, it must be observed that some of these more spectacular lamination freaks, in which one or both layers is peeled like the top of a tin can, have received some assistance from human hands. Having acquired a mild or moderate lamination freak, some collectors or members of the general public will seek to accentuate the peeling, which can be quite easily done with a screwdriver or any other object used as a prying wedge. An expert can often tell when this has been done, but still the practice has rendered lamination freaks a bit less desirable or popular than might otherwise be.

Off-Center Misstrike. These, while not particularly rare or valuable unless they occur on an old coin, are very eye-catching errors and always in demand. If you look closely at coins in ordinary pocket change, you will note an occasional specimen which slightly deviates from symmetrical striking; the design is too far near one of the edges, and the opposite edge shows too much bare metal. Even when the variation is half a millimeter it can be noticed. These coins, which are only marginally off center, give some indication of the nature of a collectible off-center misstrike. To be regarded as collectible, the design must be a minimum of 10% out of register. Without going to the difficulty of trying to determine what 10% of a coin design constitutes, one can use a much easier rule-of-thumb to ascertain whether such a specimen is collectible. If the design is entirely present, with no portion of it missing, the coin will not be regarded as a worthwhile misstrike and will have no premium value over its face value. If the design is considerably more than 10% off center, which does happen, the value will be higher in proportion.

If you wish to buy or sell variety or error coins, a number of highly qualified professional dealers are prepared to serve you. Their names and addresses may be found in the popular numismatic publications to which readers of the *Blackbook* are referred.

NEW U.S. GOLD

On December 17, 1985, President Reagan signed a bill authorizing the production of the first U.S. gold coins in more than 50 years. This, coupled with the gold Statue of Liberty commemorative "Half Eagle," issued January 1, 1986, put gold squarely in the forefront of numismatic headlines.

Collectors and investors reacted with enthusiasm to the new U.S. gold coins. The Statue of Liberty commemorative is chiefly a collector's piece, while the non-commemorative gold coins are intended for collectors and gold bullion investors. In all cases the actual market values of the coins far exceed their face values. Hence there is no possibility of them being used in actual circulation, as were early U.S. gold coins.

The Statue of Liberty commemorative was struck as part of a set, whose other coins are not of gold. It was, however, sold separately by the Mint and is now being sold by coin dealers both individually and as part of the set. The name "Half Eagle" derives from its $5 face value, as U.S. gold coins of that denomination were traditionally known as Half Eagles.

The four gold bullion coins are in denominations of $50, $25, $10 and $5. Their bullion values are not tied to their face values and they will be bought and sold as bullion, by gold content, just as are other gold bullion coins of the world. These are actually the first *new* gold coins since 1849. Though the Mint struck gold coins up to the 1930s, all those after 1849 were simply continuations of established series. There are several other "firsts" involved, too. The $50 denomination is the highest face-value gold coin ever struck by the U.S. with the exception of commemoratives. There has never been a $50 gold circulating coin. Also it will contain more gold—one troy ounce of .999 fine—than any circulating coin in U.S. history. The $25 gold piece will be the first coin, in any metal, struck in this denomination. In spite of its higher face value, however, it will contain less actual gold than the old "Double Eagles," which carried a $20 face value. Additionally, it is the first time in history that the U.S. has authorized four gold coins simultaneously.

Reentry of the U.S. government into the realm of gold coins ended years of speculation and debate. When we lifted our ban on gold ownership in 1975 the possibility of striking gold coins was immediately raised. This seemed unlikely at the time and the volatile gold bullion market of 1979–80 appeared to render gold coinage an impossibility. With gold fluctuating so markedly in price, how could face values be established and maintained?

Subsequent events proved to those at the Mint and in Congress, as well as in the White House, that collectors and investors could be well served by gold coins without the need, or even the desirability, for such coins to be used as money.

Both the Canadian Maple Leaf and South African Kruegerrand, each containing an ounce of gold, established strong popularity without any intention of being used as legal tender. This is precisely the thrust of the new U.S. gold coins. While Congress *may* give them legal tender status (that point has not yet been resolved), no one is apt to spend a coin for $50 when it contains $300 to $400 worth of gold. While technically there was no official connection between authorization of new U.S. gold coinage and the banning of imports on South Africa's Kruegerrand, the $50 gold piece will undoubtedly be bought by many investors in place of the South African coin. Content-wise it is identical. The smaller denomination coins contain a proportionate quantity of gold:

$50 face value—1 oz. .999
$25 face value—½ oz. .999
$10 face value—⅕ oz. .999
$5 face value—⅒ oz. .999

The $5 Statue of Liberty commemorative was struck on the specifications of the old Half Eagle, .900 fine, with a gold content of .24187 ounce or just slightly under one quarter ounce. It was announced by the Mint in July 1985, and promoted through an extensive advertising campaign. A surcharge of $35 was added to the ordering price, to be contributed to a fund for repairs on the historic Statue of Liberty in New York Harbor. Pre-issue orders were taken directly from the public and contracts signed with several large national retailers to sell the coins. As a result of participation by these large retailers, the coin became available "over the counter" in roughly 2,500 outlets across the country. While mail order customers were originally prepared to wait until January 1, 1986, for shipment of their orders, the heavy response and huge backlog prompted earlier release of the coin. Orders started being filled in December, all coins being sent by registered mail from the Mint's West Point, New York, facility. Many arrived before the year's end. By December 31, the deadline for placing mail orders, the Mint had collected $12,900,000 for the Statue of Liberty/Ellis Island Foundation. This amount includes revenue from the other (non-gold) coins in the series as well.

Congress authorized only half a million of the $5 gold commemoratives to be struck and pre-release orders accounted for more than 400,000 being sold. Speculation was raised on the possibility of striking more to meet the demand. This met objection on the grounds that a certain portion of the price went for scarcity, in addition to gold value, and reducing that scarcity would, in effect, be unfair to those who now own the coin. A potential alternative was to change some feature of the design so that two distinct coins, with their own scarcity levels, would result.

Collectors who missed out on ordering the Statue of Liberty Half Eagle from the Mint have not lost their chance to buy it. Even after the coin is sold out by the Mint's retail contractors, it will still be available from many coin dealers. Prices charged by retail sources are likely to fluctuate depending on the changes in bullion values.

EXPERT TIPS ON BUYING COINS

Intelligent coin buying is the key to building a good collection at reasonable cost. Today, with the added confusion of split grading, slider grading, and the devious practices of some coin sellers, it is more necessary than ever to be a skilled buyer.

In the interest of supplementing the coin pricing and identification in this book with practical advice on astute buying, the editor presents the following article. It reviews major pitfalls to which an uninformed buyer might succumb and gives specific suggestions on getting the most for your money when buying coins.

The editor wishes to state clearly that the exposure of questionable practices by some coin sellers, as detailed below, is not intended as a general indictment of the coin trade. The vast majority of professional coin dealers are ethical and try to please. Moreover it can be safely stated that if the hobbyist restricts his buying exclusively to well-established coin dealers he runs very little risk.

UNSATISFACTORY SOURCES OF COINS

Unsatisfactory sources of coins—those entailing a higher than necessary degree of risk—include flea markets, antiques shops, garage sales, private parties who are unknown to you, auction sales in which coins are offered along with non-numismatic merchandise, and advertisements in magazines and newspapers published for a general readership rather than for coin collectors. This advice is given to benefit the non-expert buyer and especially the beginner. Advanced collectors with full confidence in their coin buying skills will sometimes shop these sources to find possible bargains.

MAIL ORDER ADS IN NATIONAL MAGAZINES

The sharp rise in coin values during 1979 and 1980 encouraged many promoters to deal in coins. (Promoters are persons who aren't coin dealers in the accepted sense of the term, but who utilize coins for large-scale mail order promotions.) The objective, nearly always, is to sell coins to buyers of limited knowledge and thereby succeed in promising more, and charging more, than would a legitimate professional coin dealer. Undoubtedly such promotions are extremely successful, to judge from the number of such ads that appear regularly.

Here are some examples of the headlines they use:

"Genuine Silver Dollars Struck by the U.S. Mint . . ."

"Real John F. Kennedy Silver Half Dollars . . ."

"Cased Set of U.S. Mint Morgan Dollars . . ."

"Unbelievable But True: U.S. Silver Dollars at Only $21.95 . . ."

The ads look impressive and sound impressive. They show enlargements of the merchandise. They quote facts and figures, often with historical data. They present a variety of guarantees about the coins, and there is no misrepresentation in those guarantees. You do receive genuine coins struck by the U.S. Mint. They really are 90% silver if you order Morgan or Peace Dollars. But the price you pay is from twice to three times as much as if you bought from a *real* coin dealer. In the legitimate coin trade, the coins sold via these ads are looked upon as "junk coins." They command a very small premium over their silver bullion value. They are not only the most common dates but are usually in miserable condition.

To lend credibility, the promoters will normally use a company name which gives the appearance of being that of a full-time coin dealer. There is nothing illegal in doing this, but it does contribute to the misleading nature of such ads.

Let's examine some of the specific methods used in today's ever-increasing deceptive coin ads. You will soon see why coins, especially U.S. silver coins, have become a favorite of mail order promoters: they can be "hyped" in a most convincing manner, without making statements that are patently false. Thus the advertisers skirt around—though narrowly—allegations of mail fraud. (Fraud cannot be alleged on the basis of price, as a merchant is free to charge what he pleases for whatever he sells.)

1. *Creating the impression that the coins offered originate from a hidden or sequestered cache not previously available to the public.* This is accomplished by the use of such phrases as, "Just found, 2,367 specimens," or, "Now released to the public . . ." The assertion that they were "just found" is not wholly inaccurate, however. The advertiser has, more than likely, located a dealer who could supply wholesale quantities of junk coins. The coins themselves were never lost or hidden. "Now released to the public" has nothing to do with official government release nor release by a court. It simply means the advertiser is selling them.

In a very few isolated cases, in which mail fraud charges were brought, ads have gone beyond this kind of assertion-by-innuendo. They actually stated that the coins were from secret government stockpiles. One of them wove an elaborate tale of silver dollars being taken to special storage locations by the army during World War I. Such an event never occurred, and that is the basic difference between prosecutable and non-prosecutable ads. If an advertiser merely hints at something, but does not state it as fact, he is usually within the law.

2. *Leading the potential customer to believe the coins are scarcer or more valuable than they really are.* This is done via numerous techniques. Among the favorites is to compare the advertiser's selling price against prices for other coins of the same series. An ad offering Morgan Dollars for $27.50 may call attention to the fact that "some Morgan Dollars have sold for $20,000, $50,000 and more." Yes, they have. They are the rare, desirable dates in UNC, not the common, circulated coins you receive from the advertiser.

When half dollars are offered, it will be said that "you just can't find them in circulation any longer." It's entirely true that Walking Liberty halves, Franklins, and the lone 90% silver Kennedy half (1964) cannot be found in day-to-day circulation. But coin dealers have them by the roll and sell them for less than you will pay through such an ad. The fact that these coins are not found in circulation is not an indication of rarity. Many coins carrying very little premium value over their face value cannot be found in day-to-day circulation.

3. *Emphatic guarantee that the coins are genuine.* On this point the advertiser can speak with no fear of legal repercussion. His coins are genuine and nobody can say otherwise. But, even where absolute truth is involved, it can be—and is—presented in such a manner as to give a false impression. By strongly stressing the coins' authenticity, the message is conveyed that many non-authentic specimens exist and that you run a risk in buying from someone else. Such is far from the case. Any large coin dealer can sell you quantities of perfectly genuine Morgan Dollars, Peace Dollars, or any other coins you want.

4. *Implication that the coins offered are in some respect "special," as opposed to specimens of the same coins available at coin shops.* This presents an obvious difficulty for the advertiser, as his coins are just the opposite of special: usually heavily circulated, often with actual damage such as nicks, gouges, etc. It is not, however, insurmountable. The advertiser can keep silent about the condition of his coins and present them as some sort of special government issue. Usually this is done by selling them in quantities of four or five and referring to them as "U.S. Mint Sets," "Government Mint Sets," or something similar. The uninformed reader believes he is ordering a set assembled and packaged by the Mint. The Mint *does* assemble and package sets, as everyone knows. But it had no part in these! Assembling and packaging was done by the advertiser. Regardless of how attractive the box or case may be, it is not of official nature and lends absolutely nothing to the value. The Mint has never issued cased or boxed sets in which all the coins were of the same denomination. In these hard-sell sets you will find such combinations as two Morgan Dollars and two Peace Dollars, four Morgan Dollars, or three half dollars. Dates are a purely random selection. And, we repeat, the coins are in well-worn, circulated condition.

5. *Failure to state actual silver content.* This falls under the heading of deception by silence. The potential customer is left to draw his own conclusions and the advertiser knows full well that those conclusions will be wrong. Provided, of course, the ad is worded in such a way that it lends itself to incorrect conclusions. Typically this sort of advertiser is selling Kennedy halves dated from 1965 to 1970. During these years the Kennedy half contained some silver but not very much—just 40% (after 1970 it contained no silver at all). Its silver content was less than 1/2 that of 50¢ pieces struck prior to 1965. In fact it was even less than the silver content of pre-1965 quarters. Very few individuals, aside from coin hobbyists, are aware of this reduction of silver content in half dollars from 1965 to 1970. When *silver* coins are advertised they automatically think in terms of 90% silver. Yet the advertiser is legally within his rights in referring to 40% silver coins as silver. As the 40% silver coins look just like their 90% silver predecessors, few purchasers will suspect they've overpaid. Until they have them appraised.

6. *Creation of gimmicked names for coins.* By calling a coin something different than its traditional numismatic name, it is made to seem more unusual or special. Everyone is familiar with Kennedy half dollars but what about "Kennedy Silver Eagles"? This is a promoter's name for the Kennedy half, used in an effort to glamorize it. It is highly inappropriate, as silver coins are never referred to as eagles. This designation is reserved for a $10 coin, struck exclusively in gold, which was discontinued many years ago.

7. *False references.* Advertisements of this type are sometimes accompanied by doubtful or fairly obvious fake references on the advertiser's behalf. Taking his cue from legitimate coin dealers, whose ads nearly always refer to their membership in coin organizations and often carry other easily verifiable references as well, he feels he must present similar assurances of his background and reliability. Since he has nothing too convincing to offer in the way of genuine references, he manufactures them. He invents the name of a mythical coin organization, of which he is either a member in good standing, an officer, or perhaps even president. If he chooses not to go quite that far, as he might be caught in the deception, he can take a less volatile course and claim membership in "leading coin collector and dealer organizations." Without, of course, naming them. This is just like the ads for questionable diet aids, which say, "Tests at a leading Eastern university have shown . . ." No one is likely to check all five hundred or more Eastern universities. Or enter into a debate about which ones are leading, or what they may be leading *in.*

Of the various other unsatisfactory sources of coins, the dangers they present should be fairly obvious.

RECOMMENDED SOURCES OF COINS

As a general rule, coin purchasing should be confined to the following sources:

1. Professional coin dealers who sell coins at a shop and/or by mail order.

2. Auction sales conducted by professional coin dealers or auction houses making a specialty of coins.

3. Shows and conventions for coin collectors.

Another acceptable source, though unavailable to many coin hobbyists, is the fellow collector with duplicate or surplus specimens to sell or trade. This source is acceptable only if the individual is known to you, as transactions with strangers can result in problems.

The dangers of buying from sources other than these are overgraded and consequently overpriced coins; non-graded and likewise overpriced coins; coins that have been doctored, "whizzed," chemically treated, artificially toned, or otherwise altered. Buying from the legitimate, recommended sources greatly reduces but does not absolutely eliminate these risks. The buyer himself is the ultimate safeguard, if he has a reasonably thorough working knowledge of coins and the coin market. In this respect experience is the best teacher, but it can sometimes be costly to learn from bad coin buying experiences.

Smart coin buyers follow certain basic strategies or rules. They will not buy a rare coin that they know little or nothing about. They will do some checking first. Has the coin been frequently counterfeited? Are counterfeits recorded of that particular date and mintmark? What are the specific grading standards? What key portions of the design should be examined under magnification to detect evidence of circulation wear?

The smart coin buyer may be either a hobbyist collecting mainly for the sport of it, or an investor. In either case he learns not just about coins but the workings of the coin trade: its dealers and auctioneers and their methods of doing business. It's essential to keep up to date always, as the coin market is a continual hotbed of activity.

When buying from the recommended sources there is relatively little danger of fakes, doctored coins, or other obviously unwanted material. If such a coin does slip through and escape the vigilance of an ethical professional dealer, you are protected by his guarantee of authenticity. It is highly unlikely that you will ever be "stuck" with a counterfeit, doctored, or otherwise misrepresented coin bought from a well-established professional.

Merely avoiding fakes is, however, not the sole object of intelligent coin buying. It is, in fact, a rather minor element in the overall picture. Getting the absolute most for your money in terms of properly graded coins at fair prices is the prime consideration. Here the responsibility shifts from seller to buyer. It is the dealer's responsibility not to sell fakes or misidentified coins. But it is the *buyer's* responsibility to make certain of getting the best deal by comparing prices and condition grades of coins offered by different dealers. Quite often you *can* save by comparison shopping, even after your incidental expenses are tabulated. The very unique nature of the coin market makes this possible.

Prices do vary from one dealer to another on many coins. That is precisely the reason—or at least one of the primary reasons—for the *Blackbook.* If you could determine a coin's value merely by checking one dealer's price, or even a few dealers' prices, there would be minimal need for a published price guide. The editors review prices charged by hundreds of dealers, to arrive at the median or average market prices that are listed in the *Blackbook.* Prices are matched condition grade by condition grade, from UNC down the line. The results are often little short of astounding. One dealer may be asking $50 for a coin priced at $30 by another. And there are sure to be numerous other offerings of the coin at $35, $40, $45 and various midpoint sums.

It is important to understand why prices vary and how you can utilize this situation to your advantage.

Some readers will remark, at this juncture, that prices vary because of inaccurate grading.

It is unquestionably true that personal applications of the grading standards do contribute to price differences. What one dealer sees as an AU-55 is AU-50 or AU-52 to another, with a corresponding difference in price. It is one reason for non-uniform prices. *It is not the only one.*

Obviously the lowest priced specimens are not always those to buy. Smart numismatic buying calls for knowing when to take bargains and when to bypass them. Low price could result from something directly concerning the coins. Or it may be tied to matters having nothing to do with the coin or coins. A dealer could be oversupplied, or he may be offering coins in which he does not normally deal and wants to move them quickly. He may have a cash flow imbalance and needs to raise funds, in which event he has probably reduced most of his prices. He may be pricing a coin low because he made a fortunate purchase in which the coin cost him very little. In all of these cases—and examples of all can be found regularly in the coin trade—the lower than normal price is not a reflection upon the coin's quality or desirability. These coins, if properly graded, are well worth buying. They do save you some money and cause no problems.

Personal circumstances of the dealer are, to one degree or another, reflected in the prices of most of his coins. A dealer cannot very well charge $1000 for a 1948 Lincoln cent just because he needs the money. The traffic would not bear it. But within reasonable bounds a dealer's pricing structure for his stock reflects his circumstances. If the dealer has substantial operating costs to meet, such as shop rent and employee salaries, his overall pricing structure will reflect this. Yet his prices are not likely to be too much higher than the average, as this class of dealer is intent on quick turnover. Also, there is a certain degree of competitiveness between dealers, particularly those whose advertisements run in the same periodicals. Unfortunately this competitiveness is sometimes carried to extremes by some dealers, resulting in "bargains" that are sometimes overgraded.

Condition has always played a major role in coin prices. Even in the hobby's early, far less sophisticated days, collectors would pay more for a bright, shiny uncirculated coin than for the same coin in worn condition. The undeniable difference in value and desirability of coins in different condition grades led gradually to adoption of grading standards. In a sense, grading standards are comparable to the "scale of one to ten." Some circulated coins show more wear than others, so it is not sufficient to merely call a coin circulated. Even among uncirculated coins or UNCs, there can be differences in condition and desirability. While UNCs show no circulation wear, the majority do have tiny hair-like or lint-like scratches on both surfaces. You will not see these on casual examination, only if you look closely and in some cases only if a magnifying lens is used. These are the "average" UNCs. Uncirculated coins having very few surface abrasions are scarcer and many buyers are willing to pay extra for them. This increases their market value. Occasionally an uncirculated coin has no surface abrasions. It is then regarded as "mint state perfect," for which the designation on the grading scale is MS-70. A correctly graded specimen in MS-70 will sell higher than any other grade of condition, sometimes much higher.

The grading guidelines used for U.S. coins (no grading guidelines exist for foreign coins) are those adopted by the American Numismatic Association and are included in summarized format in this book. Any U.S. coin can be graded by these guidelines, from the very oldest obsolete types to those in current production. The principle behind the grading guidelines is simple.

A coin's design always has certain vulnerable areas. Some parts of the design are more highly raised than others. These show wear the quickest. Likewise, some of the engraved lines are shallower than others and more quickly obliterated with day-to-day handling. By carefully examining a coin and checking these vulnerable areas, one can determine if the coin grades circulated or uncirculated. If it grades circulated, its vulnerable areas will also establish its specific grade, by the amount of wear they've absorbed. Anyone can learn to grade coins, but the process does call for patience, good lighting, a magnifying lens, and objectivity. Objectivity is essential. There is always a natural tendency to believe one's coins are a shade better than they really are. This is true even of a collector who has no intention of selling and takes no particular interest in resale potential. It applies to a greater degree when the person doing the grading has intentions of selling.

Values, as you will see in this book, often jump sharply from one grade to the next higher grade. The difference in price between an AU-55 and MS-60 specimen is not 10% or 20%. It is more often 100%, 200% or more, depending on the coin, its scarcity, age, and other considerations. Hundreds, or even thousands, of dollars can be riding on the clarity of one tiny portion of its design. Even when a coin is not really rare or expensive, it will be worth quite a bit more in the higher grades of condition than in the lower.

While grading as practiced today is very precise and scientific compared to numismatics' early years, it is not foolproof. The human element still comes into play to some degree. So do situations not specifically accounted for in the grading guidelines. The human element is the great intangible. Two or three persons of equal competency may grade a coin identically. A dozen are not likely to. Someone will believe, honestly and without motive, that the coin is a grade higher or lower than the others consider it. The person who grades it differently is not necessarily careless. He may, in fact, be the most careful observer in the group. His close attention has revealed something overlooked by the rest.

Some coins invite variations in grading, for any of various reasons. These include circulated and uncirculated specimens as well as coins that appear to fall directly on the borderline between these categories. What makes certain coins more difficult to grade than others? First we have the coins, usually very old ones, that have not followed the normal patterns of wear. For reasons not always satisfactorily explained, the more vulnerable portions of their designs show less wear than other areas. By strict adherence to the established ANA standards they would grade in the higher ranks of circulated condition. A truly objective grader would hesitate to place them there. He would drop them down a bit, though just how far to drop is, in cases of this nature, mostly a matter of opinion.

Then there are coins which can be matched up easily with their proper condition grade so far as wear is concerned, but which have problems not related to wear. The ANA guidelines apply to circulation wear or its absence *only.* There are no provisions under these guidelines for grading coins with rim nicks, bruises, discoloration, oxidization, porosity, or any other defect not related to circulation wear. Such coins, which are encountered frequently, are treated in different ways by different dealers. Many will grade the coin for wear, then insert a note calling attention to its defect. Some will just grade the coin a little lower and let it go at that.

According to the ANA grading guidelines, a coin that does not fully meet the requirements for a grading level must be dropped down to the next lower category. If a coin cannot squeeze by as an AU-55 it has to be called AU-50, with the corresponding inevitable difference in retail value. As the guidelines are hardly enforceable by law, however, they are bent at will by anyone who wishes to do so. One of the by-products is so-called *slider grading,* which has become widespread. The use of slider grading is so commonplace today that some of its critics of a few years ago are adopting it. Coin dealers have an entirely logical reason for doing so. Even if a certain dealer is personally opposed to slider grading, he is in effect placing himself at a disadvantage by declining to utilize it. If his fellow dealers are slider grading their coins, his will seem inferior by comparison. His MS-60 price will be the same as another dealer charges for MS-62. Many customers, looking simply at price and the claim made for condition, will order the MS-62. So slider grading is done defensively just as much as offensively.

A slider grade is any grade outside of the accepted guidelines. It is an unofficial grade that exists in the seller's eye and which he hopes will exist in the purchaser's when he examines the coin. It is unofficial because there are no published guidelines for it. Presumably an AU-52 coin is a shade nicer than AU-50, but grading of this sort is very subjective. A great deal of personal opinion comes into play and that is directly contrary to the purpose of grading standards. They were established to remove personal opinion as much as possible from coin grading. It is certainly understandable that anyone, whether dealer or collector, would be reluctant to grade a coin AU-50 when it seems finer than most specimens of that grade. Under the present guidelines, however, there is no alternative provision for such coins. However one may feel about slider grade coins, one thing is certain: if you pay a premium for them, you take a risk. A dealer who buys your coin collection at some future time will not pay extra for your sliders. He will pay no more than for specimens in the next lower condition ranking.

Also prevalent today, to make intelligent coin buying even more challenging, is *split grading.* Split grading is seen in advertisements and coin dealers' catalogues as AU-50/55, MS-65/60, and so on. The coin is given two grades instead of one. The first stated grade, which would be AU-50 in our example of AU-50/55, refers to the front or obverse of the coin while the second refers to the back or reverse. Under normal circumstances, both sides of a coin show the same degree of surface wear or smoothing down of their designs. Nearly all coins in circulated condition have received their wear from being handled day after day, carried in pockets and change purses, taken in and out of cash drawers, and rubbing against other coins. Whatever happens to one side of a coin generally happens to the other as well, so the wear on both sides will be equal in 99 out of 100 coins. Yet there is that problematical 100th coin, which is slightly—never more than slightly—better preserved on one side than on the other.

If the coin is very old and quite rare, the sort that would have appealed to collectors of generations ago, its unevenness of wear will be attributed to a phenomenon called *cabinet friction.* Today most hobbyists store their coins in albums or individual holders made of paper or inert plastic. In the 1800s and early 1900s it was quite the fashion to keep coins in wooden cabinets with pull-out trays or drawers. This is still done in Europe by wealthy collectors. The coins rested in little slots on beds of velvet, sometimes merely on the bare wood (a very bad practice!). Collectors almost always kept all their coins face up, so for decades and decades a coin might be absorbing friction on one side, as the tray was pulled in and out. The side facing up did not rub against anything and absorbed no friction. Consequently many such coins showed greater deterioration on their reverse side than on their face. Perhaps the difference was not noticed by hobbyists of that uncritical era. Today, when every coin is meticulously inspected, the effects of "cabinet friction" become apparent. This is not to say that cabinet friction is the only possible explanation for unevenness in wear. There could be other causes that would be difficult to speculate upon without knowing the actual history of the coin, how it was handled and stored, and so forth. Obviously in the case of split grade *uncirculated* coins, cabinet friction does not come into play. These coins do not show evidence of wear on either side. They are true UNCs, but their grading is split, such as MS-63/60, because one side has fewer "bag marks" or fine hairline scratches than the other. One may even, occasionally, encounter a coin graded Mint State Perfect on one side but not on the other. This can appear in any of various ways: MS-70/68, MS-67/70, MS-70/69, etc.

There is no denying the fact that split grading, confusing though it is, is a legitimate grading practice when the coin calls for it. The alternative to split grading is to grade the coin into the lower category; in other words, use the side showing more deterioration as the grading criteria. In doing this, an AU-55/50 coin would become merely AU-50. This is objected to by most sellers, including not only dealers but private parties selling coins from their collection, on grounds that the coin is better than a plain or straight AU-50 and deserves to sell for a premium or at least attract more attention. Some individuals solve this dilemma by use of the slider grading discussed above. They would call an AU-50/55 coin AU-52 or AU-53 without entering into further explanation. This, however, is the least acceptable of the potential methods of describing such coins. Most collectors seem to agree that coins with real condition variations, from one side to the other, ought to be graded into split grades. The key word here is "real." The middle 1980s witnessed an undeniable misuse of split grading, not only on the part of some professional coin dealers but collectors, investors, auctioneers, even writers of numismatic books and magazine articles. It has become trendy to split grade a coin, as if the use of split grading indicated extra careful attention on the grader's part. Literally tens of thousands of older coins that passed through the market with a standard grade in the late 1970s reappeared later as split graders. More are sure to follow. The time may well be coming when the majority of all 18th and 19th century U.S. coins carry a split grade. Nor would it be terribly surprising, considering the proliferation of split and slider gradings, to see an onslaught of finely split grades such as AU-50/51, MS-62/63 and the like.

As with coin grading in general, split grading can be helpful to both seller and buyer in judging the desirability and cash value of a coin. It can also be utilized to confuse, mislead, and overcharge a potential buyer, so once again it becomes a matter of the care and integrity of the person doing the grading. Several precise conclusions can be drawn with regard to split grading. The true split grade coin—that is, the coin which truly merits such a grading and would be so graded by most astute persons—is not nearly so plentiful as today's market would lead one to believe. Of true split graders, those in circulated condition will generally be in better grade on the front or face.

As to quantities, here is a rough summary:

18th Century Uncirculated Coins. Here the proportion of genuine "splitters" runs rather high, as it includes coins which are uncirculated on one side but show some slight wear on the other. These coins were kept in cabinets for many years, enduring the above mentioned cabinet friction. The percentage of true split graders among UNCs of the 18th century would run at least 20%. Some of them are coins that were simply better struck on one side than the other, which technically should not enter into grading considerations—but it does. Many of these coins have uneven toning from one side to the other, which is another result of cabinet storage for long periods of time. One side was in continual contact with a possibly acid or moisture-emitting substance—such as wood—while the other was not.

18th Century Circulated Coins. The proportion of true split graders found in this category is lower than for 18th century UNCs but higher than for circulated coins of the 19th or 20th centuries by quite a wide margin. The total would probably be from 15% to 20% of all specimens if we group together copper, silver, and gold. It will always be slightly higher on gold coins, as their surface softness invited uneven wear. They suffered the most and the quickest from cabinet friction, with silver coins coming next and copper suffering least of all. Hence in all the time periods there will be somewhat fewer split grade copper coins, or coins composed of other so-called base metals. It is not just the greater durability of these metals which resisted uneven wear. Though that was a factor, a more important one was circumstances in the coin hobby. In the earlier days of coin collecting in this country, say up to about 1870, relatively few of the advanced collectors were taking an interest in copper or other base metal coins, regardless of age or rarity. They preferred the more prestigious gold and silver. Copper coins such as the Large Cent were regarded as good material for a starter collection or juvenile collection. Thus, few copper coins went into cabinets to absorb friction wear.

19th Century Uncirculated Coins. Among these you will find a moderate number of true split graders in the rarer and more popular types, such as Bust Dollars and the $10 gold pieces from the earlier part of the century. They also occur on the Double Eagles but not as frequently. The percentage of split graders with one side UNC and the other side circulated is rather substantial for the groups just mentioned, though negligible on such groups as the silver 3¢, Large Cent, 10¢ and most others. Even when these smaller coins were stored in cabinets, which was not as frequently, their lighter weight worked in their favor to reduce friction.

19th Century Circulated Coins. A considerably lower percentage of true split graders is to be found among this category than any of those previously discussed. The overall figure, taking all 19th century circulated coins into account, would be under 10%. Yet among those in the upper ranges of price there is no doubting that the percentage would run somewhat higher. The explanation is essentially the same as given above for uncirculated coins of the same time period. Those of the more common dates and types were not as frequently placed in cabinets and escaped cabinet friction. Most 19th century split grade circulated coins are the rarer Bust Dollars and Seated Liberty Dollars. True splitting is not as common on Morgan Dollars, but will be found fairly extensively on $10 and $20 gold pieces of the 19th century.

20th Century Uncirculated Coins. True split grading on these is confined mostly to Morgan and Peace Dollars and to gold coins, and is the result of one side ranking a little higher than MS-60 while the opposite side is a plain or straight MS-60. With 20th century coins, cabinet friction is not the cause of split grading, even in circulated specimens, as the use of cabinets by domestic collectors was on the decline by 1900 and went totally out of fashion a few years before World War I. Split grading on 20th century UNCs is ascribable to bag marks being more pronounced on one surface than the other. With earlier split graders you will note a pattern of the obverse (front or face of the coin) normally being in a higher grade of condition, due to cabinet storage. As split grade coins of the 20th century resulted from no such systematic procedure, but rather pure chance, the better side is just as likely to be the reverse.

20th Century Circulated Coins. The number of split grade specimens is virtually nil, less than 1%. These coins received their wear in day-to-day circulation handling and tended to wear evenly on both sides. The methods by which 20th century collectors have stored their coins have not contributed to the creation of split graders.

How should the smart collector deal with split grade coins? Should he buy them or avoid them? Should he be willing to pay premium prices for them, over and above the normal price for a specimen in the lower of the two grades?

As a general rule, split grade coins should be avoided unless you can place reasonable confidence in the person doing the grading. Many coin dealers are judicious in their use of split grading and apply such a designation only when it seems absolutely called for. Others are somewhat more frivolous with split grading, as you will quickly note by scanning the large display advertisements in numismatic newspapers and magazines. Checking these ads, including those offering coins you have no intention of buying, should be required for anyone interested in learning about the coin market. This can be most revealing. You will find, for example, ads in which one thousand coins are separately listed and priced, and two- to three hundred of them are presented as split graders. That is simply too high a percentage to occur in the normal course of events, regardless of the type of coins involved. Few numismatists could objectively grade a thousand coins and find two or three hundred "splitters." When you encounter this sort of thing it is a fairly safe assumption that the advertiser is partial to split grading. He has a predisposition to it and wants to find cause for split grading in every coin he grades. In that he is not successful, as the majority of coins offer absolutely no basis for split grading. But he does much better in finding split grade coins than people who have no special leaning toward them. Of course we are talking about the coins he sells. When he buys, he will more than likely be extremely content to go with the lower grade. Any coin that he can split grade, in offering it for sale, becomes upgraded (though only marginally) over the condition in which it was acquired, with the potential for a somewhat greater profit margin. There is absolutely nothing wrong with this if he finds true split graders among the coins he has bought. All dealers, including the most reliable, will sometimes discover upon reexamining a purchase that the coin belongs in a different grade than they had originally believed. The more reputable conscientious dealers will regrade a coin *down* when that seems appropriate, so they can hardly be censured for grading up when that appears called for. The culprit is the maniacal split grader who seems to have an obsession with it. In any given advertisement showing a large proportion of the coins as split graders, there are apt to be additional indications that the advertiser is trying to pull his coins into more desirable grades. (Please understand that an advertiser is not necessarily a dealer; some ads are placed by private parties.) Ads with a preponderance of split graders are likely to also be above the normal in slider grades.

True split grade coins are a shade more desirable than if both surfaces fell into the lower of the two grades. If you have the opportunity to buy one for no more than the price of a straight specimen—say an AU-55/50 for the price of an AU-50—fine. You can hardly be making a mistake. But when you pay any kind of premium for a split grader, however slight, it is a questionable investment. The person who eventually buys it from you is likely to say, "I don't pay extra for split grades."

PUTTING YOUR COIN BUYING KNOWLEDGE TO WORK

General Suggestions (whether buying in person at a coin shop or by other means):

1. Deal with someone in whom you can have confidence. The fact that a dealer has been in the business a long period of time may not be an absolute guarantee of his reliability, but it is definitely a point in his favor. Is he a member of coin collector or coin dealer organizations? You do not have to ask about this to find out. If he does hold membership in good standing in any of the more prestigious organizations that fact will be prominently displayed in his ads, his sales literature, and on the walls of his shop. The leading organization for coin dealers is the PNG, or Professional Numismatists' Guild. Its members are carefully screened and must, after gaining admittance, comply with its code of ethics. Complaints against PNG members *are* investigated. Those that cannot be easily resolved are brought before an arbitration panel. You are on the safest possible ground when dealing with a PNG member. As the PNG is rather a select group, however, your local dealer may not be a member. This in itself should not make him suspect. One of the requirements of PNG membership is to carry at least $100,000 retail value in coins and many dealers simply do not maintain that large an inventory. Is your dealer an American Numismatic Association member? Local Chamber of Commerce?

2. Don't expect the impossible, either in a dealer or his coins. The dealers are in business to make a profit and they could not do this by offering bargains on every coin they sell. Treat the dealers fairly. Look at things from their point of view. For example, a long "layaway" on an expensive coin may not be in the dealer's best interest. The dealers will go out of their way for established customers but, even then, they cannot be expected to place themselves at a disadvantage.

BUYING IN PERSON AT A COIN SHOP

1. Plan your visits in advance. Don't shop in a rush or on the spur of the moment. Give yourself time to look, think, examine, and decide.

2. Before entering the shop have a clear idea of the specific coins, or at least the type of coins, you want to see. If more than a few dates and mintmarks are involved, do not trust it all to memory. Write a list.

3. Look at everything that interests you before deciding to buy anything.

4. When shopping for rarities, bring along your own magnifier. A small one with attached flashlight is the most serviceable. You may not be able to conduct really in-depth examinations in a shop, but you'll learn more with a magnifier than without one. Don't be reticent about using it. The dealers will not be insulted.

5. If the shop has more than one specimen of the coin that interests you, ask to see them all. Even if all are graded identically and priced identically, you may discover that one seems a shade nicer than the rest.

6. If this is your first visit to the shop you will want to give some attention to whether or not the shop inspires confidence. An experienced collector tends to get different vibrations from each shop, to the point where he can form an opinion almost immediately—sometimes before entering. Some coin shops give the distinct impression of being more professional than others. And that impression is usually correct! There are various points on which this can be judged. Do all coins, with the exception of bullion items, have their prices marked on the holder? Is the price accompanied by a statement of condition grade? Are the holders, and the style of notations on them, fairly uniform from coin to coin? If the coins are housed in various different kinds of holders, with notations that seem to have been made by a dozen different people, they are most likely remnants from the stocks of other dealers or so-called "odd lots." Their condition grades should have been verified and they should have been transferred to uniform holders before being placed on sale. Since the shopkeeper failed to do this, he probably knows very little about their actual condition grades. He merely took the previous owners' word for it. Does the shopkeeper impress you as a person with intimate knowledge of coins? He need not love coins, as his business is selling them and not collecting them. But he should appear to regard them a little higher than "just merchandise." He ought to be appreciative of and perhaps even enthusiastic over the finer aspects of a rare coin. Under no circumstances should he treat coins as if he cares nothing about them, such as by handling them roughly or sloppily or touching their surfaces with his fingers.

7. Buying in person gives you an opportunity to converse with the dealer, and this can have its advantages. Upon expressing interest in a coin you may discover that the dealer offers a verbal discount from the market price—even without asking for one. If this does not occur, you do, of course, have the right to at least hint at the matter. Just a modest savings can often turn a borderline item into a sound purchase. Don't get a reputation of asking for a discount on every coin you buy. Let the circumstances guide you and be diplomatic. You are always in a better position to receive a discount when purchasing a number of coins at the same time. Dealers like volume buyers. Never say, "Will you take $300 for this?" or anything which could be construed as making the dealer an offer. The dealers make offers when they buy from the public and the right to make an offer is something they like to reserve for themselves. You can broach the subject in a more subtle fashion. Instead of mentioning what you would be willing to give for the coins, ask if there is a savings (savings is a much better word than discount) on large purchases. If you pay in cash you have a better bargaining position as you're saving the dealer the time required in collecting the funds. That is the essence of reasonable discounts: playing fair, not becoming a nuisance, and being willing to accept a small consideration even if just 5%. At least with the small discounts you are, or should be, getting good coins. If anyone were willing to discount a coin by 50% you could be virtually certain it was a problem item.

BUYING BY MAIL ORDER

There is no reason to shun mail order. Most coin dealing is done by mail. There are at least a dozen mail order coin dealers for every one who operates a shop. Your local shop may not specialize in your type of coins, but in dealing by mail you can reach any coin dealer in the country and obtain virtually any coin you may want.

Consider the following before doing any mail order buying.

1. Compare ads and prices, compare descriptions, compare everything from one ad to another running in the same publication. Look for evidence of the advertiser's professional standing, such as PNG membership. Read his terms of sale. There should be an unqualified guarantee of authenticity plus a guarantee of satisfaction. If you are not satisfied with your purchase for any reason you should have the option of returning it within a specific time period. This time period should be stated in the dealer's terms of sale. It will usually be ten days or two weeks. It should likewise be clearly stated that if you do choose to return the coins, you can receive a full refund or credit as *you* prefer (not as the dealer prefers). Full refund means the sum paid for the coins, with postage and registration fees deducted. Few dealers will refund postage charges. Consequently, when you return a shipment you are paying the postage both ways.

2. Send a small trial order if you haven't previously done business with the advertiser. This will give you an opportunity to judge his grading accuracy and see just what sort of coins he supplies. You will also discover how prompt and attentive he is. The results of this trial order should give a fairly good idea of what you can expect from that dealer when placing larger orders.

3. Do not xerox an ad and circle numbers. Write out your order, simply and plainly. Mention the publication and issue date. The dealer probably has different ads running in different publications.

4. Give second choices only if this is necessary to qualify for a discount. Otherwise don't. Most dealers will send you your first choice if it's still available. Some will send the second choice, even if they do still have your first choice. This is called "stock balancing." If they have two remaining specimens of your first choice, and 20 of your second choice, they would much prefer sending you the second choice. Only a relatively small proportion of dealers will ignore your wishes in this manner, but our suggestion still applies: no second choices if you can avoid them. To speed things up, make payment by money order or credit card. A personal check may delay shipment by as much as three weeks.

5. Examine the coins as soon as possible upon receiving them. If a return is necessary this must be done promptly to be fair to the dealer. Most likely you will not be permitted to remove a coin from its protective holder to examine it. The coins will be in clear mylar (an inert plastic) holders known as "flips" or "flipettes," with a staple at the top. The staple must be in place for a return to be honored. While this may seem harsh it is necessary as a means of the dealer protecting himself against unscrupulous collectors who would switch coins on him. These individuals would replace a high grade coin with one of a lower grade from their collection, and return the lower grade specimen, asking for a refund.

In the unlikely event you receive a coin in a holder which does not permit satisfactory examination, the best course is to simply return it. In making your examination be fair to yourself and to the dealer. Should you have the least doubt about its authenticity, submit the coin to the American Numismatic Association for its opinion and inform the dealer of your action. If the ANA finds the coin to be fake or doctored, you can return it even if the grace period for returns has expired. Under these circumstances many dealers will reimburse you for the ANA's expertizing cost. Chances are, however, that you will never receive a suspect coin.

6. Do not file a complaint against the dealer unless he is clearly in violation of his printed "terms of sale." When it is absolutely necessary to do so, a report of the transaction may be forwarded to the organizations in which he maintains membership, as well as the publications in which he advertises. But even if you place hundreds of mail orders, it is unlikely that the need will ever arise to register a formal complaint against a dealer.

BUYING AT AUCTION SALES

The volume of collector coins sold at auction is enormous. Auction buying is preferred by many collectors, as the opportunity exists to buy coins at somewhat less than their book values.

Not everything sold by auction is a bargain, however, and the auction house's "terms of sale" allow you far less latitude in making returns. Still, auction buying in the present day entails considerably less risk than it traditionally did. A generation ago, or even more recently, everything sold at auction was strictly "as is." Nothing could be returned for any reason whatsoever, even if grossly misdescribed or counterfeit. Today, almost all coin auctioneers will take back a fake or doctored coin, and some will take returns of those that have been incorrectly graded or otherwise misdescribed. This varies somewhat from one auction firm to another.

There are two types of auction sales: mail sales, in which all bidding is conducted by mail or phone; and so-called "floor" sales, which have in-person bidding. Even at floor sales, however, one is permitted to make an absentee bid if he cannot personally attend. When an absentee bid is successful, the bidder is notified by mail.

You have just as good a chance of being successful with an absentee bid as if you were present. The reputable auction houses will not bill you for the full amount of your bid if there was weak bidding on the coin. If you placed a bid of $500 and no one else offered more than $200, you would be billed only for an amount sufficient to beat the $200 bid. This would in most cases be $225. At some auctions, though, an automatic "buyer's premium" or surcharge in the amount of 10% is added to the price. In the example just given you would be paying a total of $247.50 plus charges for shipping. Sales at which bids are accepted exclusively by mail and phone do not, as a rule, utilize the buyer's premium. Check the terms of sale to be sure, as this obviously makes a difference in the amounts you should bid.

Whether the auction is a mail or floor sale, there will be a printed list of its contents available for those who may be interested in bidding. This list is circulated well in advance of the sale date to give everyone ample time to study it and plan their bidding. The list may appear as a full-page or multi-page advertisement in one of the numismatic magazines or newspapers. It may be issued in the form of a handsome catalogue with photos, sent to clients on the auctioneer's mailing list (and available to non-clients at a small charge). In any event it will be accompanied by a set of regulations for those participating in the sale, and a bidsheet on which prospective buyers can enter their bids. The bidsheet will mention the sale's closing date. Bids received after the closing date, or after the start of vocal bidding in a floor sale, are ineligible.

Here is some advice for auction buying.

1. Find an auctioneer who specializes in your kind of coins and order a subscription to his catalogues. Regardless of the type of coins you collect, there are some auctioneers who handle them more regularly than others and these are the catalogues you should be receiving. Subscribing brings you the catalogues as early as possible and you also receive the list of "prices realized" following each sale. This in itself is extremely useful. It shows the prices actually paid for each coin, and it shows you the coins that failed to draw any bids or were removed from the sale for other reasons. You can utilize this information when placing bids in future sales conducted by the same auction house.

2. Read the entire catalogue or list before filling out your bidsheet. Make a Xerox of the blank bidsheet in case you decide to make changes in your bids.

3. Determine whether the prices shown in the catalogue are book values, estimated selling prices, or "minimum bids." In some sales you will encounter a mixture of all three, which can become confusing. Sometimes no prices at all will be shown. When estimated selling prices (sometimes called "estimated retail value") are used, you are usually safe in assuming that the majority will sell slightly below those figures. Some will sell for more and others for a good deal less, but most are likely to go for about 10% under the estimates. Once the buyer's premium is added, assuming one is used, they hit right around the auctioneer's estimate. This pattern maintains because a large number of bidders at any given auction will bid predictably by the percentage method. When the auctioneer states $100 as an estimated selling price or estimated retail value, they will bid $90. If the auctioneer states $200, many will bid $175 or some figure in that general neighborhood. This gives them the feeling of obtaining a bargain, though of course it hardly remains a bargain when the buyer's 10% surcharge is added. Such a bid is high enough in most instances to stand a very good chance of success. Those who bid 50% or 60% of the estimates are not really intent on being successful. They would rather lose a coin than pay anything near the normal retail price for it. Occasionally a few of their bids will come through if the sale turns out disappointing. There will also be some bidders, at every sale, who bid above the estimate, as a way of annihilating the competition. Needless to say, this can be an expensive way of acquiring coins.

If minimum bids are used, no bid lower than the sum stated will be entertained. In any sale in which all the lots are provided with minimum bids, a large number will sell right at the minimum or just fractionally above it, such as $55 for a lot carrying a $50 minimum bid. Minimum bid requirements tend to have a negative psychological influence on many bidders. They feel that if the stated price is satisfactory to the auctioneer and the coin's owner, the coin cannot be worth very much more. In actual fact many lots with minimum bids are worth considerably more than the sums indicated, and you can sometimes get excellent buys at a "minimum bids" sale. It all depends on the specific nature of the sale and who is running it.

4. The auctioneers frequently stress advantages in bidding early, assuming you are placing an absentee bid. There is in fact more logic in bidding late, so long as you can be sure of making the deadline. An early bid is likely to be disclosed to other prospective bidders, who thereby have the opportunity to exceed it. A late bid may give competitors no time to react.

5. If you're interested in bidding on a coin which is not pictured in the catalogue, ask the auction house for a photo of it. In most cases they will supply a photo if your request arrives early. There may be a token charge for the photo, but if you can get a photo it's far preferable to bidding on a coin you have not seen. If you live close enough to the auction house, make a personal visit to examine any coins in the sale. In nearly all sales the coins will be available for inspection as soon as the catalogue is circulated.

6. While the "terms of sale" will not vary too drastically from one auction house to the next, it is still advisable to read them thoroughly. If the words "all coins guaranteed genuine and may be returned for full refund if proven otherwise" are not included, this is not a sale in which you should be participating. In some mail sales—never in floor sales—you will find this statement: "no bids reduced." This means you pay the full amount of your bid if you win the coin, even if the next highest bid is considerably less. If you bid the fair market value or somewhat below, you can safely place bids in such a sale.

7. If the buyer's premium of 10% is being used, automatically reduce all your bids by 10%, but always bid in round numbers. A bid of $61 or $33.25 will not be accepted.

8. When bidding in person, always have your catalogue open to the page showing the coin being sold at the moment. It is very easy to confuse one lot number with another and place a bid on the wrong coin. Once your bid has been acknowledged by the auctioneer, do not leave your hand up, as in the excitement this may be misinterpreted as a further bid—and you will be bidding against yourself. Always listen carefully to see if you have the high bid. Do not be led, by the competitive spirit of a floor sale, to bid higher than you had intended. Show no emotion whatsoever during bidding or at the conclusion of bidding. One of the basic strategies of auction bidding is to draw no attention to yourself.

The above advice should help to better explain coin buying in its various phases. Space limitations have prevented us from covering some of the more specialized aspects of buying, and we have purposely refrained from mentioning things that should be apparent to everyone. Coin collecting offers infinite possibilities as an enjoyable hobby or profitable investment. It need not be complex or problem-laden. But anyone who buys coins—even for the most modest sums—owes it to himself to learn how to buy wisely.

THE AMERICAN NUMISMATIC ASSOCIATION

Most of today's coin collectors probably know that there is an American Numismatic Association, the largest organization of "coin" collectors in the world. However, many may not realize that the Association is nearly 100 years old, with a current operating budget of more than a million dollars.

An educational, nonprofit organization, the American Numismatic Association invites and welcomes to membership all worthy persons eleven years of age and older who have a sincere interest in numismatics—whether they collect coins,

DR. GEORGE F. HEATH
FOUNDER OF ANA.

AMERICAN NUMISMATIC ASSOCIATION HEADQUARTERS IN COLORADO SPRINGS FEATURES A MUSEUM AND A REFERENCE LIBRARY, BOTH OPEN TO THE PUBLIC AT NO CHARGE.

paper money, tokens, or medals—whether advanced collectors or those noncollectors only generally interested in the subject. Members, located in every state of the Union and in many other countries, total some 40,000.

A factor that deterred the Association's development during its first three-quarters of a century was the geographic dispersal of its functional offices: the executive secretary was in Phoenix, Arizona; the treasurer in Washington, D.C.; the editor in Chicago, Illinois; and the librarian in Lincoln, Nebraska. None of the staff was full-time or received pay, and most operated out of their homes or private offices. Obviously, this situation limited and hampered communication and made for inefficient operation in general.

Since 1967 ANA operations have been centered in Colorado Springs, Colorado, and in 1982 the building was expanded to almost twice its original size. A board of governors, which establishes policy in determining all bylaws and regulations, is elected from the membership on a regular basis and serves without pay. Implementing established policy in Colorado Springs is a full-time salaried professional staff that includes an executive vice president, editor, librarian, authenticators, and assistants and clerical staff.

The principal objectives of the Association are the advancement of numismatic knowledge and better relations among numismatists. Collectors will find the annual membership dues low compared to the tremendous value to be found in the prestige and services that membership offers.

The ANA does not buy or sell coins. Its revenue comes from membership dues and is supplemented by gifts, bequests, and contributions. It receives no operating funds from any governmental body. Any net income from various activities is used on behalf of its members and for the advancement of the hobby.

When the ANA was organized in October 1891, Dr. George F. Heath, the motivating force, was honored with membership No. 1. Member No. 1,000 was admitted in March 1908; No. 10,000 in March 1944; No. 50,000 in August 1963; and No. 100,000 in August 1979. Of course, the passing of time has taken its toll, and today's membership is slightly less than a third of the total number enrolled during the Association's 99 years.

The Numismatist, the Association's monthly magazine, is actually older than the ANA itself, having been started by Dr. Heath in 1888 (September–October) and published privately through 1910. It did, however, cooperate with and champion the cause of the Association—before and after its organization. In 1910 the vice president of ANA, W.W.C. Wilson of Montreal, purchased the magazine from publisher Farran Zerbe and gifted it to the Association, which has continued its publication without interruption.

More recent and rapidly growing is the American Numismatic Association Certification Service (ANACS), available to the public, but with lower fees for members. The ANACS staff examines and conducts nondestructive tests on numismatic items and furnishes the person submitting an item with a statement of expert opinion of the item's genuineness. A permanent record is kept by ANACS of all coins it examines.

Using the system of grading established and published by the ANA, the ANACS staff will express an opinion on the condition of a U.S. coin and record it on the coin's certificate. Only authenticated coins will be graded. The fee for grading is, in most cases, appreciably less than for certification.

Collectors between the ages of 11 and 17 are encouraged in the hobby by lower membership dues, special articles in *The Numismatist,* special exhibit classes and programs at conventions, and other educational programs.

Classes of membership are as follows: **Regular**—adults 18 years of age and older (eligible for all benefits, including receipt of *The Numismatist*); **Club**—non-profit numismatic organizations (entitled to all benefits); **Junior**—11 through 17 years of age (entitled to all benefits but cannot hold office); **Associate**—limited to the spouse or child of a Regular or Life Member (cannot hold office or receive *The Numismatist*); and **Life Member**—corresponding to Regular members but a one-time fee is paid for lifetime membership. Memberships are not transferrable from one person to another, and member numbers are never reassigned.

The amounts of dues and a few other details of membership follow:

DUES

Regular *(adult)—U.S. only*	$ 26.00*
Regular *(adult)—all other countries*	28.00*
Club—*any country*	30.00*
Junior *(11 through 17 years old)*	11.00
Associate *(child or spouse of Regular or Life Member living at member's address)*	4.00
5-year individual or club	120.00
Life *(adult individual)*	750.00
Life *(club)*	1250.00
***Add $6 application fee, first year only**	
Nonmember annual subscription—*U.S. only*	$ 28.00
Subscription—*all other countries*	33.00

The Numismatist continues to be the official publication and voice of the Association. Published monthly, it contains well-illustrated articles about various phases of collecting, identifying, and caring for coins, tokens, medals, and paper money. Included are news items regarding Association activities, new issues of coins, medals, and paper money, and developments within the hobby.

The advertising pages of the magazine are open only to ANA members, who must agree to abide by a strict "Code of Ethics." Members, except Associates, receive the magazine as one of the advantages of membership.

Aside from the magazine, one of the earliest services offered to ANA members was the use of a circulating numismatic library, which has grown to be the world's largest facility of its kind. The library houses more than 12,000 books and more than 20,000 periodicals and other items, all of which are loaned by mail to members and are available to non-members for use in the Colorado Springs headquarters.

Related to the library is a visual education service that maintains and loans numismatic slide sets to member clubs for their meeting programs. These sets cover many different phases of numismatics and are available without cost except for shipping charges.

An important date in the history of ANA is May 9, 1912, when it was granted a Federal Charter by the U.S. Congress. Signed by President Taft, the Act gave the

Charter a fifty-year life. A Congressional amendment dated April 10, 1962, allowed for an increase in the number of ANA board members and perpetuated the Charter indefinitely. One of very few such charters ever granted, it has given the Association prestige and has been a stabilizing influence on its management.

The ANA produces books of articles reprinted from *The Numismatist,* as well as pamphlets about coin collecting and "ANACS Counterfeit Detection Reports." In addition, numismatic books are offered at reduced prices through the Reference Book of the Month Club. Members of the book club are not required to purchase books, although membership will be automatically renewed only if one or more titles are purchased during a calendar year. Membership is $26 for the first year and includes a subscription to *The Numismatist* magazine.

Persons having specific questions, or wanting to see a copy of *The Numismatist* or obtain an application for membership, are invited to write to: ANA Executive Vice President, 818 North Cascade Avenue, Colorado Springs, CO 80903-3729, Phone (719) 632-2646.

AMERICAN NUMISMATIC ASSOCIATION CERTIFICATION SERVICE

(ANACS) offers an independent, unbiased, and professional opinion about the authenticity and grade of numismatic items. Because the ANA grading standards apply only to United States coins, only U.S. regular issue and commemorative coins are graded by ANACS. No opinions are given regarding the value or salability of any coin. The opinions offered by ANACS represent the best judgment and experience of trained numismatic professionals based on the most accurate and up-to-date information available to them. Because ANACS employs only non-destructive techniques for counterfeit detection and because grading is always a subjective procedure, no warranties are expressed or implied in ANACS opinions. Certification does not constitute a guarantee that others will not reach a different conclusion as to grade.

As each coin is received by ANACS it is registered, photographed, weighed, and recorded on a computer. A minimum of four staff members then examine each piece for authenticity and grade, using the *Official ANA Grading Standards for United States Coins.* If the item requires further examination, it is sent to outside consultants who are acknowledged experts in various areas of numismatics.

CERTIFICATION FEES

SERVICE DESIRED	FEE
Authentication only	$15.00
Authentication & Grading	23.00
•Grading of a coin previously authenticated by ANACS	15.00
•Re-examination	15.00

•Original certificate MUST accompany request.

All fees are per item and include photographic certificate.
Write for more detailed information.

ANACS has determined this item is genuine and as described.
WARNING: See reverse for important information regarding this certificate.
USA 1881-S DOLLAR

NO.: A-0002-A **Consensus Grade Opinion:** MS63/65
REGISTERED TO: JOHN Q COLLECTOR

For additional forms or information contact:
ANACS, 818 N. Cascade Ave., Colorado Springs, CO 80903-3729
Phone (719) 632-2646

HISTORY OF COLONIAL COINS, PATTERNS, AND TOKENS

The history of our coinage begins not with the first federal issues but the coin used earlier by colonists. This period in American coin use, from exploration of Florida and the first Virginia settlements up to 1792, spans 200 years and is considered one of the most fascinating specialties for collectors. It is rich in types, designs, and methods of production. While a great deal of colonial coinage is rare, some fall into the moderate price range. Here are historical objects of undisputed significance, purchasable in some cases for less than the cost of key-date modern coins. The celebrated "Rosa Americana," circulated before George Washington was born, can be held in good condition for less than $100. Even some of the 17th century "elephant tokens" sell for under $100, though this series also includes rarities of high price. The belief that colonial coinage is only for the wealthy just isn't so.

The story of this nation's beginnings is probably better told by its early money than by any other antiquities. Pilgrim settlers are often pictured as hunters and trappers living off the land. This is partly true, but even in the 1600s there were cities with shops and a real need existed for coinage. When nothing better was available the old barter system was resorted to, as used in ancient times, with goods traded for other goods of similar value. In Massachusetts, iron nails were accepted as legal tender, as well as Indian wampum (shells strung together on cords, each having a set value). As early as the 1640s, 20 years after the Mayflower, serious thought was given by the Bay Colony to striking its own money. In 1652 the Massachusetts General Court authorized experimental efforts in this direction, the first attempts being no more than rough metal discs stamped with small symbols. Compared to Europe's elaborate coinage they were meager, but proved that this country had the ability to produce a medium of exchange. These were followed by improved domestic efforts as well as importation of coins from abroad, struck expressly for colonial use. These include the "Lord Baltimore" coins of Maryland and the Colonial Plantation Token. By the 17th century's close a variety of coins and pseudo-coins circulated. Some were private or merchant tokens, of British or Dutch manufacture. These were largely speculative issues brought to this country in large quantities by persons hoping to acquire vast land parcels. There was little confidence in the integrity of such coinage but it was nevertheless accepted, on the basis of weight.

Coins of both England and Spain, brought over by immigrants and traders, circulated pretty freely. Other foreign coins were also met with. Rather than being changed at face value they were, in the early years, valued at metal content, every merchant having a scale to weigh coins brought to him. Spain's dollar or "piece of eight" became the most familiar coin in the colonies, replaced thereafter by the coins of Great Britain. By the time of the Revolution, probably as many as 90% of the coins in American circulation were of British mintage.

Because colonial coins and tokens were not issued by a central government and were produced under challenging conditions, standardization cannot be expected. Sizes, denominations and quality of workmanship all vary, sometimes to an extreme degree. Included are crude pieces hardly recognizable as coins, and works of considerable artistic merit. Some were not milled but hammered, struck by hammering the dies into metal blanks just as the Romans and Greeks made their coins 2,000 years ago. They also vary in scarcity. The collector should not be duped into paying inflated prices for coins merely on grounds of their being pre-Revolutionary. This in itself is no assurance of rarity. Each issue has its own established value, as shown in the listings section of this book. Allowance must be made for the condition of hammered pieces (whose shape will be somewhat irregular) and for specimens of great rarity, as these are almost impossible to find in the kind of condition one would expect of later coins. On the whole, condition standards are less rigid for colonial than federal issues. On the other hand, the buyer should not accept badly damaged examples in the belief that nothing better can be found.

THE UNITED STATES MINT

For 16 years following the Declaration of Independence this country still relied upon British and other foreign coinage. This was not only unsatisfactory but objectionable to many citizens, as Britain's coins bore the likeness of the not-too-popular George III. In 1791 Congress approved the establishment of a federal Mint. Presses for milling were purchased, designers and die-cutters hired. But the question remained whether to fashion U.S. coinage after Britain's or devise an entirely new series with different denominations. After much debate the latter plan was adopted, with the dollar (named for Thalers of the Dutch, who were not our enemies) as the chief currency unit and our coinage based upon divisions or multiples of it. The metal standard was fixed at 15 parts silver to one part of gold. When finalized on April 2, 1792, the Mint Act provided for coins in values of $10, $5, $2.50, $1, 50¢, 25¢, 10¢, 5¢, 1¢ and ½¢. The 1¢ and ½¢ were of copper; other denominations up to $1, silver; those over $1, gold. The $5 piece was regarded as the equivalent to Britain's pound sterling, the 25¢ to the British shilling, while the ½¢ was the counterpart to Britain's farthing or "fourthling" (¼ part of a British penny). It may seem odd that necessity was felt for a coin valued under one cent, but at this remote period even the penny had considerable buying power and fractional pricing of goods was common—apples at 1¢ each or 5½¢ per half dozen, for example. If such a coin was not available, the situation would have invited an onslaught of merchant tokens.

Philadelphia was selected as home for the first Mint building, whose cornerstone was laid July 31, 1792. George Washington, then serving as President, contributed silverware from which the first federal coins were struck—a few half dimes or half dismes as they were called (5¢ pieces). Proceeding cautiously, the Mint's first purchase of metal was six pounds of copper. This was used for cents and half cents, delivered to the Treasurer of the United States in 1793. The following year a deposit of $80,715.73½ worth of French silver coins was made to the Mint by the State of Maryland, to be melted down and used for coinage. They yielded a quantity of 1794-dated dollars and half dollars. Gold was not obtained until 1795 when a Boston merchant turned over $2,276.72 in ingots, which were quickly transformed (apparently along with gold from other sources) into 744 Half Eagles ($5 pieces). Later that year 400 Eagles ($10) were produced. By the close of the year 1800 the Mint had milled $2,534,000 worth of coins and succeeded in distributing them throughout the then-inhabited regions of the country, as far west as Michigan and Missouri.

HOW UNITED STATES COINS ARE MINTED

THE COIN ALLOY CONTENT

In the coinage process, the first step is to prepare the alloy to be used. Except for nickels and one cent pieces, the alloys formerly (1964 and earlier) used in the coining of United States coins were as follows:

a. **Silver coins**—90% silver and 10% copper
b. **Five-cent pieces**—75% copper and 25% nickel
c. **One-cent pieces**—95% copper and 5% zinc
(The cents of 1943 consisted of steel coated with zinc; and the nickels of 1942 to 1945 consisted of 35% silver, 56% copper, and 9% manganese.) In 1982 the cent was changed to a zinc interior with copper coating.

WHAT ARE THE NEW CLAD COINS MADE OF?

a. **(1971 TO DATE)** cupro-nickel dollars and half dollars. **(1965 TO DATE)** quarters and dimes. The outer surfaces are 75% copper and 25% nickel and the inner core is 100% copper.
b. **(1965–1970)** half-dollars. The outer surface is 80% silver and 20% copper. The inner core is 21% silver and 79% copper. The overall silver content of the coin is 40%.

When clad coinage was introduced in 1965, the designs then in use were retained: the Roosevelt dime, Washington quarter and Kennedy half. (The U.S. was not at that time minting dollar coins.) The only alteration since then was for the special 1976 Bicentennial designs.

Because of the ever-increasing demand for coinage, the Mint introduced new time-saving steps in its coin minting. Raw metal is cast into giant ingots 18 feet long, 16 inches wide and 6 inches thick, weighing 6,600 pounds. Previously, they had weighed 400 pounds and were 16 times smaller in measurement. The ingot is rolled red hot and scaled to remove imperfections. It's then ready for the coins to be stamped; no longer are blanks made and annealed (heated). The excess metal that's left behind is used to make new ingots, in a continuous, never-ending process. The new coins are electronically scanned, counted, and automatically bagged. These facilities are in use at the new, ultra-modern Mint in Philadelphia. It has a production capacity of eight billion coins per year and is open to the public, featuring interesting displays and guided tours.

HOW PROOF COINS ARE MINTED

1. Perfect planchets are picked out.
2. They are washed with a solution of cream of tartar.
3. Washed again and alcohol dipped.
4. The dies for making proof coins receive a special polishing for mirror-like finish.
5. The planchets are then milled.
6. The coins are minted by special hydraulic presses at a much slower rate than regular coins. The fine lines are much more visible on a proof coin.

MINTING: FROM METAL TO COINS

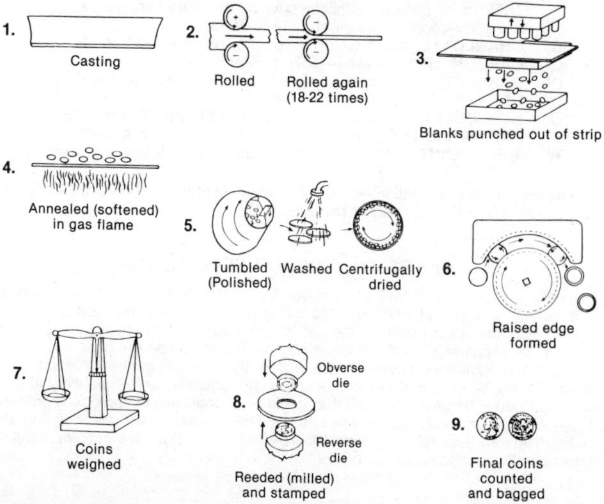

COIN TERMINOLOGY

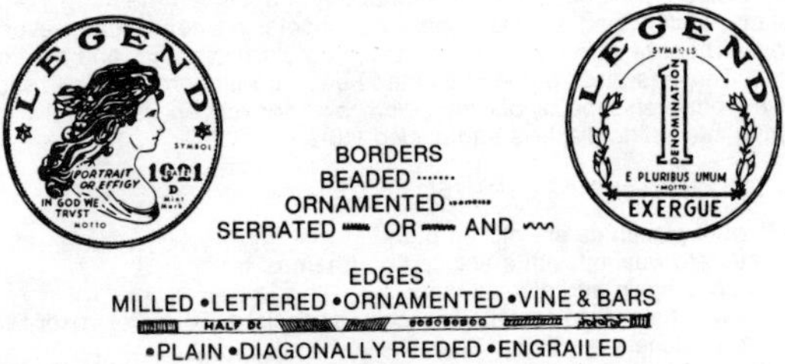

THE MINTS AND THEIR MINT MARKS

By separate Acts of Congress, the government has established mints in different parts of the country.

1. "P" **PHILADELPHIA,** *Pennsylvania*—1973 to date—No Mint Mark. Until 1973, coins minted at Philadelphia did not carry mint marks, except for the silver-content nickels of 1942 to 1945.
2. "C" **CHARLOTTE,** *North Carolina*—gold coins only, 1838 to 1861.
3. "CC" **CARSON CITY,** *Nevada*—1870 to 1893.
4. "D" **DAHLONEGA,** *Georgia*—on gold coins only, 1838 to 1861.
5. "D" **DENVER,** *Colorado*—1906 to date.
6. "O" **NEW ORLEANS,** *Louisiana*—1838 to 1861 and 1879 to 1909.
7. "S" **SAN FRANCISCO,** *California*—1854 to 1955. 1968 to date.
8. "W" **WEST POINT,** *New York*—1984 to date—used for special issues only.

The mint mark is a small letter, denoting which mint made the coin. Mint marks appear on either the obverse or reverse.

WHERE TO BUY AND SELL COINS

There are many potential sources for buying and selling coins: coin shops, auction sales, approval selections, coin shows and conventions, mail order, and other collectors. If a coin shop is located in your area, this is the best place to begin buying. By examining the many coins offered in a shop you will become familiar with grading standards. Later you may wish to try buying at auction. When buying from dealers, be sure to do business only with reputable parties. Be wary of rare coins offered at bargain prices, as they could be counterfeits or improperly graded. Some bargain coins are specimens that have been amateurishly cleaned and are not considered desirable by collectors. The best "bargains" are popular coins in good condition, offered at fair prices.

Selling Coins to a Dealer. All coin dealers buy from the public. They must replenish their stock and the public is a much more economical source of supply than buying from other dealers. Damaged, very worn, or common coins are worthless to a dealer. So, too, usually, are sets in which the "key" coins are missing. If you have a large collection or several valuable coins to sell, it might be wise to check the pages of coin publications for addresses of dealers handling major properties, rather than selling to a local shop.

Visit a coin show or convention. There you will find many dealers at one time, and you will experience the thrill of an active trading market in coins. You will find schedules of conventions and meetings of regional coin clubs listed in such publications as:

CoinAGE
2660 East Main Street
Ventura, CA 93003

Coins Magazine
Iola, WI 54945

Coin World
Post Office Box 150
Sidney, OH 45365

The Numismatist
Published by the ANA
818 North Cascade Avenue
Colorado Springs, CO 80903-3729

To find your local dealer, check the phone book under *"Coin Dealers."*

CLEANING COINS

Under no circumstances should any effort be made to clean coins. Their value is likely to be reduced by such an attempt.

ABOUT THE PRICES IN THIS BOOK

Prices shown in this book represent the current *retail* selling prices at press time. In the first column of each listing, a current *average buying price* is also indicated. This is the price at which coin dealers are buying from the public. Readers should understand that the actual prices charged or paid by any given dealer (there are more than 12,000 coin dealers in the U.S.) can vary somewhat. Hence the *Blackbook* is presented merely as a guide to the average buying and selling prices.

Prices are shown for each coin in various condition grades. It is of utmost importance that a coin be accurately graded before a value can be placed on it. So-called slider grades, such as MS-62, are not included in this book because of space limitations and the difficulties of gathering reliable information on their values. Nor are split-grade coins included (such as AU-55/MS-60), but with some simple mathematics their values can be estimated, based on the prices shown.

When a price is omitted, there is not enough reliable pricing information available. This is usually because the coin, in that particular condition grade, is seldom sold publicly. However, this should not lead to the assumption that all such coins are more valuable than those for which prices are indicated. This is not necessarily the case.

For some scarce coins which are not regularly sold, an example will be given of a specific auction sale result, along with the year in which the sale occurred. These are given purely in the interest of supplying some tangible pricing information, but *may not* (especially in the case of older prices) accurately reflect the price that would be obtained for the same coin if sold today.

When a coin is said to be "unique," this indicates that only one single specimen is recorded to exist. It does not preclude the possibility that other specimens might exist, which have escaped the notice of numismatists.

Prices are given for the major or traditionally acknowledged die varieties, for coins on which die varieties occurred. Many additional die varieties will be noticed in dealers' and auctioneers' literature. The collector status of many of these "minor" die varieties—that is, whether they deserve to be recognized as separate varieties—is a point on which no general agreement has been, or is likely to be, reached. It is important, however, to note, whether discussing major or minor die varieties, that the market values of such coins are not automatically higher than those of the normal die type. Nor can it always be assumed that the variety is scarcer than the normal die type.

In the case of common date silver and gold coins of the late nineteenth and twentieth centuries, it must be borne in mind that the values (for buying or selling) are influenced by the current value of the metal they contain. Most coin shops display the current "spot" prices for silver and gold bullion.

HOW TO USE THIS BOOK

Listings are provided in this book for all coins of the U.S. Mint plus colonial coins and several other groups of coins (please consult index).

Each listing carries the following information:

Denomination of coin.

Date (this is the date appearing on the coin, which is not necessarily the year in which it was actually manufactured).

Mintage (quantity manufactured by the Mint). In some cases this information is not available. In others, the totals announced by the Mint may not be entirely accurate. This is particularly true of coins dating before 1830.

Average Buying Price (A.B.P.). This is the price at which dealers are buying the coin in the condition grade noted. Buying prices can vary somewhat from one dealer to another.

Current Retail Value, in various grades of condition. The price columns following the A.B.P. (or Average Buying Price) show retail prices being charged by dealers. Prices for each coin are given in various grades of condition. Check the column head, then refer to the Grading Guide if you have any doubt about the condition of your coin. Be sure you have correctly identified your coin and its condition. If the date is missing from your coin, it qualifies only as a "type filler" (that is, a "type" coin in low grade condition), and its value will be lower than the price shown for a coin of that series.

OFFICIAL ANA GRADING SYSTEM

The descriptions of coin grades given in this book are intended for use in determining the relative condition of coins in various states of preservation. The terms and standards are based on the commonly accepted practices of experienced dealers and collectors. Use of these standards is recommended by the American Numismatic Association to avoid misunderstandings during transactions, cataloging, and advertising.

The method of grading described in this book should be referred to as the Official ANA Grading System. When grading by these standards, care must be taken to adhere to the standard wording, abbreviations, and numbers used in this text.

When a coin first begins to show signs of handling, abrasion, or light wear, only the highest parts of the design are affected. Evidence that such a coin is not Uncirculated can be seen by carefully examining the high spots for signs of a slight change in color, surface texture, or sharpness of fine details.

In early stages of wear the highest points of design become slightly rounded or flattened, and the very fine details begin to merge together in small spots.

After a coin has been in circulation for a short time, the entire design and surface will show light wear. Many of the high parts will lose their sharpness, and most of the original mint luster will begin to wear, except in recessed areas.

Further circulation will reduce the sharpness and relief of the entire design. High points then begin to merge with the next lower parts of the design.

After the protective rim is worn away the entire surface becomes flat, and most of the details blend together or become partially merged with the surface.

It should be understood that because of the nature of the minting process, some coins will be found which do not conform exactly with the standard definitions of wear as given in this text. Specific points of wear may vary slightly. Information given in the notes at the end of some sections does not cover all exceptions, but is a guide to the most frequently encountered varieties.

Also, the amount of mint luster (for the highest several grades) is intended more as a visual guide rather than a fixed quantity. The percentage of visible mint luster described in the text is the *minimum* allowable amount, and a higher percentage can usually be expected. Luster is not always brilliant and may be evident, although sometimes dull or discolored.

A *Choice* coin in any condition is one with an attractive, above average surface relatively free from nicks or bag marks. A *Typical* coin may have more noticeable minor surface blemishes.

In all cases, a coin in lower condition must be assumed to include all the wear features of the next higher grade in addition to its own distinguishing points of wear.

Remarks concerning the visibility of certain features refer to the *maximum* allowable amount of wear for those features.

Note: The official ANA Grading System used in this book is with the permission of the American Numismatic Association.

RECORD KEEPING

For your convenience, we suggest you use the following record-keeping system to note condition of your coin in the checklist box.

ABOUT GOOD ⧅	FINE ⊟	UNCIRCULATED ⧅
GOOD ⧄	VERY FINE ◫	PROOF ■
VERY GOOD ⊠	EXTREMELY FINE ⧅	

GRADING ABBREVIATIONS

Corresponding numbers may be used with any of these descriptions.

PROOF-70	Perfect Proof	Perf. Proof	Proof-70
PROOF-65	Choice Proof	Ch. Proof	Proof-65
PROOF-60	Proof	Proof	Proof-60
MS-70	Perfect Uncirculated	Perf. Unc.	Unc.-70
MS-65	Choice Uncirculated	Ch. Unc.	Unc.-65
MS-60	Uncirculated	Unc.	Unc.-60
AU-55	Choice About Uncirculated	Ch. Abt. Unc.	Ch. AU
AU-50	About Uncirculated	Abt. Unc.	AU
EF-45	Choice Extremely Fine	Ch. Ex. Fine	Ch. EF
EF-40	Extremely Fine	Ex. Fine	EF
VF-30	Choice Very Fine	Ch. V. Fine	Ch. VF
VF-20	Very Fine	V. Fine	VF
F-12	Fine	Fine	F
VG-8	Very Good	V. Good	VG
G-4	Good	Good	G
AG-3	About Good	Abt. Good	AG

PROOF COINS

The mirrorlike surface of a brilliant proof coin is much more susceptible to damage than are the surfaces of an Uncirculated coin. For this reason, proof coins which have been cleaned often show a series of fine hairlines or minute striations. Also, careless handling has resulted in certain proofs acquiring marks, nicks and scratches.

Some proofs, particularly nineteenth century issues, have "lintmarks." When a proof die was wiped with an oily rag, sometimes threads, bits of hair, lint, and so on would remain. When a coin was struck from such a die, an incuse or recessed impression of the debris would appear on the piece. Lintmarks visible to the unaided eye should be specifically mentioned in a description.

Proofs are divided into the following classifications:

Proof-70 (Perfect Proof). A Proof-70 or Perfect Proof is a coin with no hairlines, handling marks, or other defects; in other words, a flawless coin. Such a coin may be brilliant or may have natural toning.

Proof-65 (Choice Proof). Proof-65 or Choice Proof refers to a proof which may show some fine hairlines, usually from friction-type cleaning or friction-type drying or rubbing after dipping. To the unaided eye, a Proof-65 or a Choice Proof will appear to be virtually perfect. However, 5× magnification will reveal some minute lines. Such hairlines are best seen under strong incandescent light.

Proof-60 (Proof). Proof-60 refers to a proof with some scattered handling marks and hairlines which will be visible to the unaided eye.

Impaired Proofs; Other Comments. If a proof has been excessively cleaned, has many marks, scratches, dents, or other defects, it is described as an impaired proof. If the coin has seen extensive wear, then it will be graded one of the lesser grades—Proof-55, Proof-45, or whatever. It is not logical to describe a slightly worn proof as "AU" (Almost Uncirculated) for it never was "Uncirculated" to begin with—in the sense that Uncirculated describes a top grade normal production strike. So, the term "Impaired Proof" is appropriate. It is best to describe fully such a coin, examples being: "Proof with extensive hairlines and scuffing," or "Proof with numerous nicks and scratches in the field," or "Proof-55, with light wear on the higher surfaces."

UNCIRCULATED COINS

The term "Uncirculated," interchangeable with "Mint State," refers to a coin that has never seen circulation. Such a piece has no wear of any kind. A coin as bright as the time it was minted or with very light natural toning can be described as "Brilliant Uncirculated." A coin which has natural toning can be described as "Toned Uncirculated." Except in the instance of copper coins, the presence or absence of light toning does not affect an Uncirculated coin's grade. Indeed, among silver coins, attractive natural toning often results in the coin bringing a premium price.

The quality of luster or "mint bloom" on an Uncirculated coin is an essential element in correctly grading the piece, and has a bearing on its value. Luster may in time become dull, frosty, spotted, or discolored. Unattractive luster will normally lower the grade.

With the exception of certain Special Mint Sets made in recent years for collectors, Uncirculated or normal production strike coins were produced on high-speed presses, stored in bags together with other coins, run through counting machines, and in other ways handled without regard to numismatic posterity. As a result, it is the rule and not the exception for an Uncirculated coin to have bag marks and evidence of coin-to-coin contact, although the piece might not have seen actual commercial circulation. The amount of such marks will depend upon the coin's size. Differences in criteria in this regard are given in the individual sections under grading descriptions for different denominations and types.

Uncirculated coins can be divided into three major categories:

MS-70 (Perfect Uncirculated). MS-70 or Perfect Uncirculated is the finest quality available. Such a coin under 4× magnification will show no bag marks, lines, or other evidence of handling or contact with other coins.

A brilliant coin may be described as "MS-70, Brilliant" or "Perfect Brilliant Uncirculated." A lightly toned nickel or silver coin may be described as "MS-70, toned" or "Perfect Toned Uncirculated." Or, in the case of particularly attractive or unusual toning, additional adjectives may be in order such as "Perfect Uncirculated with attractive iridescent toning around the borders."

Copper and bronze coins: To qualify as MS-70 or Perfect Uncirculated, a copper or bronze coin must have its full luster and natural surface color, and may not be toned brown, olive, or any other color. (Coins with toned surfaces which are otherwise perfect should be described as MS-65 as the following text indicates.)

MS-65 (Choice Uncirculated). This refers to an above average Uncirculated coin which may be brilliant or toned (and described accordingly) and which has fewer bag marks than usual; scattered occasional bag marks on the surface or perhaps one or two very light rim marks.

MS-60 (Uncirculated). MS-60 or Uncirculated (typical Uncirculated without any other adjectives) refers to a coin which has a moderate number of bag marks on its surface. Also present may be a few minor edge nicks and marks, although not of a serious nature. Unusually deep bag marks, nicks and the like must be described separately. A coin may be either brilliant or toned.

Striking and Minting Peculiarities on Uncirculated Coins

Certain early United States gold and silver coins have mint-caused planchet or adjustment marks, a series of parallel striations. If these are visible to the naked eye, they should be described adjectivally in addition to the numerical or regular descriptive grade. For example: "MS-60 with adjustment marks," or "MS-65 with adjustment marks," or "Perfect Uncirculated with very light adjustment marks," or something similar.

If an Uncirculated coin exhibits weakness due to striking or die wear, or unusual (for the variety) die wear, this must be adjectivally mentioned in addition to the grade. Examples are: "MS-60, lightly struck," or "Choice Uncirculated, lightly struck," and "MS-70, lightly struck."

CIRCULATED COINS

Once again, as a coin enters circulation it begins to show signs of wear. As time goes on the coin becomes more and more worn until, after a period of many decades, only a few features may be left.

Dr. William H. Sheldon devised a numerical scale to indicate degrees of wear. According to this scale, a coin in condition 1 or "Basal State" is barely recognizable. At the opposite end, a coin touched by even the slightest trace of wear (below MS-60) cannot be called Uncirculated.

While numbers from 1 through 59 are continuous, it has been found practical to designate specific intermediate numbers to define grades. Hence, this text uses the following descriptions and their numerical equivalents:

AU-55 (Choice About Uncirculated). Only a small trace of wear is visible on the highest points of the coin. As is the case with the other grades here, specific information is listed in the following text under the various types, for wear often occurs in different spots on different designs.

AU-50 (About Uncirculated). With traces of wear on nearly all of the highest areas. At least half of the original mint luster is present.

EF-45 (Choice Extremely Fine). With light overall wear on the coin's highest points. All design details are very sharp. Mint luster is usually seen only in protected areas of the coin's surface such as between the star points and in the letter spaces.

EF-40 (Extremely Fine). With only slight wear but more extensive than the preceding, still with excellent overall sharpness. Traces of mint luster may still show.

VF-30 (Choice Very Fine). With light, even wear on the surface; design details on the highest points lightly worn, but with all lettering and major features sharp.

VF-20 (Very Fine). As preceding but with moderate wear on highest parts.

F-12 (Fine). Moderate to considerable even wear. Entire design is bold. All lettering, including the word LIBERTY (on coins with this feature on the shield or headband), visible, but with some weaknesses.

VG-8 (Very Good). Well worn. Most fine details such as hair strands, leaf details, and so on are worn nearly smooth. The word LIBERTY, if on a shield or headband, is only partially visible.

G-4 (Good). Heavily worn. Major designs visible, but with faintness in areas. Head of Liberty, wreath, and other major features visible in outline form without center detail.

AG-3 (About Good). Very heavily worn with portions of the lettering, date, and legends being worn smooth. The date barely readable.

Note: The exact descriptions of circulated grades vary widely from issue to issue. It is essential to refer to the specific text when grading any coin.

SPLIT AND INTERMEDIATE GRADES

It is often the case that because of the peculiarities of striking or a coin's design, one side of the coin will grade differently from the other. When this is the case, a diagonal mark is used to separate the two. For example, a coin with an AU-50 obverse and a Choice Extremely Fine-45 reverse can be described as: AU/EF or, alternately, 50/45.

The ANA standard numerical scale is divided into the following steps: 3, 4, 8, 12, 20, 30, 40, 45, 50, 60, 65 and 70. Most advanced collectors and dealers find that the gradations from AG-3 through Choice AU-55 are sufficient to describe nearly every coin showing wear. The use of intermediate grade levels such as EF-42, EF-43 and so on is not encouraged. Grading is not that precise, and using such finely split intermediate grades is imparting a degree of accuracy which probably will not be able to be verified by other numismatists. As such, it is discouraged.

A split or intermediate grade, such as that between VF-30 and EF-40, should be called Choice VF-35 rather than VF-EF or About EF.

An exception to intermediate grades can be found among Mint State coins, coins grading from MS-60 through MS-70. Among Mint State coins there are fewer variables. Wear is not a factor; the considerations are the amount of bag marks and surface blemishes. While it is good numismatic practice to adhere to the numerical classifications of 60, 65 and 70, it is permissible to use intermediate grades.

In all instances, the adjectival description must be of the next lower grade. For example, a standard grade for a coin is MS-60 or Uncirculated Typical. The next major category is MS-65 or Uncirculated Choice. A coin which is felt to grade, for example, MS-64, must be described as "MS-64, Uncirculated Typical." It may not be described as Choice Uncirculated, for the minimum definition of Choice Uncir-

culated is MS-65. Likewise, an MS-69 coin must be described as: MS-69, Uncirculated Choice. It is not permissible to use Uncirculated Perfect for any coin which is any degree less than MS-70.

The ANA grading system considers it to be good numismatic practice to adhere to the standard 60, 65 and 70 numerical designations. Experienced numismatists can generally agree on whether a given coin is MS-60 or MS-65. However, not even the most advanced numismatists can necessarily agree on whether a coin is MS-62 or MS-63; the distinction is simply too minute to permit accuracy. In all instances, it is recommended that intermediate grades be avoided, and if there is any doubt, the lowest standard grade should be used. The use of plus or minus signs is also not accepted practice.

SMALL CENTS—INDIAN HEAD 1859–1909

MINT STATE *(Absolutely no trace of wear.)*

MS-70 (Perfect Uncirculated)
A flawless coin exactly as it was minted, with no trace of wear or injury. Must have full mint luster and brilliance of light toning. Any unusual die or planchet traits must be described.

MS-65 (Choice Uncirculated)
No trace of wear; nearly as perfect as MS-70 except for some small blemish. Has full mint luster but may be unevenly toned or lightly fingermarked. A few barely noticeable nicks or marks may be present.

MS-60 (Uncirculated)
A strictly Uncirculated coin with no trace of wear, but with blemishes more obvious than for MS-65. May lack full mint luster, and surface may be dull or spotted. Check points for signs of abrasion: hair above ear; curl to right of ribbon; bow knot.

ABOUT UNCIRCULATED *(Small trace of wear visible on highest points.)*

AU-55 (Choice About Uncirculated)
OBVERSE: Only a trace of wear shows on the hair above the ear.
REVERSE: A trace of wear shows on the bow knot. Three-quarters of the mint luster is still present.

AU-50 (About Uncirculated)
OBVERSE: Traces of wear show on the hair above ear and curl to right of ribbon.
REVERSE: Traces of wear show on the leaves and bow knot. Half of the mint luster is still present.

REVERSE
(without shield, 1859)

OBVERSE

REVERSE
(with shield, 1860-1909)

EXTREMELY FINE *(Very light wear on only the highest points.)*

EF-45 (Choice Extremely Fine)
OBVERSE: Wear shows on hair above ear, curl to right of ribbon, and on the ribbon end. All of the diamond design and letters in LIBERTY are very plain.
REVERSE: High points of the leaves and bow are lightly worn. Traces of mint luster still show.

EF-40 (Extremely Fine)
OBVERSE: Feathers well defined and LIBERTY is bold. Wear shows on hair above ear, curl to right of ribbon, and on the ribbon end. Most of the diamond design shows plainly.
REVERSE: High points of the leaves and bow are worn.

VERY FINE *(Light to moderate even wear. All major features are sharp.)*

VF-30 (Choice Very Fine)
OBVERSE: Small flat spots of wear on tips of feathers, ribbon, and hair ends. Hair still shows half of details. LIBERTY slightly worn but all letters are sharp.
REVERSE: Leaves and bow worn but fully detailed.

VF-20 (Very Fine)
OBVERSE: Headdress shows considerable flatness. Nearly half of the details still show in hair and on ribbon. Head slightly worn but bold. LIBERTY is worn but all letters are complete.
REVERSE: Leaves and bow are almost fully detailed.

FINE *(Moderate to heavy even wear. Entire design clear and bold.)*

F-12 (Fine)
OBVERSE: One-quarter of details show in the hair. Ribbon is worn smooth. LIBERTY shows clearly with no letters missing.
REVERSE: Some details visible in the wreath and bow. Tops of leaves are worn smooth.

VERY GOOD *(Well worn. Design clear but flat and lacking details.)*

VG-8 (Very Good)
OBVERSE: Outline of feather ends shows but some are smooth. Legend and date are visible. At least three letters in LIBERTY show clearly, but any combination of two full letters and parts of two others are sufficient.
REVERSE: Slight detail in wreath shows, but the top is worn smooth. Very little outline showing in the bow.

GOOD *(Heavily worn. Design and legend visible but faint in spots.)*

G-4 (Good)
OBVERSE: Entire design well worn with very little detail remaining. Legend and date are weak but visible.
REVERSE: Wreath is worn flat but completely outlined. Bow merges with wreath.

ABOUT GOOD *(Outlined design. Parts of date and legend worn smooth.)*

AG-3 (About Good)
OBVERSE: Head is outlined with nearly all details worn away. Legend and date readable but very weak and merging into rim.
REVERSE: Entire design partially worn away. Bow is merged with the wreath.

SMALL CENTS — LINCOLN 1909 TO DATE

MINT STATE *(Absolutely no trace of wear.)*

MS-70 (Perfect Uncirculated)
A flawless coin exactly as it was minted, with no trace of wear or injury. Must have full mint luster and brilliance of light toning. Any unusual die or planchet traits must be described.

MS-65 (Choice Uncirculated)
No trace of wear; nearly as perfect as MS-70 except for some small blemish. Has full mint luster but may be unevenly toned or lightly fingermarked. A few barely noticeable nicks or marks may be present.

MS-60 (Uncirculated)
A strictly Uncirculated coin with no trace of wear, but with blemishes more obvious than for MS-65. May lack full mint luster, and surface may be dull or spotted. Check points for signs of abrasion: high points of cheek and jaw; tips of wheat stalks.

ABOUT UNCIRCULATED *(Small trace of wear visible on highest points.)*

AU-55 (Choice About Uncirculated)
OBVERSE: Only a trace of wear shows on the highest point of the jaw.
REVERSE: A trace of wear on the top of wheat stalks. Almost all of the mint luster is still present.

AU-50 (About Uncirculated)
OBVERSE: Traces of wear show on the cheek and jaw.
REVERSE: Traces of wear show on the wheat stalks. Three-quarters of the mint luster is still present.

EXTREMELY FINE *(Very light wear on only the highest points.)*

EF-45 (Choice Extremely Fine)
OBVERSE: Slight wear shows on hair above ear, on the cheek, and at the jaw.
REVERSE: High points of wheat stalks are lightly worn, but each line is clearly defined. Half of the mint luster still shows.

EF-40 (Extremely Fine)
OBVERSE: Wear shows on hair above ear, on the cheek, and on the jaw.
REVERSE: High points of wheat stalks are worn, but each line is clearly defined. Traces of mint luster still show.

VERY FINE *(Light to moderate even wear. All major features are sharp.)*

REVERSE
(wheatline, 1909-1958)

OBVERSE

REVERSE
(memorial, 1959-date)

VF-30 (Choice Very Fine)
OBVERSE: There are small flat spots of wear on cheek and jaw. Hair still shows details. Ear and bow tie slightly worn but show clearly.
REVERSE: Lines in wheat stalks are lightly worn but fully detailed.

VF-20 (Very Fine)
OBVERSE: Head shows considerable flatness. Nearly all the details still show in hair and on the face. Ear and bow tie worn but bold.
REVERSE: Lines in wheat stalks are worn but plain and without weak spots.

FINE *(Moderate to heavy even wear. Entire design clear and bold.)*

F-12 (Fine)
OBVERSE: Some details show in the hair. Cheek and jaw are worn nearly smooth. LIBERTY shows clearly with no letters missing. The ear and bow tie are visible.
REVERSE: Most details are visible in the stalks. Top wheat lines are worn but separated.

VERY GOOD *(Well worn. Design clear but flat and lacking details.)*

VG-8 (Very Good)
OBVERSE: Outline of hair shows but most details are smooth. Cheek and jaw are smooth. More than half of bow tie is visible. Legend and date are clear.
REVERSE: Wheat shows some details and about half of the lines at the top.

GOOD *(Heavily worn. Design and legend visible but faint in spots.)*

G-4 (Good)
OBVERSE: Entire design well worn with very little detail remaining. Legend and date are weak but visible.
REVERSE: Wheat is worn nearly flat but is completely outlined. Some grains are visible.

ABOUT GOOD *(Outlined design. Parts of date and legend worn smooth.)*

AG-3 (About Good)
OBVERSE: Head is outlined with nearly all details worn away. Legend and date readable but very weak and merging into rim.
REVERSE: Entire design partially worn away. Parts of wheat and motto merged with the wreath.

Note: The Memorial cents from 1959 to date can be graded by using the obverse descriptions.

The following characteristic traits will assist in grading but must not be confused with actual wear on the coins:

Matte proof cents of 1909 through 1916 are often spotted or stained.

Branch mint cents of the 1920s are usually not as sharply struck as later dates.

Many of the early dates of Lincoln cents are weakly struck either on the obverse or the reverse, especially the following dates: 1911-D, 1914-D, 1917-D, 1918-D, 1921, 1922-D, 1923, 1924, 1927-D, 1927-S and 1929-D.

1922 "plain" is weakly struck at the head, has a small I and joined RT in LIBERTY. Sometimes the wheat heads are weak on the reverse.

1924-D usually has a weak mint mark.

1931-S is sometimes unevenly struck.

1936 proof cents: early strikes are less brilliant than those made later that year.
1955 doubled die: hair details are less sharp than most cents of the period.

NICKEL FIVE CENTS — LIBERTY HEAD 1883–1912

MINT STATE *(Absolutely no trace of wear.)*

MS-70 (Perfect Uncirculated)
A flawless coin exactly as it was minted, with no trace of wear or injury. Must have full mint luster but this may range from brilliant to frosty. Any unusual die or striking traits must be described.

MS-65 (Choice Uncirculated)
No trace of wear; nearly as perfect as MS-70 except for some small weakness or blemish. Has full mint luster but may be unevenly toned, frosty, or lightly finger-marked. A few barely noticeable nicks or marks may be present.

MS-60 (Uncirculated)
A strictly Uncirculated coin with no trace of wear, but with blemishes more obvious than for MS-65. May lack full mint luster, and surface may be dull or spotted. Check points for signs of abrasion: high points of hair left of ear and at forehead, corn ears at bottom of wreath.

ABOUT UNCIRCULATED *(Small trace of wear visible on highest points.)*

AU-55 (Choice About Uncirculated)
OBVERSE: Only a trace of wear shows on the highest points of hair left of ear.
REVERSE: A trace of wear shows on corn ears. Half of the mint luster is still present.

AU-50 (About Uncirculated)
OBVERSE: Traces of wear show on hair left of ear and at forehead.
REVERSE: Traces of wear show on the wreath and on corn ears. Part of the mint luster is still present.

EXTREMELY FINE *(Very light wear on only the highest points.)*

EF-45 (Choice Extremely Fine)
OBVERSE: Slight wear shows on high points of hair from forehead to the ear.
REVERSE: High points of wreath are lightly worn. Lines in corn are clearly defined. Traces of mint luster may still show.

EF-40 (Extremely Fine)
OBVERSE: Wear shows on hair from forehead to ear, on the cheek, and on curls.

OBVERSE

"NO CENTS" REVERSE

REVERSE

REVERSE: High points of wreath are worn, but each line is clearly defined. Corn shows some wear.

VERY FINE *(Light to moderate even wear. All major features are sharp.)*

VF-30 (Choice Very Fine)
OBVERSE: Three-quarters of hair details show. The coronet has full bold lettering.
REVERSE: Leaves are worn but most of the ribs are visible. Some of the lines in the corn are clear unless weakly struck.

VF-20 (Very Fine)
OBVERSE: Over half the details still show in hair and curls. Head worn but bold. Every letter on coronet is plainly visible.
REVERSE: Leaves are worn but some of the ribs are visible. Most details in the wreath are clear unless weakly struck.

FINE *(Moderate to heavy even wear. Entire design clear and bold.)*

F-12 (Fine)
OBVERSE: Some details show in curls and hair at top of head. All letters of LIBERTY are visible.
REVERSE: Some details visible in wreath. Letters in the motto are worn but clear.

VERY GOOD *(Well worn. Design clear but flat and lacking details.)*

VG-8 (Very Good)
OBVERSE: Bottom edge of coronet, and most hair details, are worn smooth. At least three letters in LIBERTY are clear. Rim is complete.
REVERSE: Wreath shows only bold outline. Some letters in the motto are very weak. Rim is complete.

GOOD *(Heavily worn. Design and legend visible but faint in spots.)*

G-4 (Good)
OBVERSE: Entire design well worn with very little detail remaining. Stars and date are weak but visible.
REVERSE: Wreath is worn flat and not completely outlined. Legend and motto are worn nearly smooth.

ABOUT GOOD *(Outlined design. Parts of date and legend worn smooth.)*

AG-3 (About Good)
OBVERSE: Head is outlined with nearly all details worn away. Date readable but very weak and merging into rim.
REVERSE: Entire design partially worn away.

Note: The 1912-D, 1912-S and 1883 "no cents" variety are often weakly struck.

NICKEL FIVE CENTS — BUFFALO 1913–1938

MINT STATE *(Absolutely no trace of wear.)*

MS-70 (Perfect Uncirculated)
A flawless coin exactly as it was minted, with no trace of wear or injury. Must have full mint luster. Any unusual die or striking traits must be described.

MS-65 (Choice Uncirculated)
No trace of wear; nearly as perfect as MS-70 except for some small weakness or

blemish. Has full mint luster but may be unevenly toned or lightly fingermarked. A few barely noticeable nicks or marks may be present.

NICKEL FIVE CENTS — BUFFALO 1913–1938

MS-60 (Uncirculated)
A strictly Uncirculated coin with no trace of wear, but with blemishes more obvious than for MS-65. May lack full mint luster and surface may be dull or spotted. Check points for signs of abrasion: high points of Indian's cheek; upper front leg, hip, tip of tail. Shallow or weak spots in the relief are usually caused by improper striking and not wear.

ABOUT UNCIRCULATED *(Small trace of wear visible on highest points.)*

AU-55 (Choice About Uncirculated)
OBVERSE: Only a trace of wear shows on high point of cheek.
REVERSE: A trace of wear shows on the hip. Half of the mint luster is still present.

AU-50 (About Uncirculated)
OBVERSE: Traces of wear show on hair above and to left of forehead, and at the cheek bone.
REVERSE: Traces of wear show on tail, hip, and hair above and around the horn. Traces of mint luster still show.

EXTREMELY FINE *(Very light wear on only the highest points.)*

EF-45 (Choice Extremely Fine)
OBVERSE: Slight wear shows on the hair above the braid. There is a trace of wear on the temple and hair near cheek bone.
REVERSE: High points of hip and thigh are lightly worn. The horn and tip of tail are sharp and nearly complete.

EF-40 (Extremely Fine)
OBVERSE: Hair and face are lightly worn but well defined and bold. Slight wear shows on lines of hair braid.
REVERSE: Horn and end of tail are worn but all details are visible.

VERY FINE *(Light to moderate even wear. All major features are sharp.)*

VF-30 (Choice Very Fine)
OBVERSE: Hair shows nearly full details. Feathers and braid are worn but sharp.
REVERSE: Head, front leg, and hip are worn. Tail shows plainly. Horn is worn but full.

OBVERSE

REVERSE

VF-20 (Very Fine)
OBVERSE: Hair and cheek show considerable flatness, but all details are clear. Feathers still show partial detail.
REVERSE: Hair on head is worn. Tail and point of horn are visible.

FINE *(Moderate to considerable even wear. Entire design clear and bold.)*

F-12 (Fine)
OBVERSE: Three-quarters of details show in hair and braid. LIBERTY is plain but merging with rim.
REVERSE: Major details visible along the back. Horn and tail are smooth but three-quarters visible.

VERY GOOD *(Well worn. Design clear but flat and lacking details.)*

VG-8 (Very Good)
OBVERSE: Outline of hair is visible at temple and near cheek bone. LIBERTY merges with rim. Date is clear.
REVERSE: Some detail shows in head. Lettering is all clear. Horn is worn nearly flat but is partially visible.

GOOD *(Heavily worn. Design and legend visible but faint in spots.)*

G-4 (Good)
OBVERSE: Entire design well worn with very little detail remaining in central part. LIBERTY is weak and merged with rim.
REVERSE: Buffalo is nearly flat but is well outlined. Horn does not show. Legend is weak but readable. Rim worn to tops of letters.

ABOUT GOOD *(Outlined design. Parts of date and legend worn smooth.)*

AG-3 (About Good)
OBVERSE: Design is outlined with nearly all details worn away. Date and motto partially readable but very weak and merging into rim.
REVERSE: Entire design partially worn away. Rim is merged with the letters.

Note: Buffalo nickels were often weakly struck, and lack details even on Uncirculated specimens. The following dates are usually unevenly struck with weak spots in the details:

1913-S I and II, 1917-D, 1917-S, 1918-D, 1918-S, 1919-S, 1920-D, 1920-S, 1921-S, 1923-S, 1924-D, 1924-S, 1925-D, 1925-S, 1926-D, 1926-S, 1927-D, 1927-S, 1928-D, 1928-S, 1929-D, 1931-S, 1934-D and 1935-D.

1913 through 1916 matte proof coins are sometimes spotted or stained.

NICKEL FIVE CENTS — JEFFERSON 1938 TO DATE

MINT STATE *(Absolutely no trace of wear.)*

MS-70 (Perfect Uncirculated)
A flawless coin exactly as it was minted, with no trace of wear or injury. Must have full mint luster and brilliance. Any unusual striking or planchet traits must be described.

MS-65 (Choice Uncirculated)
No trace of wear; nearly as perfect as MS-70 except for some small weakness or blemish. Has full mint luster but may be unevenly toned or lightly fingermarked. A few barely noticeable nicks or marks may be present.

OBVERSE

"WARTIME"
REVERSE 1942-1945

REVERSE

MS-60 (Uncirculated)
A strictly Uncirculated coin with no trace of wear, but with weaknesses and blemishes more obvious than for MS-65. May lack full mint luster, and surface may be dull or spotted. Check points for signs of abrasion: cheek bone and high points of hair, triangular roof above pillars. Shallow or weak spots in the relief, particularly in the steps below pillars, are usually caused by improper striking and not wear.

ABOUT UNCIRCULATED *(Small trace of wear visible on highest points.)*

AU-55 (Choice About Uncirculated)
OBVERSE: Only a trace of wear shows on cheek bone.
REVERSE: A trace of wear shows on the beam above pillars. Three-quarters of the mint luster is still present.

AU-50 (About Uncirculated)
OBVERSE: Traces of wear show on cheek bone and high points of hair.
REVERSE: Traces of wear show on the beam and triangular roof above pillars. Half of the mint luster is still present.

EXTREMELY FINE *(Very light wear on only the highest points.)*

EF-45 (Choice Extremely Fine)
OBVERSE: Slight wear shows on cheek bone and central portion of hair. There is a trace of wear at bottom of the bust.
REVERSE: High points of the triangular roof and beam are lightly worn. Traces of mint luster still show.

EF-40 (Extremely Fine)
OBVERSE: Hair is lightly worn but well defined and bold. Slight wear shows on cheek bone and bottom of the bust. High points of hair are worn but show all details.
REVERSE: Triangular roof and beam are worn but all details are visible.

VERY FINE *(Light to moderate even wear. All major features are sharp.)*

VF-30 (Choice Very Fine)
OBVERSE: Hair worn but shows nearly full details. Cheek line and bottom of bust are worn but sharp.
REVERSE: Triangular roof and beam worn nearly flat. Most of the pillar lines show plainly.

VF-20 (Very Fine)
OBVERSE: Cheek line shows considerable flatness. Over half the hair lines are clear. Parts of the details still show in collar.

REVERSE: Pillars are worn but clearly defined. Triangular roof is partially visible.

FINE *(Moderate to heavy even wear. Entire design clear and bold.)*

F-12 (Fine)
OBVERSE: Some details show in hair around face. Cheek line and collar plain but very weak.
REVERSE: Some details visible behind pillars. Triangular roof is very smooth and indistinct.

VERY GOOD *(Well worn. Design clear but flat and lacking details.)*

VG-8 (Very Good)
OBVERSE: Cheek line is visible but parts are worn smooth. Collar is weak but visible. Only a few hair lines show separations.
REVERSE: Slight details shows throughout building. The arch is worn away. Pillars are weak but visible.

GOOD *(Heavily worn. Design and legend visible but faint in spots.)*

G-4 (Good)
OBVERSE: Entire design well worn with very little detail remaining. Motto is weak and merged with rim.
REVERSE: Building is nearly flat but is well outlined. Pillars are worn flat. Rim worn to tops of letters.

ABOUT GOOD *(Outlined design. Parts of date and legend worn smooth.)*

AG-3 (About Good)
OBVERSE: Design is outlined with nearly all details worn away. Date and legend readable but very weak and merging into rim.
REVERSE: Entire design partially worn away. Rim is merged with the letters.

Note: Jefferson nickels are frequently seen weakly struck, and with the horizontal step lines joined even on Uncirculated specimens. Many of the 1950 and 1955 nickels are unevenly struck with weak spots in the details.

DIMES — BARBER 1892-1916

MINT STATE *(Absolutely no trace of wear.)*

MS-70 (Perfect Uncirculated)
A flawless coin exactly as it was minted, with no trace of wear or injury. Must have full mint luster and brilliance or light toning. Any unusual die or striking traits must be described.

OBVERSE

REVERSE

MS-65 (Choice Uncirculated)
No trace of wear; nearly as perfect as MS-70 except for some small blemish. Has full mint luster but may be unevenly toned or lightly fingermarked. A few barely noticeable nicks or marks may be present.

MS-60 (Uncirculated)
A strictly Uncirculated coin with no trace of wear, but with blemishes more obvious than for MS-65. May lack full mint luster, and surface may be dull, spotted, or heavily toned. Check points for signs of abrasion: high points of cheek and hair below LIBERTY; ribbon bow and tips of leaves.

ABOUT UNCIRCULATED *(Small trace of wear visible on highest points.)*

AU-55 (Choice About Uncirculated)
OBVERSE: Only a trace of wear shows on highest points of hair below LIBERTY.
REVERSE: A trace of wear shows on ribbon bow, wheat grains, and leaf near O. Three-quarters of the mint luster is still present.

AU-50 (About Uncirculated)
OBVERSE: Traces of wear show on cheek, top of forehead, and hair below LIBERTY.
REVERSE: Traces of wear show on ribbon bow, wheat grains, and tips of leaves. Half of the mint luster is still present.

EXTREMELY FINE *(Very light wear on only the highest points.)*

EF-45 (Choice Extremely Fine)
OBVERSE: Slight wear shows on high points of upper leaves, cheek, and hair above forehead. LIBERTY is sharp and band edges are bold.
REVERSE: High points of the wreath and bow lightly worn. Lines in leaves are clearly defined. Part of the mint luster is still present.

EF-40 (Extremely Fine)
OBVERSE: Light wear shows on leaves, cheek, cap, and hair above forehead. LIBERTY is sharp and band edges are clear.
REVERSE: High points of wreath and bow are worn, but all details are clearly defined. Traces of mint luster may still show.

VERY FINE *(Light to moderate even wear. All major features are sharp.)*

VF-30 (Choice Very Fine)
OBVERSE: Wear spots show on leaves, cap, hair, and cheek. Bottom row of leaves is weak but has some visible details. LIBERTY and band are complete.
REVERSE: Wear shows on the two bottom leaves but most details are visible. Nearly all the details in the ribbon bow and corn kernels are clear.

VF-20 (Very Fine)
OBVERSE: Over half the details still show in leaves. Hair worn but bold. Every letter in LIBERTY is visible.
REVERSE: The ribbon is worn, but some details are visible. Half the details in leaves are clear. Bottom leaves and upper stalks show wear spots.

FINE *(Moderate to heavy even wear. Entire design clear and bold.)*

F-12 (Fine)
OBVERSE: Some details show in hair, cap, and facial features. All letters in

LIBERTY are weak but visible. Upper row of leaves is outlined, but bottom row is worn smooth.
REVERSE: Some details in the lower leaf clusters are plainly visible. Bow is outlined but flat. Letters in legend are worn but clear.

VERY GOOD *(Well worn. Design clear but flat and lacking details.)*

VG-8 (Very Good)
OBVERSE: Entire head weak, and most of the details in the face are worn smooth. Three letters in LIBERTY are clear. Rim is complete.
REVERSE: Wreath shows only a small amount of detail. Corn and grain are flat. Some of the bow is very weak.

GOOD *(Heavily worn. Design and legend visible but faint in spots.)*

G-4 (Good)
OBVERSE: Entire design well worn with very little detail remaining. Legend is weak but visible. LIBERTY is worn away.
REVERSE: Wreath is worn flat but is completely outlined. Corn and grains are worn nearly smooth.

ABOUT GOOD *(Outlined design. Parts of date and legend worn smooth.)*

AG-3 (About Good)
OBVERSE: Head is outlined with nearly all details worn away. Date readable but partially worn away. Legend merging into rim.
REVERSE: Entire wreath partially worn away and merging into rim.

DIMES — MERCURY 1916–1945

MINT STATE *(Absolutely no trace of wear.)*

MS-70 (Perfect Uncirculated)
A flawless coin exactly as it was minted, with no trace of wear or injury. Must have full mint luster and brilliance or light toning. Any unusual die or striking traits must be described.

MS-65 (Choice Uncirculated)
No trace of wear; nearly as perfect as MS-70 except for some small blemish. Has full mint luster but may be unevenly toned or lightly fingermarked. A few barely noticeable nicks or marks may be present.

MS-60 (Uncirculated)
A strictly Uncirculated coin with no trace of wear, but with blemishes more obvious

OBVERSE

REVERSE

than for MS-65. May lack full mint luster, and surface may be dull, spotted, or heavily toned. Check points for signs of abrasion: high points of hair and in front of ear, diagonal bands on fasces.

ABOUT UNCIRCULATED *(Small trace of wear visible on highest points.)*

AU-55 (Choice About Uncirculated)
OBVERSE: Only a trace of wear shows on highest points of hair above forehead and in front of ear.
REVERSE: A trace of wear shows on the horizontal and diagonal fasces bands. Three-quarters of the mint luster is still present.

AU-50 (About Uncirculated)
OBVERSE: Traces of wear show on hair along face, above forehead, and in front of ear.
REVERSE: Traces of wear show on the fasces bands but edges are sharply defined. Half of the mint luster is still present.

EXTREMELY FINE *(Very light wear on only the highest points.)*

EF-45 (Choice Extremely Fine)
OBVERSE: Slight wear shows on high points of feathers and at hair line. Hair along face is sharp and detailed.
REVERSE: High points of the diagonal fasces bands are lightly worn. Horizontal lines are clearly defined but not fully separated. Part of the mint luster is still present.

EF-40 (Extremely Fine)
OBVERSE: Wear shows on high points of feathers, hair, and at neck line.
REVERSE: High points of fasces bands are worn, but all details are clearly defined and partially separated. Traces of mint luster may still show.

VERY FINE *(Light to moderate even wear. All major features are sharp.)*

VF-30 (Choice Very Fine)
OBVERSE: Wear spots on hair along face, cheek, and neck line. Feathers are weak but have nearly full details.
REVERSE: Wear shows on the two diagonal bands but most details are visible. All vertical lines are sharp. All details in the branch are clear.

VF-20 (Very Fine)
OBVERSE: Three-quarters of the details still show in feathers. Hair worn but bold. Some details in hair braid are visible.
REVERSE: Wear shows on the two diagonal bands but most details are visible. All vertical lines are sharp. All details in the branch are clear.

FINE *(Moderate to considerable even wear. Entire design clear and bold.)*

F-12 (Fine)
OBVERSE: Some details show in hair. All feathers are weak but partially visible. Hair braid is nearly worn away.
REVERSE: Vertical lines are all visible but lack sharpness. Diagonal bands show on fasces but one is worn smooth at midpoint.

VERY GOOD *(Well worn. Design clear but flat and lacking details.)*

VG-8 (Very Good)
OBVERSE: Entire head is weak, and most details in the wing are worn smooth. All letters and date are clear. Rim is complete.

REVERSE: About half the vertical lines in the fasces are visible. Rim is complete.

GOOD *(Heavily worn. Design and legend visible but faint in spots.)*

G-4 (Good)
OBVERSE: Entire design well worn with very little detail remaining. Legend and date are weak but visible. Rim is visible.
REVERSE: Fasces is worn nearly flat but is completely outlined. Sticks and bands are worn smooth.

ABOUT GOOD *(Outlined design. Parts of date and legend worn smooth.)*

AG-3 (About Good)
OBVERSE: Head is outlined with nearly all details worn away. Date readable but worn. Legend merging into rim.
REVERSE: Entire design partially worn away. Rim worn half way into the legend.

Note: Coins of this design are sometimes weakly struck in spots, particularly in the lines and horizontal bands of the fasces.

The following dates are usually found poorly struck and lacking full details regardless of condition: 1916-D, 1918-S, 1921, 1921-D, 1925-D, 1925-S, 1926-S, 1927-D and 1927-S.

1920 and 1920-D usually show the zero joined to the rim.

1921 usually has a weakly struck date, especially the last two digits.

1923 often has the bottom of the three weakly struck and joined to the rim.

1945 is rarely seen with full cross bands on the fasces.

DIMES — ROOSEVELT 1946 TO DATE

MINT STATE *(Absolutely no trace of wear.)*

MS-70 (Perfect Uncirculated)
A flawless coin exactly as it was minted, with no trace of wear or injury. Must have full mint luster and brilliance or light toning. Any unusual striking traits must be described.

MS-65 (Choice Uncirculated)
No trace of wear; nearly as perfect as MS-70 except for some small blemish. Has full mint luster but may be unevenly toned or lightly fingermarked. A few barely noticeable nicks or marks may be present.

MS-60 (Uncirculated)
A strictly Uncirculated coin with no trace of wear, but with blemishes more obvious

OBVERSE

REVERSE

than for MS-65. Has full mint luster, but surface may be dull, spotted, or toned. Check points for signs of abrasion: high points of cheek and hair above ear, tops of leaves and details in flame.

ABOUT UNCIRCULATED *(Small trace of wear visible on highest points.)*

AU-55 (Choice About Uncirculated)
OBVERSE: Only a trace of wear shows on highest points of hair above ear.
REVERSE: A trace of wear shows on highest spots of the flame. Three-quarters of the mint luster is still present.

AU-50 (About Uncirculated)
OBVERSE: Traces of wear show on hair above ear.
REVERSE: Traces of wear show on flame but details are sharply defined. Half of the mint luster is still present.

EXTREMELY FINE *(Very light wear on only the highest points.)*

EF-45 (Choice Extremely Fine)
OBVERSE: Slight wear shows on high points of hair above ear. Ear is sharp and detailed.
REVERSE: High points of flame are lightly worn. Torch lines are clearly defined and fully separated. Part of the mint luster is still present.

EF-40 (Extremely Fine)
OBVERSE: Wear shows on high points of hair and at cheek line. Ear shows slight wear on the upper tip.
REVERSE: High points of flame, torch and leaves are worn, but all details are clearly defined and partially separated. Traces of mint luster may still show.

VERY FINE *(Light to moderate even wear. All major features are sharp.)*

VF-30 (Choice Very Fine)
OBVERSE: Wear spots show on hair, ear, cheek, and chin. Hair lines are weak but have nearly full visible details.
REVERSE: Wear shows on flame but some details are visible. All vertical lines are plain. Most details in the torch and leaves are clear.

VF-20 (Very Fine)
OBVERSE: Three-quarters of the details still show in hair. Face worn but bold. Some details in the ear are visible.
REVERSE: Wear shows on the flame but a few lines are visible. All torch lines are worn but bold. Most details in leaves are clear.

FINE *(Moderate to heavy even wear. Entire design clear and bold.)*

F-12 (Fine)
OBVERSE: Half the details show in hair. All of the face is weak but boldly visible. Half of inner edge of ear is worn away.
REVERSE: Vertical lines are all visible, but horizontal bands are worn smooth. Leaves show some detail. Flame is nearly smooth.

VERY GOOD *(Well worn. Design clear but flat and lacking details.)*

VG-8 (Very Good)
OBVERSE: Entire head is weak, and most of the details in hair and ear are worn smooth. All letters and date are clear. Rim is complete.

REVERSE: About half the outer vertical lines in torch are visible. Flame is only outlined. Leaves show very little detail. Rim is complete.

GOOD *(Heavily worn. Design and legend visible but faint in spots.)*

G-4 (Good)
OBVERSE: Entire design well worn with very little detail remaining. Ear is completely outlined. Legend and date are weak but visible. Rim is visible.
REVERSE: Torch is worn nearly flat but is completely outlined. Leaves are worn smooth. Legend is all visible.

ABOUT GOOD *(Outlined design. Parts of date and legend worn smooth.)*

AG-3 (About Good)
OBVERSE: Head is outlined with nearly all details worn away. Date readable but worn. Legend merging into rim.
REVERSE: Entire design partially worn away. Rim merges into the legend.

QUARTERS — BARBER 1892 – 1916

MINT STATE *(Absolutely no trace of wear.)*

MS-70 (Perfect Uncirculated)
A flawless coin exactly as it was minted, with no trace of wear or injury. Must have full mint luster and brilliance or light toning. Any unusual die or striking traits must be described.

MS-65 (Choice Uncirculated)
No trace of wear; nearly as perfect as MS-70 except for some small blemishes. Has full mint luster but may be unevenly toned or lightly fingermarked. A few barely noticeable nicks or marks may be present.

MS-60 (Uncirculated)
A strictly Uncirculated coin with no trace of wear, but with blemishes more obvious than for MS-65. May lack full mint luster, and surface may be dull, spotted, or heavily toned. Check points for signs of abrasion: high points of cheek and hair below LIBERTY, eagle's head and tips of tail and wings.

ABOUT UNCIRCULATED *(Small trace of wear visible on highest points.)*

AU-55 (Choice About Uncirculated)
OBVERSE: Only a trace of wear shows on highest points of hair below BER in LIBERTY.

OBVERSE

REVERSE

REVERSE: A trace of wear shows on head, tip of tail, and tips of wings. Three-quarters of the mint luster is still present.

AU-50 (About Uncirculated)
OBVERSE: Traces of wear show on cheek, tips of leaves, and hair below LIBERTY.
REVERSE: Traces of wear show on head, neck, tail, and tips of wings. Half of the mint luster is still present.

EXTREMELY FINE *(Very light wear on only the highest points.)*

EF-45 (Choice Extremely Fine)
OBVERSE: Slight wear shows on high points of upper leaves, cheek, and hair above forehead. LIBERTY is sharp and band edges are bold.
REVERSE: High points of head, neck, wings, and talons lightly worn. Lines in center tail feathers are clearly defined. Part of the mint luster is still present.

EF-40 (Extremely Fine)
OBVERSE: Light wear shows on leaves, cheek, cap, and hair above forehead. LIBERTY is sharp and band edges are clear.
REVERSE: High points of head, neck, wings, and tail are lightly worn, but all details are clearly defined. Leaves show trace of wear at edges. Traces of mint luster may still show.

VERY FINE *(Light to moderate even wear. All major features are sharp.)*

VF-30 (Choice Very Fine)
OBVERSE: Wear spots show on leaves, cap, hair and cheek. Bottom row of leaves is weak but has some visible details. LIBERTY and band are complete. Folds in cap are distinct.
REVERSE: Wear shows on shield but all details are visible. Most of the details in neck and tail are clear. Motto is complete.

VF-20 (Very Fine)
OBVERSE: Over half the details still show in leaves. Hair and ribbon worn but bold. Every letter in LIBERTY is visible.
REVERSE: The shield is worn, but most details are visible. Half the details in feathers are clear. Wings and legs show wear spots. Motto is clear.

FINE *(Moderate to heavy even wear. Entire design clear and bold.)*

F-12 (Fine)
OBVERSE: Some details show in hair, cap, and facial features. All letters in LIBERTY are weak but visible. Upper row of leaves is outlined, but bottom row is worn nearly smooth. Rim is full and bold.
REVERSE: Half of the feathers are plainly visible. Wear spots show in center of neck, motto, and arrows. Horizontal shield lines are merged; vertical lines are separated. Letters in legend are worn but clear.

VERY GOOD *(Well worn. Design clear but flat and lacking details.)*

VG-8 (Very Good)
OBVERSE: Entire head weak, and most details in face are worn smooth. Three letters in LIBERTY are clear. Rim is complete.
REVERSE: Eagle shows only a small amount of detail. Arrows and leaves are flat. Most of the shield is very weak. Part of the eye is visible.

GOOD *(Heavily worn. Design and legend visible but faint in spots.)*

G-4 (Good)
OBVERSE: Entire design well worn with very little detail remaining. Legend is weak but visible. LIBERTY is worn away.
REVERSE: Eagle worn flat but is completely outlined. Ribbon worn nearly smooth. Legend weak but visible. Rim worn to tops of letters.

ABOUT GOOD *(Outlined design. Parts of date and legend worn smooth.)*

AG-3 (About Good)
OBVERSE: Head is outlined with nearly all details worn away. Date readable but partially worn away. Legend merging into rim.
REVERSE: Entire design partially worn away and legend merges with rim.

QUARTERS — LIBERTY STANDING, VARIETY I 1916–1917 LIBERTY STANDING, VARIETY II 1917–1924

MINT STATE *(Absolutely no trace of wear.)*

MS-70 (Perfect Uncirculated)
A flawless coin exactly as it was minted, with no trace of wear or injury. Must have full mint luster and brilliance or light toning. Head details* (see p. 69) are an important part of this grade and must be specifically designated. Any other unusual die or striking traits must be described.

MS-65 (Choice Uncirculated)
No trace of wear; nearly as perfect as MS-70 except for some small blemish. Has full mint luster but may be unevenly toned or lightly fingermarked, may be weakly struck in one small spot. A few barely noticeable nicks or marks may be present. Head details may be incomplete.

MS-60 (Uncirculated)
A strictly Uncirculated coin with no trace of wear, but with blemishes more obvious than for MS-65. May lack full mint luster, and surface may be dull, spotted or heavily toned. One or two small spots may be weakly struck. Head details* (see p. 69) may be incomplete. Check points for signs of abrasion: mail covering breast, knee, high points of gown and shield; high points of eagle's breast and wings. Coins of this design frequently show weakly struck spots and usually lack full head details.

ABOUT UNCIRCULATED *(Small trace of wear visible on highest points.)*

AU-55 (Choice About Uncirculated)

OBVERSE

TYPE I
REVERSE

TYPE II
REVERSE

OBVERSE: Only a trace of wear shows on highest points of mail covering breast, inner shield and right knee.
REVERSE: A trace of wear shows on breast and edges of wings. Three-quarters of the mint luster is still present.

AU-50 (About Uncirculated)
OBVERSE: Traces of wear show on breast, knee, and high points of inner shield.
REVERSE: Traces of wear show on edges of wings and at center of breast. All of the tail feathers are visible. Half of the mint luster is still present.

EXTREMELY FINE *(Very light wear on only the highest points.)*

EF-45 (Choice Extremely Fine)
OBVERSE: Light wear spots show on upper right leg and knee. Nearly all of the gown lines are clearly visible. Shield details are bold. Breast is lightly worn and may show small flat spot.
REVERSE: Small flat spots show on high points of breast and on front wing edges. Tail feathers have nearly full details. Part of the mint luster is still present.

EF-40 (Extremely Fine)
OBVERSE: Wear shows on breast and right leg above and below knee. Most of the gown lines are visible. Shield details are bold. Breast is well rounded but has small flat spot.
REVERSE: High points of eagle are lightly worn. Central part of edge on right wing is well worn. Traces of mint luster may still show.

VERY FINE *(Light to moderate even wear. All major features are sharp.)*

VF-30 (Choice Very Fine)
OBVERSE: Wear spots show on breast, shield, and leg. Right leg is rounded but worn from above knee to ankle. Gown line crossing thigh is partially visible. Half of mail covering breast can be seen. Circle around inner shield is complete.
REVERSE: Breast and leg are worn but clearly separated, with some feathers visible between them. Feather ends and folds are visible in right wing.

VF-20 (Very Fine)
OBVERSE: Right leg is worn flat in central parts. Wear spots show on head, breast, shield, and foot. Beads on outer shield are visible, but those next to body are weak. Inner circle of shield is complete.
REVERSE: Entire eagle is lightly worn but most major details are visible. Breast and edge of right wing are worn flat. Top tail feathers are complete.

FINE *(Moderate to considerable even wear. Entire design clear and bold.)*

F-12 (Fine)
OBVERSE: Gown details worn but show clearly across body. Left leg is lightly worn. Right leg nearly flat and toe is worn. Breast worn but some mail is visible. Date may show some weakness at top. Rim is full. Outer edge of shield is complete.
REVERSE: Breast is worn almost smooth. Half of the wing feathers are visible, although well worn in spots. The rim is full.

VERY GOOD *(Well worn. Design clear but flat and lacking details.)*

VG-8 (Very Good)
OBVERSE: Entire design is weak, and most details in gown are worn smooth. All

letters and date are clear but tops of numerals may be flat. Rim is complete. Drapery across breast is partially outlined.
REVERSE: About one-third of the feathers are visible, and large feathers at ends of wings are well separated. Eye is visible. Rim is full and all letters are clear.

GOOD *(Heavily worn. Design and legend visible but faint in spots.)*

G-4 (Good)
OBVERSE: Entire design well worn with very little detail remaining. Legend and date are weak but visible. Top of date may be worn flat. Rim is complete.
REVERSE: Eagle worn nearly flat but is completely outlined. Lettering and stars worn but clearly visible. Rim worn to tops of legend.

ABOUT GOOD *(Outlined design. Parts of date and legend worn smooth.)*

AG-3 (About Good)
OBVERSE: Figure is outlined with nearly all details worn away. Legend visible but half worn away and may merge with rim. Date weak and readable.
REVERSE: Entire design partially worn away. Some letters merging into rim.

Note: Coins of this design are sometimes weakly struck in spots, particularly at Liberty's head, breast, knee, and shield and on the eagle's breast and wings.

*Specimens with "full head" must show the following details: Three well-defined leaves in hair; complete hairline along brow and across face; small indentation at ear. Coins of any grade other than MS-70 can be assumed to lack full head details unless the amount of visible features is specifically designated.

QUARTERS — WASHINGTON 1932 TO DATE

MINT STATE *(Absolutely no trace of wear.)*

MS-70 (Perfect Uncirculated)
A flawless coin exactly as it was minted, with no trace of wear or injury. Must have full mint luster and brilliance or light toning. Any unusual striking traits must be described.

MS-65 (Choice Uncirculated)
No trace of wear; nearly as perfect as MS-70 except for some small blemishes. Has full mint luster but may be unevenly toned or lightly fingermarked. A few barely noticeable nicks or marks may be present.

MS-60 (Uncirculated)
A strictly Uncirculated coin with no trace of wear, but with blemishes more obvious

OBVERSE

REVERSE

than for MS-65. May lack full mint luster, and surface may be dull, spotted, or heavily toned. Check points for signs of abrasion: high points of cheek and hair in front and back of ear, tops of legs and details in breast feathers.

ABOUT UNCIRCULATED *(Small trace of wear visible on highest points.)*

AU-55 (Choice About Uncirculated)
OBVERSE: Only a trace of wear shows on highest points of hair in front and in back of ear.
REVERSE: A trace of wear shows on highest spots of breast feathers. Nearly all of the mint luster is still present.

AU-50 (About Uncirculated)
OBVERSE: Traces of wear show on hair in front and in back of ear.
REVERSE: Traces of wear show on legs and breast feathers. Three-quarters of the mint luster is still present.

EXTREMELY FINE *(Light wear on most of the highest points.)*

EF-45 (Choice Extremely Fine)
OBVERSE: Slight wear shows on high points of hair around ear and along hairline up to crown. Hairlines are sharp and detailed.
REVERSE: High points of legs are lightly worn. Breast feathers are worn but clearly defined and fully separated. Half of the mint luster is still present.

EF-40 (Extremely Fine)
OBVERSE: Wear shows on high points of hair around and at hairline up to crown.
REVERSE: High points of breast, legs, and claws are lightly worn, but all details are clearly defined and partially separated. Part of the mint luster is still present.

VERY FINE *(Light to moderate even wear. All major features are sharp.)*

VF-30 (Choice Very Fine)
OBVERSE: Wear spots show on hair at forehead and ear, cheek, and jaw. Hair lines are weak but have nearly full visible details.
REVERSE: Wear shows on breast but a few feathers are visible. Legs are worn smooth. Most details in the wings are clear.

FINE *(Moderate to considerable even wear. Entire design clear and bold.)*

F-12 (Fine)
OBVERSE: Details show only at back of hair. Motto is weak but clearly visible. Part of cheek edge is worn away.
REVERSE: Feathers in breast and legs are worn smooth. Leaves show some detail. Parts of wings are nearly smooth.

VERY GOOD *(Well worn. Design clear but flat and lacking details.)*

VG-8 (Very Good)
OBVERSE: Entire head is weak, and most details in hair are worn smooth. All letters and date are clear. Rim is complete.
REVERSE: About half of the wing feathers are visible. Breast and legs only outlined. Leaves show very little detail. Rim is complete.

GOOD *(Heavily worn. Design and legend visible but faint in spots.)*

G-4 (Good)
OBVERSE: Hair is well worn with very little detail remaining. Half of motto is readable. LIBERTY and date are weak but visible. Rim merges with letters.

REVERSE: Eagle is worn nearly flat but is completely outlined. Leaves, breast, and legs are worn smooth. Legend is all visible but merges with rim.

ABOUT GOOD *(Outlined design. Parts of date and legend worn smooth.)*

AG-3 (About Good)
OBVERSE: Head is outlined with nearly all details worn away. Date readable but worn. Traces of motto are visible. Legend merging into rim.
REVERSE: Entire design partially worn away. Rim merges into legend.

Note: The obverse motto is always weak on coins of 1932 and early issues of 1934.
The reverse rim and lettering has a tendency to be very weak, particularly on coins dated 1934-D, 1935-D and S, 1936-D and S, 1937-D and S (especially), 1938-D and S, 1939-D and 1940-D.

HALF DOLLARS — BARBER 1892–1915

MINT STATE *(Absolutely no trace of wear.)*

MS-70 (Perfect Uncirculated)
A flawless coin exactly as it was minted, with no trace of wear or injury. Must have full mint luster and brilliance or light toning. Any unusual die or striking traits must be described.

MS-65 (Choice Uncirculated)
No trace of wear; nearly as perfect as MS-70 except for some small blemish. Has full mint luster but may be unevenly toned or lightly fingermarked. A few barely noticeable nicks or marks may be present.

MS-60 (Uncirculated)
A strictly Uncirculated coin with no trace of wear, but with blemishes more obvious than for MS-65. May lack full mint luster, and surface may be dull, spotted, or heavily toned. Check points for signs of abrasion: high points of cheek and hair below LIBERTY, eagle's head and tips of tail and wings.

ABOUT UNCIRCULATED *(Small trace of wear visible on highest points.)*

AU-55 (Choice About Uncirculated)
OBVERSE: Only a trace of wear shows on highest points of hair below BER in LIBERTY.
REVERSE: A trace of wear shows on head, tip of tail, and tips of wings. Three-quarters of the mint luster is still present.

OBVERSE

REVERSE

AU-50 (About Uncirculated)
OBVERSE: Traces of wear show on cheek, tips of leaves, and hair below LIBERTY.
REVERSE: Traces of wear show on head, neck, tail, and tips of wings. Half of the mint luster is still present.

EXTREMELY FINE *(Very light wear on only the highest points.)*

EF-45 (Choice Extremely Fine)
OBVERSE: Slight wear shows on high points of upper leaves, cheek, and hair above forehead. LIBERTY is sharp and band edges are bold.
High points of head, neck, wings and talons lightly worn. Lines in reverse center tail feathers are clearly defined. Part of the mint luster is still present.

EF-40 (Extremely Fine)
OBVERSE: Light wear shows on leaves, cheek, cap, and hair above forehead. LIBERTY is sharp and band edges are clear.
REVERSE: High points of head, neck, wings, and tail are lightly worn, but all details are clearly defined. Leaves show trace of wear at edges. Traces of mint luster may still show.

VERY FINE *(Light to moderate even wear. All major features are sharp.)*

VF-30 (Choice Very Fine)
OBVERSE: Wear spots show on leaves, cap, hair, and cheek. Bottom row of leaves is weak but has some visible details. LIBERTY and band are complete. Folds in cap are distinct.
REVERSE: Wear shows on shield but all details are visible. Most of the details in neck and tail are clear. Motto is complete.

VF-20 (Very Fine)
OBVERSE: Over half the details still show in leaves. Hair and ribbon worn but bold. Every letter in LIBERTY is visible. Bottom folds in cap are full.
REVERSE: Shield is worn, but all details are visible. Half the details in feathers are clear. Wings, tail and legs show small wear spots. Motto is clear.

FINE *(Moderate to considerable even wear. Entire design clear and bold.)*

F-12 (Fine)
OBVERSE: Some details show in hair, cap, and facial features. All letters in LIBERTY are weak but visible. Upper row of leaves is outlined, but bottom row is worn nearly smooth. Rim is full and bold.
REVERSE: Half the feathers are plainly visible. Wear spots show in center of neck, motto and arrows. Horizontal shield lines are merged; vertical lines are separated. Letters in legend are worn but clear.

VERY GOOD *(Well worn. Design clear but flat and lacking details.)*

VG-8 (Very Good)
OBVERSE: Entire head weak, and most details in face are heavily worn. Three letters in LIBERTY are clear. Rim is complete.
REVERSE: Eagle shows only a small amount of detail. Arrows and leaves are flat. Most of shield is very weak. Parts of eye and motto visible.

GOOD *(Heavily worn. Design and legend visible but faint in spots.)*

G-4 (Good)
OBVERSE: Entire design well worn with very little detail remaining. Legend and date weak but visible. LIBERTY is worn away.
REVERSE: Eagle worn flat but is completely outlined. Ribbon worn nearly smooth. Legend weak but visible. Rim worn to tops of letters.

ABOUT GOOD *(Outlined design. Parts of date and legend worn smooth.)*

AG-3 (About Good)
OBVERSE: Head is outlined with nearly all details worn away. Date readable but partially worn away. Legend merging into rim.
REVERSE: Entire design partially worn away and legend merges with rim.

HALF DOLLARS — LIBERTY WALKING 1916–1947

MINT STATE *(Absolutely no trace of wear.)*

MS-70 (Perfect Uncirculated)
A flawless coin exactly as it was minted, with no trace of wear or injury. Must have full mint luster and brilliance or light toning. Any unusual die or striking traits must be described.

MS-65 (Choice Uncirculated)
No trace of wear; nearly as perfect as MS-70 except for some small blemishes. Has full mint luster but may be unevenly toned or lightly fingermarked. May be weakly struck in one or two small spots. A few minute nicks or marks may be present.

MS-60 (Uncirculated)
A strictly Uncirculated coin with no trace of wear, but with blemishes more obvious than for MS-65. May lack full mint luster, and surface may be dull, spotted, or heavily toned. A few small spots may be weakly struck. Check points for signs of abrasion: hair above temple, right arm, left breast; high points of eagle's head, breast, legs, and wings. Coins of this design frequently show weakly struck spots and usually lack full head and hand details.

ABOUT UNCIRCULATED *(Small trace of wear visible on highest points.)*

AU-55 (Choice About Uncirculated)
OBVERSE: Only a trace of wear shows on highest points of head, breast, and right arm.
REVERSE: A trace of wear shows on left leg between breast and left wing. Three-quarters of the mint luster is still present.

OBVERSE

REVERSE

AU-50 (About Uncirculated)
OBVERSE: Traces of wear show on head, breast, arms, and left leg.
REVERSE: Traces of wear show on high points of wings and at center of head. All leg feathers are visible. Half of the mint luster is still present.

EXTREMELY FINE *(Very light wear on only the highest points.)*

EF-45 (Choice Extremely Fine)
OBVERSE: Light wear spots show on head, breast, arms, left leg, and foot. Nearly all gown lines are clearly visible. Sandal details are bold and complete. Knee is lightly worn but full and rounded.
REVERSE: Small flat spots show on high points of breast and legs. Wing feathers have nearly full details. Part of the mint luster is still present.

EF-40 (Extremely Fine)
OBVERSE: Wear shows on head, breast, arms, and left leg. Nearly all gown lines are visible. Sandal details are complete. Breast and knee are nearly flat.
REVERSE: High points of eagle are lightly worn. Half the breast and leg feathers are visible. Central part of feathers below neck is well worn. Traces of mint luster may still show.

VERY FINE *(Light to moderate even wear. All major features are sharp.)*

VF-30 (Choice Very Fine)
OBVERSE: Wear spots on head, breast, arms, and legs. Left leg is rounded but worn from above knee to ankle. Gown line crossing body is partially visible. Knee is flat. Outline of breast can be seen.
REVERSE: Breast and legs are moderately worn but clearly separated, with some feathers visible in right wing. Pupil in eye is visible.

VF-20 (Very Fine)
OBVERSE: Left leg is worn nearly flat. Wear spots show on head, breast, arms and foot. Lines on skirt are visible, but may be weak on coins before 1921. Breast is outlined.
REVERSE: Entire eagle is lightly worn but most major details are visible. Breast, central part of legs and top edge of right wing are worn flat.

FINE *(Moderate to considerable even wear. Entire design clear and bold.)*

F-12 (Fine)
OBVERSE: Gown stripes worn but show clearly, except for coins before 1921, where only half are visible. Right leg is lightly worn. Left leg nearly flat and sandal is worn but visible. Center of body worn but some of the gown is visible. Outer edge of rim is complete.
REVERSE: Breast is worn smooth. Half the wing feathers are visible, although well worn in spots. Top two layers of feathers are visible in left wing. Rim is full.

VERY GOOD *(Well worn. Design clear but flat and lacking details.)*

VG-8 (Very Good)
OBVERSE: Entire design is weak; most details in gown are worn smooth except for coins after 1921, where half the stripes must show. All letters and date are clear but top of motto may be weak. Rim is complete. Drapery across body is partially visible.
REVERSE: About one-third of the feathers are visible, and large feathers at ends of wings are well separated. Eye is visible. Rim is full and all letters are clear.

GOOD *(Heavily worn. Design and legend visible but faint in spots.)*

G-4 (Good)
OBVERSE: Entire design well worn with very little detail remaining. Legend and date weak but visible. Top of date may be worn flat. Rim is flat but nearly complete.
REVERSE: Eagle worn nearly flat but is completely outlined. Lettering and motto worn but clearly visible.

ABOUT GOOD *(Outlined design. Parts of date and legend worn smooth.)*

AG-3 (About Good)
OBVERSE: Figure is outlined with nearly all details worn away. Legend visible but half worn away. Date weak but readable. Rim merges with lettering.
REVERSE: Entire design partially worn away. Letters merge with rim.

Note: Coins of this design are sometimes weakly struck in spots, particularly at Liberty's head, hand holding branch and drapery lines of dress, and on the eagle's leg feathers.

HALF DOLLARS — FRANKLIN 1948 –1963

MINT STATE *(Absolutely no trace of wear.)*

MS-70 (Perfect Uncirculated)
A flawless coin exactly as it was minted, with no trace of wear or injury. Must have full mint luster and brilliance or light toning. Any unusual striking traits must be described.

MS-65 (Choice Uncirculated)
No trace of wear; nearly as perfect as MS-70 except for some small blemishes. Has full mint luster but may be unevenly toned or lightly fingermarked. A few barely noticeable nicks or marks may be present.

MS-60 (Uncirculated)
A strictly Uncirculated coin with no trace of wear, but with blemishes more obvious than for MS-65. May lack full mint luster, and surface may be dull, spotted, or heavily toned. Check points for signs of abrasion: high points of cheek, shoulder, and hair left of ear; straps around beam, lines, and lettering on bell.

ABOUT UNCIRCULATED *(Small trace of wear visible on highest points.)*

AU-55 (Choice About Uncirculated)
OBVERSE: Only a trace of wear shows on highest spots of cheek and hair left of ear.

OBVERSE

REVERSE

REVERSE: A trace of wear shows on highest points of lettering on bell. Nearly all of the mint luster is still present.

AU-50 (About Uncirculated)

OBVERSE: Traces of wear show on cheek and hair on shoulder and left of ear.
REVERSE: Traces of wear show on bell at lettering and along ridges at bottom. Three-quarters of the mint luster is still present.

EXTREMELY FINE *(Very light wear on only the highest points.)*

EF-45 (Choice Extremely Fine)

OBVERSE: Slight wear shows on cheek and high points of hair behind ear and along shoulder. Hair lines at back of head are sharp and detailed.
REVERSE: High points of straps on beam are lightly worn. Lines at bottom of bell are worn but clearly defined and separated. Lettering on bell is very weak at center. Half of the mint luster is still present.

EF-40 (Extremely Fine)

OBVERSE: Wear shows on high points of cheek and hair behind ear and at shoulder.
REVERSE: High points of beam straps and lines along bottom of bell are lightly worn, but details are clearly defined and partially separated. Lettering on bell is worn away at center. Part of the mint luster is still present.

VERY FINE *(Light to moderate even wear. All major features are sharp.)*

VF-30 (Choice Very Fine)

OBVERSE: Wear spots show on hair at shoulder and behind ear, on cheek and jaw. Hair lines are weak but have nearly full visible details.
REVERSE: Wear shows on bell lettering but some of the details are visible. Straps on beam are plain. Half of line details at bottom of bell are worn smooth.

VF-20 (Very Fine)

OBVERSE: Three-quarters of the lines still show in hair. Cheek lightly worn but bold. Some hair details around the ear are visible.
REVERSE: Wear shows on beam but most details are visible. Bell is worn but bold. Lines across bottom of bell are flat near crack.

FINE *(Moderate to considerable even wear. Entire design clear and bold.)*

F-12 (Very Fine)

OBVERSE: Hair details show only at back and side of head. Designer's initials weak but clearly visible. Part of cheek is worn flat.
REVERSE: Most of lines at bottom of bell are worn smooth. Parts of straps on beam are nearly smooth. Rim is full.

VERY GOOD *(Well worn. Design clear but flat and lacking details.)*

VG-8 (Very Good)

OBVERSE: Entire head is weak, and most details in hair from temple to ear are worn smooth. All letters and date are bold. Ear and designer's initial are visible. Rim is complete.

HALF DOLLARS — KENNEDY 1964 TO DATE

MINT STATE *(Absolutely no trace of wear.)*

MS-70 (Perfect Uncirculated)

A flawless coin exactly as it was minted, with no trace of wear or injury. Must have

OBVERSE

REVERSE

full mint luster and brilliance or light toning. Any unusual striking traits must be described.

MS-65 (Choice Uncirculated)
No trace of wear; nearly as perfect as MS-70 except for some small blemish. Has full mint luster but may be unevenly toned or lightly fingermarked. A few barely noticeable nicks or marks may be present.

MS-60 (Uncirculated)
A strictly Uncirculated coin with no trace of wear, but with blemishes more obvious than for MS-65. Has full mint luster, but surface may be dull, spotted, or heavily toned. Check points for signs of abrasion: high points of cheek and jawbone, center of neck, hair below part, bundle of arrows, center tail feather, right wing tip.

ABOUT UNCIRCULATED *(Small trace of wear visible on highest points.)*

AU-55 (Choice About Uncirculated)
OBVERSE: Only a trace of wear shows on highest points of cheek, jawbone and hair below part.
REVERSE: A trace of wear shows on central tail feather. Nearly all of the mint luster is still present.

EXTREMELY FINE *(Very light wear on only the highest points.)*

EF-40 (Extremely Fine)
OBVERSE: Slight wear shows on cheek, along jawbone, and on high points of hair below part. Hair lines are sharp and detailed.
REVERSE: High points of arrows and right wing tip are lightly worn. Central tail feathers are worn but clearly defined and fully separated. Three-quarters of the mint luster is still present.

VERY FINE *(Light to moderate even wear. All major features are sharp.)*

VF-30 (Choice Very Fine)
OBVERSE: Wear spots show on hair below part and along cheek and jaw. Hair lines are weak but have nearly full visible details.
REVERSE: Wear shows on arrow points but some details are visible. All central tail feathers are plain. Wing tips are lightly worn.

DOLLARS — MORGAN 1878 – 1921

MINT STATE *(Absolutely no trace of wear.)*

MS-70 (Perfect Uncirculated)
A flawless coin exactly as it was minted, with no trace of wear or injury. Must have

OBVERSE

REVERSE

full mint luster and brilliance or light toning. Any unusual striking traits must be described.

MS-65 (Choice Uncirculated)
No trace of wear; nearly as perfect as MS-70 except for a few minute bag marks or surface mars. Has full mint luster but may be unevenly toned. Any unusual striking traits must be described.

MS-60 (Uncirculated)
A strictly Uncirculated coin with no trace of wear, but with bag marks and other abrasions more obvious than for MS-65. May have a few small rim marks and weakly struck spots. Has full mint luster but may lack brilliance, and surface may be spotted or heavily toned. For these coins, bag abrasions and scuff marks are considered different from circulation wear. Full mint luster and lack of any wear are necessary to distinguish MS-60 from AU-55. Check points for signs of wear: hair above eye and ear, edges of cotton leaves and blossoms, high upper fold of cap, high points of eagle's breast, and tops of legs. Weakly struck spots are common and should not be confused with actual wear.

ABOUT UNCIRCULATED *(Small trace of wear visible on highest points.)*

AU-55 (Choice About Uncirculated)
OBVERSE: Slight trace of wear shows on hair above ear and eye, edges of cotton leaves, and high upper fold of cap. Luster fading from cheek.
REVERSE: Slight trace of wear shows on breast, tops of legs, and talons. Most of the mint luster is still present, although marred by light bag marks and surface abrasions.

AU-50 (About Uncirculated)
OBVERSE: Traces of wear show on hair above eye and ear, edges of cotton leaves, and high upper fold of cap. Partial detail visible on tops of cotton blossoms. Luster gone from cheek.
REVERSE: There are traces of wear on breast, tops of legs, wing tips, and talons. Three-quarters of the mint luster is still present. Surface abrasions and bag marks are more noticeable than for AU-55.

EXTREMELY FINE *(Very light wear on only the highest points.)*

EF-45 (Choice Extremely Fine)
OBVERSE: Slight wear on hair above date, forehead, and ear. Lines in hair well detailed and sharp. Slight flat spots on edges of cotton leaves. Minute signs of wear on cheek.

REVERSE: High points of breast are lightly worn. Tops of legs and right wing tip show wear. Talons are slightly flat. Half of the mint luster is still present.

EF-40 (Extremely Fine)
OBVERSE: Wear shows on hair above date, forehead, and ear. Lines in hair well detailed. Flat spots visible on edges of cotton leaves. Cheek lightly worn.
REVERSE: Almost all feathers gone from breast. Tops of legs, wing tips, and feathers on head show wear. Talons are flat. Partial mint luster is visible.

VERY FINE *(Light to moderate even wear. All major features are sharp.)*

VF-30 (Choice Very Fine)
OBVERSE: Wear shows on high points of hair from forehead to ear. Some strands visible in hair above ear. There are smooth areas on cotton leaves and at top of cotton blossoms.
REVERSE: Wear shows on leaves of wreath and tips of wings. Only a few feathers visible on breast and head.

VF-20 (Very Fine)
OBVERSE: Smooth spots visible on hair from forehead to ear. Cotton leaves heavily worn but separated. Wheat grains show wear.
REVERSE: Some leaves on wreath are well worn. Breast is smooth, and only a few feathers show on head. Tips of wings are weak but lines are complete.

FINE *(Moderate to heavy even wear. Entire design clear and bold.)*

F-12 (Fine)
OBVERSE: Hairline along face is clearly defined. Lower two cotton leaves smooth but distinct from cap. Some wheat grains merging. Cotton blossoms flat but the two lines in each show clearly.
REVERSE: One-quarter of eagle's right wing and edge of left wing are smooth. Head, neck, and breast are flat and merging. Tail feathers slightly worn. Top leaves in wreath show heavy wear.

VERY GOOD *(Well worn. Design clear but flat and lacking details.)*

VG-8 (Very Good)
OBVERSE: Most details in hair are worn smooth. All letters and date are clear. Cotton blossoms flat and leaves merging in spots. Hair of eagle's right wing and one-third of left wing are smooth. All leaves in wreath are worn. Rim is complete.

GOOD *(Heavily worn. Design and legend visible but faint in spots.)*

G-4 (Good)
OBVERSE: Hair is well worn with very little detail remaining. Date, letters, and design clearly outlined. Rim is full.
REVERSE: Eagle is worn nearly flat but is completely outlined. Design elements smooth but visible. Legend is all visible; rim is full.

ABOUT GOOD *(Outlined design. Parts of date and legend worn smooth.)*

AG-3 (About Good)
OBVERSE: Head is outlined with nearly all details worn away. Date readable but worn. Legend merging into rim.
REVERSE: Entire design partially worn away. Rim merges into legend.

Note: Some of these dollars have a prooflike surface; this should be mentioned in any description of such pieces.

Portions of the design are often weakly struck, especially on the hair above the ear and on the eagle's breast.

DOLLARS — PEACE 1921–1935

MINT STATE *(Absolutely no trace of wear.)*

MS-70 (Perfect Uncirculated)
A flawless coin exactly as it was minted, with no trace of wear or injury. Must have full mint luster or light toning. Any unusual striking traits must be described.

MS-65 (Choice Uncirculated)
No trace of wear; nearly as perfect as MS-70 except for a few minute bag marks or surface marks. Has full mint luster but may be unevenly toned.

MS-60 (Uncirculated)
A strictly Uncirculated coin with no trace of wear, but with bag marks and other abrasions more obvious than for MS-65. May have a few small rim mars, and may be weakly struck. Has full mint luster but may lack brilliance, and surface may be spotted or heavily toned. For these coins, bag abrasions and scuff marks are considered different from circulation wear. Full mint luster and lack of any wear are necessary to distinguish MS-60 from AU-55. Check points for signs of wear: high points of cheek and hair, high points of feathers on right wing and leg. Weakly struck spots are common and should not be confused with actual wear.

ABOUT UNCIRCULATED *(Small trace of wear visible on highest points.)*

AU-55 (Choice About Uncirculated)
OBVERSE: Trace of wear shows on hair over ear and above forehead. Slight wear visible on cheek.
REVERSE: High points of feathers on right wing show a trace of wear. Most of the mint luster is still present, although marred by light bag marks and surface abrasions.

AU-50 (About Uncirculated)
OBVERSE: Traces of wear visible on neck and hair over ear and above forehead. Cheek shows slight wear.
REVERSE: Traces of wear show on head and high points of feathers on right wing. Three-quarters of the mint luster is still present. Surface abrasions and bag marks are more noticeable than for AU-55.

EXTREMELY FINE *(Very light wear on only the highest points.)*

OBVERSE

REVERSE

EF-45 (Choice Extremely Fine)
OBVERSE: Hair around face shows slight wear, but most hair strands are visible. Lower edge of neck lightly worn.
REVERSE: Top of neck and head behind eye show slight wear. Central wing and leg feathers lightly worn. Half of the mint luster is still present.

EF-40 (Extremely Fine)
OBVERSE: Slight flattening visible on high points of hair; most hair strands clearly separated. Entire face and lower edge of neck lightly worn.
REVERSE: Wear shows on head behind eye and top of neck. Some flat spots visible on central wing and leg feathers. Partial mint luster is visible.

DOLLARS — EISENHOWER 1971 TO DATE

MINT STATE *(Absolutely no trace of wear.)*

MS-70 (Perfect Uncirculated)
A flawless coin exactly as it was minted, with no trace of wear or injury. Must have full mint luster and brilliance or light toning. Any unusual striking traits must be described.

MS-65 (Choice Uncirculated)
No trace of wear; nearly as perfect as MS-70 except for some small blemish. Has full mint luster but may be unevenly toned or lightly fingermarked. A few minute nicks or marks may be present.

MS-60 (Uncirculated)
A strictly Uncirculated coin with no trace of wear, but with blemishes more obvious than for MS-65. Has full mint luster, but surface may be dull, spotted or heavily toned. Check points for signs of abrasion: high points of cheek and jawbone, center of neck, edge of bust, head, high points of ridges and feathers in wings and legs.

ABOUT UNCIRCULATED *(Small trace of wear visible on highest points.)*

AU-55 (Choice About Uncirculated)
OBVERSE: Only a trace of wear shows on highest points of jawbone and at center of neck.
REVERSE: A trace of wear shows on high points of feathers in wings and legs. Nearly all of the mint luster is still present.

EXTREMELY FINE *(Very light wear on only the highest points.)*

EF-45 (Choice Extremely Fine)
OBVERSE: Slight wear shows on cheek, along jawbone, and on high points at edge of bust. Hair lines are sharp and detailed.

OBVERSE

REVERSE

REVERSE: High points of head, legs, and wing ridges are lightly worn. Central feathers are all clearly defined. Three-quarters of the mint luster is still present.

VERY FINE *(Light to moderate even wear. All major features are sharp.)*

VF-30 (Choice Very Fine)
OBVERSE: Wear spots show on hair below part and along cheek and jaw. Hair lines are weak but have nearly full visible details. Slight wear shows at center of neck and along edge of bust.
REVERSE: Wear shows on head and feathers in wings and legs but all details are visible. All central tail feathers are plain. Wing and leg ridges are lightly worn.

GOLD DOLLARS—TYPE I 1849–1854

MINT STATE *(Absolutely no trace of wear.)*

MS-70 (Perfect Uncirculated)
A flawless coin exactly as it was minted, with no trace of wear or injury. Must have full mint luster and brilliance. Any unusual die or planchet traits must be described.

MS-65 (Choice Uncirculated)
No trace of wear; nearly as perfect as MS-70 except for some small blemish. Has full mint luster and brilliance but may show slight discoloration. A few barely noticeable nicks or marks may be present.

MS-60 (Uncirculated)
A strictly Uncirculated coin with no trace of wear, but with blemishes more obvious than for MS-65. May lack full mint luster and brilliance. Check points for signs of abrasion: hair near coronet; tips of leaves.

ABOUT UNCIRCULATED *(Small trace of wear visible on highest points.)*

AU-55 (Choice About Uncirculated)
OBVERSE: There is a trace of wear at upper hairline below coronet.
REVERSE: Trace of wear visible on tips of leaves. Three-quarters of the mint luster is still present.

AU-50 (About Uncirculated)
OBVERSE: There is a trace of wear on hairlines near coronet and below the ear.
REVERSE: Trace of wear visible on tips of leaves. Half of the mint luster is still present.

EXTREMELY FINE *(Very light wear on only the highest points.)*

OBVERSE

REVERSE

EF-45 (Choice Extremely Fine)
OBVERSE: Slight wear shows on highest wave of hair, hairline, and below ear. All major details are sharp. Beads at top of coronet are well defined.
REVERSE: Leaves show visible wear at tips, but central details are clearly defined. Traces of mint luster will show.

VERY FINE *(Light to moderate even wear. All major features are sharp.)*

VF-30 (Choice Very Fine)
OBVERSE: Beads on top of coronet are well defined. LIBERTY is complete. Hair around face and neck slightly worn but strands fully separated. Star centers show some details.
REVERSE: There is light even wear on legend and date. Some details show in center of leaves.

VF-20 (Very Fine)
OBVERSE: Beads at top of coronet are partially separated. LIBERTY is complete. Hair around face and neck noticeably worn but well outlined. Some star centers show details.
REVERSE: There is light even wear on legend and date. Only traces of leaf ribs are visible. Bow knot is flat on high point.

FINE *(Moderate to heavy even wear. Entire design clear and bold.)*

F-12 (Fine)
OBVERSE: LIBERTY is complete but weak. Ear lobe is visible. Hairlines and beads on coronet are worn smooth. Stars are clearly outlined, but centers are flat.
REVERSE: Legend within wreath is worn and weak in spots. Leaves and wreath are well outlined. Rim is full and edge beveled.

VERY GOOD *(Well worn. Design clear but flat and lacking details.)*

VG-8 (Very Good)
OBVERSE: Only the outline of hair is visible. Four letters in LIBERTY are clear.
REVERSE: Only the outline of leaves is visible. Legend and numeral are worn and very weak.

GOOD *(Heavily worn. Design and legend visible but faint in spots).*

G-4 (Good)
OBVERSE: Head is outlined with nearly all details worn away. Stars are weak. Full rim shows.
REVERSE: Date and legend well worn but readable. Leaves are outlined. Full rim shows.

Note: The gold dollars struck at Charlotte and Dahlonega are crude compared to those of the Philadelphia Mint. Frequently they have rough edges, and the die work appears to be generally inferior. In grading coins from these branch mints, consideration must be given to these factors.

QUARTER EAGLES — CORONET HEAD 1840 –1907

MINT STATE *(Absolutely no trace of wear.)*

MS-70 (Perfect Uncirculated)
A flawless coin exactly as it was minted, with no trace of wear or injury. Must have full mint luster and brilliance. Any unusual die or planchet traits must be described.

OBVERSE REVERSE

MS-65 (Choice Uncirculated)
No trace of wear; nearly as perfect as MS-70 except for some small blemish. Has full mint luster and brilliance but may show slight discoloration. A few barely noticeable nicks or marks may be present.

MS-60 (Uncirculated)
A strictly Uncirculated coin with no trace of wear, but with blemishes more obvious than for MS-65. May lack full mint luster and brilliance. Check points for signs of abrasion: tip of coronet, hair, wings, claws.

ABOUT UNCIRCULATED *(Small trace of wear visible on highest points.)*

AU-55 (Choice About Uncirculated)
OBVERSE: There is a trace of wear on tip of coronet and above eye.
REVERSE: Trace of wear visible on wing tips. Three-quarters of the mint luster is still present.

AU-50 (About Uncirculated)
OBVERSE: There is a trace of wear on coronet and on hair above ear, eye, and forehead.
REVERSE: Trace of wear visible on wing tips, below eye, and on claw. Half of the mint luster is still present.

EXTREMELY FINE *(Very light wear on only the highest points.)*

EF-45 (Choice Extremely Fine)
OBVERSE: There is light wear on coronet, and on hair above ear, eye, forelocks, and top of head.
REVERSE: Light wear shows on edges and tips of wings, on neck, below eye, and on claws. Part of the mint luster is still present.

EF-40 (Extremely Fine)
OBVERSE: Light wear shows on coronet, hair above ear and eye, on forelocks, and on cheek. All major details sharp.
REVERSE: Light wear shows on edges and tips of wings, on neck, below eye, on feathers, and claws. Shield well defined. Traces of mint luster will show.

VERY FINE *(Light to moderate even wear. All major features are sharp.)*

VF-30 (Choice Very Fine)
OBVERSE: Light wear visible on coronet; hair is worn but shows considerable detail. Most stars show details. LIBERTY bold and clear.
REVERSE: Light wear shows on edges and tips of wings. Some detail shows on

head and neck feathers. Vertical shield lines complete but some not separated; horizontal lines worn in center.

VF-20 (Very Fine)
OBVERSE: Hair outlined with very little detail. Only a few stars show any details. LIBERTY clear but not bold.
REVERSE: Half of wing feathers visible. Half of lines in shield are clear.

FINE *(Moderate to heavy even wear. Entire design clear and bold.)*

F-12 (Fine)
OBVERSE: Hair and cheek smooth. Stars outlined with no visible details. LIBERTY worn but visible.
REVERSE: Wings show very little detail. Head and one claw outlined only, with no details visible. Neck almost smooth. Most of shield lines merge.

Note: Coins of this type seldom appear in grades lower than Fine. Pieces made at Charlotte, Dahlonega and New Orleans are frequently found weakly struck. Those from San Francisco often lack feather details.

QUARTER EAGLES — INDIAN HEAD 1908–1929

MINT STATE *(Absolutely no trace of wear.)*

MS-70 (Perfect Uncirculated)
A flawless coin exactly as it was minted, with no trace of wear or injury. Must have full mint luster and brilliance. Any unusual die or planchet traits must be described.

MS-65 (Choice Uncirculated)
No trace of wear; nearly as perfect as MS-70 except for some small blemish. Has full mint luster and brilliance but may show slight discoloration. A few barely noticeable nicks or marks may be present.

MS-60 (Uncirculated)
A strictly Uncirculated coin with no trace of wear, but with blemishes more obvious than for MS-65. May lack full mint luster and brilliance. Checkpoints for signs of abrasion: cheekbone, headdress, headband feathers, shoulder of eagle's left wing.

ABOUT UNCIRCULATED *(Small trace of wear visible on highest points.)*

AU-55 (Choice About Uncirculated)
OBVERSE: There is a trace of wear on cheekbone.

OBVERSE

REVERSE

REVERSE: Trace of wear visible on shoulder of eagle's left wing. Three-quarters of the mint luster is still present.

AU-50 (About Uncirculated)
OBVERSE: There is a trace of wear on cheekbone and headdress.
REVERSE: Trace of wear visible on shoulder of wing, head, and breast. Half of the mint luster is still present.

EXTREMELY FINE *(Very light wear on only the highest points.)*

EF-45 (Choice Extremely Fine)
OBVERSE: There is light wear on cheekbone, headdress, and headband.
REVERSE: Light wear shows on upper portion of wing, head, neck, and breast.

EF-40 (Extremely Fine)
OBVERSE: Light wear shows on cheekbone, jaw, and headband. Slight wear visible on feathers of headdress. Stars sharp.
REVERSE: Light wear shows on wing, head, neck, and breast. Leg has full feather detail. Traces of mint luster will show.

VERY FINE *(Light to moderate even wear. All major features are sharp.)*

VF-30 (Choice Very Fine)
OBVERSE: Cheekbone shows flat spot. Small feathers clear; large feathers show some detail. Most of headband detail visible.
REVERSE: Wear shows on wing and neck. Some breast feathers show details. Most of leg feathers visible.

VF-20 (Very Fine)
OBVERSE: Cheekbone worn about halfway. Small feathers clear but large feathers show a little detail. Hair cord knot is distinct. Headband shows some detail.
REVERSE: Little detail shows on breast and leg feathers. Top of wing and neck worn. Second layer of wing feathers shows.

FINE *(Moderate to heavy even wear. Entire design clear and bold.)*

HALF EAGLES — CORONET HEAD 1839–1908

F-12 (Fine)
OBVERSE: Cheekbone worn; all feathers worn with very little detail visible. Stars outlined, with no details visible. Hair cord knot is worn but visible.
REVERSE: Wing worn, with only partial feathers at bottom visible. All lettering worn but visible.

OBVERSE

REVERSE

Note: Coins of this type are seldom collected in grades lower than Fine. Mint marks are often weakly struck.

MINT STATE *(Absolutely no trace of wear.)*

MS-70 (Perfect Uncirculated)
A flawless coin exactly as it was minted, with no trace of wear or injury. Must have full mint luster and brilliance. Any unusual die or planchet traits must be described.

MS-65 (Choice Uncirculated)
No trace of wear; nearly as perfect as MS-70 except for some small blemishes. Has full mint luster and brilliance but may show slight discoloration. A few barely noticeable bag marks and surface abrasions may be present.

MS-60 (Uncirculated)
A strictly Uncirculated coin with no trace of wear, but with blemishes more obvious than for MS-65. Has full mint luster but may lack brilliance. Surface may be lightly marred by minor bag marks and abrasions. Check points for signs of wear: hair, coronet, wings.

ABOUT UNCIRCULATED *(Small trace of wear visible on highest points.)*

AU-55 (Choice About Uncirculated)
OBVERSE: There is a trace of wear on tip of coronet and hair above eye.
REVERSE: Trace of wear visible on wing tips. Three-quarters of the mint luster is still present.

AU-50 (About Uncirculated)
OBVERSE: There is a trace of wear on coronet, above ear and eye.
REVERSE: Trace of wear visible on wing tips, below eye and on claw. Half of the mint luster is still present.

EXTREMELY FINE *(Light wear on only the highest points.)*

EF-45 (Choice Extremely Fine)
OBVERSE: There is light wear on coronet, and on hair above ear, eye, forelocks, and top of head.
REVERSE: Light wear shows on edges and tips of wings, on neck, below eye, and on claws. Part of the mint luster is still present.

EF-40 (Extremely Fine)
OBVERSE: Light wear shows on coronet, on hair above ear and eye, on the forelock, on top of head, and on cheek. All major details are sharp.
REVERSE: Light wear visible on edges and tips of wings, on neck, below eye, on feathers, and claws. Shield is well defined. Traces of mint luster will show.

VERY FINE *(Light to moderate even wear. All major features are sharp.)*

VF-30 (Choice Very Fine)
OBVERSE: Light wear shows on coronet, hair, and stars but most details are visible. LIBERTY bold.
REVERSE: Light wear visible on edges and tips of wings. Head and neck feathers show some detail. Vertical lines in shield complete but some not separated; horizontal lines worn in center.

VF-20 (Very Fine)
OBVERSE: Hair worn but major details visible. Top line of coronet broken. Some stars show partial detail. LIBERTY clear but not bold.

REVERSE: Half of wing feathers are visible. Half of lines in shield are clear.

FINE *(Moderate to heavy even wear. Entire design clear and bold.)*

F-12 (Fine)
OBVERSE: Hair and cheekbone smooth. Top line of coronet worn. LIBERTY worn but visible.
REVERSE: Wings show very little detail. Head and one claw outlined only, with no details visible. Neck almost smooth. Most of shield lines merge. (For the 1866 through 1908 group, the motto is worn but readable.)

Note: Coins of this type are seldom collected in grades lower than Fine.

HALF EAGLES — INDIAN HEAD 1908 –1929

MINT STATE *(Absolutely no trace of wear.)*

MS-70 (Perfect Uncirculated)
A flawless coin exactly as it was minted, with no trace of wear or injury. Must have full mint luster and brilliance. Any unusual die or planchet traits must be described.

MS-65 (Choice Uncirculated)
No trace of wear; nearly as perfect as MS-70 except for some small blemish. Has full mint luster and brilliance but may show slight discoloration. A few barely noticeable bag marks and surface abrasions may be present.

MS-60 (Uncirculated)
A strictly Uncirculated coin with no trace of wear, but with blemishes more obvious than for MS-65. Has full mint luster but may lack brilliance. Surface may be lightly marred by minor bag marks and abrasions. Check points for signs of wear: cheekbone, headdress, headband feathers, shoulder of eagle's left wing.

ABOUT UNCIRCULATED *(Small trace of wear visible on highest points.)*

AU-55 (Choice About Uncirculated)
OBVERSE: There is a trace of wear on cheekbone.
REVERSE: Trace of wear visible on shoulder of eagle's left wing. Three-quarters of the mint luster is still present.

AU-50 (About Uncirculated)
OBVERSE: There is a trace of wear on cheekbone and headdress.
REVERSE: Trace of wear visible on shoulder of wing, head and breast. Half of the mint luster is still present.

EXTREMELY FINE *(Light wear on only the highest points.)*

OBVERSE

REVERSE

EF-45 (Choice Extremely Fine)
OBVERSE: There is light wear on cheekbone, headdress and headband.
REVERSE: Light wear shows on upper portion of wing, head, neck, and breast. Part of mint luster is still present.

EF-40 (Extremely Fine)
OBVERSE: Light wear shows on cheekbone, jaw, and headband. Slight wear visible on feathers of headdress. Stars are sharp.
REVERSE: Light wear shows on wing, head, neck, and breast. Leg has full feather detail. Traces of mint luster will show.

VERY FINE *(Light to moderate even wear. All major features are sharp.)*

VF-30 (Choice Very Fine)
OBVERSE: Cheekbone worn, shows flat spot. Small feathers clear; large feathers show some details. Most of headband detail visible.
REVERSE: Wear shows on wing and neck. Some breast feathers show details. Most of leg feathers visible.

VF-30 (Very Fine)
OBVERSE: Cheekbone worn about half-way. Headdress feathers show some details. Hair cord knot is distinct. Headband shows only a little detail.
REVERSE: Little detail shows on breast and leg feathers. Top of wing and neck worn. Second layer of wing feathers shows.

FINE *(Moderate to heavy even wear. Entire design clear and bold.)*

F-12 (Fine)
OBVERSE: Cheekbone worn; all feathers worn with very little detail visible. Stars outlined, with no details visible. Hair cord knot is worn but visible.
REVERSE: Wing worn, with only partial feathers at bottom visible. All lettering worn but visible.

Note: Coins of this type are seldom collected in grades lower than Fine. Mint marks are often very weakly struck.

EAGLES — CORONET HEAD 1838 –1907

MINT STATE *(Absolutely no trace of wear.)*

MS-70 (Perfect Uncirculated)
A flawless coin exactly as it was minted, with no trace of wear or injury. Must have full mint luster and brilliance. Any unusual die or planchet traits must be described.

MS-65 (Choice Uncirculated)
No trace of wear; nearly as perfect as MS-70 except for some small blemishes.

OBVERSE

REVERSE

Has full mint luster and brilliance but may show slight discoloration. A few barely noticeable bag marks and surface abrasions may be present.

MS-60 (Uncirculated)
A strictly Uncirculated coin with no trace of wear, but with blemishes more obvious than for MS-65. Has full mint luster but may lack brilliance. Surface may be lightly marred by minor bag marks and abrasions. Check points for signs of wear: hair, coronet, wings.

ABOUT UNCIRCULATED *(Small trace of wear visible on highest points.)*

AU-55 (Choice About Uncirculated)
OBVERSE: There is a trace of wear on hair above eye and on coronet.
REVERSE: Trace of wear visible on wing tips. Three-quarters of the mint luster is still present.

AU-50 (About Uncirculated)
OBVERSE: There is a trace of wear on hair at ear and above eye, and on coronet.
REVERSE: Trace of wear visible on wing tips, below eye, and on claw. Half of the mint luster is still present.

EXTREMELY FINE *(Light wear on only the highest points.)*

EF-45 (Choice Extremely Fine)
OBVERSE: There is light wear on coronet, and on hair above ear, eye, forelocks, and top of head.
REVERSE: Light wear shows on edges and tips of wings, on neck, below eye, and on claws. Part of the mint luster is still present.

EF-40 (Extremely Fine)
OBVERSE: Light wear shows on coronet, hair, cheek, and stars. All major details sharp.
REVERSE: Light wear visible on wings, head, neck, and claws. Shield is well defined. Traces of mint luster will show.

VERY FINE *(Light to moderate even wear. All major features are sharp.)*

VF-30 (Choice Very Fine)
OBVERSE: There is light wear on coronet, hair, and stars, but most details are visible. There is a break on top line of coronet over two letters in LIBERTY. Cheek worn. LIBERTY bold.
REVERSE: Light wear visible on wings and head but some details show. Vertical lines in shield complete but some are not separated; horizontal lines worn in center.

VF-20 (Very Fine)
OBVERSE: Hair worn but major details visible. Break on top line of coronet extends over at least three letters in LIBERTY. Cheek well worn. Stars worn but show most details. LIBERTY clear but shows wear.
REVERSE: About half of wing feathers are visible. Very little detail shows in head.

FINE *(Moderate to heavy even wear. Entire design clear and bold.)*

F-12 (Fine)
OBVERSE: Hair and cheekbone smooth. Top line of coronet worn. Some details show in stars. LIBERTY worn but visible.
REVERSE: Wings show very little detail. Head and one claw outlined only, with no

details visible. Neck is almost smooth. Most of shield lines merge. (In the 1866 through 1907 group, the motto is worn but readable.)

Note: Coins of this type are seldom collected in grades lower than Fine.

EAGLES — INDIAN HEAD 1907–1933

MINT STATE *(Absolutely no trace of wear.)*

MS-70 (Perfect Uncirculated)
A flawless coin exactly as it was minted, with no trace of wear or injury. Must have full mint luster and brilliance. Any unusual die or planchet traits must be described.

MS-65 (Choice Uncirculated)
No trace of wear; nearly as perfect as MS-70 except for some small blemish. Has full mint luster and brilliance but may show some slight discoloration. A few minute bag marks and surface abrasions may be present.

MS-60 (Uncirculated)
A strictly Uncirculated coin with no trace of wear, but with blemishes more obvious than for MS-65. Has full mint luster but may lack brilliance. Surface may be lightly marred by minor bag marks and abrasions. Check points for signs of wear: above eye, cheek, wing.

ABOUT UNCIRCULATED *(Small trace of wear visible on highest points.)*

AU-55 (Choice About Uncirculated)
OBVERSE: There is a trace of wear above eye.
REVERSE: Trace of wear visible on wing. Three-quarters of the mint luster is still present.

AU-50 (About Uncirculated)
OBVERSE: There is a trace of wear on hair above eye and on forehead.
REVERSE: Trace of wear visible on wing. Half of the mint luster is still present.

EXTREMELY FINE *(Light wear on only the highest points.)*

EF-45 (Choice Extremely Fine)
OBVERSE: There is light wear on hair above eye and on forehead, and on cheekbone.
REVERSE: Light wear shows on wing and head. Part of the mint luster is still present.

EF-40 (Extremely Fine)
OBVERSE: Light wear shows on hair, cheekbone and feathers.

OBVERSE

REVERSE

REVERSE: Light wear visible on wing and head. Traces of mint luster will show.

VERY FINE *(Light to moderate even wear. All major features are sharp.)*

VF-30 (Choice Very Fine)
OBVERSE: There is light wear along forehead, but most detail shows. Moderate wear visible on cheekbone. Light wear shows where feathers meet headband.
REVERSE: Left wing shows more than half the details. Some details in head are visible.

VF-20 (Very Fine)
OBVERSE: About half the hair detail is visible. Moderate wear shows on cheekbone. Some feathers do not touch headband.
REVERSE: There is moderate wear on left wing which shows only about one-quarter detail. Head almost smooth. All lettering bold.

FINE *(Moderate to heavy even wear. Entire design clear and bold.)*

F-12 (Fine)
OBVERSE: Hair smooth with no details; cheekbone almost smooth. No feathers touch headband but most feather details visible.
REVERSE: Left wing top and head are worn smooth. Lettering worn but visible.

Note: Coins of this type are seldom collected in grades lower than Fine.

DOUBLE EAGLES — LIBERTY HEAD 1850 –1907

MINT STATE *(Absolutely no trace of wear.)*

MS-70 (Perfect Uncirculated)
A flawless coin exactly as it was minted, with no trace of wear or injury. Must have full mint luster and brilliance. Any unusual die or planchet traits must be described.

MS-65 (Choice Uncirculated)
No trace of wear; nearly as perfect as MS-70 except for some small blemishes. Has full mint luster and brilliance but may show slight discoloration. A few minute bag marks and surface abrasions are usually present.

MS-60 (Uncirculated)
A strictly Uncirculated coin with no trace of wear, but with blemishes more obvious than for MS-65. Has full mint luster but may lack brilliance. Surface is usually lightly marred by minor bag marks and abrasions. Check points for signs of wear: hair, coronet, eagle's neck and wing, top of shield.

ABOUT UNCIRCULATED *(Small trace of wear visible on highest points.)*

OBVERSE

REVERSE

AU-55 (Choice About Uncirculated)
OBVERSE: There is a trace of wear on hair.
REVERSE: Trace of wear visible on wing tips and neck. Three-quarters of the mint luster is still present.

AU-50 (About Uncirculated)
OBVERSE: There is a trace of wear on hair at top and over eye, and on coronet.
REVERSE: Trace of wear visible on wing tips, neck, and at top of shield. Half of the mint luster is still present.

EXTREMELY FINE *(Light wear on only the highest points.)*

EF-45 (Choice Extremely Fine)
OBVERSE: There is light wear on hair and coronet prongs.
REVERSE: Light wear shows on edges and tips of wings, on head and neck, and on horizontal shield lines. Part of the mint luster is still present.

EF-40 (Extremely Fine)
OBVERSE: Light wear shows on hair, coronet prongs and cheek.
REVERSE: Light wear visible on wings, head, neck, horizontal shield lines, and tail. Traces of mint luster will show.

VERY FINE *(Light to moderate even wear. All major features are sharp.)*

VF-30 (Choice Very Fine)
OBVERSE: About one-quarter of hair detail below coronet visible; half the detail shows above coronet. Cheek and some coronet prongs worn. Stars show wear but all details visible.
REVERSE: Most of wing details visible. Top part of shield shows moderate wear. About half the detail in tail visible.

VF-20 (Very Fine)
OBVERSE: Less than half the hair detail above coronet visible. About half the coronet prongs are considerably worn. Stars are flat but show most details. LIBERTY shows wear but is very clear.
REVERSE: Some wing details visible. Shield shows very little detail at top. Tail is worn with very little detail.

FINE *(Moderate to heavy even wear. Entire design clear and bold.)*

F-12 (Fine)
OBVERSE: All hairlines are well worn with very little detail visible. About one-quarter of details within coronet visible. Stars show little detail. LIBERTY readable.
REVERSE: Wings show very little detail. Head and neck smooth. Eye visible. Tail and top of shield smooth.

Note: Coins of this type are seldom collected in grades lower than Fine. The hair curl under the ear is sometimes weakly struck.

In the group between 1866 and 1876, the reverse motto is sometimes weakly struck.

Pieces made at the Carson City Mint are usually found weakly struck and heavily bag marked.

DOUBLE EAGLES — SAINT-GAUDENS 1907–1932

MINT STATE *(Absolutely no trace of wear.)*

MS-70 (Perfect Uncirculated)
A flawless coin exactly as it was minted, with no trace of wear or injury. Must have full mint luster and brilliance. Any unusual die or planchet traits must be described.

MS-65 (Choice Uncirculated)
No trace of wear; nearly as perfect as MS-70 except for some small blemishes. Has full mint luster and brilliance but may show slight discoloration. A few minute bag marks and surface abrasions are usually present.

MS-60 (Uncirculated)
A strictly Uncirculated coin with no trace of wear, but with blemishes more obvious than for MS-65. Has full mint luster but may lack brilliance. Surface is usually lightly marred by minor bag marks and abrasions. Check points for signs of wear: forehead, breast, knee, nose, eagle's wings and breast.

ABOUT UNCIRCULATED *(Small trace of wear visible on highest points.)*

AU-55 (Choice About Uncirculated)
OBVERSE: There is a trace of wear on left breast and left knee.
REVERSE: Trace of wear visible on high point of wing. Three-quarters of the mint luster is still present.

AU-50 (About Uncirculated)
OBVERSE: There is a trace of wear on nose, breast, and knee.
REVERSE: Trace of wear visible on wings. Half of the mint luster is still present.

EXTREMELY FINE *(Light wear on only the highest points.)*

EF-45 (Choice Extremely Fine)
OBVERSE: There is light wear on forehead, nose, breast and knee.
REVERSE: Light wear shows on wings and breast, but all feathers are bold. Part of the mint luster is still present.

EF-40 (Extremely Fine)
OBVERSE: Light wear shows on forehead, nose, breast, knee, and just below left knee. Drapery lines on chest visible.
REVERSE: Light wear visible on wings and breast but all feathers bold. Traces of mint luster will show.

VERY FINE *(Light to moderate even wear. All major features are sharp.)*

VF-30 (Choice Very Fine)
OBVERSE: There is light wear on all features, extending above and below left knee and along part of right leg. Some of garment lines on chest are visible.

OBVERSE

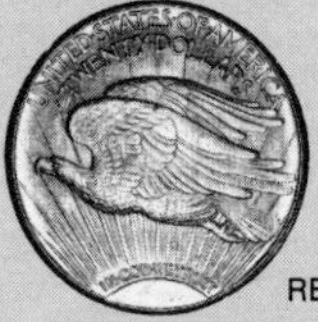

REVERSE

REVERSE: Light wear visible on left wing and breast; feathers show but some are weak.

VF-20 (Very Fine)

OBVERSE: Forehead moderately worn. Contours of breast worn. Only a few garment lines on chest are visible. Entire right leg shows moderate wear.
REVERSE: Half of feathers are visible in wings and breast.

FINE *(Moderate to heavy even wear. Entire design clear and bold.)*

F-12 (Fine)

OBVERSE: Forehead and garment smooth; breasts flat. Both legs worn with right bottom missing.
REVERSE: Less than half the wing details are visible. Only a little breast detail is visible.

Note: Coins of this type are seldom found in grades lower than Fine.

COLONIAL COINS, PATTERNS, AND TOKENS

The most extensively circulated—and faithfully trusted—coin of early colonial America was the Spanish silver dollar or "piece of eight." Introduced to this country by the Spanish explorers and later imported in abundance by traders, it had a value of eight *reals,* each real or "bit" being worth 12½ cents. Thus, the quarter or 25 cent piece came to be known as "two bits."

"Two-bits"

"Four-bits"

THE SPANISH MILLED DOLLAR
The "Piece of Eight"

The following pages contain descriptions and price valuations for most types of monies used in the American colonies, excluding foreign coins intended to serve currency needs abroad. Most can only be classed as tokens, as they either had no face value or were struck without government sanction. These include merchant pieces and other speculative issues. However, the colonists, being ever-resourceful, attempted from time to time to strike semi-official or official coinage, and these will be found listed as well. Colonial coinage on the whole is not handsome. It was generally produced under conditions inferior to that of government issued money, often designed and struck by persons who had little or no prior experience in such work. It is, nevertheless, of great interest from both a numismatic and historical point of view and much of it is extremely rare. As a general rule the collector should be wary of counterfeits and reproductions, as the majority of these pieces have at one time or other been copied, either as legitimate souvenirs or fraudulently.

SOMMER ISLANDS (BERMUDA)

This so-called "Hog money" is thought to be the first coinage of the American colonies. A hog is pictured on one side and a sailing vessel on the other. The workmanship is English. Hogs were not native to the islands but introduced around 1515 by the Spaniard Juan Bermudez, from whom Bermuda takes its name. They apparently increased and multiplied vastly within the next hundred years, serving as an important article of food for the inhabitants. The suggestion that the coins were intended to represent the market value of a hog, just as early Greek coins were sometimes stamped with a likeness of an animal whose price they equaled, is no longer given serious consideration. It was used merely as an emblem. These coins are of lightly silvered brass, inscribed "SOMMER ISLANDS." The edges are, as to be expected, irregular, having been produced by the hammering technique rather than milling.

SHILLING

TYPE OF COIN	ABP	AG-3 About Good	G-4 Good	F-12 Fine
☐ Shilling	800.00	1900.00	2700.00	7500.00

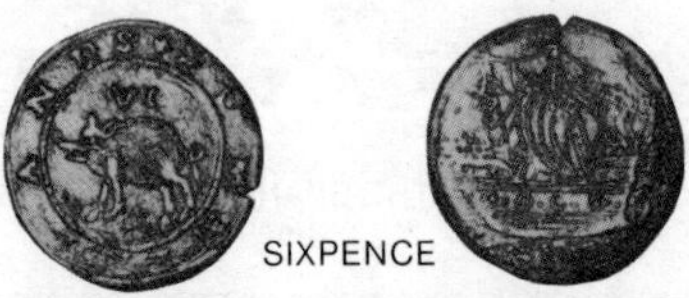

SIXPENCE

TYPE OF COIN	ABP	AG-3 About Good	G-4 Good	F-12 Fine
☐ Sixpence	600.00	1100.00	2100.00	3900.00
☐ Threepence				VERY RARE
☐ Twopence	700.00	1300.00	2500.00	4400.00

MASSACHUSETTS — NEW ENGLAND COINAGE

This is the earliest coinage struck on the North American continent. Its history is briefly detailed in the section on Colonial Coins, Patterns, and Tokens. This crude coinage may not be appealing aesthetically but its historical significance is as great, or greater, than any coins subsequently issued in this country. It was produced in limited quantities for local circulation in the Boston area and is extremely rare. When the decision was reached to attempt a native currency, the Massachusetts General Court appointed John Hull "mintmaster." The "mint" was an iron works operated by Joseph Jenks at Saugus, just north of Boston. These coins were made of silver by the ancient process of hammering—beating the designs into them by holding the die against the metal blank and striking it with a mallet. There was in fact no design at all. The coins were issued in three denominations—threepence, sixpence and twelvepence (shilling)—and each carried the letters "NE" on one side and the value in roman numerals on the other, most of the surface being blank. Variations in size, shape and placement of the markings are common. They date to 1652, but no date appears upon them.

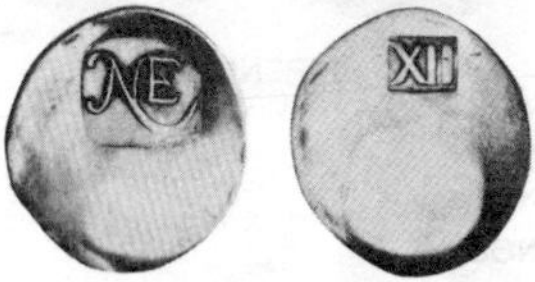

NE SHILLING

NE SIXPENCE

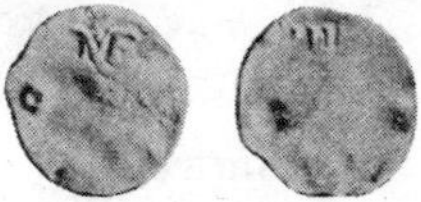

NE THREEPENCE

TYPE OF COIN	ABP	G-4 Good	F-12 Fine
☐NE Shilling	2600.00	5000.00	14000.00
☐NE Sixpence...Less than 8 known	24000.00	35000.00	70000.00
☐NE Threepence...Less than 3 known		EXTREMELY RARE	

WILLOW TREE COINS

After about four months of circulation of the Massachusetts–New England coinage (above), it was decided they were unsatisfactory. The legend and numeral of value were so simplistic that anyone possessing smith's tools could reproduce them. There was the further problem—not a new one, as it was faced by English mints in the middle ages—that the large expanses of unstamped metal invited "clipping," a practice in which unscrupulous persons trimmed down the edges and collected quantities of silver while still passing the coins at face value. It was impossible to improve the method of manufacture, there being no milling machines available. But the designs could be improved by the use of more fully engraved dies. This was accomplished with the so-called Willow Tree Coinage, introduced in 1653. On the obverse appears a very abstract rendition of a willow tree, surrounded by the place name, with the date and value designation on the reverse

(III stood for threepence, VI for sixpence and XII for shilling). Although struck at odd moments from 1653 to 1660 (there was no regular or continuous production), all specimens are dated 1652.

SHILLING

SIXPENCE

THREEPENCE

TYPE OF COIN	ABP	G-4 Good	F-12 Fine
☐ Willow Tree Shilling	4000.00	5000.00	20000.00
☐ Willow Tree Sixpence	14000.00	12000.00	35000.00
☐ Willow Tree Threepence		EXTREMELY RARE	

OAK TREE COINS

Successors to the Willow Tree Coins, these were likewise of Massachusetts origin and, like them, showed a tree on the obverse with the date and numeral of value on the reverse. They were introduced in 1660, the year of the English Restoration (the return of the Stuarts to the throne), an item of no small significance numismatically. While the previous regime, the Protectorate of Oliver Cromwell, was composed of politicians who supported the pilgrim cause, there was genuine fear that the new king—Charles II—might deal harshly with the colonists for being so bold as to strike coins. They attempted to camouflage this activity by retaining the old date, 1652, during the eight years that Oak Tree Coins were struck; and in fact it remained unaltered for the 16 years of their successors, Pine Tree Coins. In terms of design, these Oak Tree Coins were an improvement on their predecessors, being much sharper and bolder. Whether this can be attributed to more deeply engraved dies, more careful hammering, or (a usually overlooked possibility) better annealing or heating of the blanks, is uncertain. The mintmaster was still the same: John Hull. But this much is sure: the Oak Tree Coins were turned out in far larger quantities than previous Massachusetts coins.

SHILLING

SIXPENCE

THREEPENCE

TYPE OF COIN	ABP	G-4 Good	F-12 Fine	EF-40 Ex. Fine
☐Shilling	210.00	370.00	1300.00	3400.00
☐Sixpence	250.00	380.00	1200.00	3500.00
☐Threepence	210.00	380.00	1500.00	3400.00
☐Twopence	100.00	360.00	1200.00	3000.00

PINE TREE COINS

The final version of the Bay Colony *"tree"* coin, it featured a much clearer, if not more botanically accurate, portrait of a tree. Though struck in the same three denominations as the earlier types, there is a "Large Planchet" and "Small Planchet" version of the shilling, the large being slightly rarer. Both are of the same weight; the metal was simply hammered thinner on the "Large Planchet." It had been demonstrated, by the use of large planchets for the Willow and Oak Tree shillings, that the coin did not stand up well to handling and could be rendered sturdier by reducing its size and thereby increasing the thickness. It was also possible to strike the design more deeply with a thicker planchet. All coins from this series are dated 1652. They were actually struck from 1667 to 1682, during the reign of Britain's Charles II. After 1682 the issuing of coinage was discontinued by the Bay Colony. Many varieties exist in this series.

SHILLING, Large Planchet

SHILLING, Small Planchet

SIXPENCE

THREEPENCE

TYPE OF COIN	ABP	G-4 Good	F-12 Fine	EF-40 Ex. Fine
☐ Pine Tree Shilling, Large Planchet	180.00	280.00	810.00	2700.00
☐ Pine Tree Shilling, Small Planchet	180.00	270.00	800.00	2500.00
☐ Pine Tree Sixpence	180.00	260.00	770.00	2100.00
☐ Pine Tree Threepence	160.00	260.00	670.00	2100.00

MARYLAND

Maryland was the second colony, next to Massachusetts, to have coinage of its own. The origins of these coins bear little relation to those of the Bay Colony. While the Massachusetts pieces had been natively designed and struck, Maryland's coins were entirely a foreign product. They date from 1658. At this time Maryland was very sparsely inhabited, its only residents being small colonies of English immigrants, and could not have suffered too seriously from a shortage of coinage. Though not strictly classified as private issues they might well merit that designation. Maryland's first coins were the brainchild of Cecil Calvert, Lord Baltimore (for whom the colony's chief city was named). Calvert did not, as popularly supposed, "own Maryland." He did however possess large areas of its land and had the title of Lord Proprietor of Maryland. As an English lord with typical lordly pride, Calvert looked with disdain upon the prospect of Englishmen—his subjects, technically—trading with beads or iron or other objects of barter. So he ordered a batch of English-quality coins to be struck in Britain for use in the colony. They comprised a shilling, sixpence, fourpence or groat, and a penny. The first three were of silver, following the British tradition, the penny in copper. As a result of their production in an established, well-equipped mint, these coins are considerably more professional in appearance than those of Massachusetts. Lord Calvert placed his own portrait upon them. There was no need to fear censure from the king for this brazen act, as the English Civil War had already swept the king (Charles I) from his throne and Britain was not again to be ruled by a king until 1660. The reverses of the silver pieces carry Calvert's heraldic insignia with the value in roman numerals. The penny's obverse shows a regal crown surmounted by staffs and banners. There is no numeral of value on the penny but instead the word "denarium," the name of an ancient Roman coin from which the British penny evolved. (To this day the symbol for "penny" in Britain is the letter "d," meaning denarium. The cent sign, ¢, is never used.) Lord Calvert's portrait is a shoulder-length bust without crown, wreath of laurel, or other symbol of rulership. The penny is the scarcest of the denominations, as this is believed to have been a pattern only, not actually placed in use.

FOURPENCE

SHILLING

TYPE OF COIN	ABP	G-4 Good	F-12 Fine
☐ Maryland Shilling	600.00	1200.00	4200.00
☐ Maryland Sixpence	550.00	1100.00	3000.00
☐ Maryland Fourpence	600.00	1200.00	3700.00
☐ Maryland Denarium (Penny)		EXTREMELY RARE	

MARK NEWBY OR ST. PATRICK HALFPENCE

The coinage shortage in the early colonies, and the voraciousness with which anything resembling coinage was seized upon as a medium of exchange, is clearly demonstrated by the Newby or St. Patrick Halfpence. The coins are really misnamed, as they existed not only in halfpence but farthing denomination (in the British currency system a farthing or "fourthling" was equal to one quarter of a penny). Mark Newby was neither an explorer nor royal governor but apparently a private Irish citizen who came from Dublin and settled in New Jersey in the year 1681. He brought with him a quantity of tokens—they could only very charitably be called coins—which are thought to have been struck at Dublin about eight years earlier. These were coppers. On the obverse they depict a crowned king kneeling and playing a harp, almost certainly intended as the biblical King David, who is often represented in art as a harpist. St. Patrick, the legendary and patron saint of Ireland, appears on the reverse. On the halfpence he holds a crozier and cross (often mistaken for a clover) while giving benediction to a worshipper; on the farthing he is shown in a similar pose, driving the snakes out of Ireland, one of the many accomplishments with which this saint is credited. The obverse legend is "FLOREAT REX," which can be translated as "PROSPERITY TO THE KING." These are not at all bad-looking pieces and they feature an intriguing detail: the large crown on the obverse was inlaid in brass, to contrast in color with the copper and give the appearance of being golden. It is, however, sometimes lacking. The origin of this St. Patrick money is not clearly known. The possibility that it was struck for circulation in America seems very remote, as (a) there is no record of supportive legislation on either side of the Atlantic, and (b) the coins were apparently not brought to this country until long after striking, which hardly would have been the case had they been designed for use here. In any event the General Assembly of the New Jersey Province authorized their use as legal tender in May 1682, and for some while thereafter they served as the common currency of New Jersey. The most logical conclusion to be drawn is that Newby was a commercial trader who sought to profit from the shortage of coinage in America, and that he settled in New Jersey because this area was virtually without money of any kind.

If so, he would not have been the only colonist to do this. Silver and gold patterns of the farthing were struck, of which the silver is very rare and the gold unique. There may have been similar patterns of the ½ penny but they have not been discovered. In their normal metal, copper, neither is a coin of extreme scarcity.

ST. PATRICK HALFPENCE

ST. PATRICK FARTHING

TYPE OF COIN	ABP	G-4 Good	F-12 Fine
☐ St. Patrick Halfpence	73.00	125.00	360.00
☐ St. Patrick Farthing (Brass Insert on Obverse)	55.00	85.00	260.00
☐ St. Patrick Farthing (Without Brass Insert)	55.00	85.00	220.00
☐ St. Patrick Farthing (Silver Pattern)	400.00	750.00	2000.00
☐ St. Patrick Farthing (Gold Pattern)			UNIQUE

COLONIAL PLANTATION TOKEN

The so-called Plantation Token was the first coinage authorized for use in the American colonies by the British government. Its history is of great interest. Throughout the middle 17th century it was well known in England that the American provinces or "plantations" as they were called abroad (largely by persons unaware of the extent of population) suffered from a shortage of coinage. In 1688 an Englishman named John Holt petitioned the king (James II) for a patent or franchise for the striking of coinage for distribution in the colonies. In Britain at this time the system of "patents of exclusivity" was commonplace. Printers would pay a fee to have the exclusive right on putting out Bibles; merchants paid for a franchise to sell a particular product without fear of competition. The fee, which was considerable, had to be paid each year while the franchise was in force. Holt was convinced that the supply of coinage to America would be a very profitable endeavor. The government approved his request for a franchise and shortly thereafter he began to strike his coins, better called tokens. Large in size, they were made of tin and had the face value of ¼ of a Spanish real or "piece of eight," say about fourpence. On their obverse they pictured an equestrian likeness of James II, regal-looking in this design but soon to be driven out of the country into exile. It is important to note that they were not intended for use in any special region but could be exchanged anywhere in the provinces; thus they carry no place name. The original dies were preserved and restrikes made from them in the late 1820s; their appearance is quite similar to the original and could well be a cause of confusion to beginners. A very rare variety exists, in which the numeral "4" in the value legend on the reverse is positioned vertically instead of horizontally.

PLANTATION TOKEN

TYPE OF COIN	ABP	G-4 Good	F-12 Fine	EF-40 Ex. Fine	MS-60 Unc.
☐James II Plantation Token ...	120.00	200.00	310.00	750.00	2100.00
☐James II Plantation Token, vertical "4"					RARE

Restrikes exist which are worth slightly less.

ELEPHANT TOKENS

These extremely popular, intriguing pieces have been the subject of much study and debate. Their origins are only sketchily known. There are three specific types: London token, Carolina token, and New England token. All have the same obverse, a portrait of an elephant without legend or inscription of any kind. These pieces are coppers and were modeled as halfpennies, though they carry no indication of value. The extent to which they circulated in the American colonies is not established. Based on what little information is available, their history may be pieced together as follows.

First in the series was the London token, which on some specimens carries the wording "God Preserve London" on the reverse, on others merely "London," accompanying a heraldic shield. The belief is that they were struck in 1664 when the population of that city was being decimated by an outbreak of bubonic plague, which apparently is the danger from which preservation was sought. So far this theory makes some historical sense though it fails to explain the selection of an elephant as the obverse symbol. Could it be that this was a reference to "stamping out" the plague, and that the elephant, as the largest of creatures, would be best equipped to do so? That elephants were well known in London in the 1660s is well established. There were no zoos for the display of wild beasts but elephants and tigers (both from India) were kept in enclosed dungeons in the Tower of London for the amusement of visitors. Natural history drawing was still in an archaic state at that time, which explains why the elephant on Elephant Tokens looks rather strange. For a long while thereafter there appears to have been no effort to revive the Elephant Token, perhaps because the plague subsided. Then in 1694 it reappeared, in an edition bearing two different reverses: "God Preserve Carolina and the Lord's Proprietors" and "God Preserve New England." Just how these pieces came to be, what their intent was, and how they were circulated, is totally unknown. It may be presumed that "God Preserve" was used merely in the sense of "God Bless," after the fashion of the slogan "God Save the King," not as implication that either Carolina or New England suffered from any specific difficulty.

There is little doubt, based on physical evidence, that they were struck in England, as these tokens are handsomely milled (not hammered) and it is doubtful that such work could have been accomplished in the colonies. It has been said that the London variety was intended for circulation in Tangier but even if that were so, there is no evidence of it being an official issue. The Carolina and New England pieces could have been entirely speculative. Their distribution may have been local (in England) with no intention of exporting or using them for actual currency in the colonies. This seems the logical answer, especially in view of the extremely small quantities struck. Of the London token there were considerably larger numbers struck but to classify this as a piece designed for colonial use seems very presumptive. Some specimens undoubtedly reached the colonies at an early date but, if they did, it was only accidentally, in the baggage or pockets of immigrants or traders, just as almost everything else made abroad found its way across the Atlantic.

There are a number of types and varieties. The London token exists in both thin and thick planchet; with interlacing in the central portion of the shield; with sword in the second quarter of the shield (transposed from the first, where it is commonly found); and with the inscription "London" rather than "God Preserve London." Of these the transposed sword is the rarest. The chief variety on the Carolina issue is the alteration from "Proprieters" to the more correct spelling, "Proprietors," accomplished not by the introduction of a fresh die but re-engraving the original. If closely inspected the letter "e," or what remains of it, can be observed.

1694 NEW ENGLAND

1694 PROPRIETORS

1694 PROPRIETERS

1664 GOD PRESERVE LONDON

1664 GOD PRESERVE LONDON (SWORDS)

1664 LON DON

TYPE OF COIN	ABP	G-4 Good	F-12 Fine
☐ 1664 God Preserve London (thin)	43.00	75.00	230.00
☐ 1664 God Preserve London (thick)	36.00	72.00	210.00
☐ 1664 God Preserve London (diag.)	87.00	170.00	340.00
☐ 1664 God Preserve London (swords)		EXTREMELY RARE	
☐ 1664 Lon Don	200.00	390.00	1350.00
☐ 1694 New England		770.00	22000.00
☐ 1694 Proprieters (overstrike)	420.00	780.00	2900.00
☐ 1694 Proprieters		EXTREMELY RARE	

NEW YORKE TOKEN

The New York colony (referring to the state, not the city) had no coinage of its own in the 17th century. Though settled somewhat later than Massachusetts, the population of New York came close to equaling it by the century's close and the volume of business transacted was at least comparable. It is curious that tiny Maryland and equally tiny New Jersey had coins during the 17th century while New York did not. The closest it came to having one was the New Yorke Token, but this can hardly be classed with the Massachusetts, Maryland, or even the New Jersey coinage, as there is no evidence it received official sanction. It was very likely nothing more than a merchant token. This is a smallish piece, roughly equal to our nickel, of which some were struck in brass and others in pewter. On the obverse it carries a rather scrawny eagle with an allegorical design (Cupid is one of the figures) on the reverse. The obverse legend reads "NEW YORKE IN AMERICA." Of its origins practically nothing is known. The belief that this coin was struck in Holland is founded more upon assumption, because of New York's extensive Dutch population, than evidence. Its date has been the subject of controversy. The spelling of New York as "New Yorke" suggests a dating in the 17th century, but as this spelling lingered on into the 18th century it is quite possible that the coin or token is not so old as commonly presumed. It is very likely that even in the second quarter of the 18th century a European designing such a piece would have used the "New Yorke" spelling, even if it was no longer current in America. The likelihood that the New Yorke Token was struck in Manhattan from dies prepared in Holland is a romantic but not convincing theory.

UNDATED BRASS

TYPE OF COIN	ABP	G-4 Good	F-12 Fine
☐ New Yorke Token, undated: Brass	1250.00	2700.00	5800.00
☐ New Yorke Token, undated: Tin (Pewter)...........	2200.00	4200.00	

GLOUCESTER TOKEN

Very few specimens exist of this early amateur token and information about it is likewise scanty. It is apparently the first private token struck on American soil. The composition is brass, leading to the assumption that it might have been a pattern for a silver shilling that was never produced. Whether the brass pieces were intended to circulate is highly doubtful. The Gloucester Token is thought to have been the work of Richard Dawson of Gloucester, Virginia. On one side appears a five-pointed star, with a building of modest design on the other. Known specimens are so thoroughly worn that the inscription surrounding this building is unreadable. The best guess is that it was intended to represent the Gloucester County Courthouse or some other public structure. It does not appear to be a place of worship. The Gloucester Token dates to 1714.

SHILLING BRASS

TYPE OF COIN	ABP	G-4 Good	F-12 Fine
☐ Gloucester Shilling (brass)			29000.00

ROSA AMERICANA

These extremely handsome coins, thoroughly European in appearance and workmanship, are often referred to as Wood Tokens—not from being made of wood (their composition is copper, zinc, and silver) but from William Wood, the Englishman who originated them. Nearly 40 years before their appearance, John Holt, another Englishman, had gained a patent from the then-king, James II, to strike coinage for circulation in the American colonies. Upon expiration of the Holt patent or franchise there had been little enthusiasm for its renewal, as Holt's coins—the so-called Plantation Tokens—had not proved very successful. As time passed and the population of such cities as Boston, New York, and Philadelphia increased, the prospects for coinage seemed to brighten. William Wood, of whom there is not very much known, obtained a franchise from George I to supply coinage to America, as well as to Ireland. This resulted in the Rosa Americana tokens. These were struck in small denominations only, from a halfpence to twopence. The earliest, which apparently were struck in 1722, carried no date. Later a date was added and these pieces saw fairly large production in the years 1722, 1723 and 1724. After an interval of nearly ten years in which none were produced, a Rosa Americana pattern proof was struck off in 1733. As best as can be ascertained, the Wood patent had fallen into other hands, as Wood died in 1730. His successors probably toyed with the idea of reinstituting the Rosa Americana coins but never got beyond the stage of this single proof. To judge by the relative commonness of the coin (except for certain varieties, which are rare), they must have been turned out at least in the hundreds and possibly the thousands. The obverses are all alike, picturing George I in profile facing the viewer's right (it was switched to the left on the 1733 trial proof). This is not the king against whom America went to war in the Revolution but the first English monarch of that name, a German who could speak but a few words of English. Surrounding the portrait is, generally, a legend giving the names of the countries over which the king ruled: Great Britain, France, and Hibernia (Ireland). The claim that he ruled France was a purely speculative one, a reference to the victories of Marlborough over Louis XIV's armies which had ended France's ambition to capture England but in no way gave England rulership over that nation. The reverse shows the Rose, sometimes alone, sometimes surmounted by a crown. There is one variation (on the 1724 penny) where the rose is not pictured symbolically but as an actual flower growing up from the ground. These pieces gain their name from the reverse inscription, not present on all, reading "ROSA AMERICANA UTILE DULCI," or, roughly, "American Rose, utility and pleasure." The rose had been a symbol of the Tudor kings and queens well before colonization of America. In their extent and variety the Rosa Americana coins are unmatched by any others intended for circulation in America. The opinion held of them today was not shared by colonists, however, who protested that the coins were short weighted and refused to accept them.

1722 HALFPENNY "DEI GRATIA REX"

1723 PENNY

TYPE OF COIN	ABP	G-4 Good	F-12 Fine	EF-40 Ex. Fine
☐Twopence, No Date	42.00	78.00	270.00	720.00
☐Twopence, No Date, Motto Sans Label			EXTREMELY RARE	
☐1722 Halfpenny, D. G. REX	42.00	78.00	250.00	700.00
☐1722 Halfpenny, DEI GRATIA REX	36.00	65.00	190.00	600.00
☐1722 Halfpenny, VTILE DVLCI	480.00	880.00	2800.00	
☐1722 Twopence, Period after REX	38.00	75.00	240.00	630.00
☐1722 Twopence, No Period after REX.	38.00	75.00	240.00	650.00
☐1722 Penny, UTILE DULCI	34.00	58.00	160.00	450.00
☐1722 Penny, VTILE DVLCI	35.00	62.00	180.00	480.00
☐1722 Penny, Georgivs			EXTREMELY RARE	
☐1723 Twopence	53.00	87.00	250.00	700.00
☐1723 Penny	37.00	65.00	170.00	490.00
☐1723 Halfpenny	44.00	73.00	180.00	600.00
☐1723 Halfpenny, Rose without Crown			EXTREMELY RARE	
☐1724 Penny (Pattern)			EXTREMELY RARE	
☐1724 Penny, No Date, ROSA: SINE: SPINA			EXTREMELY RARE	
☐1724 Twopence (Pattern)			EXTREMELY RARE	
☐1733 Twopence (Pattern Proof)			EXTREMELY RARE	

WOOD'S COINAGE OR HIBERNIA

These coins, more properly called tokens, were issued under the patent granted to William Wood to strike coinage for America and Ireland (see Rosa Americana). "Hibernia" was the Latin name for Ireland. They are included here because these pieces proved unpopular in Ireland—just as did the Rosa Americanas in America—and Wood sought to recover his investment by circulating them in America. History does not record their fate on this side of the Atlantic but it is doubtful that they received a warm reception. They were struck in such enormous numbers, thanks to excessive over-confidence, that most types can be had inexpensively. George I appears on the obverse. There are two reverse types, both picturing a seated female with a harp representing Hibernia, the Irish equivalent of Britannia. There is no need to speculate on the reason for Type I being changed: the figure is portrayed in so ungainly a manner as to appear comical. Type II is only a slight improvement.

1723 OVER 22 HALFPENNY

1723 HALFPENNY

TYPE OF COIN	ABP	G-4 Good	F-12 Fine	EF-40 Ex. Fine
☐1722 Farthing, D.G.REX	78.00	145.00	260.00	630.00
☐1722 Halfpenny, Harp Facing Left	17.00	32.00	92.00	270.00

TYPE OF COIN	ABP	G-4 Good	F-12 Fine	EF-40 Ex. Fine
☐1722 Halfpenny, Harp Facing Right...	17.00	28.00	85.00	280.00
☐1722 Halfpenny, D.G. REX...........			EXTREMELY RARE	
☐1723 Halfpenny	12.00	20.00	60.00	210.00
☐1723 Over 22 Halfpenny.............	26.00	45.00	112.00	340.00
☐1723 Halfpenny, Silver (Pattern)			EXTREMELY RARE	
☐1723 Farthing, Silver (Pattern)........	260.00	500.00	1275.00	2450.00
☐1723 Farthing, DEL, GRATIA REX....	1250.00	24.00	47.00	210.00
☐1723 Farthing, D.G. REX	39.00	75.00	210.00	600.00
☐1724 Halfpenny	19.00	38.00	72.00	270.00
☐1724 Farthing	26.00	50.00	100.00	300.00

HIGLEY COINAGE

The Higley or Granby tokens were entirely private issues. Had they been imported for circulation from abroad they might be of modest interest at best but these are, in fact, *the first privately produced tokens struck on American soil that actually reached circulation.* All are extremely rare. Dr. Samuel Higley, a Connecticut resident and graduate of Yale University, deplored the coinage shortage in his state and took matters into his own hands. Unsupported by legislation and unsponsored by government funds, Higley engraved his own dies and for coin metal used copper from a mine he owned located near Granby, Connecticut (hence the alternate title of these pieces). Considering their amateur origin the designs and workmanship are of higher quality than might be expected. On the obverse appears a deer surrounded by inscription. There are two reverse types, one featuring a trio of small hammers, the other a broad-bladed cleaver. As originally issued in 1737 they carried the value of threepence, stated on the obverse legend. Though well received at first, protest was later raised by persons skeptical of their copper content. This inspired the ever-resourceful Higley to add the inscription "I AM GOOD COPPER." When this failed to silence critics, who persisted in their belief that the face value was too high and that Higley was gaining a profit from circulating them, the statement of value was replaced by the not-too-subtle suggestion to "VALUE ME AS YOU PLEASE." Even so, the Roman numeral III remained. This placed them in the category of bartering pieces which could be exchanged on basis of weight. We are told that the local supply was numerous but this is hardly reflected by their present rarity. It can only be assumed that many individuals hoarded the Higley tokens and melted them. The inscription on the second reverse type (the cleaver) states "I CUT MY WAY THROUGH." The "I" is sometimes stated to be a "J," but in fact was intended merely to represent an ornamental "I" with loop at the base.

The collector is cautioned that reproductions of the Higley Tokens exist, made by electrotyping and casting, and are of sufficient quality to confuse an inexperienced buyer.

1737 THREEPENCE "CONNECTICVT"

1737 VALVE.ME.AS.YOU.PLEASE
I.AM.GOOD.COPPER

1737 VALUE.ME.AS.Y.OU.PLEASE
I.CUT.MY.WAY.THROUGH

TYPE OF COIN	ABP	G-4 Good	VG-8 Very Good
☐ 1737 THE VALUE OF THREEPENCE (3 hammers CONNECTICUT)	2950.00	5200.00	7500.00
☐ 1737 THE VALUE OF THREEPENCE (3 hammers, I AM GOOD COPPER)	3350.00	6400.00	10500.00
☐ 1737 VALUE ME AS YOU PLEASE (3 hammers, I AM GOOD COPPER)	2850.00	5000.00	7400.00
☐ 1737 VALUE ME AS YOU PLEASE (3 hammers, I AM GOOD COPPER)		EXTREMELY RARE	
☐ 1737 VALUE ME AS YOU PLEASE (broad axe, I CUT MY WAY THROUGH)	3400.00	5600.00	9900.00
☐ 1739 VALUE ME AS YOU PLEASE (broad axe, I CUT MY WAY THROUGH)	4600.00	7200.00	14800.00

VOCE POPULI COINAGE

These impressive pieces are exclusively private issues and not of American origin. They were struck in Dublin, Ireland, in 1760, by a firm whose chief occupation was the making of buttons for military uniforms. Its proprietor was named Roche. The 17th and 18th centuries both witnessed an inordinate quantity of private tokens and pseudo-money struck in Ireland, much of which reached America. It could all logically be included within the realm of Americana but the Voce Populi Tokens have become special favorites of collectors, probably on strength of design more than anything else. The obverse features a classical style portrait profile crowned with laurel wreath. It has traditionally been assumed to be George III but no actual evidence exists to support this belief. The inscription makes no reference to the king but merely carries the words "VOCE POPULI," or "Voice of the People." Various interpretations (too lengthy to be discussed here) could be placed upon the use of this common slogan. The reverse pictures a female with harp, a standard Irish symbol, and the word "HIBERNIA." This was the Latin name for Ireland. The date is shown in the exergue beneath the figure. It should always be 1760; however, on one occasion a defective die was used for the halfpenny, causing it to read 1700. That the token was actually struck in 1700 can easily be refuted on stylistic as well as other evidence. There is also a variety in which the inscription reads "VOOE POPULI."

1760 "VOCE POPULI" HALFPENNY

1760 "VOCE POPULI" FARTHING

TYPE OF COIN	ABP	G-4 Good	F-12 Fine
☐ 1700 Halfpenny (die-cutter's error)	640.00	1050.00	2150.00
☐ 1760 Halfpenny	2500.00	44.00	120.00
☐ 1760 Halfpenny, P beneath bust	44.00	73.00	175.00
☐ 1760 Halfpenny, P beside face	45.00	74.00	175.00
☐ 1760 Halfpenny, VOOE POPULI (die-cutter's error)	28.00	50.00	165.00
☐ 1760 Farthing	125.00	195.00	425.00
☐ 1760 Farthing, small lettering		EXTREMELY RARE	

PITT TOKENS

William Pitt, for whom Pittsburgh is named, is associated with these tokens only to the extent that his portrait appears on them. He apparently was connected in no way with their issuance. Two denominations were struck, or rather pieces in the *sizes* of two denominations (as they bear no value markings): farthing and halfpenny. They carry the date 1766. Just what their purpose was is not clear. The suggestion has been put forward that they were issued in the nature of medals as an honor to Pitt, who, for his stand against the British stamp tax, was held in high regard by agitators for self-government. The long-held popular belief that Pitt Tokens were designed by Paul Revere would probably be best relegated to the ranks of numismatic folklore until some firm evidence is discovered. The similarly long-held belief that the engraver was Smithers of Philadelphia is more acceptable. The obverse has Pitt's likeness in profile with the legend "NO STAMPS: THE RESTORE OF COMMERCE: 1766." The reverse shows a handsomely rendered sailing ship with the inscription "THANKS TO THE FRIENDS OF LIBERTY AND TRADE." Next to the ship is the word "AMERICA," which apparently suggests that the vessel is traveling from some foreign port with cargo for this country. "The Restore of Commerce" was a reference to the fact that British-imposed taxes were periling American commerce by rendering goods so costly that the public could not buy nearly so much as it wished to. The halfpenny is known to have been used briefly as coinage. No such use has been established for the farthing, which is much rarer.

1766 HALFPENNY

1766 FARTHING

TYPE OF COIN	ABP	G-4 Good	F-12 Fine
☐ 1766 Halfpenny	76.00	145.00	280.00
☐ 1766 Farthing	1650.00	2950.00	4950.00

FRENCH COLONIES IN AMERICA

A number of coins were struck in France for use in that nation's colonies during the 18th century. These were non-geographical pieces that could be exchanged in any French province and carried inscriptions in French and Latin rather than in local languages. It is important to remember in collecting these coins that they were *not* expressly struck for use in America, though they did see use in areas such as Louisiana (named for Louis XIV).

1722 SOU

1767 SOU

COUNTERSTAMPED "RF"

1670 5 SOLS SILVER

TYPE OF COIN	ABP	G-4 Good	F-12 Fine
☐ 1670 5 sols	92.00	195.00	440.00
☐ 1670 15 sols	2550.00	4700.00	10500.00
☐ 1709–1713 30 deniers, mint mark AA	42.00	66.00	145.00
☐ 1709–1713 30 deniers, mint mark D	38.00	67.00	145.00
☐ 1710–1713 15 deniers	50.00	90.00	220.00
☐ 1738–1748 ½ sou marque	26.00	38.00	86.00
☐ 1738–1760 sou marque	14.00	21.00	46.00
☐ 1717 6 deniers		EXTREMELY RARE	
☐ 1720 6 deniers		EXTREMELY RARE	
☐ 1717 12 deniers		EXTREMELY RARE	
☐ 1721 SOU, mint mark B for ROUEN	39.00	68.00	245.00
☐ 1721 SOU, mint mark H for ROCHELLE	25.00	42.00	135.00
☐ 1722 SOU, mint mark H	26.00	42.00	130.00
☐ 1722 Over 1721	36.00	66.00	180.00
☐ 1767 SOU	24.00	42.00	145.00
☐ 1767 SOU, counterstamped RF	16.00	27.00	96.00

VIRGINIA

Plagued by a coinage shortage, Virginia's colonists petitioned George III for supplies of trading pieces. He responded by authorizing the striking of a copper halfpenny, with his likeness on the obverse and the Virginia seal on its reverse. Proposals were also made for a penny and shilling, or coins which, to judge by the size of the few specimens struck, were intended for these denominations. They never reached circulation and are very rare. The halfpenny was struck in large quantities.

SHILLING

TYPE OF COIN	ABP	G-4 Good	F-12 Fine	MS-60 Unc.
☐ 1773 Halfpenny (Period After GEORGIVS)	21.00	36.00	77.00	680.00
☐ 1773 Halfpenny (No Per. After GEORGIVS)	29.00	47.00	100.00	790.00
☐ 1773 Penny	PROOF			6000.00
☐ 1774 Shilling (SILVER)	PROOF			17900.00

STATE OF NEW HAMPSHIRE

New Hampshire has the distinction of being the first state to attempt a local coinage following the Declaration of Independence. In 1776 it authorized William Moulton to produce an experimental batch of copper pieces. The small numbers that have been traced indicate this coin never attained general circulation, though it probably circulated in a small way. The chief type has a tree on the obverse and a harp on the reverse. Other types are known but their status has not been positively established.

1776 PINE TREE

1776 WM COPPER

TYPE OF COIN	VG-8 VERY GOOD
☐ 1776 New Hampshire Copper	12500.00
☐ 1776 New Hampshire Copper, WM in center (Pattern Piece)	EXTREMELY RARE

STATE OF VERMONT

Vermont's post-revolutionary coinage, probably the best known for its designs of any regional pieces, was struck by Reuben Harmon of Rupert, Vermont, and some by Thomas Machin of Newburgh, New York. This extensive series most often employed portraits of George III but is best known for its "plough money," an obverse design picturing a farm plough in a field against a background of tree laden mountains. This is sometimes referred to as the most original, creative, and authentically American design to be found on our colonial or federal-era coins. William Coley, a New York goldsmith, was the die-cutter for this design.

1785 VERMONTS

1786 VERMONTENSIUM

1787 BRITANNIA

TYPE OF COIN	ABP	G-4 Good	F-12 Fine
☐ 1785 Immune Colombia	600.00	1175.00	2500.00
☐ 1785 VERMONTS	76.00	160.00	550.00
☐ 1785 VERMONTIS	130.00	215.00	590.00
☐ 1786 VERMONTENSIUM	56.00	120.00	450.00
☐ 1786 Baby Head	87.00	175.00	570.00
☐ 1786 Bust faces left	55.00	115.00	490.00
☐ 1787 Bust faces right	50.00	88.00	280.00
☐ 1787 BRITANNIA reverse; it is thought that the reverse of the Brittania piece was struck from a worn, discarded die for a counterfeit British halfpenny	32.00	57.00	210.00
☐ 1788 Cent	45.00	82.00	260.00
☐ 1788 ET LIB INDE	72.00	180.00	480.00
☐ 1788 VERMON AUCTORI; reversed C			VERY RARE
☐ 1788 GEORGIVS III REX	95.00	180.00	570.00

STATE OF CONNECTICUT

Connecticut struck more coins in the period from the Revolution to the establishment of a federal currency than any other state. Or, it might be better put, more varieties, as they represent numerous variations of three basic issues. The mint at which they were struck was established by authority of the state in 1785. It was located at New Haven. The chief die-cutters were Abel Buel and James Atlee.

1.
1785 CENT

2.
1785 AFRICAN HEAD

3a.
1786 CENT

4.
1786 CENT

5.
1786 CENT

6.
1786 CENT

7.
1786 CENT

8.
1787 CENT

9.
1787 CENT

10.
1787 CENT

11a.
1787 CENT

12.
1787 CENT

13a.
1787 CENT

14.
1788 CENT

15a.
1788 CENT

16.
1788 CENT

TYPE OF COIN	ABP	G-4 Good	F-12 Fine
☐1. 1785 Cent, Bust right	24.00	47.00	115.00
☐2. 1785 Cent, Bust right: African head	30.00	53.00	175.00
☐3. 1785 Cent, Bust left	78.00	140.00	360.00
☐3a. 1786 Cent, ET LIB INDE	33.00	56.00	175.00
☐4. 1786 Cent, Large Bust Faces Right	42.00	76.00	285.00
☐5. 1786 Cent, Mailed Bust Left	21.00	36.00	140.00

TYPE OF COIN	ABP	G-4 Good	F-12 Fine
☐6. 1786 Cent, Mailed Bust Left (Hercules Head)	42.00	72.00	240.00
☐7. 1786 Cent, Draped Bust	38.00	67.00	215.00
☐8. 1787 Cent, Mailed Bust, Small Head Faces Right, ET LIB ENDE	42.00	78.00	230.00
☐9. 1787 Cent, Mailed Bust Faces Right, INDE ET LIB	45.00	88.00	250.00
☐10. 1787 Cent, Muttonhead: INDE ET LIB	41.00	75.00	220.00
☐11. 1787 Cent, Mailed Bust Faces Left	19.00	32.00	87.00
☐11a. 1787 Cent, Horned Bust	19.00	32.00	100.00
☐12. 1787 Cent, CONNECT	35.00	56.00	170.00
☐13. 1787 Cent, Draped Bust Faces Left	16.00	27.00	62.00
☐13a. 1787 Cent, Bust Left: AUCIORI	18.00	32.00	80.00
☐13b. 1787 Cent: AUCTOPI	19.00	32.00	92.00
☐13c. 1787 Cent: AUCTOBI	19.00	39.00	125.00
☐13d. 1787 Cent: CONNFC	22.00	34.00	87.00
☐13e. 1787 Cent: FNDE	19.00	37.00	86.00
☐13f. 1787 Cent: ETLIR	19.00	37.00	84.00
☐13g. 1787 Cent: ETIIB	17.00	32.00	77.00
☐14. 1788 Cent, Mailed Bust Faces Right	21.00	36.00	125.00
☐14a. 1788 Cent: Small Head	93.00	175.00	550.00
☐15. 1788 Cent, Mailed Bust Faces Left	19.00	32.00	95.00
☐15a. 1788 Cent, Mailed Bust Left: CONNLC	20.00	37.00	115.00
☐16. 1788 Cent, Draped Bust Faces Left	19.00	32.00	92.00
☐16a. Same: CONNLC	36.00	58.00	180.00
☐16b. 1788 Same: INDL ET LIB	28.00	46.00	150.00

STATE OF NEW JERSEY

No coinage was struck for New Jersey in the colonial period, but see Mark Newby Halfpence (p. 101). As the state's population increased, a serious coin shortage was experienced and, on June 1, 1786, its legislature authorized the striking of three million copper pieces, each to weigh "six pennyweight and six grains apiece." The contract for these tokens was awarded to Thomas Goadsby, Walter Mould, and Albion Cox. The full quantity was to be delivered by June 1788, with partial deliveries to be made in quarterly installments of 300,000 each. Soon after work had begun, Goadby and Cox requested and were granted permission to divide up the quantities and strike them separately, each operating his own facility. Mould set up at Morristown, New Jersey, Cox at Rahway. Goadsby's location is not established but is thought to also have been Rahway. The obverses of all these tokens show a horse's head and a plough, symbolic of the state's economy being founded largely on agriculture. The legend "NOVA CAESAREA" is simply New Jersey in Latin. On the reverse is a U.S. shield and "E PLURIBUS UNUM." A number of varieties are to be encountered.

1. 1786

3. 1786

8. 1787

11. 1788

12. 1788

TYPE OF COIN	ABP	G-4 Good	F-12 Fine
☐1. 1786 Date Under Plough Handle		VERY RARE	
☐2. 1786 Normal Legends	27.00	150.00	89.00
☐3. 1786 No Colter	83.00	150.00	460.00
☐4. 1786 Bridle Variety (NOT ILLUS.)	26.00	42.00	100.00
☐5. 1786 Narrow Shield (NOT ILLUS.)	24.00	36.00	112.00
☐6. 1786 Wide Shield (NOT ILLUS.)	28.00	43.00	116.00
☐7. 1787 Normal Legends (NOT ILLUS.)	18.00	32.00	86.00
☐8. 1787 PLURIBS	29.00	48.00	150.00
☐9. 1787 "Serpent Head" (NOT ILLUS.)	28.00	46.00	150.00
☐10. 1788 Normal Legends (NOT ILLUS.)	19.00	30.00	96.00
☐11. 1788 Horse's Head Faces Right, Running Fox	36.00	58.00	180.00
☐12. 1788 Horse's Head Left	76.00	165.00	416.00

STATE OF NEW YORK

The history of New York's local coinage prior to the Revolution reveals only the supposed Dutch merchant token discussed above and various coins and tokens struck for use elsewhere that, in the ordinary course of trade, found their way to the state. For more than a hundred years it was without locally authorized coinage. This void was filled by Dutch, British, French, and, to a lesser extent, Spanish monies, which came to New York through its great port and disseminated throughout the region. Apparently no pressing need was felt for a local coinage because none was officially instituted, even after independence. However, quantities of privately struck money did circulate. Some were the work of Thomas Machin of Newburgh, New York (where Washington had a headquarters during the war), who operated what he surreptitiously called a "hardware manufactory." It was, in fact, a copper mill, whose chief products were tokens. Other New York coins were produced at Rupert, Vermont, by a team of millers (Reuben Harmon and William Coley) who also made coins for Vermont and Connecticut. There is much yet to be learned about New York's federal-era coinage but quite a good deal has already been determined. The theory, once popularly maintained, that coins bearing the inscription "NOVA EBORAC" are of foreign origin, is now known to be false. Nova Eborac is not some sort of mysterious foreign term. It is simply New York in Latin. (If you wonder how there could be a Latin name for New York, when there are none for railroad and television and other things discovered after the Latin language died, the explanation is quite simple. The Romans did not know of New York but they certainly knew of *old* York in Britain, which they called Eborac. To change this into New York you need only add the Latin word for new—nova—and you have Nova Eborac.)

All the New York coins (or tokens) are coppers. They carry various designs, of which the portrait of George Clinton is most famous. There was also an Indian figure (not too impressively portrayed), a New York coat-of-arms, and profile bust pretty confidently believed to be George Washington. Though the designs are not very well drawn, the coins themselves are very professionally struck.

1.
1786

2.
1787

3.
1787

4.
1787

5.
1787

6c.
1787

TYPE OF COIN	ABP	F-12 Fine	VF-20 V. Fine
☐1. 1786 NON VI VIRTUTE VICI; Thought to be the head of George Washington	2100.00	3900.00	6400.00
☐2. 1787 EXCELSIOR; Eagle on Obv. faces left	910.00	1450.00	4000.00
☐3. 1787 EXCELSIOR; Eagle on Obv. faces right	1000.00	1670.00	4300.00
☐3a. 1787 EXCELSIOR; Large Eagle on reverse (NOT ILLUS.)			VERY RARE
☐3b. 1787 EXCELSIOR; George Clinton reverse (NOT ILLUS.)	4150.00	8400.00	14800.00
☐3c. 1787 EXCELSIOR; Indian Standing reverse (NOT ILLUS.)	3250.00	6800.00	10000.00
☐3d. 1787 EXCELSIOR; Indian Standing Eagle on globe (NOT ILLUS.)	3600.00	7400.00	12200.00
☐4. 1787 LIBERTATEM; Indian Standing, George III		EXTREMELY RARE	
☐5. 1787 NOVA EBORAC; Rev. seated figure faces left	125.00	220.00	440.00
☐5a. 1787 NOVA EBORAC; Rev. seated figure faces right (NOT ILLUS.)	150.00	270.00	530.00
☐5b. 1787 NOVA EBORAC; Small head (NOT ILLUS.)	969.00	1650.00	3100.00
☐6c. 1787 NOVA EBORAC; Large head	320.00	580.00	1400.00

BRASHER DOUBLOONS

Perhaps the most celebrated, at any rate the most glamorized, U.S. colonial coin is the Brasher Doubloon. Though traditionally referred to as colonial it should correctly be termed a federal-era piece, as it was struck after our independence had been gained. This is a private issue. Ephraim Brasher was a goldsmith from New York who became acquainted with George Washington when the latter resided there following the war. To classify this handsome gold piece as a speculative coin would be a mistake. Brasher, artist and patriot, appears to have manufactured it not for purposes of general circulation but as a memorial to the nation's independence and, possibly, a model from which federal coiners could gain inspiration. It dates to 1787, before the introduction of federal coinage but not before much speculation and debate on the matter. The Brasher Doubloon, as the name suggests, was modeled after the Spanish coin of that name. It contained 408 grains of gold. As a goldsmith Brasher would have encountered no difficulty securing the needed bullion for a small quantity of such pieces, but it is doubtful that he had either the resources or intention to strike this coin in large numbers. The obverse pictures the sun rising over a mountain, with the American eagle emblem on the back. The reverse bears the impressed letters E.B., the initials of Brasher's name.

Obviously they were not clandestine issues or their origin would not have been so plainly identified. At the time of its issue the Brasher Doubloon had a value of about $16. There was also a Half Doubloon worth $8. All are extremely rare, the variety in which the initials appear on the eagle's breast being preserved in a single specimen only.

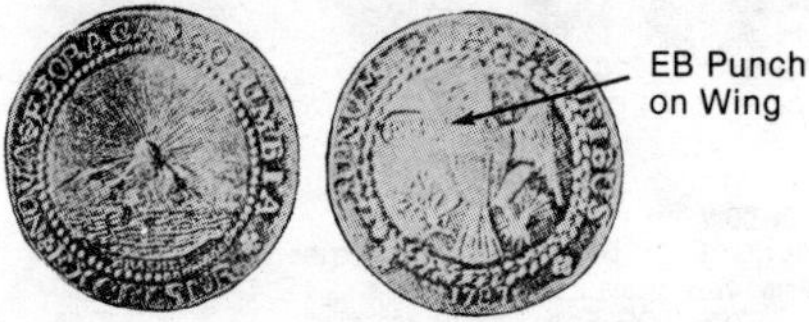

TYPE OF COIN	VG-8 VERY GOOD
☐ 1787 (GOLD) DOUBLOON, EB punch on breast	ALL TYPES EXTREMELY RARE
☐ 1787 (GOLD) DOUBLOON, EB punch on wing......	ALL TYPES EXTREMELY RARE
☐ 1787 (GOLD) HALF DOUBLOON..................	ALL TYPES EXTREMELY RARE
Garrett Sale November, 1979 ....725,000.00	
Yale University Specimen, 1980 ....600,000.00	
Estimated Current Value ....Under 600,000.00	

STATE OF MASSACHUSETTS

Massachusetts, the first colony to strike its own coins in pre-revolutionary days, also had its own coinage in the period between independence and the establishment of the U.S. Mint. On October 17, 1786, the General Court of that state authorized the setting up of a mint, "for the coinage of gold, silver, and copper." A stipulation was made that the design for coinage should employ the "figure of an Indian with bow and arrow and a star on one side with the word Commonwealth, on the reverse a spread eagle with the words Massachusetts 1787." The ambitiousness of this project was never fully realized. While coppers were struck in some quantities, a coinage of silver and gold never appeared. In 1789 the mint was abandoned, having proven costly to operate.

1788 CENT

1788 HALF CENT

TYPE OF COIN	ABP	G-4 Good	F-12 Fine
☐1787 Cent, Arrows in Left Talon	24.00	39.00	89.00
☐1787 Cent, Arrows in Right Talon	1700.00	3850.00	6200.00
☐1787 Cent, Horned Eagle (Die Break)	22.00	38.00	86.00
☐1787 Half Cent	29.00	52.00	115.00
☐1788 Cent	22.00	37.00	92.00
☐1788 Half Cent	30.00	54.00	125.00

MASSACHUSETTS PINE TREE COPPER

The origin of this unique coin is undetermined. Only one specimen is known, undoubtedly a pattern piece, and but for the greatest of good luck it would have been undiscovered. It turned up, buried beneath a Boston street, during an excavation in the 1800s, having probably been entombed nearly a century. Only the sharp eyes of a laborer prevented it from being discarded along with rubbish. Despite this imprisonment its condition is surprisingly good. It shows a pine tree on the obverse, obviously inspired by the Pine Tree Coinage of a century earlier, and a figure of Liberty posed as Britannia on the reverse, complete with globe and dog. The date 1776 appears beneath the reverse figure. Whether this was the year of striking or was used merely symbolically to denote our independence from Britain is unknown. The obverse inscription is "MASSACHUSETTS STATE" while the reverse reads "LIBERTY AND VIRTUE." This unique item is owned today by the Massachusetts Historical Society. Reproductions exist.

1776 PINE TREE
(UNIQUE)

MASSACHUSETTS HALFPENNY

This intriguing coin, classical in appearance, is dated 1776 and is often referred to as the Janus Copper or Janus Halfpenny. This is a reference (though not quite historically accurate) to the obverse design, which shows a three-sided head with faces looking forward, left, and right. The mythological god Janus had only two faces, looking right and left (the month of January is named for him; one face looks to the old year, one to the new). On the reverse is a seated representation of Liberty. The Massachusetts Halfpenny is a unique pattern piece. The only known specimen sold for $40,000 in 1979.

MASSACHUSETTS
HALFPENNY

KENTUCKY TOKEN

This novel piece was not of American origin, but struck in England around the year 1792. It is thought to have been occasioned by admission of Kentucky into the Union. On the obverse is a hand holding a petition reading "OUR CAUSE IS JUST" surrounded by the wording "UNANIMITY IS THE STRENGTH OF SOCIETY." The reverse is composed of a star in which are circular ornaments, each bearing the initial letter of a state. As K for Kentucky appears at the top, this piece is identified with that state. Some specimens have plain edges while others are stamped "Payable at Bedworth," "Payable in Lancaster," etc. It is vital to take note of these markings, as they have a great influence on the value.

1792 TOKEN

TYPE OF COIN	ABP	G-4 Good	F-12 Fine	MS-60 Unc.
☐ 1792 Token, plain edge	22.00	42.00	82.00	680.00
☐ 1792 Token, engrailed edge	68.00	120.00	220.00	1450.00
☐ 1792 Token, lettered edge, Payable at I. Fielding, etc.			EXTREMELY RARE	
☐ 1792 Token, lettered edge, Payable at Bedworth, etc.			EXTREMELY RARE	
☐ 1792 Token, lettered edge, Payable at Lancaster, London, or Bristol	30.00	54.00	100.00	720.00

MARYLAND–CHALMERS

The Chalmers tokens were the second group of coins to be struck for circulation in Maryland, preceded by the Lord Baltimore money of a century earlier. Unlike these early pieces, which were of foreign manufacture, the Chalmers coins evolved locally. They were minted at Annapolis in 1783. Apparently they came into being because of the coinage shortage which then existed in Maryland and the hesitancy of that state's legislature to take official action. John Chalmers, their maker, was a goldsmith. He struck them in silver in denominations of threepence, sixpence, and one shilling (twelve pence). Their odd geometrical designs give them an almost cabalistic appearance. All are quite scarce but the majority are obtainable.

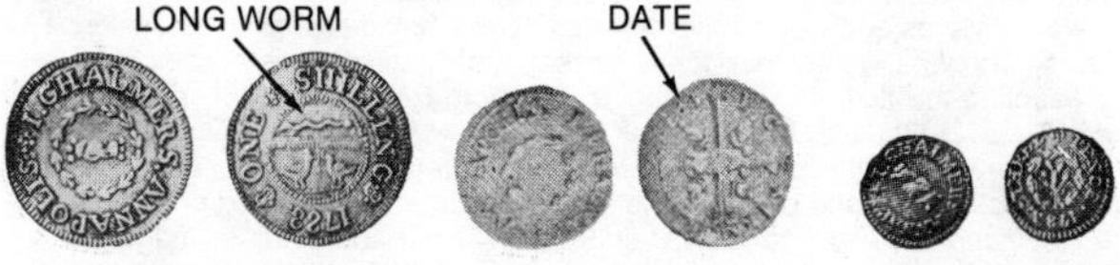

1783 SHILLING 1783 SIXPENCE 1783 THREEPENCE

TYPE OF COIN	ABP	G-4 Good	F-12 Fine
☐1783 Shilling, short worm	230.00	400.00	1450.00
☐1783 Shilling, long worm	280.00	450.00	1575.00
☐1783 Shilling, rings on reverse		EXTREMELY RARE	
☐1783 Sixpence, small date	360.00	680.00	1550.00
☐1783 Sixpence, large date	320.00	620.00	1410.00
☐1783 Threepence	280.00	450.00	1250.00

BALTIMORE, MARYLAND/STANDISH BARRY

Standish Barry was a private citizen of Baltimore who worked at various craft trades including watchmaking and silversmithing. In 1790 he struck, in very limited quantities, a silver threepenny token bearing a portrait on one side and the words "THREE PENCE" on the other. Due to the low face value and the fact of its being made of silver the physical size is quite small, about comparable to our dime. Barry's motive is not known with certainty. That he wished to alleviate the shortage of small-denomination coinage in his neighborhood is a possibility, but he produced so few specimens that this goal, if such was his intent, could not have been achieved. A more likely suggestion is that the Barry token was intended chiefly as an advertising piece. This is supported by the appearance of his name, spelled out in full on the reverse, which commonly was done only with tradesmen's tokens. The obverse portrait is thought to have been intended as George Washington, which fails to resemble him only because of artistic inability. Not only the year but the month is stated and the day as well: July 4, 90. The whole appearance is crude and amateurish, but collectors treasure it.

TYPE OF COIN	ABP	G-4 Good	F-12 Fine
☐1790 Silver Threepence	850.00	1750.00	3500.00

RHODE ISLAND TOKEN

The Rhode Island Ship Token has been variously classified as a coin, token, and medal, and its status is hardly clearer today than when research first began. Struck in 1778 or 1779 (the obverse carries one date, the reverse another), the piece is known in a variety of base metals: copper, brass, tin, and pewter, the composition having little influence on its value. That it was intended as a coin for ordinary circulation and exchange appears remote as it carries no mark of value and would have had to trade on the basis of weight. Being made of different metals, the weight varies and would have resulted in no small measure of confusion. The obverse shows a well-drawn ocean vessel. On the reverse is a complex scene representing the flight of Continental troops from Rhode Island. The inscriptions are in Dutch but the old belief that this production was of Dutch or Dutch-American origin is now given little support. Based upon the reverse theme it could well have been struck in England or by royalists in America. It should be kept in mind that the Revolutionary war had not yet ended in 1778–9 and coins or medals had a certain propaganda value. Reproductions are known to exist.

1778-1779 "VLUGTENDE"

1778-1779 WREATH

TYPE OF COIN	ABP	VF-20 V. Fine	EF-40 Ex. Fine
☐ 1778–1779 "VLUGTENDE" Below Ship			RARE
☐ 1778–1779 "VLUGTENDE" Removed.............	320.00	580.00	1210.00
☐ 1778–1779 Wreath Below Ship....................	360.00	660.00	1350.00

1776 CONTINENTAL CURRENCY

The Continental Dollar and its affiliates were struck as pattern pieces only, based upon the latest research, and never reached general circulation. They are believed to represent the first attempt at coinage by the Continental Congress, at any rate the first to achieve physical form. Upon declaring its independence from Britain, the United States was cut off from supplies of British currency and anticipated an extreme shortage within the coming months. Actually this shortage did not materialize to the degree feared. Continental Currency is crown-size and struck in silver, pewter, and brass. Though the sizes are identical and the coins bear no indication of value, it is presumed the silver pieces were intended as dollars and the base metal varieties as divisions thereof. The exact history of their origin is not recorded, the documentation of it having apparently been swept away in the turbulent times of war. We know that the engraver bore the initials E.G. because he signed his work. An exhaustive search of goldsmiths, silversmiths, and other metalworkers active at that time, having the initials E.G., has led to the conclusion that the 1776 Continental Currency was the work of Elisha Gallaudet of Philadelphia. If this is the case, they would undoubtedly have been struck in that city as well. Considering that it was headquarters of the Continental Congress, it seems to fit together historically. The legends include "WE ARE ONE" and "MIND YOUR BUSINESS," the latter not, probably, having been directed toward the British but used merely as a piece of sage advice in the spirit of Ben Franklin. Copies exist, struck at the 1876 Centennial exposition.

1776
CURENCY
Brass, Pewter,
Silver

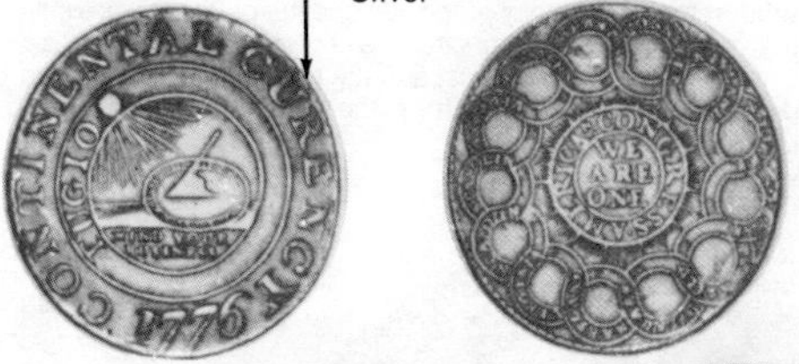

1776
CURRENCY
E. G. FECIT
Pewter, Silver

TYPE OF COIN	ABP	F-12 Fine	EF-40 Ex. Fine
☐1776 CURENCY, Brass			VERY RARE
☐1776 CURENCY, Pewter	1350.00	2300.00	4600.00
☐1776 CURENCY, Silver			VERY RARE
☐1776 CURRENCY, Pewter	1600.00	2650.00	6400.00
☐1776 CURRENCY, E.G. FECIT, Pewter	1450.00	2600.00	4900.00
☐1776 CURRENCY, E.F. FECIT, Silver		2600.00	UNIQUE
☐1776 CURRENCY, Pewter			UNIQUE

NOVA CONSTELLATIO SILVER

These Nova Constellatio silvers are pattern pieces for a federal coinage, the first such pattern pieces of silver struck by the newly born government. They date from 1783, shortly after the War of Independence had been concluded. Supposedly the brainchild of Governor Morris, a signer of the Declaration of Independence and Assistant Financier of the Confederation, their designer was Benjamin Dudley. At this point the system of cents and dollars, later agreed upon, had not yet evolved; but there was no wish to continue use of the British pound standard. Morris evolved a currency system in which the chief denomination was a mark, consisting of 1,000 units. Divisions of this coin—also included among the Nova Constellatio patterns—were the quint, equal to 500 units or half a mark, and the bit, with a value of 100 units or a tenth of a mark. Further divisions could then supposedly be made of base metal, in 50 or 10 units of whatever seemed practical. If we think of Morris' mark as the equivalent of the dollar (which in reality it was), then the 500 unit piece was the counterpart of 50¢ and the 100 unit piece of 10¢. Morris won little support for his currency proposals and the patterns were never approved for general circulation. Just one specimen is known to exist of each example; however, there are two types (and consequently two known specimens) of the 500 unit piece, one having an inscription on the obverse and the other bearing no inscription.

1783 MARK

1783 QUINT

1783 CENT

SECOND VARIETY

1783 QUINT

TYPE OF COIN	VG-8 VERY GOOD
☐ 1783 MARK—1000 Mills, Silver	ALL TYPES EXTREMELY RARE
☐ 1783 QUINT—500 Mills, Silver	ALL TYPES EXTREMELY RARE
☐ 1783 QUINT—Second Variety, Silver	ALL TYPES EXTREMELY RARE
☐ 1783 Cent—100 Mills, Silver	ALL TYPES EXTREMELY RARE
☐ 1783 "S" Copper	ALL TYPES EXTREMELY RARE

NOVA CONSTELLATIO COPPERS

Though their name and design are similar to the Nova Constellatio silver, it is important to note that these coins had quite different origins and purposes. The concept for both was that of Governor Morris, who, in addition to being a legislator, was also a prominent businessman in the late colonial/early federal age. While the silvers were pattern pieces for a proposed federal coinage, these coppers were struck as a personal speculative venture. It is quite likely that their place of origin was not America but Birmingham, England, and that their dies were engraved by an Englishman named Wyon. Upon importation to this country, Morris placed them into circulation as best he could. To judge from the fairly large quantities that exist of most types, their production must have reached the tens of thousands, if not higher.

CONSTELATIO 1783 BLUNT RAYS

1785 CENT

TYPE OF COIN	ABP	G-4 Good	F-12 Fine
☐ 1783 Cent, CONSTELLATIO, Pointed Rays, Large U.S.	26.00	40.00	120.00
☐ 1783 Cent, CONSTELLATIO, Pointed Rays, Small U.S.	20.00	35.00	120.00
☐ 1783 Cent, CONSTELLATIO, Blunt Rays	21.00	42.00	115.00
☐ 1785 Cent, CONSTELLATIO, Blunt Rays	25.00	42.00	140.00
☐ 1785 Cent, CONSTELLATIO, Pointed Rays	21.00	39.00	115.00
☐ 1786 Cent, CONSTELLATIO, Pointed Rays			VERY RARE

IMMUNE COLUMBIA

It is believed that these tokens, whose obverse designs are in some instances similar to those of the Nova Constellatio Coppers, were struck from dies engraved by Thomas Wyon of Birmingham, England. Their history is otherwise shrouded in mystery. That they represent pattern pieces which did not actually circulate seems unquestionable, as they exist in extremely limited quantities. There are several varieties, chiefly in copper, but the piece does exist in silver. A single gold specimen, dated 1785, is included in the government's collection at Washington. It was obtained by trade with the collector Stickney, who accepted a duplicate 1804 silver dollar for it. A later version of the Immune Columbia token, dated 1787, was struck from dies by James Atlee. Justice with scales is the reverse theme with a number of different obverses, including a portrait of the then not too popular George III.

OBVERSE 1785
IMMUNE COLUMBIA

1785
REVERSE
"NOVA"

IMMUNIS COLUMBIA
1787

TYPE OF COIN	ABP	G-4 Good	F-12 Fine
☐1785 Cent, Copper			
☐1785 Cent, Silver			
☐1785 Cent, Copper, Extra Star in Reverse			ALL RARE
☐1785 Cent, Copper—CONSTELATIC—Blunt Rays			
☐1785 Cent, VERMON AUCTORI	660.00	1200.00	2600.00
☐1785 Cent, GEORGE III OBVERSE	720.00	1270.00	2900.00
☐1787 Immunis Columbia	120.00	215.00	550.00

CONFEDERATIO

The Confederatio Cent, also known as Confederatio Coppers, is a hybrid coin found with various obverse and reverse designs. Regardless of the designs these are all pattern pieces that never reached circulation and all are extremely rare. Identity of the die cutters is not known but it is believed that at least some were the work of Thomas Wyon of Birmingham, England, and undoubtedly they were struck abroad. One of the obverse motifs features George Washington.

1785 CENT

1785 WASHINGTON

TYPE OF COIN	ABP	G-4 Good	F-12 Fine
☐1785 Cent, Stars in Small Circle		7500.00	12300.00
☐1785 Cent, Stars in Large Circle		7500.00	12300.00
☐1785 Cent, George Washington		EXTREMELY RARE	

SPECIMEN PATTERNS

A number of copper pattern pieces were struck in or about 1786 for possible use as token currency. Their history is not well established and all are extremely rare. The shield design and "E PLURIBUS UNUM" inscription on the reverses of some were subsequently used on New Jersey tokens, but the following patterns cannot be classified as belonging to any given locality.

TYPE OF COIN	ABP	G-4 Good	F-12 Fine
☐1786 IMMUNIS COLUMBIA, shield reverse		EXTREMELY RARE	
☐1786 IMMUNIS COLUMBIA, eagle reverse		EXTREMELY RARE	
☐1786 Eagle on obverse		EXTREMELY RARE	
☐1786 Washington/eagle		EXTREMELY RARE	
☐Undated, Washington obverse		EXTREMELY RARE	

NORTH AMERICAN TOKEN

This is a private piece, one of a number issued following the Revolution, that circulated in this country. Its origin is Irish, having been struck in Dublin. Undoubtedly it represented the effort of an Irish merchant or metalsmith to take advantage of America's coin shortage. The date shown is 1781 but belief is strong that it was actually produced at some later time, possibly in the late 1790s or early 1800s. The U.S. was experiencing a coin shortage during the presidency of Thomas Jefferson, so it could well date from that era. This situation was well known abroad, as foreigners melting down our coinage were chiefly responsible. On the obverse it pictures a sailing ship with the word "COMMERCE" and a seated likeness of Hibernia (symbol of Ireland) with her harp on the reverse, inscribed "NORTH AMERICAN TOKEN." It may well be that the side of this token traditionally regarded as the obverse was intended as the reverse. Quantities in which the North American Token were distributed in the U.S. are not known. The piece is far from rare. Its size is roughly equivalent to a quarter.

TYPE OF COIN	ABP	G-4 Good	F-12 Fine
☐1781 Token	14.00	22.00	63.00

MACHIN COPPERS

Thomas Machin operated a copper mill at Newburgh, New York. From 1786 to 1789 he was active in the production of tokens, some designed for use in the State of New York (listed under New York) and others that were nothing but counterfeits of the British copper halfpenny. He attempted to profit by placing these counterfeits, of lighter than standard weight, into immense circulation. To avoid suspicion he used a variety of dates, going back as far as 1747. But the majority are dated in the early 1770s. The design is always the same: a portrait of the king on the obverse with Britannia on the reverse. As these pieces are not collected by date, their values are constant irrespective of date. They can easily be distinguished from genuine British halfpennies by their cruder die engraving. However, the Machin fakes were not the only ones made of this coin.

TYPE OF COIN	ABP	G-4 Good	F-12 Fine
☐Halfpenny, various dates	30.00	56.00	195.00

GEORGIUS TRIUMPHO TOKEN

This controversial coin, dating from 1783, is made of copper. On the obverse is a male portrait in profile with the inscription "GEORGIUS TRIUMPHO," which cannot be translated in any other fashion but "George Has Triumphed." Considering that the War for Independence had recently ended with an American victory, the triumphal George should be Washington. But the portrait much more closely resembles George III, the British monarch who sought to preserve American colonization. Just how this George could be regarded to have triumphed at that moment is puzzling. Perhaps the explanation is that Washington was intended but the engraver, being unskilled and having no likeness at hand from which to copy, merely fashioned the portrait after that on English money. A similar situation prevailed at the time among illustrators who designed copperplate portraits for books, the likeness often being guessed at. As photography did not exist and few citizens actually saw celebrities in the flesh, it was not really known if such works were accurate. The reverse pictures Liberty holding an olive branch, and thirteen bars representing the confederation. Its inscription is "VOCE POPOLI," an error for Voce Populi or "Voice of the People."

TYPE OF COIN	ABP	G-4 Good	F-12 Fine	VF-20 Fine
☐1783 GEORGIUS TRIUMPHO	21.00	40.00	155.00	360.00

AUCTORI PLEBIS TOKEN

Not much is known of this copper piece, other than the fact that it closely resembles the early coinage of Connecticut. It is thought to have been struck in England and may never have been intended for American circulation. It has, however, traditionally been included in American colonial and federal-era collections. It bears a date of 1787 and carries a male portrait profile on the obverse with a seated figure of Liberty on the reverse. The workmanship is not especially skilled.

TYPE OF COIN	ABP	G-4 Good	F-12 Fine	VF-20 Fine
☐1787 AUCTORI PLEBIS Token	30.00	49.00	140.00	265.00

MOTT TOKEN

An early trade token, this piece had no official sanction nor any legal value as money. Its issuers were William and John Mott, who operated a business on Water Street in the downtown area of Manhattan. Mott Street, now the central boulevard of New York's Chinatown, was named for this family. The Mott Token is of copper, picturing on one side the American eagle emblem and (quite unusual) a shelf clock on the other. The clock served an advertising purpose, as the Motts dealt in goldware, silverware, and fancy goods, including importations. This token dates from 1789. Of too high a quality for local production, it seems evident they were manufactured in England.

TYPE OF COIN	ABP	G-4 Good	F-12 Fine	EF-40 Ex. Fine
☐1789 Mott Token, thick planchet	40.00	72.00	175.00	550.00
☐1789 Mott Token, thin planchet	56.00	100.00	220.00	660.00
☐1789 Mott Token, engrailed edge.....	67.00	121.00	415.00	1250.00

BAR CENT

The Bar Cent is a very simply designed coin whose name derives from the fact that its reverse design is composed of a grid containing thirteen bars (one for each state of the confederation). On the obverse are the letters USA in large size, intertwined. Beyond this there is no further ornament or inscription and the origin of this piece has proven a dilemma. It is almost surely a foreign product, made possibly by Wyon (of Nova Constellatio copper frame) of Birmingham, England. Its first public appearance was made in New York in late 1785. It may be presumed that the date of minting was either that year or possibly 1784. Reproductions were produced during the Civil War, against which collectors are cautioned.

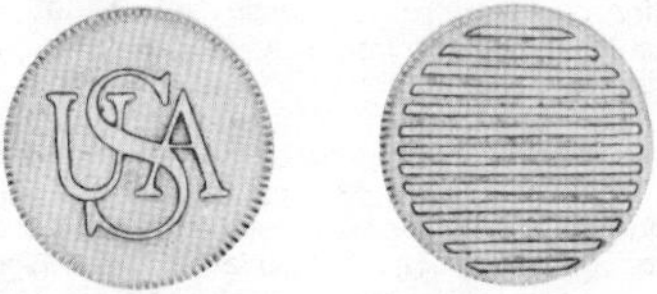

TYPE OF COIN	ABP	G-4 Good	F-12 Fine	EF-40 Ex. Fine
☐ Undated, Bar Cent	130.00	215.00	500.00	1200.00

TALBOT, ALLUM, AND LEE CENTS

These are trade tokens, circulated by a firm of importers known as Talbot, Allum, and Lee, who were headquartered at 241 Pearl Street, New York, in what is now the financial district but then was given over largely to import/export because of its access to the Battery docks. There is no question but that they were struck in England. The corporation's name appears on one side, sometimes with and sometimes without its place of location. The earliest date is 1794 and at this point they carried a value legend of one cent. In 1794 this was removed, possibly out of fear of government protest, and an inscription added to the edge: "WE PROMISE TO PAY THE BEARER ONE CENT." There are, however, specimens of the 1795 edition with unlettered edge, which are considerably scarcer. This practice of issuing tokens redeemable at a certain place of business became widespread in the 19th century, especially during the small-change shortage of the Civil War.

1794 NEW YORK

1795 CENT

TYPE OF COIN	ABP	G-4 Good	F-12 Fine	EF-40 Ex. Fine
☐ 1794 Cent with "NEW YORK"	20.00	42.00	86.00	195.00
☐ 1794 Cent without "NEW YORK"	89.00	185.00	440.00	910.00
☐ 1795 Cent	16.00	31.00	82.00	400.00

GEORGE WASHINGTON PIECES

Following the Revolution, George Washington became a national hero and idol to such degree that he was virtually worshipped. Books were written on his life, engravers published pictures of him, and his likeness was set into snuff boxes, jewelry cases, and other fancy goods. It is only natural that Washington would also be the subject of numerous tokens and pseudo-coins. These were issued beginning in 1783 and (for practical purposes) ceasing about 1795, after official federal coinage began circulating. No exact date can be placed on their discontinuance, however, as tokens and medals honoring Washington appeared from time to time thereafter. Those listed below are not strictly classed as commemoratives but might just as well be. They were primarily coppers and contained a cent's worth of that metal. They could therefore be used as money, but the extent to which this was done is not known and can be presumed to have been limited, as none was struck in large quantities. The best title for them might be "celebration pieces." Building a complete collection is outside the realm of possibility, because of the extreme scarcity of some issues. A fair assembly of them can, however, be made. Their origins are not well established. Some are believed to have been designed and struck in England. This would seem logical on the basis of workmanship. Those made abroad were surely not designed for circulation there, but for export and distribution within the United States. One of the Washington tokens—in ½ penny value—declares itself a Welsh product; it carries the inscription "NORTH WALES" on the reverse. Another was a London tradesman's token. As for their dates, the presumption is that some, at least, were struck subsequent to the year indicated, perhaps in the first decade of the 19th century or even later. Most have distinctive reverses and are known chiefly by these reverse types. So far as the portraiture is concerned, there is a rich and interesting variety, differing not only in artistic quality but concept. On some, Washington is shown as a Roman-style emperor, wearing a laurel wreath. The majority portray him in military dress. Though a few coins of amateurish design are included in this group there are likewise several of the most skilled and impressive workmanship, which, if executed as sculptures, would be regarded as important works of art. The likelihood that Washington sat for any of the die-cutters is remote, but apparently they either had prior experience drawing or sculpting him or worked from some of the better oil pictures, such as those of Stuart. They could not have achieved such faithful portraiture merely from descriptions of his physical appearance.

1.
1783 CENT

2.
1783 CENT

3.
1783 CENT

4.
1783 CENT (DOUBLE HEAD)

6.
1791 CENT

7.
1791 CENT

8.
1791 HALFPENNY

9.
1792 CENT

10.
1792 CENT

11.
1792 HALF DOLLAR

12.
1792 ROMAN HEAD

13.
1792 EAGLE

14.
1793 HALFPENNY

15.
1795 HALFPENNY

16.
1795 PENNY

17.
1795 HALFPENNY

18.
TOKEN

19.
TOKEN

20.
TOKEN

TYPE OF COIN	ABP	G-4 Good	F-12 Fine
☐ 1. 1783 Cent, Large Military Bust	19.00	30.00	48.00
☐ 1a. 1783 Cent, Small Military Bust...........	21.00	36.00	57.00
☐ 1b. 1783 Cent, Small Military Bust, engraved edge	27.00	42.00	68.00

TYPE OF COIN	ABP	G-4 Good	F-12 Fine
☐ 2. 1783 Cent, Draped Bust	24.00	40.00	67.00
☐ 2a. 1783 Cent, Draped Bust, button on cloak	30.00	46.00	92.00
☐ 2b. 1783 Cent, Draped Bust, silver restrike	22.00	PROOF: $610.00	
☐ 3. 1783 Cent, Draped Bust: Unity States	18.00	37.00	89.00
☐ 4. 1783 Cent (Undated) Double Head		30.00	69.00
☐ 5. 1784 (Ugly Head) (NOT ILLUS.)			RARE
☐ 6. 1791 Cent, Small Eagle	42.00	79.00	180.00
☐ 7. 1791 Cent, Large Eagle	42.00	79.00	175.00
☐ 8. 1791 Liverpool Halfpenny	135.00	225.00	500.00
☐ 9. 1792 Cent, WASHINGTON PRESIDENT	815.00	1610.00	3300.00
☐ 10. 1792 Cent, BORN VIRGINIA	470.00	880.00	2150.00
☐ 11. 1792 Silver		EXTREMELY RARE	
☐ 11a. 1792 Copper	710.00	1450.00	4100.00
☐ 11b. 1792 Large Eagle			UNIQUE
☐ 12. 1792 Roman Head		PROOF RARE	
☐ 13. 1792 Eagle, Copper			
☐ 13a. 1792 Eagle, Silver		EXTREMELY RARE	
☐ 13b. 1792 Eagle, Gold			
☐ 14. 1793 Ship Halfpenny	47.00	76.00	120.00
☐ 15. 1795 Halfpenny, Reeded Edge, "GRATE," small buttons	50.00	97.00	150.00
☐ 15a. 1795 Halfpenny, Reeded Edge, "GRATE," large buttons	22.00	40.00	82.00
☐ 15b. 1795 Halfpenny, Lettered Edge, "GRATE," large buttons	82.00	155.00	250.00
☐ 16. 1795 Penny, Undated, LIBERTY AND SECURITY	47.00	90.00	150.00
☐ 17. 1795 Halfpenny, Dated, LIBERTY AND SECURITY, London	37.00	57.00	112.00
☐ 17a. 1795 Halfpenny, LIBERTY AND SECURITY, Birmingham	37.00	58.00	110.00
☐ 17b. 1795 Halfpenny, Dated, LIBERTY AND SECURITY, Asylum	42.00	76.00	180.00
☐ 17c. 1795 Halfpenny, Dated, LIBERTY AND SECURITY, Plain Edge	37.00	62.00	108.00
☐ 18. Success Token, Large	52.00	96.00	175.00
☐ 19. Success Token, Small	52.00	96.00	172.00
☐ 20. 1795 Halfpenny, NORTH WALES	52.00	96.00	195.00

FRANKLIN PRESS TOKEN

This copper token was struck in England as a merchant piece and its use apparently restricted there. Because of its connection with Benjamin Franklin it has interest for collectors of American coinage. The obverse pictures an old-fashioned screw press (driven by jerking a lever), with the words "PAYABLE AT THE FRANKLIN PRESS LONDON" on the opposite side. It carries a date of 1794. As Franklin died in 1790 he could not have seen this token. Reproductions exist.

TYPE OF COIN	ABP	G-4 Good	F-12 Fine	EF-40 Ex. Fine
☐ 1794 Token	24.00	39.00	100.00	290.00

CASTORLAND

Royalists who fled France following the revolution's outbreak in 1791 scattered to many parts of the globe. A small colony settled in the New York State farmlands (near Carthage) and called the locality Castorland. The Castorland medal or token is said to be a pattern piece struck in France for a proposed currency. It never reached beyond the experimental stage and both varieties, in silver and copper, are extremely rare. They carry a date of 1796.

TYPE OF COIN	ABP	G-4 Good	VG-8 Very Good	F-12 Fine
☐ 1796 Silver Original, Reeded Edge....	BOTH TYPES RARE			
☐ 1796 Copper Original, Reeded Edge ..				

FUGIO CENTS

The Fugio Cents, so called because that word is a component in the obverse inscription, were the first officially sanctioned U.S. federal coinage. It was resolved by Congress in 1787 that a contract be put out with a private miller, James Jarvis, for 300 tons of copper coins. The arrangement was for Jarvis to secure the metal himself and pay all expenses, then sell the coins to the government at face value—his profit arising from the difference between his cost and the total face value. It was a venture of enormous proportions, considering that the U.S. had not previously authorized any coins. The matter of designing was not left to the contractor. Congress specifically spelled out what these coins should look like: "thirteen circles linked together, a small circle in the middle with the words 'United States' around it, and in the center the words 'We are one'; on the other side of the same piece the following device, viz: a dial with the hours expressed on the face of it; a meridian sun above on one side of which is the word 'Fugio.' " Fugio is Latin for "time flies." As the obverse carries the saying "Mind your Business," often attributed to Benjamin Franklin, this is sometimes called the Franklin Cent; such terminology is, however, misleading and confusing. The dies were produced by Abel Buel of New Haven, Connecticut, and most of the striking was apparently carried out in that city. Jarvis failed to deliver the agreed-on number of coins, was prosecuted for breach of contract and imprisoned.

1787 CENT

TYPE OF COIN	ABP	G-4 Good	F-12 Fine
☐ 1787 Cent, Club Rays, Rounded Ends	48.00	90.00	280.00
☐ 1787 Cent, Club Rays, Concave Ends, FUCIO (NOT ILLUS.)			
☐ 1787 Cent, Club Rays, Concave Ends, FUGIO		ALL VERY RARE	
☐ 1787 Cent, Club Rays, States United			
☐ 1787 Cent, Pointed Rays, UNITED above, STATES below			
☐ 1787 Cent, Pointed Rays, UNITED STATES at side of circle (NOT ILLUS.)	40.00	69.00	165.00
☐ 1787 Cent, Pointed Rays, STATES UNITED at side of circle; Cinquefoils	40.00	69.00	165.00
☐ 1787 Cent, Pointed Rays, STATES UNITED at sides, 8 pointed star on reverse band (NOT ILLUS.)	52.00	105.00	275.00
☐ 1787 Cent, Pointed Rays, STATES UNITED, raised edge on reverse band	60.00	120.00	400.00
☐ 1787 Cents, Pointed Rays, UNITED STATES, No Cinquefoils	112.00	200.00	640.00
☐ 1787 Cent, Pointed Rays, STATES UNITED, No Cinquefoils	225.00	240.00	720.00
☐ 1787 Cent, AMERICAN CONGRESS, with Rays (NOT ILLUS.)			VERY RARE

NEW HAVEN RESTRIKES

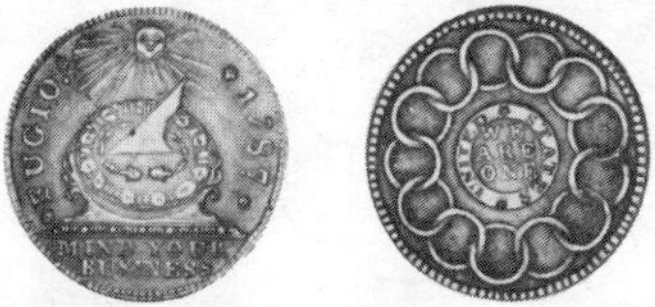

1787 CENT

In 1858, C. Wyllys Betts found three sets of dies in New Haven. Restrikes in various metals were made. The restrikes were not made directly from these dies but copies fashioned from them.

TYPE OF COIN	ABP	MS-60 Unc.
☐Copper	170.00	310.00
☐Silver	350.00	630.00
☐Brass	175.00	330.00
☐Gold	EXTREMELY RARE	

FIRST UNITED STATES OF AMERICA MINT ISSUES

1792 BIRCH CENT

The 1792 Birch Cent was the first coin to be struck at the newly established U.S. Mint in Philadelphia and the first governmental issue struck by the government as opposed to private contractors. This coin was not circulated but produced as a trial piece only. Along with it there were also trial or pattern pieces of half disme, disme, and quarter dollar denominations, all of which are extremely rare. A motion is said to have been made for placing George Washington's likeness on these pieces but that Washington, when informed of this plan, declined to be honored in such a manner. It was then decided to use a portrait of the Goddess of Liberty. The better-known version of the Birch Cent is large in size and composed entirely of copper. A smaller cent was also produced, containing a droplet of silver at the center. This was done entirely experimentally, in an effort to determine whether a penny coin in small size might be publicly more acceptable than one made exclusively of base metal. The pattern quarter dollar has more the appearance of a medal than a coin. The Birch Cent derives its name from Robert Birch, its designer. Birch is thought also to have been among the die-cutters for the half disme and disme.

1792 BIRCH CENT

1792 HALF DISME

1792 DISME

TYPE OF COIN	VG-8 VERY GOOD
☐ 1792 (Silver), DISME	
☐ 1792 (Copper), DISME	ALL COINS ARE RARE,
☐ 1792 (Silver), HALF DISME	VERY RARE, OR UNIQUE
☐ 1792 BIRCH CENT (Copper)	
☐ 1792 BIRCH CENT (White Metal)	EXTREMELY RARE
☐ 1792 QUARTER DOLLAR (Pattern, Copper)	EXTREMELY RARE
☐ 1792 QUARTER DOLLAR (Pattern, White Metal)	EXTREMELY RARE

1792 SILVER CENTER CENT

TYPE OF COIN	VG-8 VERY GOOD
☐ 1792 Silver Center Cent	ALL COINS ARE VERY RARE
☐ 1792 Cent, No Silver Center	OR UNIQUE

HALF CENTS, 1793–1857

That the lowly half cent survived into the second half of the 19th century is looked upon as remarkable today by persons not well acquainted with the economic conditions of that time. Despite its minute face value, and the grumblings of many citizens that it did little but clutter their pockets, it served an important function in trade. Many articles in shops were priced fractionally and without the half cent difficulty would have been encountered in making change for such purchases. Their availability was, however, frequently abused. Merchants, anxious to rid themselves of half cents, would often give them instead of pennies. As first introduced in 1793, the coin bore a portrait of Liberty facing left on its obverse and a wreathed reverse with the words "HALF CENT" and "UNITED STATES OF AMERICA." The designer was Adam Eckfeldt. The original weight was 6.74 grams and the composition pure copper. The coin has a diameter of 22 mm. and is stamped along the edge, "TWO HUNDRED FOR A DOLLAR." After being struck for a single year it was decided to redesign the coin (coin redesigning occurred frequently in the Mint's early days of operation), the new design being the work of Robert Scot. Liberty was switched round to face right, her features streamlined, and her cap (the "cap of liberty," a reference to caps worn by freed slaves in Roman times) enlarged. The reverse was restyled but not materially altered. Planchets were of the same weight but slightly larger physically, measuring 23½ mm. Another fresh version was placed into use in 1795, this one the work of John S. Gardner; its specifications were the same as its predecessor's. It was later concluded that the weight had been set too high. This ushered in the so-called "thin planchet" half cent, weighing 5.44 grams and still measuring 23½ mm. "TWO HUNDRED FOR A DOLLAR" was removed from the edge. The varieties of this "Liberty Cap" half cent are numerous, despite the brief period of its manufacture.

The Liberty Cap half cent was followed in 1800 by introduction of the Draped Bust design, after a period of two years in which coins of this denomination were not minted (they could hardly have been in short supply as well over 200,000 had been circulated). Liberty's cap was removed and her hairstyle made somewhat more fashionable. The portrait was lengthened somewhat to include a suggestion of shoulders, over which a classical-style garment was placed. The designer was Robert Scot, who had done the 1794 version. Specifications remained the same as before. It was resolved to get these coins into very extensive circulation, resulting in a mintage quantity of more than one million in the year 1804 alone. By the end of 1808, the last year for this design, more than three million had been struck. The new half cent was the so-called "Classic Head" variety, designed by John Reich. Apparently this title was bestowed in the belief that Reich's Liberty more closely approximated Grecian sculpture than had the other types. The face, if stronger, became less physically attractive and more masculine. Stars were set at either side of the portrait and Liberty was given a band round her head with her name imprinted on it. The next design, and the last, was introduced in 1840 but used for proofs only, as the half cent did not return to general circulation until 1849. Christian Gobrecht was the designer and his rendition of Liberty has come to be known as the "Braided Hair Type." A sharp departure from the Reich approach, it pictured Liberty with Roman nose and considerable loss of bulk. This could well be considered the most attractive design, portrait-wise, of the half cent series.

HALF CENTS — LIBERTY CAP, 1793–1797

1793

1794 Pole to Cap

DATE	MINTAGE	ABP	G-4 Good	F-20 Fine	VF-20 V. Fine
☐ 1793 (Facing Left)	31,534	780.00	1520.00	2850.00	8900.00
☐ 1794 (Facing Right)	81,600	165.00	300.00	760.00	1300.00
☐ 1795 Plain Edge		165.00	260.00	600.00	1050.00
☐ 1795 Lettered Edge	25,600	165.00	290.00	600.00	1210.00
☐ 1796 With Pole	5,090	1750.00	3500.00	8000.00	12900.00
☐ 1796 No Pole			EXTREMELY RARE		
☐ 1797 Plain Edge		190.00	300.00	620.00	1200.00
☐ 1797 Lettered Edge	119,214	620.00	960.00	2500.00	5000.00
☐ 1797 1 Above 1		125.00	270.00	560.00	1100.00

HALF CENTS — DRAPED BUST, 1800–1808

1804

Plain 4

Crosslet 4

Spiked Chin Variety

DATE	MINTAGE	ABP	G-4 Good	F-12 Fine	VF-20 V. Fine	EF-40 Ex. Fine
☐ 1800	211,530	19.00	35.00	68.00	115.00	265.00
☐ 1802 with 1800 reverse ...		1250.00	2050.00	6300.00	15800.00	
☐ 1802	14,366	98.00	192.00	880.00	2700.00	5100.00
☐ 1803	87,900	18.00	35.00	60.00	86.00	360.00
☐ 1804 Plain 4		18.00	35.00	57.00	86.00	220.00
☐ 1804 Crosslet	1,055,312	18.00	32.00	53.00	82.00	220.00
☐ 1804 Spiked Chain		17.00	30.00	48.00	77.00	178.00
☐ 1805	814,464	18.00	34.00	50.00	90.00	230.00
☐ 1806	356,000	17.00	29.00	48.00	77.00	225.00
☐ 1806 Small 6, Stems		46.00	86.00	230.00	330.00	760.00
☐ 1807	476,000	16.00	30.00	54.00	89.00	260.00
☐ 1808 Normal Date	400,000	16.00	31.00	59.00	89.00	360.00
☐ 1808 Over 7		35.00	69.00	265.00	610.00	1750.00

HALF CENTS — TURBAN HEAD, 1809–1837

1837

1837 TOKEN

DATE	MINTAGE	ABP	G-4 Good	F-12 Fine	VF-20 V. Fine	EF-40 Ex. Fine
☐ 1809	1,154,572	11.00	21.00	41.00	62.00	86.00
☐ 1809 over 6		11.00	24.00	40.00	62.00	95.00
☐ 1809 Circle Inside O		15.00	25.00	42.00	71.00	125.00
☐ 1810	215,000	16.00	28.00	50.00	110.00	200.00
☐ 1811	63,140	40.00	90.00	340.00	750.00	1450.00
☐ 1811 Restrike with 1802 Reverse					EXTREMELY RARE	
☐ 1825	63,000	12.00	29.00	42.00	72.00	140.00
☐ 1826	234,000	11.00	26.00	38.00	71.00	95.00
☐ 1828 12 Stars	606,000	11.00	29.00	42.00	70.00	105.00
☐ 1828 13 Stars		11.00	24.00	37.00	50.00	70.00
☐ 1829	487,000	11.00	22.00	37.00	52.00	74.00
☐ 1831-8 known	2200		Business	Strikes-	Original	5600.00
☐ 1831 SMALL BERRIES ...			Proof Only-	Restrike		7800.00
☐ 1831 LARGE BERRIES ...			Proof Only-	Restrike		6700.00
☐ 1832	154,000	11.00	22.00	34.00	51.00	76.00
☐ 1833	120,000	11.00	22.00	34.00	51.00	76.00
☐ 1834	141,000	11.00	22.00	34.00	51.00	76.00
☐ 1835	398,000	11.00	22.00	34.00	51.00	76.00
☐ 1836		Proof Only	Original	7000.00	Restrike	7300.00
☐ 1837 (Token) pure copper		21.00	35.00	65.00	160.00	200.00

HALF CENTS — BRAIDED HAIR, 1840–1857

DATE		ABP		PRF-65 Proof
☐ 1840		3000.00	Proof Only	4500.00
☐ 1841		3000.00	Proof Only	4400.00
☐ 1842	ORIGINAL	3000.00	Proof Only	4300.00
☐ 1843	AND RESTRIKE	3000.00	Proof Only	4300.00

DATE		ABP		PRF-65 Proof
□ 1844	PROOFS ONLY	3000.00	Proof Only	4250.00
□ 1845	1840–1849	3000.00	Proof Only	4300.00
□ 1846	NO MINTAGE	3000.00	Proof Only	4350.00
□ 1847	RECORDS	3000.00	Proof Only	4200.00
□ 1848	AVAILABLE	3000.00	Proof Only	4350.00
□ 1849		3000.00	Proof Only	4350.00

DATE	MINTAGE	ABP	G-4 Good	F-12 Fine	VF-20 V. Fine	EF-40 Ex. Fine
□ 1849	39,864	20.00	42.00	57.00	64.00	92.00
□ 1850	39,812	21.00	40.00	46.00	64.00	86.00
□ 1851	147,672	17.00	27.00	42.00	56.00	72.00
□ 1852			Proofs Only—Original and Restrike: $4200.00			
□ 1853	129,964	15.00	27.00	44.00	58.00	74.00
□ 1854	55,358	15.00	27.00	44.00	58.00	74.00
□ 1855	56,500	15.00	31.00	44.00	58.00	74.00
□ 1856	40,430	21.00	36.00	52.00	62.00	82.00
□ 1857	35,180	24.00	50.00	60.00	72.00	92.00

LARGE CENTS—1793–1857

The shrinkage of the cent from its introduction in 1793 to its present size is ample evidence of inflation; the present Lincoln cent weighs only about one third as much as its distant ancestor. But what the penny has lost in bulk and buying power has been compensated for, at least in part, by its greater convenience. The series began with the Flowering Hair/Chain Reverse type designed by Henry Voight. Its weight was set at 13.48 grams of pure copper, precisely twice that of the half cent. (The government set rigid standards of weight, fearing that without such regulations its coinage would not inspire confidence.) There were no long suspensions of production, as with the half cent. A quantity—varying, of course, in number—was minted each year from the coin's inception until conclusion of the large cent in 1857, with the single exception of 1815 because of a metal shortage. The first design, aptly named as Liberty, is shown with billowing hair that appears breeze-blown. Her features are delicate and the overall composition is pleasing. It will be noted that the reverse design bears very close resemblance to the Fugio cent or Franklin cent, struck in 1787. The diameter of this coin varies from 26 to 27 mm. It is consequently not very much smaller than the present 50¢ piece. After three months of striking coins from these dies, during which time more than 36,000 were produced, a new design was introduced. The work of Adam Eckfeldt, designer of the first half cent, it retained the Flowing Hair portrait on the obverse but employed a wreath rather than the chained reverse, enclosing the words "ONE CENT." Its weight was unchanged but the diameter varies from 26 to 28 mm. or slightly larger than its predecessor. Along the edge is stamped the inscription "ONE HUNDRED FOR A DOLLAR."

This design got somewhat further, resulting in a mintage of more than 60,000 pieces, but before the year was out another had taken its place. The Flowing Hair portrait, subjected to criticism in the press (to which the government seems to have been more sensitive than subsequently), was removed in favor of a "Liberty Cap" type, designed by Joseph Wright. Here the bust of Liberty is positioned somewhat to the right of center; over her left shoulder she balances a staff, on the tip of which rests a conical-shaped cap—the "cap of liberty," symbolic of freedom from slavery in Roman times. This version, too, was assailed, but minters were so weary of making alterations that they continued using it until 1796. The staff and cap looked like an Indian arrow in the opinion of some; others fancied that Liberty was wearing an oversized bow in her hair. The weight was retained but the planchet grew slightly larger, to 29 mm. In 1795, still using the same design, the weight was dropped to 10.89 grams, diameter remained 29 mm., and new dies were engraved. The artist was John S. Gardner. His work is often said to be superior to other efforts. The "Draped Bust Type," first struck in mid-1796, was an effort to render more classicism to the portrait. Designed by Robert Scot, it deleted the much-maligned liberty cap and, while not materially altering Miss Liberty's facial features, gave her the appearance of chubbiness. Specifications remained as previously. In 1808 the so-called "Classic Head" made its bow, designed by John Reich. Here Liberty wears a coronet with the word "LIBERTY" spelled out upon it and the bust is shortened with drapery removed. She grows chubbier still. The reverse is very close to that of a modern "wheat" cent: the words "ONE CENT" encircled in laurel, surrounded by the legend "UNITED STATES OF AMERICA." There are numerous varieties, as enumerated below. The classic head survived until the copper shortage which followed close upon the heels of the War of 1812, when production of large cents was temporarily halted. When resumed in 1816 the design was new. The work of Robert Scot, it was referred to as "Matron Head," as Liberty appears to have taken on added years. She, in fact, was growing old with her coinage. A youth in 1792 when the series began, she had now advanced into middle age. The bust is shortened even further; stars now totally encircle it (except for the space containing the date); but the reverse remains the same.

In 1837 the last large cent design was put into production. The next two decades yielded many varieties of it, from die re-engravings. This is the Gobrecht version, basically a handsome portrait which returns the youthful goddess image to Liberty and slims her down. The weight was 10.89 grams (the penny was never to return to its old weight-standard), the diameter 27½ mm. Chief variations are the Silly Head and Booby Head, neither of which really merited such ridicule. There was also a Petite Head and Mature Head and ample differences in letter and numeral sizes.

LARGE CENTS — FLOWING HAIR, 1793

1793 Chain

1793 Wreath

DATE	MINTAGE	ABP	G-4 Good	VG-8 V. Good	F-12 Fine	VF-20 V. Fine
□ 1793 Chain AMERI	36,103	800.00	2100.00	3000.00	4100.00	6800.00
□ 1793 Chain AMERICA		800.00	2100.00	3000.00	4100.00	6800.00
□ 1793 Chain type, period after date and Liberty		800.00	2000.00	2500.00	3800.00	6200.00
□ 1793 Wreath type, edge has vine and bars	63,353	600.00	1150.00	1300.00	1900.00	3000.00
□ 1793 Wreath type, lettered edge, one leaf on edge ...		600.00	1150.00	1300.00	1900.00	2900.00
□ 1793 Wreath type lettered edge, double leaf on edge		600.00	1150.00	1300.00	1900.00	2900.00

LARGE CENTS — LIBERTY CAP, 1793–1796

1793 LIBERTY CAP

1795 JEFFERSON HEAD

ONE CENT
in Center of Wreath

ONE CENT
High in Wreath

DATE	MINTAGE	ABP	G-4 Good	VG-8 V. Good	F-12 Fine	VF-20 V. Fine
□ 1793	11,056	1000.00	2200.00	3200.00	4200.00	6400.00
□ 1794		80.00	180.00	290.00	480.00	860.00
□ 1794*	ALL KINDS	140.00	350.00	550.00	1310.00	2300.00
□ 1794**		80.00	170.00	240.00	420.00	760.00
□ 1794***	918,521	80.00	170.00	200.00	420.00	760.00
□ 1794****		1200.00	3400.00	4900.00	9000.00	22000.00
□ 1795 Jefferson Head ...		1100.00	2100.00	3600.00	6200.00	14400.00
*Head of 1793 **Head of 1795 ***No Fraction Bar ****Stars on Back						
□ 1795† Lettered Edge* ..		80.00	185.00	280.00	490.00	1375.00
□ 1795† Lettered Edge** .		90.00	210.00	310.00	550.00	1450.00
□ 1795†† Plain Edge*		72.00	170.00	260.00	420.00	750.00
□ 1795†† Plain Edge**		72.00	170.00	260.00	420.00	750.00

DATE	MINTAGE	ABP	G-4 Good	VG-8 V. Good	F-12 Fine	VF-20 V. Fine
□ 1796††† Liberty Cap		80.00	185.00	295.00	470.00	990.00

†Total Mintage: 82,000 ††Total Mintage: 456,500 †††Total Mintage: 109,825
*"ONE CENT" in Center of Wreath **"ONE CENT" High in Wreath

LARGE CENTS — DRAPED BUST, 1796–1800

LIHERTY 1796 (error)

DATE	MINTAGE	ABP	G-4 Good	VG-8 V. Good	F-12 Fine	VF-20 V. Fine
□ 1796†		39.00	76.00	120.00	215.00	420.00
□ 1796† "LIHERTY" (error) .		45.00	87.00	162.00	312.00	600.00
□ 1796†† Stems on Wreath .		32.00	70.00	116.00	200.00	420.00
□ 1797†† Stemless Wreath .		32.00	70.00	126.00	260.00	800.00
□ 1797†† Stems on Wreath .		21.00	48.00	82.00	135.00	300.00
□ 1797†† Gripped		20.00	45.00	82.00	142.00	300.00
□ 1797†† Plain Edge		21.00	45.00	86.00	152.00	350.00
□ 1798††† over 97		34.00	80.00	140.00	230.00	500.00
□ 1798††† Small Date		18.00	36.00	60.00	145.00	350.00
□ 1798††† Large Date		18.00	34.00	60.00	145.00	350.00
□ 1798†††*		18.00	42.00	80.00	180.00	420.00
□ 1799** over 98		400.00	900.00	1500.00	2600.00	5100.00
□ 1799** Normal Date		400.00	850.00	1500.00	2300.00	4900.00
□ 1800*** over 1798		15.00	36.00	52.00	120.00	310.00

†Total Mintage: 363,372 ††Total Mintage: 897,509 †††Total Mintage: 979,700
*Reverse of 96. Single leaf Reverse. Total Mintage: 904,584 ***Part of 2,822,170

LARGE CENTS — DRAPED BUST, 1800–1801

Normal Date—Normal Die

1800 Over 179

DATE	MINTAGE	ABP	G-4 Good	VG-8 V. Good	F-12 Fine	VF-20 V. Fine
□ 1800 over 79, Style I Hair .		14.00	30.00	47.00	105.00	310.00
□ 1800† over 79 Style II Hair		14.00	30.00	47.00	105.00	310.00
□ 1800† Unfinished Cyphers		14.00	30.00	47.00	105.00	310.00

DATE	MINTAGE	ABP	G-4 Good	VG-8 V. Good	F-12 Fine	VF-20 V. Fine
☐ 1800† Normal Date		14.00	30.00	47.00	115.00	290.00
☐ 1801†† Normal Dies, Blunt "1"		20.00	37.00	62.00	142.00	360.00
☐ 1801†† First "1" Pointed .		16.00	30.00	50.00	116.00	295.00
☐ 1801†† 3 Errors—1/1000, one stem, and UNITED ...		24.00	38.00	96.00	196.00	410.00

†Total Mintage: 2,822,170†† Total Mintage (all 1801 Varieties) 1,362,837

LARGE CENTS — DRAPED BUST, 1801–1804

1802- 1/100

ERROR 1/100 OVER 1/000

DATE	MINTAGE	ABP	G-4 Good	VG-8 V. Good	F-12 Fine	VF-20 V. Fine
☐ 1801†† 1/000		18.00	42.00	74.00	146.00	320.00
☐ 1801†† 1/100 Over 1/000		20.00	46.00	83.00	150.00	360.00
☐ 1802††† Normal Dies		12.00	26.00	40.00	90.00	290.00
☐ 1802††† Stemless Wreath		14.00	32.00	52.00	121.00	295.00
☐ 1802††† Fraction 1/000 ..		15.00	33.00	40.00	147.00	335.00
☐ 1803* Sm. Date, Sm. Fract.		12.00	22.00	40.00	93.00	330.00
☐ 1803* Sm. Date, Lg. Fract.		12.00	22.00	40.00	93.00	325.00
☐ 1803* Lg. Date, Sm. Fract.			RARE (ABOUT 20 KNOWN)			
☐ 1803* Lg. Date, Lg. Fract.		12.00	22.00	42.00	86.00	315.00

Total Mintage: ††1,362,837 †††3,435,100 *2,471,350

LARGE CENTS — DRAPED BUST, 1803–1804

"Mumps" Obverse

"Normal" Obverse

DATE	MINTAGE	ABP	G-4 Good	VG-8 V. Good	F-12 Fine	VF-20 V. Fine
☐ 1803† Mumps Obverse ...		12.00	29.00	47.00	98.00	290.00
☐ 1803† Stemless Wreath ..		12.00	29.00	47.00	98.00	290.00
☐ 1803† 1/100 over 1/000 .		12.00	29.00	47.00	98.00	290.00
☐ 1804 Normal Dies	756,837	200.00	510.00	750.00	1150.00	2200.00
☐ 1804 Broken Obverse Die		200.00	510.00	750.00	1150.00	2200.00

DATE	MINTAGE	ABP	G-4 Good	VG-8 V. Good	F-12 Fine	VF-20 V. Fine
□ 1804 Broken Obverse & Reverse Die		200.00	510.00	790.00	1250.00	2190.00

†Part of 2,471,350

LARGE CENTS — DRAPED BUST, 1804–1807

1804
Normal Die

1804
Restruck
in 1860

Small Fraction   Large Fraction   Comet Variety, 1807

DATE	MINTAGE	ABP	G-4 Good	VG-8 V. Good	F-12 Fine	VF-20 V. Fine
□ 1804 Restrike of 1860					UNC.	370.00
□ 1805 Blunt "1" in Date ...	941,115	16.00	35.00	52.00	121.00	315.00
□ 1805 Pointed "1" in Date .		16.00	35.00	52.00	121.00	315.00
□ 1806	348,000	20.00	46.00	82.00	145.00	325.00
□ 1807 over 6 lg. 7		16.00	32.00	48.00	120.00	325.00
□ 1807 over 6 sm. 7				RARE-ABOUT 21 KNOWN		
□ 1807 Small Fraction	727,000	16.00	31.00	48.00	120.00	325.00
□ 1807 Large Fraction		16.00	31.00	48.00	120.00	325.00
□ 1807 Comet Variety		16.00	31.00	48.00	120.00	325.00

LARGE CENTS — TURBAN HEAD, 1808–1814

DATE	MINTAGE	ABP	G-4 Good	VG-8 V. Good	F-12 Fine	VF-20 V. Fine
☐ 1808 13 Stars		17.00	38.00	63.00	110.00	310.00
☐ 1808 12 Stars	1,109,000	17.00	38.00	63.00	110.00	310.00
☐ 1809	222,867	30.00	76.00	140.00	250.00	620.00
☐ 1810 over 9		10.00	32.00	47.00	86.00	290.00
☐ 1810	1,458,400					
Normal Date		10.00	29.00	47.00	92.00	290.00
☐ 1811 over 10		32.00	70.00	121.00	182.00	485.00
☐ 1811	218,025					
Normal Date		28.00	70.00	116.00	180.00	470.00
☐ 1812						
Small Date		12.00	30.00	44.00	86.00	285.00
☐ 1812	1,075,500					
Large Date		12.00	30.00	46.00	86.00	290.00
☐ 1813						
Close Stars		21.00	47.00	79.00	132.00	370.00
☐ 1813	418,000					
Distant Stars		20.00	50.00	79.00	132.00	375.00
☐ 1814 Plain 4		15.00	33.00	46.00	93.00	280.00
☐ 1814	357,830					
Crosslet 4		15.00	33.00	46.00	94.00	280.00

LARGE CENTS—CORONET, 1816–1838

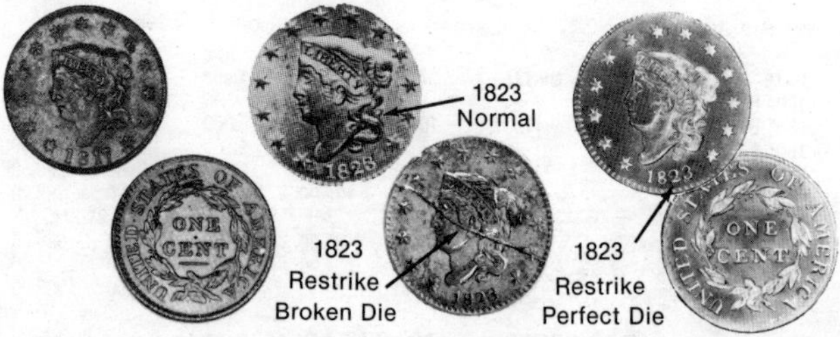

DATE	MINTAGE	ABP	G-4 Good	VG-8 V. Good	F-12 Fine	VF-20 V. Fine	MS-60 Unc.
☐ 1816	2,820,982	7.50	12.00	17.00	31.00	54.00	365.00
☐ 1817 Wide Date		7.50	10.00	14.00	21.00	42.00	310.00
☐ 1817	3,984,400	7.50	10.00	14.00	21.00	42.00	305.00
☐ 1817 (15 Stars)		7.00	11.00	22.00	34.00	76.00	700.00
☐ 1818	3,167,000	6.50	10.00	14.00	21.00	37.00	375.00
☐ 1819 over 18		6.50	12.00	13.00	21.00	37.00	375.00
☐ 1819 Large Date	2,671,000	6.50	12.00	13.00	21.00	37.00	375.00
☐ 1819 Small Date		6.50	12.00	13.00	21.00	37.00	375.00

DATE	MINTAGE	ABP	G-4 Good	VG-8 V. Good	F-12 Fine	VF-20 V. Fine	MS-60 Unc.
☐ 1820 over 19		7.00	10.00	14.00	24.00	41.00	380.00
☐ 1820 Small Date	4,407,550	6.50	11.00	12.00	20.00	35.00	290.00
☐ 1820 Large Date		6.50	11.00	12.00	20.00	35.00	290.00
☐ 1821 Wide Date	389,000	9.00	14.00	31.00	54.00	121.00	2100.00
☐ 1821 Close Date	389,000	9.00	14.00	31.00	54.00	118.00	2100.00
☐ 1822 Wide Date	2,075,339	7.00	9.00	15.00	21.00	46.00	400.00
☐ 1822 Close Date		7.00	9.00	15.00	21.00	46.00	400.00
☐ 1823 over 22, Part of	855,730	12.00	30.00	48.00	80.00	200.00	2100.00
☐ 1823 Normal Date		18.00	30.00	55.00	110.00	275.00	3400.00
☐ 1823 Restrike from Broken Obv. Die		150.00		UNCIRCULATED ONLY			370.00
☐ 1823 Restrike from Perfect Die	49 Known				EXTREMELY RARE		
☐ 1824 over 22		10.00	20.00	34.00	66.00	120.00	1870.00
☐ 1824 Wide Date	1,262,090	8.00	12.00	20.00	31.00	62.00	750.00
☐ 1824 Close Date		8.00	12.00	20.00	31.00	62.00	750.00
☐ 1825 Small A's	1,461,000	6.00	9.00	14.00	25.00	55.00	480.00
☐ 1825 Large A's		6.00	9.00	14.00	25.00	55.00	480.00
☐ 1826 over 25		10.00	18.00	32.00	60.00	121.00	520.00
☐ 1826 Wide Date	1,517,422	5.00	10.00	14.00	19.00	52.00	485.00
☐ 1826 Close Date		5.00	10.00	14.00	19.00	52.00	475.00
☐ 1827	2,357,733	5.00	10.00	12.00	17.00	46.00	500.00
☐ 1828 Small Date	2,260,625	7.50	11.00	15.00	24.00	54.00	460.00
☐ 1828 Large Date		5.00	10.00	12.00	18.00	42.00	370.00
☐ 1829 Small Letters	1,414,500	7.50	12.00	18.00	23.00	55.00	430.00
☐ 1829 Large Letters	1,414,500	6.00	10.00	14.00	19.00	43.00	390.00
☐ 1830 Small Letters		6.00	12.00	16.00	21.00	48.00	415.00
☐ 1830 Large Letters		5.00	8.00	10.00	14.00	30.00	350.00
☐ 1831 Small Letters	3,359,260	5.00	8.00	10.00	12.00	30.00	360.00
☐ 1831 Large Letters		5.00	8.00	10.00	12.00	30.00	360.00
☐ 1832 Small Letters	2,362,000	5.00	8.00	10.00	12.00	39.00	365.00
☐ 1832 Large Letters	2,362,000	5.00	8.00	10.00	12.00	39.00	365.00
☐ 1833 Small Letters	2,739,000	5.00	8.00	10.00	12.00	31.00	335.00
☐ 1833 Large Letters		5.00	8.00	10.00	12.00	31.00	335.00
☐ 1834*		5.00	9.00	11.00	16.00	38.00	410.00
☐ 1834**	1,855,110	5.00	8.00	10.00	14.00	35.00	360.00
☐ 1834***		5.00	8.00	10.00	15.00	35.00	360.00
☐ 1835 Sm. Date—Sm. Stars		5.00	8.00	11.00	17.00	39.00	330.00
☐ 1835 Lg. Date Lg. Stars	3,878,397	5.00	8.00	10.00	13.00	32.00	320.00
☐ 1835 Type of 1836		4.00	8.00	9.00	13.00	31.00	340.00
☐ 1836	2,111,000	4.00	8.00	11.00	12.00	32.00	310.00
☐ 1837 Plain Hair Cord —Small Letters		5.00	9.00	12.00	12.00	31.00	315.00
☐ 1837 Plain Hair Cord —Large Letters	5,558,301	5.00	9.00	12.00	12.00	29.00	320.00
☐ 1837 Beaded Hair Cord —Small Letters		5.00	9.00	12.00	12.00	32.00	320.00

DATE	MINTAGE	ABP	G-4 Good	VG-8 V. Good	F-12 Fine	VF-20 V. Fine	MS-60 Unc.
□ 1838	6,370,200	4.50	8.50	10.00	14.00	24.00	310.00

*Large Date—Large Stars—Large Letters Reverse **Small Date—Small Stars—Small Letters Reverse ***Large Date—Small Stars—Small Letters Reverse.

LARGE CENTS — BRAIDED HAIR, 1839–1857

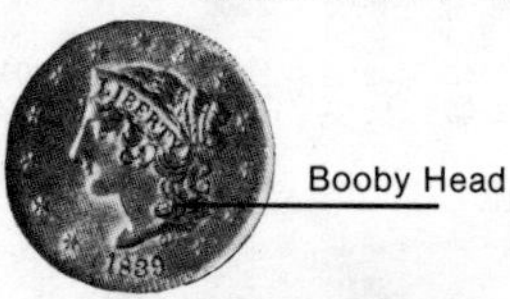

DATE	MINTAGE	ABP	G-4 Good	VG-8 V. Good	F-12 Fine	VF-20 V. Fine	MS-60 Unc.
□ 1839 over 36		77.00	162.00	270.00	340.00	800.00	3600.00
□ 1839 Type							
□ 1838 Line under Cent		6.00	8.50	13.00	14.00	40.00	390.00
□ 1839 Silly Head	ALL KINDS						
□ No Center Dot		6.00	10.00	12.00	20.00	44.00	500.00
□ 1839 Booby Head	3,128,662						
□ Head		4.50	8.50	11.00	20.00	43.00	360.00
□ 1839 Petite Head		4.50	8.50	11.00	19.00	37.00	360.00
□ 1840 Small Date		4.50	8.50	10.00	15.00	27.00	290.00
□ 1840 Large Date	2,462,700	4.50	8.50	10.00	15.00	25.00	290.00
□ 1841	1,597,366	4.50	8.50	10.00	17.00	28.00	310.00
□ 1842 Small Date		4.00	8.50	10.00	14.00	23.00	270.00
□ 1842 Large Date	2,383,390	4.00	8.50	10.00	14.00	23.00	270.00
□ 1843 Obv. and Rev. 1842		4.00	8.50	10.00	16.00	27.00	280.00
□ 1843 Obv. 1842 Rev. 1844		4.00	8.50	10.00	15.00	26.00	270.00
□ 1844		4.00	8.50	10.00	14.00	20.00	260.00
□ 1844 over 81	2,398,752	8.00	17.00	24.00	34.00	68.00	240.00
□ 1845	3,894,805	4.50	7.00	9.00	12.00	18.00	260.00
□ 1846 Small Date		4.50	7.00	9.00	12.00	18.00	260.00
□ 1846 Med. Date	4,120,800	4.50	7.00	9.00	12.00	18.00	260.00
□ 1846 Tall Date		4.50	7.00	9.00	12.00	18.00	260.00

DATE	MINTAGE	ABP	G-4 Good	VG-8 V. Good	F-12 Fine	VF-20 V. Fine	MS-60 Unc.
□ 1847		4.50	7.00	9.00	12.00	18.00	260.00
□ 1848	6,320,680	4.00	7.00	8.00	12.50	16.50	250.00
□ 1849	4,260,111	4.00	7.00	8.00	12.50	16.50	250.00
□ 1850	4,426,844	3.40	7.00	8.00	11.00	18.00	300.00
□ 1851		3.40	7.00	8.00	11.00	18.00	300.00
□ 1851 over 81	9,899,700	7.00	12.00	15.00	22.00	37.00	450.00
□ 1852	5,063,094	4.00	7.00	7.50	11.00	18.00	250.00
□ 1853	6,641,131	4.00	7.00	7.50	11.00	18.00	250.00
□ 1854	4,236,156	4.00	7.00	7.50	11.00	18.00	225.00
□ 1855 Upright 5's		4.00	7.00	7.50	11.00	18.00	225.00
□ 1855 Slanting 5's	1,574,829	4.00	7.00	7.50	11.00	18.00	225.00
□ 1855 Slanting 5's Knob on Ear		4.00	7.00	7.50	11.00	18.00	260.00
□ 1856 Upright 5	2,690,465	4.00	7.00	7.50	11.00	18.00	260.00
□ 1856 Slanting 5		4.00	7.00	7.50	11.00	18.00	260.00
□ 1857 Small Date	333,456	14.00	28.00	38.00	48.00	68.00	350.00
□ 1857 Large Date		12.00	26.00	32.00	40.00	62.00	350.00

SMALL CENTS

FLYING EAGLE, 1856–1858

It would be hard to find a coin in the standard U.S. series that proved so unpopular as the Flying Eagle Cent—unpopular, that is, originally. It has since become a favorite of collectors. During 1856, while the large cent continued in production, plans were underway to replace it with a smaller coin of the same value. A number of patterns of the Flying Eagle were struck that year at the Philadelphia Mint but were not circulated because the large cent was discontinued and minting switched over to this new piece, with a huge output in that one year of nearly 17,500,000 coins. The public balked. It charged that the government was forcing the small cent on it. Not only didn't the public care much for that idea, it was also not too fond of the coin. Instead of being struck in pure copper and having the substantial appearance that a cent was supposed to have, its composition was 88% copper and 12% nickel, yielding a coin that was sufficiently pale in color to be called white. (If one wonders about the bickerings over coin sizes, designs, and compositions in the 18th and 19th centuries, it should be realized that far greater attention was focused upon money in those days, when few persons used checks and credit cards were unknown.) The Flying Eagle Cent was designed by James Longacre. Its weight was 4.67 grams and its diameter 19 mm. As a designer, Longacre was not unskilled. He proved his abilities with the Indian Head Cent, which replaced the Flying Eagle in 1859.

DATE	MINTAGE	ABP	G-4 Good	F-12 Fine	EF-40 Ex. Fine	MS-60 Unc.	PRF-65 Proof
□ 1856	Approx. 1,000	750.00	1500.00	2100.00	2600.00	4000.00	7500.00
□ 1857	17,450,000	4.50	9.00	14.00	65.00	250.00	5000.00
□ 1858 Small Letters		4.50	9.00	14.00	65.00	250.00	5000.00
□ 1858 Large Letters	24,600,000	4.50	9.00	14.00	68.00	250.00	5000.00

SMALL CENTS — INDIAN HEAD, 1859–1909

Probably the most famous of all U.S. coins (its only challenger for that honor being the Morgan Dollar), the Indian Head Cent remained in production without change in design for half a century. After the disaster of the Flying Eagle Cent, rejected by the public because of its almost white color, the government knew that it must manufacture a cent whose appearance was that of good metal, even if it was not to return to the large cent. The question remained: would a small copper piece be accepted, when large cents, containing a much greater quantity of metal, were still widely circulating? The new cent had the same composition as its predecessor, 88% copper and 12% nickel. The first batch of Indian Heads, released in 1859, amounted to 36,400,000 pieces, more than had ever been coined of a single denomination in one year: $364,000 worth of pennies. Beginning in 1864 the copper content was increased to 95%, the nickel removed entirely and replaced with a 5% alloy of tin and zinc. This was so successfully absorbed into the copper that the resulting coin was hardly different in color than if copper alone were used. Finally the problem was solved, and the Indian Head Cent was on the road to a long successful existence. Its designer was James Longacre. The weight was 4.67 grams and the diameter 19 mm., these specifications being the same as the Flying Eagle Cent. The portrait is that of an Indian maiden. As first designed, the reverse carried no shield but this was added in 1860, the second year of issue. The Indian Head became the first U.S. coin struck in a quantity of more than 100 million in a year, when 108 million specimens were turned out in 1907. This exceeded the country's population. It is interesting to note that the 1908 and 1909 editions, representing the last two years of this design, are the only dates to be found with mint marks. The origin of the portrait has been for many years a matter of discussion. It was at one time thought that Longacre had taken it from life, using an Indian girl as his model. This was dismissed when the suggestion was advanced that the profile resembled Longacre's daughter. It is now generally believed that no live model sat for the likeness but that it was based upon classical statuary, of which Longacre was known to be a collector. The Indian Head Cent portrait is neither as realistic nor impressive as that featured on the Buffalo Nickel, but this is nevertheless an important coin whose design represented a bold innovation.

1901

1860–1864 Wreath on Shield

DATE	MINTAGE	ABP	G-4 Good	F-12 Fine	EF-40 Ex. Fine	MS-60 Unc.	PRF-65 Proof
☐ 1859 Copper-Nickel	36,400,000	1.80	3.70	9.00	60.00	300.00	3200.00
☐ 1860 Copper-Nickel	20,566,000	2.10	4.20	8.50	22.00	160.00	2000.00
☐ 1861 Copper-Nickel	10,100,000	6.00	11.00	8.50	40.00	210.00	2000.00
☐ 1862 Copper-Nickel	28,075,000	1.75	4.00	8.00	24.00	120.00	2000.00
☐ 1863 Copper-Nickel	49,840,000	1.75	4.00	6.10	16.00	120.00	2000.00
☐ 1864 Copper-Nickel	13,740,000	4.00	8.00	14.00	31.00	130.00	2000.00
☐ 1864 Bronze	39,233,714	1.70	4.10	9.00	29.00	110.00	2200.00
☐ 1864 L on Ribbon		18.00	42.00	60.00	160.00	320.00	15800.00
☐ 1865	35,429,286	1.75	6.00	10.00	31.00	76.00	1250.00
☐ 1866	9,826,500	9.50	19.00	30.00	88.00	172.00	1250.00
☐ 1867	9,821,000	9.50	19.00	30.00	88.00	172.00	1250.00
☐ 1868	10,266,500	9.50	19.00	30.00	88.00	172.00	1250.00
☐ 1869	6,420,000	14.00	21.00	60.00	150.00	400.00	1250.00
☐ 1869 over 8		42.00	90.00	200.00	550.00	900.00	
☐ 1870	5,275,000	12.00	20.00	60.00	121.00	270.00	1250.00
☐ 1871	3,929,500	17.00	30.00	65.00	135.00	300.00	1250.00
☐ 1872	4,042,000	15.00	32.00	80.00	182.00	360.00	1250.00
☐ 1873	11,676,500	4.50	11.00	18.00	54.00	170.00	1200.00
☐ 1873 Doubled Liberty						EXTREMELY RARE	
☐ 1874	14,187,500	4.50	8.00	18.00	60.00	165.00	1200.00
☐ 1875	13,528,000	4.50	8.00	18.00	60.00	165.00	1200.00
☐ 1876	7,944,000	8.00	16.00	25.00	60.00	180.00	1200.00
☐ 1877	852,500	93.00	130.00	360.00	750.00	1500.00	4250.00
☐ 1878	5,799,850	8.00	14.00	29.00	60.00	215.00	1100.00
☐ 1879	16,231,200	1.10	2.10	8.50	23.00	70.00	700.00
☐ 1880	38,964,955	.62	2.50	4.50	15.00	74.00	700.00
☐ 1881	39,211,575	.62	2.50	4.50	15.00	74.00	700.00
☐ 1882	38,581,100	.62	2.50	4.50	15.00	74.00	700.00
☐ 1883	45,598,109	.62	2.50	4.50	17.00	74.00	700.00
☐ 1884	23,261,742	.83	2.50	8.50	36.00	78.00	700.00
☐ 1885	11,765,384	1.50	3.00	12.00	36.00	90.00	700.00
☐ 1886	17,654,290	1.00	2.00	9.10	29.00	79.00	700.00
☐ 1887	45,226,483	.55	1.15	3.60	12.00	75.00	700.00
☐ 1888	37,494,414	.55	1.15	3.60	12.00	75.00	700.00

DATE	MINTAGE	ABP	G-4 Good	F-12 Fine	EF-40 Ex. Fine	MS-60 Unc.	PRF-65 Proof
☐ 1889	48,868,361	.40	1.00	2.75	12.00	40.00	700.00
☐ 1890	57,182,854	.40	1.00	2.75	12.00	40.00	700.00
☐ 1891	47,072,350	.40	1.00	2.75	12.00	40.00	700.00
☐ 1892	37,649,832	.40	1.00	2.75	12.00	40.00	700.00
☐ 1893	46,642,195	.40	1.00	2.75	12.00	40.00	700.00
☐ 1894	16,752,132	.60	2.00	7.50	20.00	58.00	700.00
☐ 1895	38,343,636	.40	1.00	1.60	9.00	40.00	700.00
☐ 1896	39,057,293	.40	1.00	1.60	9.00	40.00	700.00
☐ 1897	50,466,330	.40	1.00	1.60	9.00	40.00	700.00
☐ 1898	49,923,079	.40	1.00	1.60	9.00	40.00	700.00
☐ 1899	53,600,031	.40	1.00	1.60	9.00	40.00	700.00
☐ 1900	66,833,764	.40	1.00	1.60	9.00	30.00	500.00
☐ 1901	79,611,143	.40	1.00	1.60	9.00	30.00	500.00
☐ 1902	87,376,722	.40	1.00	1.60	9.00	30.00	500.00
☐ 1903	85,094,493	.40	1.00	1.60	9.00	30.00	500.00
☐ 1904	61,328,015	.38	.80	1.00	7.10	30.00	500.00
☐ 1905	80,719,163	.38	.80	1.00	7.10	30.00	500.00
☐ 1906	96,022,255	.38	.80	1.00	7.10	30.00	500.00
☐ 1907	108,138,618	.38	.80	1.00	7.10	30.00	500.00
☐ 1908	32,327,987	.38	.80	1.00	7.10	30.00	500.00
☐ 1908S	1,115,000	11.00	22.00	26.00	45.00	160.00	500.00
☐ 1909	14,370,645	.58	1.20	2.60	9.00	56.00	500.00
☐ 1909S	309,000	49.00	110.00	145.00	220.00	380.00	500.00

SMALL CENTS — LINCOLN HEAD, 1909 TO DATE

It is quite likely that, despite having remained in use for 50 years, the Indian Head design would have been retained for the cent beyond 1909, had not President Roosevelt pressed for its removal. The year 1909 marked the 100th anniversary of Abraham Lincoln's birth and Roosevelt (who, not coincidentally, was a member of the same political party) wished to memorialize the anniversary by placing a likeness of Lincoln on the penny. His suggestion was adopted, the result being a design that has survived in continuous use longer than any other in the Mint's history: 76 years, with no indication that it will soon be replaced. The Indian Head Cents were so popular that criticism was risked by their removal. Had they been abandoned in favor of any other design a public outcry might have ensued. But for Lincoln, allowances could be made. This was incidentally the first time an American citizen appeared on coinage of the Mint, as George Washington, though depicted on numerous coins and tokens, was never portrayed on an issue of the federal Mint. Designer of the Lincoln Cent was Victor D. Brenner. Rather than using a close-up profile, Brenner showed Lincoln in quarter-length, with beard, as he appeared in the last few years of his life. It is not known whether the likeness was adapted from a specific photograph, from statuary, or merely from a study of various photos and other artworks. As first struck, the coin carried Brenner's initials and this variety is known as the VDB Cent. They were removed midway through production of the 1909 issue and not reinstated until 1918, when they were switched from the reverse to the obverse. Specimens of the 1909 coin with initials, especially those struck at San Francisco, where less than half a million were produced, eventually became favorite collectors' items. At the time little notice was taken of them.

Originally the reverse was composed of the wording "ONE CENT—UNITED STATES OF AMERICA" enshrouded by wheat sheaves. In 1959 a new reverse was introduced, on the occasion of the 150th anniversary of Lincoln's birth and the 50th of the coin's use. Designed by Frank Gasparro, it pictures the Lincoln Memorial building in Washington, D.C. From 1909 to 1942 the Lincoln Cent had a composition of 95% copper and 5% tin and zinc with a weight of 3.11 grams and a diameter of 19 mm.

In 1943 it was made of steel-coated zinc. From 1944 to 1946 what are known as "Shell Case Cents" were made from spent shell casings; their content was 95% copper and 5% tin and zinc, until September of 1962 when the tin was removed from the cent for the last time. The content of the cent from 1962 until 1981 was 95% copper and 5% zinc. Beginning in 1982, the cent has been made of a zinc core with copper coating. Thus, it is now another clad coin, leaving only the nickel as the lone non-clad U.S. coin.

1909

No V.D.B.

V.D.B. Restored

DATE	MINTAGE	ABP	G-4 Good	F-12 Fine	VF-20 V. Fine	EF-40 Ex. Fine	MS-60 Unc.	PRF-65 Proof
(1909–1942 COMPOSITION-95% COPPER WITH 5% TIN AND ZINC)								
☐ 1909	72,702,618	.24	.60	.70	1.00	2.00	13.50	
☐ 1909 V.D.B. .	27,995,000	1.25	2.20	3.60	3.50	3.50	13.50	
☐ 1909S	1,825,000	21.00	48.00	58.00	66.00	93.00	180.00	
☐ 1909S V.D.B.	484,000	120.00	230.00	300.00	340.00	400.00	500.00	800.00
☐ 1910	146,801,218	.12	.19	.26	.60	4.10	16.50	
☐ 1910S	6,045,000	2.50	7.20	9.00	12.00	21.00	80.00	
☐ 1911	101,177,787	.10	.23	.40	1.70	4.50	17.50	
☐ 1911D	12,672,000	1.60	4.10	5.00	11.00	24.00	90.00	
☐ 1911S	4,026,000	5.00	11.00	15.00	20.00	30.00	130.00	
☐ 1912	68,53,060	.21	.51	1.75	4.10	6.50	30.00	
☐ 1912D	10,411,000	2.00	6.10	8.00	12.00	31.00	120.00	220.00
☐ 1912S	4,431,000	5.00	11.00	14.00	18.00	27.00	115.00	215.00
☐ 1913	76,532,352	.17	.37	1.50	3.50	7.00	20.00	
☐ 1913D	15,804,000	.90	2.50	4.70	6.50	19.00	82.00	
☐ 1913S	6,101,000	3.00	8.50	10.00	12.00	20.00	99.00	
☐ 1914	75,238,432	.22	.58	1.60	4.10	6.00	53.00	
☐ 1914D	1,193,000	33.00	63.00	88.00	160.00	370.00	920.00	1550.00
☐ 1914S	4,137,000	4.70	9.50	13.00	18.00	33.00	195.00	
☐ 1915	29,092,120	.43	1.30	3.10	7.00	27.00	90.00	
☐ 1915D	22,050,000	.30	1.10	1.70	3.00	12.00	43.00	

DATE	MINTAGE	ABP	G-4 Good	F-12 Fine	VF-20 V. Fine	EF-40 Ex. Fine	MS-60 Unc.	PRF-65 Proof
□ 1915S	4,833,677	4.20	9.00	12.50	13.00	23.00	105.00	
□ 1916	131,838,677	.09	.24	.26	.92	2.10	11.00	200.00
□ 1916D	35,956,000	.11	.29	1.10	1.72	6.50	52.00	
□ 1916S	22,510,000	.37	.92	1.70	2.60	7.20	58.00	
□ 1917	196,429,785	.09	.21	.32	.66	2.00	13.00	
□ 1917D	55,120,000	.12	.31	.76	2.10	5.70	53.00	
□ 1917S	32,620,000	.20	.40	.76	2.10	5.70	59.00	
□ 1918	288,104,634	.09	.21	.52	1.00	2.10	14.00	
□ 1918D	47,830,000	.12	.22	.68	1.15	6.50	52.00	
□ 1918S	34,680,000	.12	.27	.62	1.75	6.50	63.00	
□ 1919	392,021,000	.08	.17	.30	.60	2.10	9.50	
□ 1919D	57,154,000	.12	.22	.62	1.90	3.50	44.00	
□ 1919S	139,760,000	.08	.17	.30	.72	2.50	35.00	
□ 1920	310,165,000	.08	.12	.25	.60	2.00	11.00	
□ 1920D	49,280,000	.10	.16	.52	1.43	4.00	52.00	
□ 1920S	46,220,000	.10	.16	.35	1.46	3.70	61.00	
□ 1921	39,157,000	.12	.21	.35	.92	4.00	40.00	
□ 1921S	15,274,000	.31	.68	1.66	2.80	11.00	124.00	
□ 1922 Plain (No Mint Mark)*		82.00	160.00	290.00	420.00	680.00	3200.00	
□ 1922D	7,160,000	2.00	4.20	6.00	9.50	21.00	79.00	
□ 1923	74,723,000	.10	.15	.32	.60	2.10	13.00	
□ 1923S	8,700,000	.70	1.72	2.70	4.10	13.00	192.00	
□ 1924	75,178,000	.07	.11	.23	.63	2.10	25.00	
□ 1924D	2,520,000	6.00	11.00	19.00	20.00	40.00	230.00	
□ 1924S	11,696,000	.28	.65	1.60	2.10	7.20	115.00	
□ 1925	139,949,000	.08	.11	.41	.66	2.20	9.75	
□ 1925D	22,580,000	.16	.23	.90	1.30	4.20	52.00	
□ 1925S	26,380,000	.11	.12	.50	.96	4.20	62.00	
□ 1926	157,088,000	.07	.12	.25	.40	2.10	8.60	
□ 1926D	28,022,022	.12	.15	.80	2.20	3.70	52.00	
□ 1926S	4,550,000	1.60	2.50	6.50	7.00	12.00	90.00	
□ 1927	144,440,000	.07	.11	.40	.65	2.10	8.60	
□ 1927D	27,170,000	.10	.17	.40	.65	3.30	32.00	
□ 1927S	14,276,000	.25	.50	2.20	3.00	5.10	66.00	
□ 1928	134,116,000	.08	.11	.40	.60	1.70	8.50	
□ 1928D	31,170,000	.09	.15	.35	.60	2.10	24.00	
□ 1928S	17,266,000	.16	.26	.58	.90	3.50	50.00	
□ 1929	185,262,000	.11	.11	.28	.40	1.70	7.10	
□ 1929D	41,730,000	.11	.14	.34	.50	1.30	18.00	
□ 1929S	50,148,000	.11	.13	.30	.40	1.30	11.00	
□ 1930	157,415,000	.07	.13	.28	.50	1.30	7.60	
□ 1930D	40,100,000	.07	.13	.28	.60	1.30	15.00	
□ 1930S	24,286,000	.07	.13	.32	.60	1.30	8.75	
□ 1931	19,396,000	.17	.35	.96	1.40	2.20	18.00	
□ 1931D	4,480,000	.99	2.10	3.20	3.50	2.20	52.00	
□ 1931S	866,000	14.00	27.00	41.00	46.00	50.00	89.00	
□ 1932	9,062,000	.62	1.70	2.40	2.70	4.30	21.00	

DATE	MINTAGE	ABP	G-4 Good	F-12 Fine	VF-20 V. Fine	EF-40 Ex. Fine	MS-60 Unc.	PRF-65 Proof
□ 1932D**	10,500,000	.26	.50	1.30	1.60	2.00	19.00	
□ 1933	14,360,000	.30	.82	2.10	2.30	2.65	20.00	
□ 1933D	6,200,000	.70	1.75	3.10	3.80	4.50	24.00	
□ 1934	219,080,000	.07	.09	.20	.22	.33	7.50	
□ 1934D	28,446,000	.07	.09	.22	.41	.76	25.00	
□ 1935	245,388,000	.07	.08	.22	.26	.35	3.50	
□ 1935D	47,000,000	.07	.09	.25	.34	.52	7.50	
□ 1935S	38,702,000	.07	.09	.24	.34	.50	12.00	
□ 1936	309,637,569	.07	.08	.23	.26	.37	2.50	
□ 1936D	40,620,000	.07	.10	.27	.37	.45	3.10	
□ 1936S	29,130,000	.07	.10	.27	.37	.52	3.20	
□ 1937	309,179,320	.05	.08	.23	.27	.34	1.60	215.00
□ 1937D	50,430,000	.05	.09	.26	.28	.34	2.00	
□ 1937S	35,500,000	.07	.10	.25	.28	.34	2.40	
□ 1938	156,696,734	.05	.07	.24	.26	.32	1.80	130.00
□ 1938D	20,010,000	.06	.10	.31	.40	.56	3.20	
□ 1938S	15,180,000	.07	.19	.43	.60	.68	3.30	

*Beware of Removed Mintmark

**Note: More than 15,000 specimens of the 1932D cent were included in the Dr. Jerry Buss Collection, sold in 1985. This was the largest quantity ever sold at one time.

DATE	MINTAGE	ABP	G-4 Good	F-12 Fine	VF-20 V. Fine	EF-40 Ex. Fine	MS-60 Unc.	PRF-65 Proof
□ 1939	316,479,520	.05	.08	.15	.18	.32	.80	108.00
□ 1939D	15,160,000	.14	.31	.46	.58	.70	5.30	
□ 1939S	52,070,000	.06	.13	.21	.28	.38	2.80	
□ 1940	586,825,872	.05	.06	.12	.18	.22	.95	95.00
□ 1940D	83,190,000	.05	.06	.12	.18	.22	1.90	
□ 1940S	112,940,000	.05	.06	.12	.18	.22	2.10	
□ 1941	887,039,100	.05	.06	.12	.18	.22	1.80	85.00
□ 1941D	128,700,000	.05	.06	.12	.18	.22	3.80	
□ 1941S	92,360,000	.06	.06	.12	.18	.22	4.60	
□ 1942	657,828,600	.06	.06	.12	.18	.22	.87	86.00
□ 1942D	206,698,000	.05	.06	.12	.18	.22	1.15	
□ 1942S	85,590,000	.05	.06	.12	.18	.31	7.10	
(1943 WARTIME STEEL COMPOSITION-STEEL COATED WITH ZINC)								
□ 1943	684,628,670	.05	.07	.13	.19	.29	2.60	
□ 1943D	217,660,000	.06	.13	.18	.23	.37	3.30	
□ 1943S	191,550,000	.06	.12	.22	.32	.41	5.50	
(1944–1946 "SHELL CASE" COPPER COMPOSITION-95% COPPER AND 5% ZINC)								
□ 1944	1,435,400,000	.06			.12	.21	.60	
□ 1944D	430,578,000	.06			.11	.28	.92	
□ 1944S	282,760,000	.06			.12	.26	.83	
□ 1945	1,040,515,000	.05			.11	.14	.46	
□ 1945D	226,268,000	.05			.11	.18	.85	
□ 1945S	181,770,000	.05			.11	.18	.67	
□ 1946	991,655,000	.05			.11	.15	.45	
□ 1946D	315,690,000	.05			.11	.15	.45	
□ 1946S	198,100,000	.05			.11	.18	.82	
(1947–1962 COMPOSITION-95% COPPER AND 5% TIN AND ZINC)								
□ 1947	190,555,000	.04			.11	.19	.90	
□ 1947D	194,750,000	.04			.11	.14	.72	

DATE	MINTAGE	ABP	G-4 Good	F-12 Fine	VF-20 V. Fine	EF-40 Ex. Fine	MS-60 Unc.	PRF-65 Proof
☐ 1947S......	99,000,000	.04			.12	.17	.75	
☐ 1948	317,570,000	.04			.10	.15	.70	
☐ 1948D	172,637,500	.04			.12	.19	.85	
☐ 1948S......	81,735,000	.04			.14	.25	1.00	
☐ 1949	217,490,000	.04			.10	.15	1.50	
☐ 1949D	154,370,500	.04			.10	.15	1.20	
☐ 1949S......	64,290,000	.04			.13	.35	3.10	
☐ 1950	272,686,386	.04				.12	1.00	84.00
☐ 1950D	334,950,000	.04				.12	.80	
☐ 1950S......	118,505,000	.04			.13	.12	.70	
☐ 1951	294,633,500	.04				.12	.83	55.00
☐ 1951D	625,355,000	.04				.12	.44	
☐ 1951S......	100,890,000	.04			.11	.25	1.70	
☐ 1952	186,856,980	.04				.13	.75	40.00
☐ 1952D	746,130,000	.04				.13	.34	
☐ 1952S......	137,800,004	.04			.11	.21	1.20	
☐ 1953	256,883,800	.04				.14	.25	24.00
☐ 1953D	700,515,000	.04				.13	.25	
☐ 1953S......	181,835,000	.04				.19	.53	
☐ 1954	71,873,350	.04			.11	.25	.58	11.00
☐ 1954D	251,552,500	.04				.12	.33	
☐ 1954S......	96,190,000	.04			.10	.18	.50	
☐ 1955	330,958,200	.04				.13	.23	9.00
☐ 1955 Double Die				190.00	390.00	410.00	720.00	
☐ 1955D	563,257,500	.04				.10	.23	
☐ 1955S......	44,610,000	.10		.15	.22	.26	.70	
☐ 1956	421,414,384	.04				.08	.21	2.80
☐ 1956D	1,098,201,100	.04				.08	.21	
☐ 1957	283,787,952	.04				.08	.21	2.10
☐ 1957D	1,051,342,000	.04				.08	.21	
☐ 1958	253,400,652	.04				.08	.21	2.30
☐ 1958D	800,953,000	.04				.08	.21	

LINCOLN MEMORIAL DESIGN

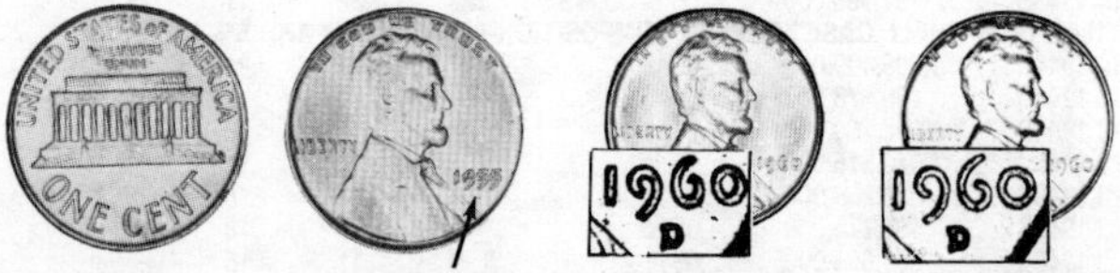

LINCOLN MEMORIAL — 1955 DOUBLE DIE — SMALL DATE — LARGE DATE

COIN	MINTAGE	ABP	EF-40 Ex. Fine	MS-60 Unc.	PRF-65 Proof
☐ 1959	610,864,291			.08	1.40
☐ 1959D	1,279,760,000			.08	
☐ 1960 Small Date	588,096,602	.25	1.65	3.40	15.50
☐ 1960 Large Date				.15	
☐ 1960D Small Date	1,580,884,000			.35	
☐ 1960D				.17	
☐ 1961	756,373,244			.09	1.15
☐ 1961D	1,753,266,700			.09	1.15
(SEPTEMBER 1961–1981 COMPOSITION-95% COPPER AND 5% ZINC)					
☐ 1962	609,263,019			.09	1.00
☐ 1962D	1,793,148,400			.09	1.00
☐ 1963	757,185,645			.09	1.00
☐ 1963D	1,744,020,400			.09	1.00
☐ 1964	2,652,525,762			.09	1.00
☐ 1964D	3,799,071,500			.09	1.00
☐ 1965	1,497,224,900			.09	1.00
☐ 1966	2,188,147,783			.09	1.00
☐ 1967	3,048,667,077			.09	1.00
☐ 1968	1,707,880,965			.20	1.00
☐ 1968D	2,886,269,590			.07	1.00
☐ 1968S	261,311,500			.07	1.00
☐ 1969	1,136,910,000			.30	1.00
☐ 1969D	4,002,832,200			.07	1.00
☐ 1969S	547,309,631			.07	1.00
☐ 1970	1,898,315,000			.28	1.00
☐ 1970D	2,891,438,900			.07	1.00
☐ 1970S	693,192,814			.07	1.00
☐ 1970S					1.00
☐ Small Date		.23	.60	7.20	1.00
☐ 1971	1,919,490,000			.19	1.00
☐ 1971D	2,911,045,600			.12	1.00
☐ 1971S	528,354,192			.18	1.00
☐ 1972	2,933,255,000			.09	1.00
☐ 1972 Double Die		74.00	160.00	220.00	1.00
☐ 1972D	2,665,071,400			.10	1.00
☐ 1972S	380,200,104			.08	1.00
☐ 1973	3,728,245,000			.08	1.00
☐ 1973D	3,549,576,588			.08	1.00
☐ 1973S	319,937,634			.08	1.00
☐ 1974	4,232,140,523			.08	1.00
☐ 1974D	4,235,098,000			.08	1.00
☐ 1974S	412,039,228			.11	1.40
☐ 1975	4,505,275,300			.06	
☐ 1975D	5,505,275,300			.08	
☐ 1975S Proof Only	2,909,369				5.40
☐ 1976	4,674,292,426			.07	
☐ 1976D	4,221,595,455			.07	
☐ 1976S Proof Only	4,149,945				2.60

COIN	MINTAGE	ABP	EF-40 Ex. Fine	MS-60 Unc.	PRF-65 Proof
☐ 1977	4,469,972,000			.03	
☐ 1977D	4,149,055,800			.05	
☐ 1977S Proof Only	3,250,895				2.70
☐ 1978	5,266,905,000			.06	
☐ 1978D	4,280,233,400			.06	
☐ 1978S Proof	3,127,781				3.75
☐ 1979P	6,018,515,201			.06	
☐ 1979D	4,139,357,000			.06	
☐ 1979S Proof	3,677,200				3.70
☐ 1979S Proof (II)					5.20
☐ 1980	7,414,705,002			.06	
☐ 1980D	5,140,098,675			.06	
☐ 1980S Proof Only	3,547,130				2.70
☐ 1981	7,491,750,500			.06	
☐ 1981D	5,373,235,000			.06	
☐ 1981S Proof (I)	4,065,000				2.75
☐ 1981S Proof (II)					3.90
☐ 1982 Introduction of zinc cent	10,712,520,000			.06	
☐ 1982D	6,013,000			.06	
☐ 1982S Proof Only	3,857,480				3.75
☐ 1983*	7,752,354,900			.06	
☐ 1983D	6,468,000,000			.06	
☐ 1983S Proof Only	3,228,650				7.00
☐ 1984	8,183,657,000			.05	
☐ 1984D	5,570,000,000			.05	
☐ 1984S Proof Only					6.70
☐ 1985	5,842,628,000			.05	
☐ 1985D	5,329,742,000			.05	
☐ 1985S Proof Only	3,412,110				6.60
☐ 1986	4,622,410,712			.05	
☐ 1986D	4,287,870,420			.05	
☐ 1986S Proof Only	3,211,110				6.60
☐ 1987	4,427,867,241			.04	
☐ 1987D	4,782,420,670			.04	
☐ 1987S					6.00
☐ 1988				.03	
☐ 1988D				.03	
☐ 1988S Proof					5.50
☐ 1989				.03	
☐ 1989D				.03	
☐ 1989S Proof					5.00

Note: The 1982 cent was the first U.S. coin struck in a quantity of more than ten billion. *Double die reverses occurred on some 1983 cents struck at Philadelphia. As yet these coins have not established a clear market value. The doubling is very slight and for this reason the variety may not become popular with collectors.

TWO-CENT PIECES

TWO CENT (BRONZE), 1864–1873

The two-cent piece was a short-lived coin whose impact upon the world fell far short of its impact on modern numismatists. Small change was growing increasingly scarce during the Civil War, to the point where postage stamps, encased in holders, were being used for money. The government sought to alleviate this by increased production of the penny and introduced the two-cent piece to take the penny's place in areas where it might not be in sufficient supply. Enormous quantities were struck at the outset, approaching 20 million per year, the composition being the same as that of the penny, 95% copper to 5% of tin and zinc. The diameter was 23 mm. Designer of the two-cent piece was James Longacre, who did most of the Mint's designing at that time. There is no portrait on the coin; it carries a U.S. shield on one side and a value statement on the other. The lack of portraiture was undoubtedly an effort to prevent this coin from being confused with the penny. Though larger by 4 mm. in diameter than the penny, it must be remembered that large cents were still found in circulation in 1864—they had been discontinued less than ten years earlier—and one almost needed a scoreboard to keep track of the denominations of coins passing through his hands. Production totals of the two-cent piece decreased each year of its minting, until only 65,000 were turned out in 1872 and nothing but proofs and restrikes the following year. It died a very silent death.

1864 Small Motto

First Coin to Bear the Motto "In God We Trust"

1864 Large Motto

DATE	MINTAGE	ABP	G-4 Good	F-12 Fine	EF-40 Ex. Fine	MS-60 Unc.	PRF-65 Proof
☐ 1864 Small Motto	19,847,500	30.00	63.00	105.00	266.00	560.00	13800.00
☐ 1864 Large Motto		2.20	4.10	9.50	34.00	160.00	3100.00
☐ 1865	13,640,000	2.00	4.00	9.50	34.00	165.00	1500.00
☐ 1866	3,177,000	2.70	5.00	12.00	35.00	162.00	1500.00
☐ 1867	3,915,000	2.50	5.00	12.50	37.00	170.00	1500.00
☐ 1867 Double Die					EXTREMELY RARE		
☐ 1868	3,252,000	3.00	5.00	12.00	37.00	170.00	1500.00
☐ 1869	1,546,500	3.50	7.00	14.00	45.00	200.00	1500.00

DATE	MINTAGE	ABP	G-4 Good	F-12 Fine	EF-40 Ex. Fine	MS-60 Unc.	PRF-65 Proof
□ 1870	861,250	5.00	11.00	20.00	64.00	300.00	1500.00
□ 1871	721,250	6.00	12.00	22.00	80.00	350.00	1500.00
□ 1872	65,000	40.00	72.00	160.00	350.00	900.00	2100.00
□ 1873 Closed 3	600				PROOFS ONLY		2700.00
□ 1873 Open 3 (Restrike)	480	1295.00			PROOFS ONLY		3200.00

THREE-CENT PIECES

THREE CENT (SILVER), 1851–1873

America's burgeoning population, plus conditions brought about by the California gold strike, resulted in a shortage of small change during the middle 19th century. The decision was made to strike a coin in three cents denomination and to have its composition of silver, alloyed with 25% copper. Because of its low face value and precious metal content the coin was extremely small physically. Its designer was James Longacre. Rather than portraiture, a symbolic obverse was used, consisting of a six-pointed star and shield. This was done to avoid confusion with the half dime, whose size and color were similar. On the reverse was the Roman numeral III enclosed within an ornamental letter C (for "cents") and surrounded by small stars. The weight was only 4/5 of a gram—the lightest coin ever struck by the Mint—with a diameter of just 14 mm. It was tiny, indeed. Undoubtedly the government expected that this coin, despite serving an important purpose, would not prove popular. It didn't. After striking about 35 million in the first three years of its production, quantities were sharply reduced thereafter. It was subsequently replaced by the "nickel" three-cent piece following the Civil War, which contained no silver whatever. Though the basic design of the silver three-cent piece was maintained throughout its lifetime—they continued being struck until 1873, though rarely circulated after 1862—some minor changes were introduced. In 1854 the obverse star was redrawn with a triple border. The final version, put into use in 1859, has a double border. As there are no great rarities among the circulating dates of this series, a complete collection is well within the realm of possibility. In 1854 there was a change of composition to 90% silver/10% copper and the weight was brought down to ¾ of a gram. From then until conclusion of the series all minting was carried out in Philadelphia. Previously the manufacture of this coin had been divided between Philadelphia and New Orleans.

The Mint Mark "O" is on the Reverse to the Right of the III

DATE	MINTAGE	ABP	G-4 Good	F-12 Fine	EF-40 Ex. Fine	MS-60 Unc.	PRF-65 Proof
□ 1851	5,447,400	4.50	12.00	18.00	66.00	270.00	
□ 1851O	720,000	7.00	17.00	34.00	120.00	500.00	
□ 1852	18,663,500	4.75	9.00	17.00	46.00	250.00	
□ 1853	11,400,000	4.75	9.00	17.00	46.00	250.00	
□ 1854	671,000	4.80	10.00	18.00	90.00	350.00	
□ 1855	139,000	11.00	20.00	42.00	150.00	600.00	5500.00
□ 1856	1,458,000	4.75	10.00	19.00	85.00	380.00	5100.00
□ 1857	1,042,000	5.00	9.00	19.00	90.00	410.00	5100.00
□ 1858	1,604,000	6.00	10.00	18.00	93.00	370.00	5000.00
□ 1859	365,000	6.00	10.00	18.00	60.00	250.00	2500.00
□ 1860	287,000	6.00	10.00	18.00	60.00	250.00	2500.00
□ 1861	498,000	6.00	10.00	18.00	60.00	250.00	2500.00
□ 1862	363,550	6.00	10.00	18.00	60.00	250.00	2500.00
□ 1862, 2 over 1		6.00	10.00	18.00	120.00	350.00	2600.00
□ 1863	21,460	350.00				800.00	2600.00
□ 1863, 3 over 2		400.00				700.00	3000.00
□ 1864	470	400.00				710.00	3000.00
□ 1865	8,500	400.00				710.00	3000.00
□ 1866	22,725	400.00				710.00	2900.00
□ 1867	4,625	400.00				710.00	3700.00
□ 1868	4,100	400.00				750.00	3800.00
□ 1869	5,100	400.00				750.00	3800.00
□ 1870	4,000	400.00				760.00	3000.00
□ 1871	4,260	400.00				760.00	3700.00
□ 1872	1,950	400.00				800.00	4000.00
□ 1873	600	1500.00	PROOF ONLY				4100.00

THREE CENT (NICKEL), 1865–1889

For all practical purposes the three-cent piece had been out of circulation during most of the Civil War. Upon the war's conclusion its manufacture was resumed, but no longer was the composition chiefly of silver. In fact, the new version contained no precious metal at all. It was composed of 75% copper and 25% nickel. What the three-cent piece lost metallically it gained physically: its weight more than doubled, rising to 1.94 grams, and its diameter increased to 17.0 mm. It may be wondered why a coin containing 75% copper would be referred to as a "nickel" rather than a "copper." The explanation is that the term "copper" was already in use for the cent. Americans picked up this nickname from the British, who had long been calling their pennies "coppers." As the new three-cent coin represented the greatest use made of nickel by the Mint up to that time, the name "nickel" seemed appropriate. The coin was somewhat better received than its predecessor, as there was not so much danger of confusing it with another denomination. The fact that its life was not particularly long (it was discontinued in 1889) can be attributed more to inflation than any fault of its own. By 1889 there was simply no longer a pressing need for three-cent pieces. At least 20 million were in circulation at that time and this was deemed more than enough to meet whatever demand might exist. The five-cent piece, which began in 1866 to be composed of the same copper-nickel ratio as the three cent, was adequately filling whatever need the three cent had earlier satisfied.

The three cent Nickel carried a Liberty head on its obverse and a large Roman numeral III on the reverse. Like the silver version it was designed by James Longacre. All were struck at Philadelphia. Throughout the quarter-century of production no changes occurred in its design.

DATE	MINTAGE	ABP	G-4 Good	F-12 Fine	EF-40 Ex. Fine	MS-60 Unc.	PRF-65 Proof
□ 1865	11,382,000	2.00	3.00	6.50	19.00	106.00	3600.00
□ 1866	4,801,000	2.00	3.10	6.50	19.00	106.00	2000.00
□ 1867	3,915,000	2.00	3.10	6.50	19.00	106.00	1100.00
□ 1868	3,252,000	2.00	3.10	6.50	19.00	106.00	1100.00
□ 1869	1,604,000	2.70	4.90	7.00	19.00	106.00	1100.00
□ 1870	1,335,000	2.70	4.90	7.00	19.00	110.00	1100.00
□ 1871	604,000	2.70	4.90	8.00	24.00	250.00	1100.00
□ 1872	862,000	2.70	4.90	7.00	22.00	250.00	1100.00
□ 1873 Closed 3	1,173,000	2.70	4.90	8.00	23.00	170.00	1100.00
□ 1873 Open 3		2.70	4.90	8.00	23.00	170.00	1100.00
□ 1874	790,000	2.70	4.90	8.00	23.00	210.00	1100.00
□ 1875	228,000	3.50	8.00	15.00	30.00	210.00	1100.00
□ 1876	162,000	5.20	11.00	19.00	40.00	210.00	1100.00
□ 1877	510	2000.00		PROOF			4000.00
□ 1878	2,350	1200.00		PROOF			2800.00
□ 1879	41,200	23.00	45.00	80.00	130.00	300.00	2100.00
□ 1880	24,955	32.00	65.00	100.00	131.00	310.00	2100.00
□ 1881	1,080,575	2.70	6.50	9.00	20.00	200.00	2000.00
□ 1882	25,300	25.00	58.00	80.00	120.00	400.00	2100.00
□ 1883	10,609	72.00	150.00	180.00	250.00	500.00	2100.00
□ 1884	5,642	120.00	270.00	350.00	410.00	600.00	2100.00
□ 1885	4,790	150.00	350.00	500.00	600.00	1000.00	2100.00
□ 1886	4,290			PROOF			2100.00
□ 1887	7,961	120.00	210.00	330.00	400.00	600.00	2100.00
□ 1887 over 86		1000.00		PROOF			2200.00
□ 1888	41,083	25.00	50.00	87.00	100.00	400.00	1900.00
□ 1889	21,561	30.00	66.00	112.00	140.00	450.00	1900.00

A.B.P. is for coins in fine condition or better. Superbly struck uncirculated coins bring proportionately more than price listed.

NICKELS

SHIELD, 1866–1883

Though the silver half dime was still being struck in 1866, its production was too limited to serve as a general circulating coin. This noble old soldier, its origins dating back to the Mint's beginnings, was suffering the effects of general inflation and the bullion shortage of the Civil War, caused in part by a scarcity of laborers for the silver mines. Not knowing what the future might hold, the government had no wish to terminate the silver half dime but it wanted, at the same time, to introduce a coin of proportionate value made of base metal, and attempt to popularize it. Thus was born the five-cent piece Nickel or "true nickel," as opposed to the three-cent coin that was also called a nickel. The five-cent Nickel was authorized by Congress on May 16, 1866. It was to have a weight of 5 grams and be composed of three parts copper and one part nickel. The diameter was 20½ mm. James Longacre, chief engraver of the Mint, was called upon to design it and produced a portraitless coin consisting of a shielded obverse with arabic numeral "5" on the reverse surrounded by stars and rays (or bars). "IN GOD WE TRUST" appears on the obverse above the shield. Nearly 15,000,000 pieces were struck in the first year of issue. In the following year, 1867, after production had continued briefly, the rays were removed from the reverse, resulting in a rarity of moderate proportions for the "with rays" type. This is not, however, an expensive coin except in uncirculated condition. It may be asked why the 1867 variety with rays and the standard 1866 date are valued almost equally, when only 2,019,000 of the former and 14,742,500 of the latter were struck, yielding a scarcity ratio of 7-to-1. The answer is simply that the 1866 would *not* be worth so much, if it wasn't the first date of its series. There are many collectors buying "first dates" who buy no other coins of the series. For this reason the first year of minting of *any* U.S. coin carries a premium over and above the quantity struck or available in the market. (Compare the 1866 value with that of the 1872, of which fewer than half as many were struck; the former is more common but worth more.)

1866–83

1866–67
With rays

1867–83
Without rays

DATE	MINTAGE	ABP	G-4 Good	F-12 Fine	EF-40 Ex. Fine	MS-60 Unc.	PRF-65 Proof
☐ 1866 w/rays	14,742,500	4.00	12.00	24.00	86.00	315.00	6000.00
☐ 1867 w/rays	30,909,500	4.00	12.00	30.00	110.00	500.00	10000.00
☐ 1867 no rays		3.20	6.00	12.00	30.00	180.00	1500.00
☐ 1868	28,817,000	3.10	6.00	12.00	30.00	168.00	1500.00

DATE	MINTAGE	ABP	G-4 Good	F-12 Fine	EF-40 Ex. Fine	MS-60 Unc.	PRF-65 Proof
□ 1869	16,395,000	3.10	6.00	11.00	30.00	195.00	1500.00
□ 1870	4,806,000	4.20	8.00	15.00	40.00	195.00	1500.00
□ 1871	561,000	14.00	30.00	52.00	100.00	300.00	1700.00
□ 1872	6,036,000	4.10	8.00	14.00	40.00	195.00	1500.00
□ 1873 closed 3	4,550,000	4.10	8.00	15.00	40.00	200.00	1500.00
□ 1873 open 3		4.10	8.00	16.00	40.00	190.00	1500.00
□ 1874	3,538,000	4.70	10.00	16.00	45.00	190.00	1500.00
□ 1875	2,097,000	4.70	10.00	17.00	56.00	230.00	1500.00
□ 1876	2,530,000	4.70	10.00	17.00	50.00	210.00	1500.00
□ 1877	500	1400.00		PROOF			3000.00
□ 1878	2,350	1200.00		PROOF			2600.00
□ 1879	29,100	120.00	256.00	350.00	520.00	700.00	2000.00
□ 1879 9 over 8						EXTREMELY RARE	
□ 1880	19,955	130.00	290.00	450.00	600.00	860.00	1900.00
□ 1881	72,375	100.00	210.00	330.00	400.00	710.00	1900.00
□ 1882	11,476,600	4.50	8.00	16.00	35.00	260.00	1600.00
□ 1883	1,456,919	6.50	14.00	20.00	35.00	260.00	1600.00
□ 1883 over 2		30.00	61.00	115.00	178.00	350.00	2200.00

NICKEL—LIBERTY HEAD, 1883–1912

When production of the silver half dime picturing Liberty ceased in the 1870s, designers were free to transfer the likeness of this goddess to our nickel five-cent piece. This, however, was not immediately done and when finally undertaken in 1883 the portrait was not the full figure used for half dimes but a profile bust. The new design was created by Charles E. Barber and gained for this piece the name "Barber Nickel," which was once used commonly but seems to have lost popularity. Like its predecessor, it was made of 75% copper and 25% nickel and had a weight of 5 grams. The diameter was slightly larger, measuring 21.2 mm., and striking was done at Philadelphia, Denver, and San Francisco. An embarrassing difficulty occurred with this coin at the outset of production. As first designed, the reverse carried the Roman numeral V (for 5) without the word "cents" or any sign indicating that cents was intended. Very shortly, unscrupulous persons began gilding the coin with gold wash and passing it to foreigners and other uninformed individuals as a $5 gold piece. The government put a halt to this activity by having the die re-engraved and the word "Cents" added. From then until 1913, when a new design was introduced (the famous Buffalo/Indian), no changes were made in designing. The Liberty Head was struck in great quantities throughout almost its entire run of production, with the total output reaching well into the hundreds of millions. It could still be found in general circulation, though not with much frequency, as late as the 1940s. The 1913 Liberty Head, America's most valuable base-metal coin, has long proved an enigma. The Mint claims not to have struck any Liberty Heads that year, asserting that its production consisted entirely of the Buffalo/Indian. It is certainly believable that no regular production occurred, otherwise the total in existence would not be as small as just five specimens. Even assuming that minting for the year was started with the Liberty Head design and was switched off to the new type after a few days, thousands of coins would by that time have been struck. There seems no logical way in which just five pieces could have been manufactured. The likelihood—though it may slightly tarnish this rarity's appeal—is that 1913 dies were produced, then put aside when the change of design was authorized and used (possibly clandestinely) to strike just a few specimens by a person or persons unknown. This theory is supported by the fact that originally, when first brought to public light, *all five* were owned by the same individual: Colonel Edward H. R. Green of New York, a noted collector of coins, stamps and art in the World War I era. If struck by the Mint and dispersed, it is almost beyond the realm of possibility that they could have been acquired by one collector within so short a period of time. (Colonel Green, incidentally, is equally noted for being the purchaser of the sheet of 24¢ inverted-center airmail stamps issued in 1918, which he *broke up and sold;* his approach to collecting was rather like that of a dealer or speculator, and one can only wonder at the reason for his association with the 1913 Liberty Head five-cent piece.)

1883

Without "CENTS"

1887 Cents

DATE	MINTAGE	ABP	G-4 Good	F-12 Fine	EF-40 Ex. Fine	MS-60 Unc.	PRF-65 Proof
☐ 1883 no cents	5,479,519	1.20	2.50	3.10	10.00	45.00	1400.00
☐ 1883 w/cents	16,032,983	2.90	6.00	12.00	32.00	250.00	910.00
☐ 1884	11,273,942	3.20	6.50	13.00	35.00	260.00	910.00
☐ 1885	1,476,490	100.00	210.00	400.00	700.00	1300.00	2500.00
☐ 1886	3,330,290	24.00	52.00	100.00	240.00	610.00	1800.00
☐ 1887	15,263,652	2.70	6.00	11.00	36.00	230.00	750.00
☐ 1888	10,720,483	3.00	7.00	13.00	42.00	230.00	750.00
☐ 1889	15,881,361	2.30	5.00	10.00	34.00	220.00	750.00
☐ 1890	16,259,272	2.30	5.00	12.00	34.00	210.00	750.00
☐ 1891	16,834,350	1.70	3.80	10.00	34.00	250.00	760.00
☐ 1892	11,699,642	1.70	3.25	13.00	34.00	250.00	760.00
☐ 1893	13,370,195	1.70	3.20	12.00	34.00	230.00	760.00
☐ 1894	5,413,132	2.00	5.00	18.00	65.00	300.00	760.00
☐ 1895	9,979,884	1.70	3.10	9.00	30.00	200.00	760.00
☐ 1896	8,842,920	1.70	3.10	11.00	30.00	200.00	760.00
☐ 1897	20,428,735	.57	1.10	4.00	20.00	200.00	760.00
☐ 1898	12,532,087	.57	1.25	4.00	20.00	210.00	760.00
☐ 1899	26,029,031	.30	.58	4.00	20.00	170.00	760.00
☐ 1900	27,255,995	.30	.58	3.50	20.00	130.00	760.00
☐ 1901	26,480,213	.30	.58	3.50	20.00	130.00	760.00
☐ 1902	31,480,579	.30	.58	3.50	20.00	130.00	725.00
☐ 1903	28,006,725	.30	.58	3.50	20.00	130.00	725.00
☐ 1904	21,404,984	.30	.58	3.50	20.00	130.00	725.00
☐ 1905	29,827,276	.30	.58	3.50	20.00	130.00	725.00

DATE	MINTAGE	ABP	G-4 Good	F-12 Fine	EF-40 Ex. Fine	MS-60 Unc.	PRF-65 Proof
□ 1906	38,613,725	.30	.58	3.10	21.00	110.00	700.00
□ 1907	39,214,800	.30	.58	3.10	21.00	110.00	700.00
□ 1908	22,686,177	.30	.58	3.10	21.00	110.00	700.00
□ 1909	11,590,526	.30	.58	3.10	21.00	110.00	700.00
□ 1910	30,169,353	.30	.58	3.10	21.00	110.00	690.00
□ 1911	39,559,372	.30	.58	3.10	21.00	110.00	690.00
□ 1912	26,236,714	.30	.58	3.10	21.00	110.00	690.00
□ 1912D	8,474,000	.53	1.25	4.50	50.00	300.00	
□ 1912S	238,000	25.00	48.00	80.00	350.00	670.00	
□ 1913* Not a Regular Mint Issue—5 Known—BUSS SALE 1985: $365,000.00							

NICKELS — BUFFALO OR INDIAN HEAD, 1913–1938

Undoubtedly the most dramatic, artistic and original set of designs employed for a U.S. coin, the Buffalo/Indian Head Nickel went into production in 1913. The composition was 75% copper and 25% nickel, with a weight of five grams. Its diameter was 21.2 mm. James E. Fraser, the designer, was not one to go half way. He hired an Indian to sit for the obverse portrait and took his sketching gear to the Bronx Zoo to get a likeness of a buffalo in the flesh. The artwork of this coin is little short of superb: each motif fully fills the planchet ground and is unencumbered by large inscriptions or miscellaneous symbols. Unfortunately the rate of wear in handling was such that few individuals aside from collectors had the opportunity to see the coin at its best. Just like the noble animal it pictured, the American bison, this coin proved to be a rapidly disappearing species. Within only 20 years after its discontinuation in 1938 it had all but vanished from circulation, despite enormous production output. Critics of the Buffalo/Indian Head Nickel were few. Those who spoke against it raised the objection that the buffalo was endangered by extinction because of its hunting by the Indians, and that to place both on the same coin was similar to picturing a woolly mastodon and a caveman. However, the intent, very well accomplished, was to use the medium of coinage to portray a subject genuinely American rather than endlessly repeating such symbols of foreign origin as Liberty. So popular did the bison likeness become that the coin, unlike most others, came to be popularly known by its reverse rather than its obverse. In 1916 a double die error resulted on some specimens, producing a twin or ghost impression of the date. Of regularly struck pieces, those from the San Francisco mint in the early and middle 1920s are scarcest.

1913-1938

1913-
Type I
Buffalo on High Mound

Mint Mark
is on the
Reverse, Under
"Five Cents"

1913
Type 2
Buffalo on Level Ground

DATE	MINTAGE	ABP	G-4 Good	F-12 Fine	EF-40 Ex. Fine	MS-60 Unc.	PRF-65 Proof
□ 1913 Type-1	30,993,520	1.30	3.00	4.00	14.00	36.00	2300.00
□ 1913D Type-1	5,337,000	3.20	6.00	10.00	23.00	78.00	
□ 1913S Type-1	2,105,000	4.70	8.50	18.00	42.00	89.00	
□ 1913 Type-2	29,858,700	1.70	3.50	8.00	12.00	36.00	3300.00
□ 1913D Type-2	4,156,000	17.00	36.00	55.00	110.00	210.00	
□ 1913S Type-2	1,209,000	40.00	80.00	120.00	210.00	350.00	
□ 1914	20,665,738	1.70	6.00	7.00	15.00	66.00	3300.00
□ 1914D	3,912,000	11.00	20.00	42.00	102.00	275.00	
□ 1914S	3,470,000	5.50	8.50	15.00		130.00	
□ 1915	20,987,270	1.60	2.70	6.00	15.00	75.00	3300.00
□ 1915D	7,569,500	2.40	6.00	16.00	52.00	160.00	
□ 1915S	1,505,000	7.20	16.00	31.00	110.00	275.00	
□ 1916 Double Die Obverse		320.00	710.00	1500.00	2650.00	4400.00	
□ 1916	63,498,000	.41	.70	1.60	6.00	41.00	3600.00
□ 1916D	13,333,000	2.30	4.60	9.10	50.00	160.00	
□ 1916S	11,860,000	1.75	3.50	7.00	50.00	160.00	
□ 1917	51,424,029	.41	.80	2.10	10.00	51.00	
□ 1917D	9,910,800	3.20	6.00	12.00	84.00	245.00	
□ 1917S	4,193,000	3.20	6.00	14.00	76.00	246.00	
□ 1918	32,086,314	.60	1.00	2.75	18.00	86.00	
□ 1918D	8,362,000	2.10	5.00	14.00	87.00	312.00	
□ 1918D over 17		210.00	530.00	900.00	2800.00	8000.00	
□ 1918S	4,882,000	2.34	5.00	13.00	90.00	285.00	
□ 1919	60,868,000	.32	.65	1.50	10.00	42.00	
□ 1919D	8,006,000	2.10	4.80	15.00	115.00	360.00	
□ 1919S	7,521,000	1.62	4.20	10.00	85.00	310.00	
□ 1920	63,093,000	.31	.60	1.50	11.00	42.00	
□ 1920D	9,418,000	1.60	3.30	10.00	125.00	330.00	
□ 1920S	9,689,000	1.15	2.40	7.00	90.00	215.00	
□ 1921	10,683,000	.43	.86	3.00	21.00	86.00	
□ 1921S	1,557,000	8.00	19.00	40.00	350.00	620.00	
□ 1923	35,715,000	.34	.62	1.50	8.00	45.00	
□ 1923S	6,142,000	1.10	2.20	5.00	65.00	150.00	
□ 1924	21,620,000	.32	.75	1.60	12.00	58.00	
□ 1924D	5,258,000	1.25	3.00	7.50	78.00	216.00	
□ 1924S	1,437,000	3.10	6.00	13.00	350.00	700.00	
□ 1925	35,565,100	.34	.60	1.50	9.00	39.00	
□ 1925D	4,450,000	2.30	6.20	13.00	90.00	310.00	
□ 1925S	6,256,000	1.60	3.30	7.00	75.00	230.00	
□ 1926	44,693,000	.24	.47	1.00	7.00	39.00	
□ 1926D	5,638,000	1.70	3.20	12.00	100.00	160.00	
□ 1926S	970,000	3.00	6.10	13.00	400.00	600.00	
□ 1927	37,981,000	.20	.45	.90	6.50	36.00	
□ 1927D	5,730,000	.67	1.20	3.10	40.00	99.00	
□ 1927S	3,430,000	.57	1.00	2.20	60.00	175.00	
□ 1928	23,411,000	.28	.40	1.00	6.50	37.00	
□ 1928D	6,436,000	.43	.77	2.10	15.00	50.00	

DATE	MINTAGE	ABP	G-4 Good	F-12 Fine	EF-40 Ex. Fine	MS-60 Unc.	PRF-65 Proof
□ 1928S	6,936,000	.27	.66	1.40	10.00	72.00	
□ 1929	36,446,000	.27	.42	1.00	7.00	30.00	
□ 1929D	8,370,000	.24	.41	1.00	11.00	54.00	
□ 1929S	7,754,000	.20	.41	.96	10.00	40.00	
□ 1930	22,849,000	.20	.35	.86	6.10	34.00	
□ 1930S	5,435,000	.24	.45	1.10	8.10	52.00	
□ 1931S	1,200,000	1.60	3.00	4.40	12.00	58.00	
□ 1934	20,313,000	.20	.40	.78	4.00	30.00	
□ 1934D	7,480,000	.20	.36	.95	5.00	50.00	
□ 1935	58,264,000	.17	.30	.56	3.00	20.00	
□ 1935D	12,092,000	.20	.40	.78	6.00	46.00	
□ 1935S	10,300,000	.20	.40	.65	4.00	28.00	
□ 1936	119,001,420	.20	.30	.47	2.00	17.00	2300.00
□ 1936D	24,418,000	.20	.40	.65	4.00	18.00	
□ 1936S	14,390,000	.20	.33	.57	3.00	21.00	
□ 1937	79,485,769	.20	.30	.51	2.10	13.00	2300.00
□ 1937D	17,826,000	.20	.30	.63	2.00	16.00	
□ 1937D—3 Legged Buffalo*		35.00	83.00	130.00	255.00	600.00	
□ 1937S	5,635,000	.20	.37	.66	2.10	15.00	
□ 1938D	7,020,000	.20	.37	.65	2.10	12.00	
□ 1938D over S		1.35	2.35	9.00	8.00	25.00	

*Beware of altered coins

NICKELS — JEFFERSON, 1938 TO DATE

In 1938 Thomas Jefferson became the third president to be pictured on an American coin (preceded by Lincoln and Washington), when his likeness was installed on the five-cent piece replacing the Buffalo/Indian Head. When the decision was made to use Jefferson's portrait on this coin a public competition was instituted to select the best design, accompanied by an award of $1,000. A total of 390 entries was received, the winning one being that of Felix Schlag. Jefferson is shown in profile facing left on the obverse with his home at Monticello pictured on the reverse. No alteration has ever been made in the design of this coin but some changes occurred in composition and modeling of the dies. In 1966 Schlag's initials were added, the feeling being that he deserved this honor as much as the designer of the Lincoln Cent, whose initials were incorporated into the design. The coin has always weighed five grams and measured 21.1 mm. Originally its content was 75% copper and 25% nickel. Due to a shortage of nickel during World War II, because of its use in military production, this metal was entirely removed from the coin in 1942 and substituted by a composition of 56% copper, 35% silver and 9% manganese. Wartime nickels consequently carry a premium value because of their silver content, though the silver additive was so small that the premium is only minimal. In 1946 the pre-war composition was resumed, and has since remained constant. Prior to 1968 the mint mark was on the reverse, to the right of the design. On wartime specimens (1942–45) it is considerably enlarged and placed above Monticello's dome. From 1968 on, it appears on the obverse between the date and portrait.

DATE	MINTAGE	ABP	G-4 Good	F-12 Fine	EF-40 Ex. Fine	MS-60 Unc.	PRF-65 Proof
☐ 1938	19,515,365	.09	.17	.32	.60	2.65	90.00
☐ 1938D	5,376,000	.37	.85	1.40	2.10	6.15	
☐ 1938S	4,105,000	.64	1.20	2.20	5.00	8.80	
☐ 1939	120,627,535	.12	.16	.21	.41	2.10	84.00
☐ 1939D	3,514,000	1.25	3.50	5.70	7.50	36.00	
☐ 1939S	6,630,000	.27	.53	.74	2.50	27.00	
☐ 1940	176,499,158				.41	1.20	62.00
☐ 1940D	43,540,000				.40	2.60	
☐ 1940S	39,690,000				.45	2.60	
☐ 1941	203,283,730				.21	.90	57.00
☐ 1941D	53,432,000				.40	2.85	
☐ 1941S	43,445,000				.40	4.10	
☐ 1942	49,818,600				.40	2.10	53.00
☐ 1942D	13,938,000	.11	.18	.31	1.70	24.00	
WARTIME SILVER NICKELS							
☐ 1942P	57,900,600	.20	.31	.70	2.00	12.50	280.00
☐ 1942S	32,900,000	.20	.31	.70	1.70	8.00	
☐ 1943P	271,165,000	.20	.30	.70	1.70	3.00	
☐ 1943D	15,294,000	.20	.30	.70	1.70	3.50	
☐ 1943S	104,060,000	.20	.29	.70	1.70	4.00	
☐ 1944P	119,150,000	.20	.29	.70	1.70	4.00	
☐ 1944D	32,309,000	.20	.29	.70	1.70	7.00	
☐ 1944S	21,640,000	.20	.29	.70	1.70	6.50	
☐ 1945P	119,408,100	.20	.29	.70	1.70	5.00	
☐ 1945D	37,158,000	.20	.29	.70	1.70	4.50	
☐ 1945S	58,939,000	.20	.29	.70	1.70	4.00	
REGULAR PRE-WAR TYPE							
☐ 1946	161,116,000				.24	.45	
☐ 1946D	45,292,200				.30	.60	
☐ 1946S	13,560,000				.42	.60	
☐ 1947	95,000,000				.22	.52	
☐ 1947D	37,882,000				.35	.60	
☐ 1947S	24,720,000			.12	.24	.60	
☐ 1948	89,348,000				.22	.40	
☐ 1948D	44,734,000			.15	.35	1.00	
☐ 1948S	11,300,000			.25	.55	1.00	

DATE	MINTAGE	ABP	G-4 Good	F-12 Fine	EF-40 Ex. Fine	MS-60 Unc.	PRF-65 Proof
☐ 1949	60,652,000				.30	1.00	
☐ 1949D	36,498,000			.20	.35	1.15	
☐ 1949, "D" over "S" ...				25.00	75.00	380.00	
☐ 1949S	9,716,000	.12	.20	.35	.70	2.10	
☐ 1950	9,847,386	.17	.25	.45	.80	1.90	72.00
☐ 1950D	2,530,000	2.75	4.00	6.00	9.00	13.00	
☐ 1951	28,689,500				.35	.98	53.00
☐ 1951D	20,460,000				.35	1.10	
☐ 1951S	7,776,000	.12	.22	.40	.75	2.70	
☐ 1952	64,069,980				.18	.62	32.00
☐ 1952D	30,638,000			.23	.30	1.75	
☐ 1952S	20,572,000			.10	.25	.82	
☐ 1953	46,772,800				.18	.40	23.00
☐ 1953D	59,878,600				.20	.32	
☐ 1953S	19,210,900			.15	.28	.45	
☐ 1954	47,917,350					.25	9.75
☐ 1954D	117,183,060					.38	
☐ 1954S	29,834,000			.10	.20	.42	
☐ 1954, S over D				6.00	18.00	36.00	
☐ 1955	8,266,200	.12	.25	.50	.60	1.15	8.20
☐ 1955D	74,464,100		.25			.30	
☐ 1955, D over S				5.50	17.00	27.00	
☐ 1956	35,885,384					.36	2.75
☐ 1956D	67,222,940					.36	
☐ 1957	39,655,952					.36	1.45
☐ 1957D	136,828,900				.34		
☐ 1958	17,963,653					.39	2.80
☐ 1958D	168,249,120					.25	
☐ 1959	28,397,291					.25	1.30
☐ 1959D	160,738,240		Circulated			.25	
☐ 1960	57,107,602		coins			.25	.80
☐ 1960D	192,582,180		of			.25	.80
☐ 1961	76,668,344		these			.25	.80
☐ 1961D	229,342,760		dates			.25	
☐ 1962	100,602,019		are			.25	.80
☐ 1962D	280,195,720		not			.25	
☐ 1963	178,851,645		bought			.25	.80
☐ 1963D	276,829,460		by			.25	
☐ 1964	1,028,622,762		dealers			.25	.80
☐ 1964D	1,787,297,160					.25	
☐ 1965	136,131,380					.16	
☐ 1966	156,208,283					.16	
☐ 1967	107,324,750					.16	
☐ 1968D	91,227,800					.16	
☐ 1968S	103,437,510					.16	.80
☐ 1969D	202,807,500					.16	
☐ 1969S	128,099,631					.16	.80
☐ 1970D	515,485,380					.16	

DATE	MINTAGE	ABP	G-4 Good	F-12 Fine	EF-40 Ex. Fine	MS-60 Unc.	PRF-65 Proof
☐ 1970S	241,464,814					.20	1.35
☐ 1971	108,884,000					.20	
☐ 1971D	316,144,800					.18	
☐ 1971S	3,224,138					1.40	
☐ 1972	202,036,000					.18	
☐ 1972D	351,694,600					.18	
☐ 1972S	3,267,667						1.35
☐ 1973	384,396,000					.18	
☐ 1973D	261,405,400					.18	
☐ 1973S Proof Only	2,769,624						1.35
☐ 1974	601,752,000					.18	1.35
☐ 1974D	277,373,000		Circulated			.16	
☐ 1974S Proof Only	2,617,350		coins				1.25
☐ 1975	181,772,000		of			.16	
☐ 1975D	401,875,300		these			.16	
☐ 1975S Proof Only	2,909,369		dates				.96
☐ 1976	376,124,000		are			.16	
☐ 1976D	563,964,147		not			.16	
☐ 1976S Proof Only	4,149,945		bought				.70
☐ 1977	585,175,250		by			.16	
☐ 1977D	297,325,618		dealers			.16	
☐ 1977S Proof Only	3,250,095						.82
☐ 1978	391,308,000					.16	
☐ 1978D	313,092,780					.16	
☐ 1978S Proof Only	3,127,781						1.20
☐ 1979	463,188,123					.15	
☐ 1979D	325,867,600					.15	
☐ 1979S Proof (I)	3,677,200						1.40
☐ 1979S Proof (II)							2.50
☐ 1980P	593,004,060					.15	
☐ 1980D	502,324,000					.15	
☐ 1980S Proof Only	3,554,800						.80
☐ 1981P	657,503,295					.12	
☐ 1981D	364,802,000					.12	
☐ 1981S Proof (I)	4,000,000						.80
☐ 1981S Proof (II)							2.15
☐ 1982P	292,350,000					.12	
☐ 1982D	373,725,500					.12	
☐ 1982S Proof (I)	3,856,995						1.75
☐ 1982S Proof (II)							3.60
☐ 1983P	560,750,000					.12	
☐ 1983D	536,726,000					.12	
☐ 1983S Proof	3,228,537						2.00
☐ 1984P	750,000,000					.12	
☐ 1984D	518,000,000					.12	
☐ 1984S Proof							2.00
☐ 1985P	676,222,421					.12	
☐ 1985D	463,621,747					.12	

DATE	MINTAGE	ABP	G-4 Good	F-12 Fine	EF-40 Ex. Fine	MS-60 Unc.	PRF-65 Proof
☐ 1985S Proof..........	3,241,412						1.60
☐ 1986P	572,842,600					.10	
☐ 1986D	382,610,212					.10	
☐ 1986S Proof..........	3,101,640						2.50
☐ 1987P	362,111,406					.10	
☐ 1987D	411,690,114					.10	
☐ 1987S Proof..........						.10	1.45
☐ 1988P						.09	
☐ 1988D						.09	
☐ 1988S Proof..........							1.40
☐ 1989P						.09	
☐ 1989D						.09	
☐ 1989S							1.40

HALF DIMES, 1794–1873

The first half dimes did not technically reach manufacture until 1795 but carried a 1794 date, as the dies had been engraved that year and there was no desire to redo this work. The weight was 1.35 grams, the composition consisting of .8924 silver and .1076 copper; or, to speak in rounded figures, nine parts silver to one part copper. After more than 40 years of being unchanged compositionally the silver content was raised to a full nine parts in 1837, which necessitated a weight reduction to 1.34 grams. The original obverse type was the Flowing Hair Liberty, similar to that of other silver coinage of the time. Its designer was Robert Scot. On the reverse appeared the standing eagle and legend "UNITED STATES OF AMERICA." This was replaced by the Draped Bust type with similar reverse in 1796, and the shield eagle reverse in 1800. Beginning in 1829 the Capped Bust was introduced, along with a modified version of the shield eagle (wings downward instead of upturned). The sharpest departure occurred in 1837, with the introduction of a design that was to remain—with modifications—until the series closed out in 1873. This was the Seated Liberty, an attractive bit of classical portraiture but one to which some objection was voiced, on grounds that it closely resembled the figure of Britannia on British coins. The reverse carried the wording "HALF DIME" within an open wreath, encircled by "UNITED STATES OF AMERICA." There was initially no decoration of the obverse beyond the figure of Liberty. In 1838 a series of stars was added as a half-frame to the portrait. Arrows were placed by the date in 1853. The chief revision came in 1860 when the words "UNITED STATES OF AMERICA" were removed from the reverse and placed on the obverse, supplanting the stars. The reverse wreath was redesigned and made larger and frillier to fill the vacancy.

1794–1795 HALF DIMES, LIBERTY WITH FLOWING HAIR

DATE	MINTAGE	ABP	G-4 Good	F-12 Fine	VF-20 V. Fine
☐ 1794	86,416	500.00	1110.00	1700.00	2600.00
☐ 1795		420.00	720.00	1100.00	1800.00

(Both the 1794 and 1795 were struck in 1795)

HALF DIMES — DRAPED BUST, SMALL EAGLE, 1796–1797

DATE	MINTAGE	ABP	G-4 Good	F-12 Fine	VF-20 V. Fine
☐ 1796 over 5		450.00	850.00	1350.00	2100.00
☐ 1796	10,230	400.00	800.00	1300.00	2000.00
☐ 1796 LIKERTY		400.00	800.00	1300.00	1980.00
☐ 1797 (13 stars)		400.00	800.00	1200.00	1900.00
☐ 1797 (15 stars)	44,527	375.00	750.00	1200.00	1850.00
☐ 1797 (16 stars)		375.00	750.00	1200.00	1850.00

HALF DIMES — DRAPED BUST, LARGE EAGLE, 1800–1805

DATE	MINTAGE	ABP	G-4 Good	F-12 Fine	VF-20 V. Fine
☐ 1800		330.00	600.00	1000.00	1400.00
☐ 1800 LIBEKTY	24,000	330.00	600.00	1000.00	1400.00
☐ 1801	33,910	330.00	600.00	1000.00	1400.00
☐ 1802 (Very Rare)	13,010	1550.00	7000.00	12000.00	20000.00
☐ 1803	37,850	300.00	650.00	1000.00	1400.00
☐ 1805	15,600	395.00	800.00	1100.00	1600.00

HALF DIMES — LIBERTY CAP, 1829–1837

DATE	MINTAGE	ABP	G-4 Good	F-12 Fine	EF-40 Ex. Fine	MS-63 Unc.
☐ 1829	1,230,000	7.00	14.00	24.00	110.00	720.00
☐ 1830	1,240,000	7.00	14.00	24.00	110.00	700.00
☐ 1831	1,242,700	7.00	14.00	24.00	110.00	700.00
☐ 1832	965,000	7.00	14.00	24.00	110.00	710.00
☐ 1833	1,370,000	7.00	14.00	24.00	110.00	700.00
☐ 1834	1,480,000	7.00	14.00	24.00	110.00	700.00
☐ 1835*	2,760,000	7.00	14.00	24.00	110.00	700.00
☐ 1836	1,900,000	7.00	14.00	24.00	110.00	700.00
☐ 1837 large $.05	2,276,000	7.00	14.00	24.00	110.00	700.00
☐ 1837 small $.05		11.00	20.00	50.00	150.00	1500.00

*1835 Large Date—Large $.05, Large Date—Small $.05, Same prices
Small Date—Small $.05, Small Date—Large $.05, Same prices

HALF DIMES — LIBERTY SEATED, 1837–1859

1837–1839O no Stars

1838–1859 with Stars

1837–1859

Mint Mark is on the Reverse Under the Value

DATE	MINTAGE	ABP	G-4 Good	F-12 Fine	EF-40 Ex. Fine	MS-60 Unc.	PRF-65 Proof
☐ 1837 Small Date, No Stars		15.00	28.00	59.00	250.00	740.00	
☐ 1837 Large Date, No Stars	2,250,000	13.00	26.00	56.00	230.00	670.00	
☐ 1838O No Stars	70,000	50.00	98.00	217.00	760.00	2700.00	
☐ 1838 w/Stars	2,255,000	3.15	6.00	13.00	62.00	430.00	
☐ 1839	1,069,150	3.15	6.00	13.00	62.00	520.00	
☐ 1839O	1,096,550	5.50	11.00	18.00	83.00	540.00	
☐ 1840 No Drapery	1,344,085	4.00	6.00	12.00	70.00	535.00	
☐ 1840 Drapery		10.00	24.00	56.00	172.00	1690.00	
☐ 1840O Drapery		15.00	36.00	87.00	265.00	2100.00	
☐ 1840O No Drapery		6.00	12.00	22.00	89.00	630.00	
☐ 1841	1,500,000	3.00	7.00	10.00	47.00	290.00	
☐ 1841O	815,000	4.00	11.00	22.00	85.00	680.00	
☐ 1842	815,000	3.50	6.00	9.00	52.00	410.00	
☐ 1842O	350,000	17.00	32.00	70.00	410.00		
☐ 1843	1,165,000	3.00	6.10	8.50	46.00	330.00	
☐ 1844	430,000	4.00	8.00	8.00	62.00	365.00	
☐ 1844O	220,000	34.00	75.00	190.00	920.00		
☐ 1845	1,564,000	3.00	7.00	8.50	46.00	315.00	
☐ 1846	27,000	72.00	160.00	290.00	815.00	315.00	
☐ 1847	1,274,000	3.00	7.00	10.00	48.00	315.00	
☐ 1848 (Medium Date)	668,000	3.70	8.00	15.00	68.00	315.00	
☐ 1848 (Large Date)		13.00	23.00	43.00	165.00	470.00	
☐ 1848O	600,000	7.50	16.00	29.00	98.00	650.00	
☐ 1849	1,309,000	2.70	7.00	12.00	52.00	630.00	
☐ 1849 over 46	1,309,000	6.70	16.00	21.00	82.00	420.00	
☐ 1849 over 48	1,309,000	6.70	16.00	28.00	110.00	550.00	
☐ 1849O	140,000	19.00	35.00	85.00	490.00		
☐ 1850	955,000	2.70	7.00	10.00	47.00	400.00	
☐ 1850O	690,000	7.10	16.00	25.00	100.00	880.00	
☐ 1851	781,000	2.70	6.00	10.00	47.00	420.00	
☐ 1851O	860,000	5.10	12.00	24.00	84.00	800.00	
☐ 1852	1,000,000	2.70	7.00	10.00	50.00	280.00	
☐ 1852O	260,000	16.00	32.00	75.00	220.00	280.00	
☐ 1853 w/arrows	13,210,020	2.10	6.00	7.10	55.00	380.00	7500.00

DATE	MINTAGE	ABP	G-4 Good	F-12 Fine	EF-40 Ex. Fine	MS-60 Unc.	PRF-65 Proof
☐ 1853 no arrows	135,000	11.00	26.00	61.00	210.00	830.00	
☐ 1853O w/arrows	2,360,000	4.00	7.50	15.00	62.00	390.00	
☐ 1853O no arrows	160,000	70.00	165.00	280.00	820.00		
☐ 1854 w/arrows	5,740,000	2.20	6.00	12.00	54.00	375.00	7300.00
☐ 1854O w/arrows	1,560,000	3.70	9.00	14.00	80.00	710.00	
☐ 1855 w/arrows	1,750,000	3.20	7.00	12.00	61.00	350.00	7300.00
☐ 1855O w/arrows	600,000	6.70	16.00	30.00	98.00	980.00	
☐ 1856	4,880,000	2.60	6.00	9.00	43.00	295.00	9600.00
☐ 1856O	1,100,000	5.20	11.00	22.00	86.00	680.00	
☐ 1857	7,280,000	2.20	6.00	7.70	42.00	280.00	4200.00
☐ 1857O	1,380,000	4.20	11.00	15.00	78.00	670.00	
☐ 1858	3,500,000	2.70	6.00	8.00	48.00	290.00	4200.00
☐ 1858 over inverted date		17.00	36.00	84.00	210.00	750.00	
☐ 1858O	1,660,000	4.60	10.00	16.00	75.00	660.00	
☐ 1859†	340,000	5.60	13.00	23.00	94.00	350.00	4200.00
☐ 1859O	560,000	6.10	12.00	19.00	92.00	700.00	

†There are two recognized patterns in this series, the transitional pieces of 1859 and 1860: 1859—proof: $9,000.00; 1860—unc: $4,000.00

HALF DIMES — LIBERTY SEATED, 1860–1873 WITH "UNITED STATES OF AMERICA" ON OBVERSE

Mint Marks are Under or Within Wreath on Reverse

DATE	MINTAGE	ABP	G-4 Good	F-12 Fine	EF-40 Ex. Fine	MS-60 Unc.	PRF-65 Proof
☐ 1860 Legend	799,000	3.00	7.00	13.00	47.00	230.00	2500.00
☐ 1860O	1,060,000	3.00	7.00	16.00	51.00	420.00	
☐ 1861	3,361,000	3.00	7.00	10.00	35.00	265.00	2500.00
☐ 1862	1,492,550	3.00	7.00	10.00	35.00	265.00	2500.00
☐ 1863	18,460	57.00	130.00	220.00	410.00	890.00	2500.00
☐ 1863S	100,000	9.00	17.00	41.00	150.00	980.00	
☐ 1864	48,470	120.00	250.00	415.00	680.00	1200.00	2500.00
☐ 1864S	90,000	12.00	24.00	63.00	210.00		
☐ 1865	13,500	93.00	190.00	380.00	610.00	1400.00	2500.00
☐ 1865S	120,000	7.00	13.00	31.00	125.00	1200.00	
☐ 1866	10,725	80.00	180.00	315.00	560.00	980.00	2500.00
☐ 1866S	120,000	8.00	12.00	30.00	135.00	980.00	
☐ 1867	8,625	140.00	300.00	520.00	710.00	1350.00	2500.00
☐ 1867S	120,000	7.00	14.00	31.00	130.00	910.00	
☐ 1868	89,200	16.00	36.00	83.00	210.00	650.00	2450.00
☐ 1868S	280,000	6.00	10.00	21.00	72.00	700.00	

DATE	MINTAGE	ABP	G-4 Good	F-12 Fine	EF-40 Ex. Fine	MS-60 Unc.	PRF-65 Proof
□ 1869	280,000	4.60	9.00	20.00	68.00	420.00	2450.00
□ 1869S	230,000	4.60	9.00	21.00	70.00	540.00	
□ 1870*	536,000	3.10	6.00	13.00	38.00	470.00	2450.00
□ 1871	1,873,960	3.10	6.00	11.00	38.00	420.00	2450.00
□ 1871S	161,000	7.00	15.00	32.00	85.00	620.00	
□ 1872	2,947,950	2.15	6.00	10.00	36.00	425.00	2450.00
□ 1872S in wreath	837,000	3.10	6.00	10.00	38.00	425.00	
□ 1872S below wreath ..		3.10	6.00	10.00	37.00	430.00	
□ 1873	712,600	3.10	6.00	9.00	38.00	425.00	2450.00
□ 1873S	324,000	4.60	7.00	16.00	42.00	520.00	

*1870S is unique—only one known

DIMES

EARLY DIMES, 1796–1891

A coin valued at 1⁄10 of a dollar was among the first to be authorized by the U.S. Mint, though production did not begin until 1796. Had the dime made its debut even just a year sooner there is every likelihood it would have carried the Flowing Hair design, but by 1796 there was no longer much enthusiasm for this rendition of Liberty and so the coin got its start with the Draped Bust portrait. This version of Liberty, familiar on other silver pieces, lacks the "cap of liberty" and shows the goddess with a somewhat more fashionable hairdo. On the reverse was the standing eagle, encircled by branches and the inscription "UNITED STATES OF AMERICA." Stars were placed in a circular pattern on the obverse, ranging in number from 13 to 16. The designer was Robert Scot. The weight of this coin was 2.70 grams and its original composition was .8924 silver and .1076 copper, the same as that of the Half Dime (or, approximately, nine parts of silver to one part of copper). Its diameter was generally 19 mm. but slight variations are observed. In 1798 the standing eagle was replaced by the heraldic or shield eagle on the reverse, over which is a series of stars. Just like the stars on the original obverse, these too can vary in quantity from 13 to 16. In 1809 the portrait was changed to the Capped Bust, whose chief characteristic (aside from Liberty's headgear) is that the profile is switched round to face left instead of right. The reverse type is now the eagle-on-branch, still bearing a shield but with its wings down instead of opened wide. The year 1837 witnessed the most significant alteration up to the time; a likeness of Liberty seated replaced the bust type and the eagle's place on the reverse was taken by the wording "ONE DIME" within a wreath, surrounded by "UNITED STATES OF AMERICA." At first there were no stars on the obverse but these were added in 1838 and arrows were placed at the date in 1853. These, however, were of little duration as they disappeared in 1856.

DIMES — DRAPED BUST, 1796–1807 EAGLE ON REVERSE

1798–1807

1796–1797
Small Eagle

1798–1807
Large Eagle

DATE	MINTAGE	ABP	G-4 Good	F-12 Fine	VF-20 V. Fine
☐ 1796	22,135	400.00	1000.00	1650.00	2500.00
☐ 1797 (13 stars)		420.00	1110.00	1650.00	2550.00
☐ 1797 (16 stars)	25,261	450.00	1110.00	1500.00	2550.00
☐ 1798		400.00	770.00	1300.00	1700.00
☐ 1798 over 97 w/13 stars on reverse					VERY RARE
☐ 1798 small 8	27,500				VERY RARE
☐ 1798 over 97 w/16 stars on reverse		300.00	600.00	1200.00	2000.00
☐ 1800	21,760	330.00	620.00	1000.00	1900.00
☐ 1801	34,640	330.00	640.00	1000.00	1800.00
☐ 1802	10,975	400.00	750.00	1200.00	2200.00
☐ 1803	33,040	370.00	710.00	1000.00	2000.00
☐ 1804 w/13 stars on reverse	8,265	700.00	1100.00	2200.00	4200.00
☐ 1804 w/14 stars on reverse	8,265	700.00	1100.00	2200.00	4200.00
☐ 1805 w/4 berries	120,780	285.00	510.00	900.00	1300.00
☐ 1805 w/5 berries	120,780	285.00	510.00	900.00	1300.00
☐ 1807	165,000	285.00	510.00	900.00	1350.00

DIMES — LIBERTY CAP, 1809–1837

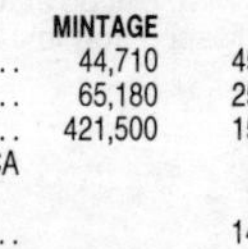

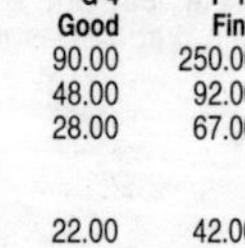

DATE	MINTAGE	ABP	G-4 Good	F-12 Fine	EF-40 Ex. Fine	MS-60 Unc.
☐ 1809	44,710	45.00	90.00	250.00	600.00	4200.00
☐ 1811 over 9	65,180	25.00	48.00	92.00	360.00	3800.00
☐ 1814 (Small Date)	421,500	15.00	28.00	67.00	360.00	1500.00
☐ 1814 STATESOFAMERICA (No Breaks Between Words: Large Date)		14.00	22.00	42.00	325.00	1400.00

DATE	MINTAGE	ABP	G-4 Good	F-12 Fine	EF-40 Ex. Fine	MS-60 Unc.
□ 1820	942,587	14.00	24.00	40.00	340.00	1300.00
□ 1821	1,186,512	14.00	24.00	40.00	340.00	1300.00
□ 1822	100,000	100.00	215.00	630.00	1100.00	4900.00
□ 1823 over 22	440,000	13.00	26.00	41.00	320.00	1300.00
□ 1824 over 22		13.00	26.00	45.00	320.00	1300.00
□ 1825 (Mintage includes 1824)	510,000	12.00	23.00	38.00	320.00	1300.00
□ 1827	1,215,000	8.00	19.00	30.00	325.00	1275.00
□ 1828 Large Date	125,000	16.00	35.00	65.00	350.00	3100.00
□ 1828 Small Date	125,000	12.00	29.00	54.00	280.00	1900.00
□ 1829 Small $.10	770,000	6.50	14.00	24.00	220.00	1500.00
□ 1829 Large $.10	770,000	13.50	28.00	57.00	250.00	1650.00
□ 1830*	510,000	5.50	12.00	22.00	240.00	1500.00
□ 1830, 30 over 29		22.00	40.00	130.00	350.00	2300.00
□ 1831	771,350	6.00	11.00	22.00	210.00	1550.00
□ 1832	522,500	6.00	11.00	22.00	210.00	1575.00
□ 1833	485,000	6.00	11.00	22.00	210.00	1550.00
□ 1834**	635,000	6.00	11.00	22.00	210.00	1550.00
□ 1835	1,410,000	6.00	11.00	22.00	210.00	1250.00
□ 1836	1,190,000	6.00	11.00	22.00	210.00	1250.00
□ 1837 ALL KINDS	359,500	6.00	11.00	22.00	220.00	1250.00

*1830—Small $.10, 1830—Large $.10: Same Price
**1834 Small 4, 1834—Large 4: Same Price

DIMES — LIBERTY SEATED, 1837–1860

1837–38O
no stars

1837–91

1838–60
with stars

DATE	MINTAGE	ABP	G-4 Good	F-12 Fine	EF-40 Ex. Fine	MS-60 Unc.
□ 1837 No Stars*	682,500	12.00	27.00	60.00	350.00	1100.00
□ 1838O No Stars	402,404	21.00	41.00	88.00	480.00	3200.00
□ 1838 Small Stars		11.00	24.00	55.00	200.00	2100.00
□ 1838 Large Stars	1,992,500	2.40	7.00	18.00	64.00	920.00
□ 1838 Partial Drapery		15.00	36.00	100.00	400.00	1600.00
□ 1839	1,053,115	2.20	7.00	17.00	59.00	480.00
□ 1839O	1,243,272	5.40	11.00	22.00	87.00	890.00
□ 1840 No Drape	1,358,580	2.15	5.00	16.00	64.00	470.00
□ 1840O No Drape	1,175,000	5.20	11.00	27.00	96.00	1450.00

*Small and Large date same price

DATE	MINTAGE	ABP	G-4 Good	F-12 Fine	EF-40 Ex. Fine	MS-60 Unc.
☐ 1840 Drapery added	377,541	14.00	26.00	80.00	350.00	
☐ 1841	1,622,500	3.00	5.00	11.00	49.00	375.00
☐ 1841O	2,007,500	3.50	7.00	15.00	72.00	1300.00
☐ 1842	1,887,500	2.75	6.00	10.00	41.00	400.00
☐ 1842O	2,020,000	3.50	6.00	14.00	76.00	

DATE	MINTAGE	ABP	G-4 Good	F-12 Fine	EF-40 Ex. Fine	MS-60 Unc.	PRF-65 Proof
☐ 1843	1,370,000	3.10	6.00	12.00	51.00	375.00	
☐ 1843O	150,000	23.00	46.00	124.00	670.00		
☐ 1844	72,500	15.00	30.00	90.00	320.00	15.00	
☐ 1845	1,755,000	3.10	6.00	11.00	49.00	360.00	
☐ 1845O	230,000	9.10	19.00	58.00	525.00		
☐ 1846	31,300	35.00	70.00	135.00	620.00		
☐ 1847	245,000	7.60	14.00	32.00	160.00	1200.00	
☐ 1848	451,000	5.10	12.00	19.00	76.00	800.00	
☐ 1849	839,000	4.60	10.00	14.00	50.00	400.00	
☐ 1849O	300,000	5.60	12.00	30.00	180.00		
☐ 1850	1,931,500	3.10	6.00	11.00	46.00	400.00	
☐ 1850O	510,000	5.60	12.00	22.00	89.00	1000.00	
☐ 1851	1,026,500	3.00	6.00	12.00	40.00	400.00	
☐ 1851O	400,000	5.60	12.00	16.00	90.00	1500.00	
☐ 1852	1,535,500	3.10	6.00	11.00	53.00	400.00	
☐ 1852O	430,000	7.00	14.00	34.00	200.00	1500.00	
☐ 1853 No arrows	95,000	34.00	60.00	100.00	300.00	1050.00	
☐ 1853 w/arrows	12,173,010	2.10	3.00	7.00	46.00	415.00	4950.00
☐ 1853O	1,100,000	3.60	6.00	12.00	95.00	850.00	
☐ 1854	4,470,000	3.10	5.00	8.00	46.00	490.00	10900.00
☐ 1854O	1,770,000	3.10	5.00	9.00	68.00	780.00	
☐ 1855	2,075,000	3.10	5.00	8.00	48.00	875.00	11000.00
☐ 1856 (Small Date)	5,780,000	3.10	5.00	8.00	36.00	560.00	8000.00
☐ 1856 (Large Date)		4.20	8.00	14.00	60.00	735.00	
☐ 1856O	1,180,000	3.20	6.00	14.00	65.00	850.00	
☐ 1856S	70,000	42.00	90.00	180.00	460.00		
☐ 1857	5,580,000	1.80	3.00	8.00	40.00	400.00	7300.00
☐ 1857O	1,540,000	3.10	6.00	11.00	60.00	830.00	
☐ 1858	1,540,000	1.80	3.00	9.00	42.00	400.00	7000.00
☐ 1858O	290,000	8.20	17.00	30.00	130.00	1100.00	
☐ 1858S	60,000	50.00	90.00	160.00	410.00		
☐ 1859†	430,000	2.70	6.00	11.00	60.00	925.00	4400.00
☐ 1859O	480,000	4.20	9.00	17.00	72.00	1100.00	
☐ 1859S	60,000	55.00	110.00	180.00	500.00		
☐ 1860S	140,000	10.00	19.00	36.00	170.00		

†There is a recognized pattern in this series—1859 Transitional Pattern Proof: $28,000

DIMES — LIBERTY SEATED, 1860–1891 WITH "UNITED STATES OF AMERICA" ON OBVERSE

Mint Marks Under or Within Wreath on Reverse

DATE	MINTAGE	ABP	G-4 Good	F-12 Fine	EF-40 Ex. Fine	MS-60 Unc.	PRF-65 Proof
☐ 1860	607,000	3.10	6.00	11.00	42.00	530.00	2400.00
☐ 1860O	40,000	120.00	270.00	610.00	1800.00		
☐ 1861	1,924,000	2.50	5.00	9.00	30.00	510.00	2400.00
☐ 1861S	172,500	12.00	20.00	40.00	140.00		
☐ 1862	847,550	3.70	7.00	10.00	41.00	480.00	2410.00
☐ 1862S	180,750	11.00	20.00	30.00	141.00		
☐ 1863	14,460	130.00	270.00	450.00	600.00	1100.00	2300.00
☐ 1863S	157,000	10.00	19.00	40.00	140.00	1200.00	
☐ 1864	39,070	140.00	300.00	500.00	680.00	1100.00	
☐ 1864S	230,000	7.10	15.00	30.00	110.00	1200.00	
☐ 1865	10,500	165.00	340.00	500.00	720.00	1300.00	2200.00
☐ 1865S	175,000	9.10	18.00	30.00	110.00		
☐ 1866	8,725	140.00	300.00	600.00	820.00	1300.00	2400.00
☐ 1866S	135,000	10.00	20.00	40.00	140.00	1450.00	
☐ 1867	6,625	240.00	500.00	750.00	1000.00	1880.00	2300.00
☐ 1867S	140,000	12.00	20.00	40.00	150.00	1200.00	
☐ 1868	466,250	4.10	9.00	14.00	60.00	600.00	2300.00
☐ 1868S	260,000	6.10	10.00	20.00	86.00	900.00	
☐ 1869	256,600	7.20	12.00	30.00	90.00	650.00	2300.00
☐ 1869S	450,000	5.10	8.00	15.00	74.00	750.00	
☐ 1870	471,500	4.00	8.00	12.00	50.00	450.00	2300.00
☐ 1870S	50,000	61.00	120.00	190.00	410.00	2600.00	
☐ 1871	753,610	3.20	7.00	11.00	40.00	350.00	2200.00
☐ 1871CC	20,100	221.00	460.00	800.00	2600.00		
☐ 1871S	320,000	7.00	12.00	30.00	120.00	900.00	
☐ 1872	2,396,450	3.00	5.00	8.00	35.00	340.00	2300.00
☐ 1872CC	24,000	140.00	300.00	600.00	2450.00		
☐ 1872S	190,000	13.00	22.00	50.00	190.00	1100.00	
☐ 1873*	2,378,500	4.50	7.00	19.00	90.00	700.00	3400.00
☐ 1873** Open "3"	1,508,600	13.00	20.00	50.00	160.00	950.00	
☐ 1873** Closed "3"	60,000	4.00	6.00	13.00	30.00	220.00	2400.00
☐ 1873CC**	12,400	UNIQUE—ONLY ONE KNOWN					
☐ 1873CC*	18,791	200.00	500.00	900.00	2800.00		
☐ 1873S*	455,000	6.00	12.00	26.00	140.00	1400.00	
☐ 1874 w/arrows	2,940,000	4.10	8.00	20.00	110.00	700.00	3400.00
☐ 1874CC w/arrows	10,817	400.00	800.00	2000.00	4200.00		

DATE	MINTAGE	ABP	G-4 Good	F-12 Fine	EF-40 Ex. Fine	MS-60 Unc.	PRF-65 Proof
☐ 1874S w/arrows	240,000	19.00	28.00	66.00	160.00	1275.00	
☐ 1875	10,350,000	1.75	3.30	6.30	23.00	240.00	2425.00
☐ 1875CC in Wreath		3.00	5.00	7.00	35.00	265.00	
☐ below Wreath	4,645,000	3.00	5.00	11.00	34.00	280.00	
☐ 1875S in Wreath		3.00	4.00	8.00	29.00	320.00	
☐ below Wreath	9,070,000	3.00	3.80	8.10	24.00	280.00	
☐ 1876	11,461,150	1.80	3.60	7.00	24.00	250.00	2350.00
☐ 1876CC	8,270,000	1.80	3.60	7.00	24.00	260.00	
☐ 1876S	10,420,000	1.80	3.60	7.00	24.00	250.00	
☐ 1877	7,310,510	1.80	3.60	7.00	24.00	260.00	2350.00
☐ 1877CC	7,700,000	1.80	3.60	7.00	24.00	250.00	
☐ 1877S	2,340,000	1.80	3.60	7.00	24.00	260.00	
☐ 1878	1,678,300	1.80	3.60	7.00	24.00	260.00	2350.00
☐ 1878CC	200,000	17.00	32.00	91.00	240.00	700.00	
☐ 1879	15,100	80.00	160.00	250.00	430.00	700.00	2300.00
☐ 1880	37,355	55.00	130.00	200.00	320.00	600.00	2300.00
☐ 1881	24,975	70.00	135.00	220.00	330.00	650.00	2300.00
☐ 1882	3,911,100	2.00	3.30	7.00	22.00	250.00	2300.00
☐ 1883	7,675,712	2.00	3.30	7.00	22.00	250.00	2200.00
☐ 1884	3,366,380	2.00	3.30	7.00	22.00	250.00	2200.00
☐ 1884S	564,969	6.00	12.00	22.00	62.00	400.00	
☐ 1885	2,533,427	2.10	4.00	7.00	23.00	250.00	2350.00
☐ 1885S	43,690	90.00	150.00	300.00	510.00	2500.00	
☐ 1886	6,377,570	1.80	4.00	7.00	23.00	275.00	2200.00
☐ 1886S	206,524	9.00	20.00	38.00	86.00	500.00	
☐ 1887	11,283,939	1.20	4.00	6.50	22.00	220.00	2200.00
☐ 1887S	4,454,450	1.20	4.00	6.50	22.00	210.00	
☐ 1888	5,496,487	1.20	4.00	6.50	22.00	220.00	2250.00
☐ 1888S	1,720,000	4.00	7.00	12.00	22.00	260.00	
☐ 1889	7,380,711	2.00	3.50	7.00	22.00	260.00	2300.00
☐ 1889S	972,678	4.50	9.90	20.00	60.00	400.00	
☐ 1890	9,911,541	1.80	4.00	6.50	24.00	270.00	2300.00
☐ 1890S	1,423,076	6.00	11.00	20.00	40.00	400.00	
☐ 1891	15,310,600	1.80	3.50	7.00	24.00	300.00	2200.00
☐ 1891O	4,540,000	2.20	4.00	7.00	25.00	300.00	
☐ 1891S	3,196,116	2.20	4.00	7.00	24.00	300.00	

*With Arrows **No Arrows

DIMES — LIBERTY HEAD OR BARBER, 1892–1916

After many years of using a seated figure of Liberty on the dime, it was decided in 1892 to return to a facial portrait. The designer was Charles E. Barber, resulting in the coin coming to be popularly known among collectors as the "Barber Dime." Liberty wears a wreath and is encircled by the inscription "UNITED STATES OF AMERICA," with the date appearing below the portrait. The reverse is unchanged from that used earlier, the words "ONE DIME" enclosed in a wreath. This coin's weight was set at 2½ grams. Its composition was nine parts silver to one part copper and its diameter 17.9 mm. It was struck at Philadelphia, Denver, San Francisco, and New Orleans. The very rare 1894 San Francisco minting, of which only 24 were produced, is the stellar item of this series. In 1916 the Liberty Head design was replaced by the so-called Mercury Head.

DATE	MINTAGE	ABP	G-4 Good	F-12 Fine	EF-40 Ex. Fine	MS-60 Unc.	PRF-65 Proof
☐ 1892	12,121,245	1.60	2.00	6.00	27.00	170.00	2250.00
☐ 1892O	3,841,700	2.00	4.30	8.50	30.00	200.00	
☐ 1892S	990,710	11.00	24.00	40.00	100.00	250.00	
☐ 1893	3,340,792	1.60	3.00	8.00	33.00	170.00	2250.00
☐ 1893, 3 over 2						EXTREMELY RARE	
☐ 1893O	1,760,000	3.40	11.00	24.00	60.00	230.00	

Mint Mark is Under Wreath on the Reverse

DATE	MINTAGE	ABP	G-4 Good	F-12 Fine	EF-40 Ex. Fine	MS-60 Unc.	PRF-65 Proof
☐ 1893S	2,491,401	4.00	6.00	15.00	40.00	210.00	
☐ 1894	1,330,972	3.00	7.00	20.00	60.00	190.00	2250.00
☐ 1894O	720,000	16.00	30.00	66.00	210.00	900.00	8000.00
☐ 1894S	EXTREMELY RARE, BUSS SALE 1985, MS-60: $46,000.00						
☐ 1895	690,880	27.00	50.00	85.00	200.00	560.00	2300.00
☐ 1895O	440,000	80.00	130.00	210.00	410.00	950.00	
☐ 1895S	1,120,000	6.50	16.00	26.00	60.00	235.00	
☐ 1896	2,000,672	3.00	5.50	12.00	40.00	180.00	2300.00
☐ 1896O	610,000	19.00	40.00	70.00	200.00	560.00	
☐ 1896S	575,056	16.00	32.00	65.00	140.00	390.00	
☐ 1897	10,869,264	1.00	1.50	4.00	25.00	160.00	2300.00
☐ 1897O	666,000	16.00	36.00	70.00	180.00	625.00	
☐ 1897S	1,342,844	2.70	6.00	16.00	60.00	230.00	
☐ 1898	16,320,735	.80	1.40	4.00	20.00	170.00	2250.00
☐ 1898O	2,130,000	1.80	3.30	12.00	50.00	290.00	
☐ 1898S	1,702,507	1.60	3.10	11.00	33.00	200.00	
☐ 1899	19,580,846	1.10	2.00	5.00	21.00	160.00	2350.00
☐ 1899O	2,650,000	1.60	3.00	12.00	50.00	290.00	
☐ 1899S	1,867,493	1.60	3.00	10.00	32.00	200.00	
☐ 1900	17,600,912	.80	1.30	5.00	20.00	170.00	2250.00
☐ 1900O	2,010,000	2.50	5.00	17.00	67.00	315.00	
☐ 1900S	5,168,270	.70	2.00	5.00	26.00	190.00	
☐ 1901	18,860,478	.70	1.30	5.00	21.00	160.00	2200.00
☐ 1901O	5,620,000	.70	1.90	6.00	43.00	280.00	
☐ 1901S	593,022	17.00	34.00	76.00	210.00	700.00	
☐ 1902	21,380,777	.70	1.30	4.00	20.00	180.00	2200.00
☐ 1902O	4,500,000	.70	1.90	5.00	34.00	230.00	
☐ 1902S	2,070,000	1.40	3.25	11.00	55.00	250.00	

DATE	MINTAGE	ABP	G-4 Good	F-12 Fine	EF-40 Ex. Fine	MS-60 Unc.	PRF-65 Proof
□ 1903	19,500,755	.70	1.25	3.10	20.00	190.00	2000.00
□ 1903O	8,180,000	.70	1.90	6.00	26.00	235.00	
□ 1903S	613,300	15.00	26.00	50.00	150.00	570.00	
□ 1904	14,601,027	.70	1.50	5.00	20.00	190.00	2000.00
□ 1904S	800,000	9.00	20.00	36.00	137.00	540.00	
□ 1905	14,552,350	.60	1.35	4.00	20.00	170.00	2000.00
□ 1905O	3,400,000	.60	2.00	8.00	30.00	210.00	
□ 1905S	6,855,199	.60	1.80	6.10	27.00	220.00	
□ 1906	19,958,406	.60	1.30	3.10	20.00	170.00	2000.00
□ 1906D	4,060,000	.60	1.90	6.00	27.00	220.00	
□ 1906O	2,610,000	.60	2.10	9.00	35.00	210.00	
□ 1906S	3,136,640	.60	1.95	7.00	30.00	210.00	
□ 1907	22,220,575	.60	1.15	3.25	20.00	180.00	2000.00
□ 1907D	4,080,000	.60	1.85	5.50	25.00	220.00	
□ 1907O	5,058,000	.60	1.85	5.50	24.00	170.00	
□ 1907S	3,178,470	.60	1.90	5.50	30.00	220.00	
□ 1908	10,600,545	.60	1.30	4.00	20.00	180.00	2000.00
□ 1908D	7,490,000	.60	1.60	4.60	20.00	170.00	
□ 1908O	1,789,000	.95	2.15	10.00	38.00	260.00	
□ 1908S	3,220,000	.60	1.90	5.00	26.00	210.00	
□ 1909	10,240,650	.60	1.40	4.00	21.00	180.00	2100.00
□ 1909D	954,000	1.35	3.00	12.00	50.00	300.00	
□ 1909O	2,287,000	.60	2.30	6.00	30.00	190.00	
□ 1909S	2,000,000	1.50	3.00	12.00	55.00	275.00	
□ 1910	11,520,551	.60	1.50	4.00	21.00	180.00	2100.00
□ 1910D	3,490,000	.60	1.65	5.00	31.00	280.00	
□ 1910S	1,240,000	.60	1.90	7.00	29.00	210.00	
□ 1911	18,870,543	.60	1.25	3.10	19.00	180.00	2100.00
□ 1911D	11,209,000	.60	1.25	4.00	20.00	190.00	
□ 1911S	3,530,000	.60	1.80	5.10	26.00	195.00	
□ 1912	19,350,700	.60	1.25	2.75	20.00	180.00	2100.00
□ 1912D	11,760,000	.60	1.25	2.75	20.00	180.00	
□ 1912S	3,420,000	.60	1.60	4.00	21.00	195.00	
□ 1913	19,760,000	.60	1.15	2.50	19.00	180.00	2100.00
□ 1913S	510,000	3.00	6.00	25.00	130.00	300.00	
□ 1914	17,360,655	.60	1.25	2.70	20.00	160.00	2700.00
□ 1914D	11,908,000	.60	1.25	2.90	20.00	210.00	
□ 1914S	2,100,000	.60	1.80	5.00	26.00	190.00	
□ 1915	5,620,450	.60	1.50	3.25	19.00	210.00	2700.00
□ 1915S	960,000	.60	1.95	7.00	30.00	220.00	
□ 1916	18,490,000	.60	1.20.	3.00	19.00	180.00	
□ 1916S	5,820,000	.60	1.20	3.50	19.00	170.00	

DIMES — MERCURY DIMES, 1916–1945

The Mercury Dime is misnamed. The likeness on its obverse is not that of Mercury (a male god) but Liberty, the same mythological figure who had graced dimes since their introduction in 1796. Confusion resulted from the attachment of small wings to Liberty's headdress, which, to students of Greek and Roman folklore, could only represent Mercury, the "quick messenger," whom the gods equipped with wings to better execute his duties. To give Liberty wings was a bit of poetic license; the intended meaning was "liberty of thought," but so vague was this concept that its purpose remained unserved. On the reverse was an object that caused only slightly less confusion, a vertical column of some kind that only the most astute observers could identify. This was designed as a bundle of fasces or sticks with axe protruding. In Roman times, an imperial or senatorial procession was often accompanied by "fasces bearers" who carried these bundles of wood sticks throughout the streets. Their meaning was supposedly symbolic but they likewise served a practical function: when dusk fell they could be lighted to illuminate the path. Designer of the Mercury Dime was Adolph Weinman. Its specifications are the same as those of the Barber Dime. The mint mark appears on the reverse, between the words "ONE" and "DIME," to the left of the fasces. The Mercury Dime was composed of 90% silver and 10% copper. It has a weight of 2½ grams and diameter of 17.9 mm.

Mint Mark is on Reverse at Bottom to Left of Branches

Enlargement Showing 1942 Over 41 Dime

DATE	MINTAGE	ABP	G-4 Good	F-12 Fine	VF-20 V. Fine	EF-40 Ex. Fine	MS-60 Unc.
□ 1916	22,180,000	.65	2.10	4.00	5.00	9.00	35.00
□ 1916D	264,000	170.00	375.00	800.00	1000.00	1500.00	2500.00
□ 1916S	10,450,000	.75	3.10	6.10	8.00	15.00	47.00
□ 1917	55,230,000	.60	1.30	2.50	6.00	7.00	28.00
□ 1917D	9,402,000	1.00	3.00	8.00	15.00	33.00	110.00
□ 1917S	27,330,000	.60	1.65	3.75	6.00	10.00	50.00
□ 1918	26,680,000	.60	1.65	4.00	11.00	22.00	59.00
□ 1918D	22,674,800	.60	1.65	3.75	9.00	20.00	80.00
□ 1918S	19,300,000	.60	1.65	3.20	7.00	13.50	46.00
□ 1919	35,740,000	.60	1.50	3.10	5.00	8.50	39.00
□ 1919D	9,939,000	.60	2.00	6.00	15.00	31.00	130.00
□ 1919S	8,850,000	.60	2.10	6.00	14.00	29.00	141.00
□ 1920	59,030,000	.60	1.20	2.40	5.00	9.00	31.00
□ 1920D	19,171,000	.60	1.40	3.50	7.00	15.00	77.00
□ 1920S	13,820,000	.60	1.40	3.50	7.00	13.00	70.00
□ 1921	1,230,000	12.00	21.00	64.00	127.00	330.00	760.00
□ 1921D	1,080,000	14.00	31.00	86.00	165.00	340.00	760.00
□ 1923*	50,130,000	.60	1.40	3.00	4.25	7.00	23.00
□ 1923S	6,440,000	.60	1.75	5.00	7.10	20.00	76.00

*All dimes with 23D date are counterfeit

DATE	MINTAGE	ABP	G-4 Good	F-12 Fine	VF-20 V. Fine	EF-40 Ex. Fine	MS-60 Unc.
☐ 1924	24,010,000	.60	1.80	3.00	4.60	8.00	52.00
☐ 1924D	6,810,000	.60	1.80	3.90	7.10	19.00	93.00
☐ 1924S	7,120,000	.50	1.50	4.10	7.00	16.00	90.00
☐ 1925	25,610,000	.50	1.35	3.00	5.00	7.00	42.00
☐ 1925D	5,117,000	2.10	4.50	9.00	22.00	62.00	260.00
☐ 1925S	5,850,000	.65	1.40	5.00	7.50	18.00	120.00
☐ 1926	32,160,000	.60	1.20	2.50	4.10	6.00	25.00
☐ 1926D	6,828,000	.60	1.30	4.00	5.00	14.00	70.00
☐ 1926S	1,520,000	3.00	8.00	16.00	30.00	80.00	380.00
☐ 1927	28,080,000	.60	1.20	3.00	4.00	7.00	25.00
☐ 1927D	4,812,000	1.50	2.75	6.00	14.00	31.00	175.00

DATE	MINTAGE	ABP	G-4 Good	F-12 Fine	VF-20 V. Fine	EF-40 Ex. Fine	MS-60 Unc.	PRF-65 Proof
☐ 1927S	4,770,000	.60	1.80	3.00	6.10	13.00	80.00	
☐ 1928	19,480,000	.60	1.20	2.30	4.00	5.50	21.00	
☐ 1928D	4,161,000	.60	3.00	7.00	15.00	31.00	130.00	
☐ 1928S	7,400,000	.60	1.60	2.75	5.00	12.00	65.00	
☐ 1929	25,970,000	.60	1.20	2.00	3.90	5.00	16.00	
☐ 1929D	5,034,000	.60	2.00	4.00	7.50	10.00	45.00	
☐ 1929S	4,730,000	.60	1.60	2.60	5.00	7.00	50.00	
☐ 1930	6,770,000	.60	1.40	2.60	5.00	7.00	25.00	
☐ 1930S	1,843,000	.60	3.10	5.00	7.00	12.00	70.00	
☐ 1931	3,150,000	.60	2.00	3.10	5.00	9.00	40.00	
☐ 1931D	1,260,000	3.00	6.00	11.00	17.00	29.00	98.00	
☐ 1931S	1,800,000	.65	3.00	5.10	7.00	12.00	70.00	
☐ 1934	24,080,000	.60	.75	1.30	2.00	3.10	19.00	
☐ 1934D	6,772,000	.60	1.55	1.60	2.75	5.00	34.00	
☐ 1935	58,830,000	.60	.75	1.30	2.00	3.00	14.00	
☐ 1935D	10,477,000	.60	.75	1.25	2.25	6.75	43.00	
☐ 1935S	15,840,000	.60	.75	1.25	2.25	5.00	21.00	
☐ 1936	87,504,130	.60	.75	1.30	2.25	2.90	16.00	1200.00
☐ 1936D	16,132,000	.60	.75	1.30	2.25	4.50	30.00	
☐ 1936S	9,210,000	.60	.75	1.30	2.25	2.75	21.00	
☐ 1937	56,865,756	.60	.75	1.25	2.25	2.75	13.00	835.00
☐ 1937D	14,146,000	.60	.75	1.25	2.25	3.30	26.00	
☐ 1937S	9,740,000	.60	.75	1.25	2.25	3.10	18.00	
☐ 1938	22,198,728	.60	.75	1.10	1.75	3.00	13.00	790.00
☐ 1938D	5,537,000	.60	.75	1.10	1.75	3.00	24.00	
☐ 1938S	8,090,000	.60	.75	1.10	1.75	3.10	16.00	
☐ 1939	67,749,321	.60	.75	1.10	1.75	2.75	12.00	745.00
☐ 1939D	24,394,000	.60	.75	1.10	1.75	2.75	13.00	
☐ 1939S	10,540,000	.60	.75	1.10	1.75	2.75	28.00	
☐ 1940	65,361,827	.60	.75	1.10	1.30	2.00	8.00	600.00
☐ 1940D	21,560,000	.60	.75	1.10	1.30	2.00	16.00	
☐ 1940S	21,560,000	.60	.75	1.10	1.30	2.00	9.00	
☐ 1941	175,106,557	.60	.75	1.10	1.30	2.00	9.00	500.00
☐ 1941D	45,634,000	.60	.75	1.10	1.30	2.00	13.00	
☐ 1941S	43,090,000	.60	.75	1.10	1.30	2.00	13.00	
☐ 1942	205,432,329	.60	.75	1.10	1.30	2.00	10.00	600.00

DATE	MINTAGE	ABP	G-4 Good	F-12 Fine	VF-20 V. Fine	EF-40 Ex. Fine	MS-60 Unc.	PRF-65 Proof
□ 1942 Part of Above over 41		85.00	158.00	215.00	240.00	310.00	1000.00	
□ 1942/41-D ..		92.00	180.00	240.00	260.00	380.00	1210.00	
□ 1942D	60,740,000	.55	.80	1.10	1.30	2.20	11.00	
□ 1942S	49,300,000	.55	.80	1.10	1.30	2.20	16.00	
□ 1943	191,710,000	.55	.80	1.10	1.30	2.20	12.00	
□ 1943D	71,949,000	.55	.80	1.10	1.30	2.20	10.00	
□ 1943S	60,400,000	.55	.80	1.10	1.30	2.20	11.00	
□ 1944	231,410,000	.55	.80	1.10	1.30	2.20	9.00	
□ 1944D	62,224,000	.55	.80	1.10	1.30	2.20	9.50	
□ 1944S	49,490,000	.55	.80	1.10	1.30	2.20	9.50	
□ 1945	159,130,000	.55	.80	1.10	1.30	2.20	9.50	
□ 1945D	40,245,000	.55	.80	1.10	1.30	2.20	9.50	
□ 1945S	41,920,000	.55	.80	1.10	1.30	2.20	14.00	
□ 1945S (Micros)		1.00	1.50	2.00	2.00	3.00	19.00	

DIMES — ROOSEVELT, 1946 TO DATE

The Roosevelt Dime series is significant for the change made to clad composition in 1965. Upon the death of President Roosevelt in 1945 there was considerable public sentiment to install his likeness on a coin. The penny, nickel, and quarter were not seriously considered, as they already carried portraits of former Presidents. As no dollars were being struck, this left only the dime and half dollar, which both carried representations of Liberty, as suitable choices. The dime was selected, probably because of the much wider distribution of this coin. The designer was John Sinnock. Roosevelt is shown in profile facing left, with the word "LIBERTY" and the inscription "IN GOD WE TRUST." The bundle of fasces was retained as the central element for the reverse type, which was redrawn. Originally the mint mark appeared on the reverse, as it had on the Mercury Dime, then was switched to the obverse on clad pieces. The weight was 2½ grams. The composition of this coin, originally 90% silver and 10% copper, was altered in 1965 to three parts copper/one part nickel outer covering with an interior of pure copper, yielding a weight of 2.27 grams. The diameter remained 17.9 mm. In the first year of striking the clad dime, more pieces were manufactured than had ever been turned out of a ten-cent piece in the Mint's history, more than 1.6 billion. A serious shortage of dimes had resulted from spectators hoarding the silver coins and this abundant new supply was intended to replace those lost from circulation. A mintage figure of more than two billion was achieved in 1967, or more than $1 worth of dimes for every U.S. citizen.

Mint Mark is on Reverse of Left, Bottom of Torch.

From 1968 Mint Mark at Base of Neck.

DATE	MINTAGE	ABP	MS-60 Unc.	PRF-65 Proof
□ 1946	255,250,000	.50	1.80	
□ 1946D	61,043,500	.50	3.75	
□ 1946S	27,900,000	.50	4.10	
□ 1947	121,500,000	.50	4.00	
□ 1947D	46,835,000	.50	6.00	
□ 1947S	34,840,000	.50	6.00	
□ 1948	74,950,000	.50	7.50	
□ 1948D	52,841,000	.50	7.00	
□ 1948S	35,520,000	.50	8.10	
□ 1949	30,940,000	.50	21.00	
□ 1949D	26,034,000	.50	10.00	
□ 1949S	13,510,000	.50	50.00	
□ 1950	50,181,500	.50	4.75	65.00
□ 1950D	46,803,000	.50	4.75	
□ 1950S	20,440,000	.50	17.00	
□ 1951	103,937,602	.50	2.50	
□ 1951D	52,191,800	.50	2.25	55.00
□ 1951S	31,630,000	.50	12.00	
□ 1952	99,122,073	.50	2.70	34.00
□ 1952D	122,100,000	.50	2.50	
□ 1952S	44,419,500	.50	5.00	
□ 1953	53,618,920	.50	2.10	24.00
□ 1953D	156,433,000	.50	2.10	
□ 1953S	39,180,000	.50	1.50	
□ 1954	114,243,503	.50	1.50	8.00
□ 1954D	106,397,000	.50	1.50	
□ 1954S	22,860,000	.50	1.50	
□ 1955	12,828,381	.50	1.60	8.00
□ 1955D	13,959,000	.50	2.00	
□ 1955S	18,510,000	.50	2.00	
□ 1956	109,309,384	.50	1.80	3.00
□ 1956D	108,015,100	.50	1.80	
□ 1957	161,407,952	.50	1.80	2.70
□ 1957D	113,354,330	.50	1.80	
□ 1958	32,785,652	.50	1.80	2.90
□ 1958D	136,564,600	.50	1.60	
□ 1959	86,929,291	.50	1.60	2.15
□ 1959D	164,919,790	.50	1.60	

DATE	MINTAGE	ABP	MS-60 Unc.	PRF-65 Proof
☐ 1960	72,081,602	.50	1.45	1.90
☐ 1960D	200,160,400	.50	1.45	
☐ 1961	96,756,244	.50	1.45	1.90
☐ 1961D	209,146,550	.50	1.45	
☐ 1962	75,668,019	.50	1.45	1.90
☐ 1962D	334,948,380	.50	1.45	
☐ 1963	126,725,645	.50	1.45	1.90
☐ 1963D	421,476,530	.50	1.45	
☐ 1964	933,310,762	.50	1.45	1.90
☐ 1964D	1,357,517,180	.50	1.45	
☐ 1965 Clad Coinage Begins	1,652,140,570		.40	
☐ 1966	1,382,734,540		.40	
☐ 1967	2,244,077,300		.40	
☐ 1968	424,470,400		.40	
☐ 1968D	480,748,280		.40	
☐ 1968S Proof Only	3,041,508			.85
☐ 1969	145,790,000		.40	
☐ 1969D	563,323,870		.40	
☐ 1969S Proof Only	2,934,631			.85
☐ 1970	345,570,000		.40	
☐ 1970D	754,942,000		.40	
☐ 1970S Proof Only	2,632,810			.85
☐ 1971	162,690,000		.40	
☐ 1971D	377,914,240		.40	
☐ 1971S Proof Only	3,244,138			.85
☐ 1972	431,540,000		.40	
☐ 1972D	330,290,000		.40	
☐ 1972S Proof Only	3,267,667		.40	.85
☐ 1973	315,670,000		.35	
☐ 1973D	455,032,426		.35	
☐ 1973 Proof Only	2,769,624			.85
☐ 1974	470,248,000		.35	
☐ 1974D	571,083,000		.35	
☐ 1974S Proof Only	2,617,350			.80
☐ 1975	585,673,900		.35	
☐ 1975D	313,705,250		.35	
☐ 1975S Proof Only	2,909,369			.80
☐ 1976	568,760,000		.35	
☐ 1976D	695,222,774		.35	
☐ 1976S Proof Only	4,149,945			.80
☐ 1977	796,900,480		.35	
☐ 1977D	376,610,420		.35	
☐ 1977S Proof Only	3,250,895			.80
☐ 1978	663,908,000		.35	
☐ 1978D	282,847,540		.35	
☐ 1978S Proof Only	3,127,781			.80
☐ 1979	315,440,007		.35	
☐ 1979D	390,921,285		.35	

DATE	MINTAGE	ABP	MS-60 Unc.	PRF-65 Proof
□ 1979S Proof (I)	3,677,200			1.70
□ 1979 Proof (II)				2.00
□ 1980P	735,170,079		.35	
□ 1980D	719,354,382		.35	
□ 1980S Proof Only	3,547,130			.90
□ 1981P	676,000,000		.35	
□ 1981D	712,285,000		.35	
□ 1981S Proof (I)	4,063,080			.90
□ 1982P*	519,474,983		.35	
□ 1982D	541,721,064		.35	
□ 1982S Proof (I)	3,857,000			.90
□ 1983P	646,124,004		.30	
□ 1983D	730,130,000		.30	
□ 1983S Proof	3,228,650			1.40
□ 1984P	856,670,936		.30	
□ 1984D	704,731,827		.30	
□ 1984S Proof	3,000,210			1.75
□ 1985P	712,182,461		.30	
□ 1985D	589,641,000		.30	
□ 1985S Proof	3,121,410			1.75
□ 1986P	670,210,401		.22	
□ 1986D	476,420,831		.22	
□ 1986S Proof	3,110,120			1.50
□ 1987P	774,621,460		.22	
□ 1987D	676,294,210		.22	
□ 1987S				1.10
□ 1988P			.21	
□ 1988D			.21	
□ 1988S Proof				1.10
□ 1989P			.20	
□ 1989D			.20	
□ 1989S Proof				1.10

Note: In 1983, dimes dated 1982 and bearing no mint mark began to be discovered. At first they caused a furor as it was believed they might be great rarities (largely because a whole year had passed before any were noticed). During the first month or two of trading, prices on MS-65 specimens reached as high as $600. At that time it was thought that as few as 300 or 400 might exist. Later it was revealed that a midwest source owned 4,000, and the existing total is now estimated at around 8,000. At the time of going to press, prices on MS-65 specimens were in the $170.00 range. Beware of removed mint mark.

TWENTY-CENT PIECES — LIBERTY SEATED, 1875–1878

The 20¢ piece has the unenviable distinction of being the shortest-lived of any U.S. coin. Authorized by a Congressional Act on March 3, 1875, it was placed into production immediately thereafter, with manufacture divided up between the Philadelphia, San Francisco, and Carson City mints (mints on the east and west coasts being employed in hopes the coin would distribute more evenly in circulation than if released exclusively from a single source of production). Designed by William

Barber, it pictured a figure of the goddess Liberty seated on the obverse, framed by stars, with an eagle on the reverse. It was composed of nine-tenths silver and one-tenth copper, with a weight of five grams and a diameter of 22 mm. Despite high hopes, the 20¢ piece never achieved popularity, the chief reason for its rejection being the physical similarity to the quarter. Production was greatly cut back in 1876 and discontinued two years thereafter. All told, less than a million and a half were struck.

DATE	MINTAGE	ABP	G-4 Good	F-12 Fine	EF-40 Ex. Fine	MS-60 Unc.	PRF-65 Proof
☐ 1875	39,700	30.00	52.00	90.00	275.00	1100.00	5800.00
☐ 1875CC	133,290	30.00	52.00	90.00	260.00	1100.00	
☐ 1875S	1,155,000	17.00	36.00	62.00	210.00	1100.00	
☐ 1876	15,900	60.00	100.00	140.00	360.00	1200.00	5800.00
☐ 1876CC	10,000				(EXTREMELY RARE)		75000.00
☐ 1877	510	4000.00		PROOFS ONLY			10000.00
☐ 1878	600	4000.00		PROOFS ONLY			10500.00

QUARTERS

EARLY QUARTERS, 1796 – 1866

It became evident from a very early period that the quarter or 25¢ piece would be the most significant division of the dollar in everyday commerce. However, the effect was not fully felt until the 19th century. Striking of the quarter dollar was authorized in 1792 along with other denominations, upon establishment of a national currency. No actual specimens came into circulation until 1796. The earliest design was the Draped Bust portrait of Liberty, common to other silver coinage, with eagle reverse and the legend "UNITED STATES OF AMERICA." Stars appeared alongside Liberty on the obverse and her name was affixed above the portrait, with the date below. The designer was Robert Scot. The original quarter dollar was composed of .8924 silver alloyed with .1076 copper, or roughly a nine-to-one ratio. Its weight was 6.74 grams and the diameter generally 27½ mm. with slight variations to be observed according to the flatness of the planchet. Only 6,146 pieces were struck in 1796 as a trial issue (influenced in some measure by a shortage of silver) and this date has become scarce, even in less than the best condition. Production of quarters was not resumed until 1804, when discontinuation of dollar coins increased the need for them. The Draped Bust type was retained but the reverse changed to the Heraldic or Shield Eagle design. John Reich designed a new quarter dollar in 1815, identical in composition to its predecessors but having a slightly smaller diameter, 27 mm. This was the Capped Bust type, with naturalistic shielded eagle on the reverse. Production got off to a small start but was rapidly expanded. No further change occurred until 1831 when the coin was brought down in size to 24.3 mm. but was made a bit thicker, retaining the old weight of 6.74 grams. The designer of this new 25¢ piece was William Kneass (pronounced Niece) and all striking was done at Philadelphia. There is a "small letters" and "large letters" variety of this design, with little influence on value. The portrait is a somewhat streamlined Capped Liberty who appears more noble than previously. This design was of short duration, replaced by the Seated Liberty type in

1838. On the reverse was the shield eagle, beneath which appeared the words "QUAR. DOL." (The use of abbreviations did not fully meet the approval of artistic-minded persons.) There was an accompanying change in specifications as well. The silver content was slightly raised, to an even 90%; the copper dropped to an even 10%; and the weight went down to 6.68 grams. The diameter was the same as previously. Designer of this coin was Christian Gobrecht. It was struck at both Philadelphia and New Orleans. A further reduction in weight was made to 6.22 grams in 1853; arrows were placed at the dates to remind users of the coin that it contained less silver than previously. Compositionally it was unaltered, with nine parts silver to one of copper. On the reverse, sunrays sprang from behind the eagle, an area of the design which previously had been blank. This addition was made for the same reason as the arrows.

QUARTERS — DRAPED BUST, 1796–1807

1796–1807

1796 Small Eagle

1804–1807 Large Eagle

DATE	MINTAGE	ABP	G-4 Good	F-12 Fine	VF-20 V. Fine	MS-60 Unc.
□ 1796	5,894	1500.00	3200.00	5400.00	9000.00	24000.00
□ 1804	6,738	400.00	900.00	2400.00	4400.00	21000.00
□ 1805	121,394	150.00	275.00	600.00	1100.00	6800.00
□ 1806	206,124	150.00	275.00	600.00	1100.00	6800.00
□ 1806 over 5		150.00	275.00	600.00	1100.00	6800.00
□ 1807	220,643	150.00	275.00	600.00	1100.00	6800.00

QUARTERS — LIBERTY CAP, 1815–1838

1815–1838

1815–1828 Motto Over Eagle

1831–1838 Without Motto

DATE	MINTAGE	ABP	G-4 Good	F-12 Fine	VF-20 V. Fine	MS-60 Unc.	PRF-65 Proof
□ 1815	89,235	22.00	48.00	110.00	260.00	2950.00	
□ 1818	361,174	22.00	48.00	110.00	260.00	2700.00	
□ 1818 over 15	361,174	22.00	48.00	100.00	270.00	2350.00	
□ 1819*	144,000	22.00	44.00	90.00	250.00	2300.00	
□ 1820**	127,440	22.00	44.00	90.00	250.00	2100.00	

*1819—Small 9, 1819—Large 9. **1820—Small o, 1820—Large O; Same Price

DATE	MINTAGE	ABP	G-4 Good	F-12 Fine	VF-20 V. Fine	MS-60 Unc.	PRF-65 Proof
□ 1821	216,850	22.00	44.00	90.00	250.00	2100.00	
□ 1822	64,084	24.00	60.00	90.00	250.00	2200.00	
□ 1822 (25 over $.50)		120.00	210.00	475.00	910.00	3800.00	
□ 1823 over 22†	17,821	2000.00	4200.00	10000.00	13800.00		29000.00
□ 1824		22.00	40.00	99.00	250.00	2800.00	
□ 1825 over dates	168,000	22.00	40.00	120.00	260.00	2800.00	
□ 1827 (original)††	4,000	FEW PIECES KNOWN—RARE $200,000.00					
□ 1828	102,000	22.00	40.00	97.00	240.00	2200.00	
□ 1828 (25 over $.50)	102,000	40.00	110.00	210.00	400.00	3500.00	
REDUCED SIZE—NO MOTTO ON REVERSE							
□ 1831***	398,000	12.00	29.00	52.00	110.00	1100.00	
□ 1832	320,000	12.00	29.00	52.00	110.00	1100.00	
□ 1833	156,000	12.00	29.00	52.00	160.00	1500.00	
□ 1834	286,000	12.00	29.00	52.00	90.00	1100.00	
□ 1835	1,952,000	12.00	29.00	52.00	90.00	1100.00	
□ 1836	472,000	12.00	29.00	52.00	90.00	1100.00	
□ 1837	252,000	12.00	29.00	52.00	90.00	1100.00	
□ 1838	832,000	12.00	29.00	52.00	90.00	1100.00	

***1831—Small Letters, 1831—Large Letters: Same Price. †Stack's Auction, March 1977
††Stack's Auction, 1977: also 1827 restrike proof 12,500.00

QUARTERS — LIBERTY SEATED, 1838–1865 NO MOTTO ABOVE EAGLE

1838–1865

1853 With Rays

Mint Mark is Below Eagle on Reverse 1838–1852 1854–1865 Without Rays

DATE	MINTAGE	ABP	G-4 Good	F-12 Fine	EF-40 Ex. Fine	MS-60 Unc.	PRF-65 Proof
□ 1838*	832,000	6.50	11.00	27.00	165.00	1700.00	
□ 1839*	491,146	6.50	11.00	27.00	165.00	1700.00	
□ 1840**	188,127	15.00	28.00	82.00	270.00	1700.00	
□ 1840O*		6.50	11.00	29.00	160.00	1950.00	
□ 1840O**	425,200	17.00	27.00	60.00	200.00	1600.00	
□ 1841	120,000	33.00	50.00	110.00	300.00	1100.00	
□ 1841O	452,000	13.00	18.00	40.00	200.00	1000.00	
□ 1842	88,000	53.00	90.00	180.00	300.00	2600.00	
□ 1842O Small Date		190.00	300.00	800.00	2300.00		
□ 1842O Large Date	769,000	7.00	14.00	90.00	200.00		
□ 1843	645,000	6.00	12.00	19.00	90.00	800.00	
□ 1843O Small "O"	968,000	8.00	16.00	36.00	210.00		
□ 1843O Large "O"		8.00	16.00	36.00	205.00		

*No Drapery **Drapery

DATE	MINTAGE	ABP	G-4 Good	F-12 Fine	EF-40 Ex. Fine	MS-60 Unc.	PRF-65 Proof
☐ 1844	421,000	5.00	10.00	20.00	90.00	1000.00	
☐ 1844O	740,000	5.00	10.00	20.00	109.00	1100.00	
☐ 1845	922,000	5.00	10.00	19.00	80.00	680.00	
☐ 1846	510,000	5.00	10.00	19.00	80.00	680.00	
☐ 1847	734,000	5.00	10.00	19.00	80.00	680.00	
☐ 1847O	368,000	12.00	24.00	60.00	200.00	985.00	
☐ 1848	146,000	15.00	26.00	140.00	250.00	985.00	
☐ 1849	340,000	8.00	16.00	60.00	150.00	900.00	
☐ 1849O	16,000	200.00	400.00	900.00	3200.00		
☐ 1850	190,800	12.00	18.00	70.00	170.00	950.00	
☐ 1850O	412,000	11.00	24.00	60.00	170.00	1000.00	
☐ 1851	160,000	13.00	18.00	90.00	180.00	900.00	
☐ 1851O	88,000	90.00	200.00	410.00	1250.00		
☐ 1852	177,060	16.00	25.00	70.00	200.00	1100.00	
☐ 1852O	96,000	90.00	215.00	475.00	1250.00	2200.00	
☐ 1853***	15,210,020	6.00	9.00	19.00	120.00	2200.00	
☐ 1853/4		28.00	68.00	150.00	650.00	2300.00	
☐ 1853††	44,200	80.00	200.00	350.00	825.00	3400.00	
☐ 1853O***	1,332,000	7.00	12.00	28.00	160.00	2600.00	
☐ 1854†	12,380,000	4.50	9.00	20.00	90.00	800.00	
☐ 1854O† Large "O"	1,484,000	7.00	17.00	30.00	110.00	2000.00	
☐ 1854O Huge "O"		60.00	90.00	275.00	700.00		
☐ 1855†	2,857,000	5.00	9.00	20.00	100.00	900.00	6500.00
☐ 1855O†	176,000	20.00	46.00	92.00	350.00	1800.00	
☐ 1855S†	396,400	14.00	40.00	85.00	310.00	1700.00	
☐ 1856	7,264,000	5.00	9.00	21.00	55.00	650.00	5500.00
☐ 1856O	968,000	6.00	12.00	40.00	110.00	850.00	
☐ 1856S		19.00	30.00	60.00	300.00		
☐ 1856S over S	286,000	38.00	60.00	300.00	900.00		
☐ 1857	9,644,000	5.00	9.00	19.00	70.00	460.00	5500.00
☐ 1857O	1,180,000	7.50	11.00	21.00	70.00	900.00	
☐ 1857S	82,000	22.00	47.00	110.00	540.00		
☐ 1858	7,368,000	5.00	9.00	19.00	58.00	470.00	4150.00
☐ 1858O	520,000	7.00	11.00	30.00	90.00	900.00	
☐ 1858S	121,000	15.00	36.00	90.00	400.00		
☐ 1859	1,344,000	4.00	8.00	19.00	55.00	700.00	3800.00
☐ 1859O	260,000	10.00	16.00	45.00	110.00	800.00	
☐ 1859S	80,000	30.00	58.00	160.00	460.00		
☐ 1860	805,400	5.00	9.00	19.00	56.00	600.00	3700.00
☐ 1860O	388,000	6.00	11.00	40.00	90.00	1050.00	
☐ 1860S	56,000	30.00	76.00	250.00	700.00		
☐ 1861	4,854,000	5.00	9.00	19.00	52.00	460.00	3600.00
☐ 1861S	96,000	17.00	30.00	110.00	310.00	2100.00	
☐ 1862	932,550	5.00	9.00	16.00	70.00	600.00	3500.00
☐ 1862S	67,000	26.00	46.00	120.00	350.00		
☐ 1863	192,060	12.00	18.00	40.00	90.00	740.00	3600.00
☐ 1864	94,070	30.00	40.00	90.00	210.00	940.00	3600.00
☐ 1864S	20,000	70.00	120.00	300.00	1100.00		

DATE	MINTAGE	ABP	G-4 Good	F-12 Fine	EF-40 Ex. Fine	MS-60 Unc.	PRF-65 Proof
□ 1865	59,300	28.00	40.00	90.00	220.00	1000.00	3500.00
□ 1865S	41,000	30.00	45.00	115.00	400.00	2300.00	

1866 Only One Known—Hydeman Sale 1961 Proof—$24,500.00
***W Arrows and Rays †W/Arrows and no Rays ††Over 52, No Arrows

QUARTERS — LIBERTY SEATED, 1866–1891 MOTTO ABOVE EAGLE

In 1866 the words "IN GOD WE TRUST" were added to the reverse, on a banner between the eagle and the inscription "UNITED STATES OF AMERICA." When the weight was changed slightly to 6.25 grams in 1873 the arrows were returned but no further use was made of sunrays on the reverse. The arrows were removed in 1875.

DATE	MINTAGE	ABP	G-4 Good	F-12 Fine	EF-40 Ex. Fine	MS-60 Unc.	PRF-65 Proof
□ 1866	17,525	90.00	200.00	380.00	700.00	1450.00	3100.00
□ 1866S	28,000	80.00	160.00	300.00	800.00	1850.00	
□ 1867	20,625	70.00	90.00	200.00	500.00	1300.00	3200.00
□ 1867S	48,000	38.00	60.00	180.00	300.00	2800.00	
□ 1868	30,000	50.00	75.00	160.00	350.00	1100.00	3100.00
□ 1868S	96,000	21.00	38.00	86.00	210.00	2000.00	
□ 1869	16,600	70.00	180.00	280.00	700.00	1200.00	3000.00
□ 1869S	76,000	60.00	130.00	230.00	300.00		
□ 1870	87,400	21.00	30.00	90.00	160.00	1000.00	3000.00
□ 1870CC	8,340	500.00	1000.00	2600.00	4600.00		
□ 1871	171,232	8.00	16.00	40.00	90.00	800.00	3000.00
□ 1871CC	10,890	260.00	500.00	1150.00	3100.00	2700.00	
□ 1871S	30,900	90.00	135.00	450.00	860.00	2800.00	
□ 1872	182,950	8.50	12.00	32.00	90.00	600.00	3000.00
□ 1872CC	9,100	130.00	230.00	500.00	2100.00		
□ 1872S	103,000	100.00	160.00	400.00	700.00	4500.00	
□ 1873*	1,263,700	7.00	12.00	26.00	160.00	1800.00	4000.00
□ 1873** Open "3"	220,600	16.00	30.00	60.00	220.00	600.00	
□ 1873** Closed "3"		35.00	70.00	130.00	400.00		3000.00
□ 1873CC*	12,462	230.00	510.00	920.00	2510.00		
□ 1873CC**	4,000			RARE—Auction 1980—$200,000.00			
□ 1873S*	160,000	17.00	30.00	70.00	260.00	1250.00	
□ 1874*	471,900	8.00	12.00	34.00	180.00	1100.00	4200.00
□ 1874S**	392,000	11.00	21.00	41.00	220.00	1200.00	

DATE	MINTAGE	ABP	G-4 Good	F-12 Fine	EF-40 Ex. Fine	MS-60 Unc.	PRF-65 Proof
□ 1875	4,293,500	5.00	8.00	17.00	60.00	500.00	2500.00
□ 1875CC	140,000	20.00	40.00	110.00	400.00	1420.00	
Arrows Removed Starting 1875							
□ 1875S	680,000	9.50	12.00	35.00	90.00	590.00	
□ 1876	17,817,150	4.00	8.00	18.00	60.00	400.00	2500.00
□ 1876CC	4,944,000	4.00	9.00	21.00	90.00	490.00	
□ 1876S	8,596,000	4.00	8.00	19.00	70.00	450.00	
*W/Arrows **No Arrows							
□ 1877	10,911,710	4.00	8.00	19.00	72.00	400.00	2500.00
□ 1877CC	4,192,000	5.00	10.00	25.00	90.00	600.00	
□ 1877S	8,996,000	5.00	10.00	28.00	60.00	400.00	
□ 1878	2,260,000	4.70	8.00	21.00	80.00	400.00	2600.00
□ 1878CC	996,000	14.00	21.00	70.00	200.00	500.00	
□ 1878S	140,000	19.50	48.00	115.00	250.00	1700.00	
□ 1879	14,700	63.00	90.00	160.00	300.00	660.00	2700.00
□ 1880	14,955	63.00	90.00	160.00	280.00	645.00	2700.00
□ 1881	12,975	60.00	80.00	160.00	280.00	645.00	2700.00
□ 1882	16,300	60.00	80.00	160.00	280.00	650.00	2700.00
□ 1883	15,439	60.00	80.00	160.00	280.00	650.00	2700.00
□ 1884	8,875	70.00	90.00	180.00	300.00	700.00	2700.00
□ 1885	14,530	50.00	80.00	130.00	300.00	660.00	2700.00
□ 1886	5,886	90.00	110.00	260.00	400.00	780.00	2700.00
□ 1887	10,710	60.00	90.00	120.00	300.00	680.00	2700.00
□ 1888	10,833	60.00	90.00	120.00	300.00	680.00	2700.00
□ 1888S	1,216,000	6.00	11.00	21.00	60.00	400.00	
□ 1889	12,711	60.00	90.00	125.00	200.00	650.00	2500.00
□ 1890	80,590	30.00	50.00	70.00	200.00	650.00	2500.00
□ 1891	3,920,600	5.00	9.00	17.00	60.00	500.00	2500.00
□ 1891O	68,000	50.00	120.00	210.00	500.00		
□ 1891S	2,216,000	6.00	9.00	21.00	70.00	450.00	

QUARTERS — BARBER OR LIBERTY HEAD, 1892–1916

The Barber or Liberty Head Quarter with its classical portrait bust was introduced in 1892 after a design by Charles E. Barber. Liberty faces right and wears a cap and laurel wreath. On the reverse is a shield eagle holding arrows and branch, with (at long last) the words "QUARTER DOLLAR" spelled out without abbreviation. This was without doubt the handsomest design in the quarter dollar series and has become extremely popular with collectors. It was struck at Philadelphia, Denver, New Orleans, and San Francisco. The Barber quarter has a composition of 90% silver and 10% copper with a weight of 6¼ grams and a diameter of 24.3 mm.

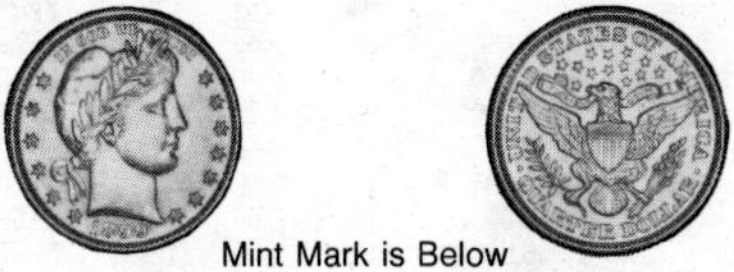

Mint Mark is Below
the Eagle on Reverse

DATE	MINTAGE	ABP	G-4 Good	F-12 Fine	EF-40 Ex. Fine	MS-60 Unc.	PRF-65 Proof
☐ 1892	8,237,245	2.00	3.50	10.00	52.00	300.00	2500.00
☐ 1892O	2,640,000	2.00	6.50	14.00	60.00	360.00	
☐ 1892S	964,079	5.00	16.00	30.00	82.00	430.00	
☐ 1893	5,444,815	2.10	3.00	11.00	51.00	300.00	2600.00
☐ 1893O	3,396,000	2.10	5.00	14.00	60.00	360.00	
☐ 1893S	1,454,535	2.10	6.00	18.00	70.00	400.00	
☐ 1894	3,432,972	2.10	4.00	11.00	51.00	300.00	2900.00
☐ 1894O	2,852,000	2.10	4.00	12.00	60.00	360.00	
☐ 1894S	2,648,821	2.10	4.00	12.00	65.00	360.00	
☐ 1895	4,440,880	2.10	3.75	11.00	56.00	300.00	2900.00
☐ 1895O	2,816,000	2.10	5.00	15.00	60.00	420.00	
☐ 1895S	1,764,681	2.10	6.00	18.00	75.00	400.00	
☐ 1896	3,874,762	2.10	5.00	11.00	62.00	310.00	2900.00
☐ 1896O	1,484,000	2.10	5.00	16.00	90.00	820.00	
☐ 1896S	188,039	110.00	230.00	500.00	1500.00	3600.00	
☐ 1897	8,140,731	2.10	3.00	9.00	50.00	300.00	2900.00
☐ 1897O	1,414,800	3.20	6.10	21.00	100.00	840.00	
☐ 1897S	542,229	4.10	9.50	26.00	95.00	400.00	
☐ 1898	11,100,735	2.00	3.00	10.00	52.00	300.00	2800.00
☐ 1898O	1,868,000	2.10	4.00	14.00	68.00	500.00	
☐ 1898S	1,020,592	2.10	4.00	12.00	55.00	300.00	
☐ 1899	12,624,846	1.60	3.00	11.00	49.00	320.00	2900.00
☐ 1899O	2,644,000	2.10	5.10	14.00	66.00	410.00	
☐ 1899S	708,000	3.00	7.00	28.00	70.00	410.00	
☐ 1900	10,016,912	2.10	3.50	9.10	52.00	300.00	2900.00
☐ 1900O	3,416,000	2.10	5.00	14.00	60.00	400.00	
☐ 1900S	1,858,585	2.10	4.00	12.00	60.00	370.00	
☐ 1901	8,892,813	2.10	2.75	10.00	51.00	400.00	2700.00
☐ 1901O	1,612,000	6.00	9.00	40.00	120.00	780.00	
☐ 1901S	72,664	375.00	910.00	1800.00	3700.00	11000.00	
☐ 1902	12,197,744	1.70	3.00	9.00	51.00	290.00	2900.00
☐ 1902O	4,748,000	2.10	3.20	11.00	60.00	420.00	
☐ 1902S	1,524,612	2.10	6.00	16.00	80.00	420.00	
☐ 1903	9,670,064	1.70	2.75	10.00	52.00	290.00	2900.00
☐ 1903O	3,500,000	2.10	3.10	11.00	70.00	350.00	
☐ 1903S	1,036,000	2.10	6.00	16.00	90.00	420.00	
☐ 1904	9,588,813	2.10	3.00	9.00	51.00	300.00	2800.00
☐ 1904O	2,456,000	2.10	4.00	16.00	90.00	720.00	

DATE	MINTAGE	ABP	G-4 Good	F-12 Fine	EF-40 Ex. Fine	MS-60 Unc.	PRF-65 Proof
☐ 1905	4,968,250	1.70	2.90	9.00	51.00	260.00	2900.00
☐ 1905O	1,230,000	2.10	4.90	16.00	70.00	370.00	
☐ 1905S	1,884,000	2.10	4.50	11.00	58.00	330.00	
☐ 1906	3,656,435	1.70	3.00	9.00	55.00	270.00	2900.00
☐ 1906D	3,280,000	2.10	3.00	11.00	60.00	350.00	
☐ 1906O	2,056,000	2.10	4.00	12.00	66.00	310.00	
☐ 1907	7,192,575	1.70	2.60	9.00	50.00	290.00	2900.00
☐ 1907D	2,484,000	2.10	4.00	12.00	55.00	310.00	
☐ 1907O	4,560,000	2.15	3.00	10.00	50.00	310.00	
☐ 1907S	1,360,000	2.15	3.50	12.00	61.00	410.00	
☐ 1908	4,232,545	1.70	2.90	9.00	56.00	290.00	2800.00
☐ 1908D	5,788,000	2.10	2.80	9.00	52.00	310.00	
☐ 1908O	6,244,000	1.70	2.70	9.00	50.00	310.00	
☐ 1908S	784,000	2.15	5.00	16.00	60.00	440.00	
☐ 1909	9,268,650	1.50	2.80	8.00	53.00	370.00	2800.00
☐ 1909D	5,114,000	1.50	2.80	8.00	53.00	315.00	
☐ 1909O	712,000	3.00	7.00	31.00	140.00	650.00	
☐ 1909S	1,348,000	1.50	3.10	9.00	52.00	360.00	
☐ 1910	2,244,551	1.50	2.80	9.00	52.00	300.00	2800.00
☐ 1910D	1,500,000	1.50	3.00	9.20	55.00	330.00	
☐ 1911	3,270,543	1.50	2.80	9.00	50.00	350.00	2800.00
☐ 1911D	933,600	1.50	3.00	16.00	85.00	340.00	
☐ 1911S	988,000	1.50	3.00	16.00	74.00	370.00	
☐ 1912	4,400,700	1.50	2.80	8.00	50.00	290.00	2800.00
☐ 1912S	708,000	1.50	2.80	12.00	71.00	350.00	
☐ 1913	484,613	3.00	7.00	38.00	360.00	900.00	3000.00
☐ 1913D	1,450,800	1.50	3.00	12.00	60.00	340.00	
☐ 1913S	40,000	161.00	310.00	620.00	1700.00	3600.00	
☐ 1914	6,244,610	1.50	2.80	7.50	42.00	315.00	3300.00
☐ 1914D	3,046,000	1.50	2.80	8.10	40.00	680.00	
☐ 1914S	264,000	6.00	14.00	38.00	230.00	1250.00	
☐ 1915	3,480,450	1.50	2.50	8.00	48.00	315.00	3200.00
☐ 1915D	3,694,000	1.50	2.50	8.50	48.00	315.00	
☐ 1915S	704,000	1.50	2.50	12.00	72.00	315.00	
☐ 1916	1,788,000	1.50	2.50	8.00	51.00	300.00	
☐ 1916D	6,540,000	1.50	2.50	7.10	51.00	300.00	

QUARTERS — STANDING LIBERTY, 1916–1930

The Standing Liberty Quarter was introduced in 1916 during World War I and its theme was intended to reflect the nation's sentiments at that time. The goddess is portrayed in full length holding a shield with which she, presumably, fends off the defilers of liberty. An eagle in flight is pictured on the obverse, with the words "UNITED STATES OF AMERICA" and "E PLURIBUS UNUM." The designer was Herman A. MacNeil. Specifications are the same as for the Barber Quarter. This design carried so much fine detailing that very moderate handling resulted in obvious wear, making uncirculated specimens more valuable, proportionately, than in the case of most other coins. The chief point of vulnerability was the date, so small in size, and positioned in such a way as to receive heavy wear, that many specimens lost their date after only a few years of circulation. The government wished to correct this fault without totally redesigning the obverse and in 1925 hit upon the plan of showing the date in incuse—that is, pressed into the coin rather than raised from its surface. While this did not totally prevent wear it helped keep the dates readable for a longer time. A series of minor alterations was made in 1917, the second year of issue, including a dressing up of Liberty to satisfy public criticism that the figure was displaying a scandalous amount of flesh. Three stars were added beneath the eagle on the reverse.

Note: Prices listed for MS-60 specimens of Standing Liberty Quarters are for ordinary strikes. Exceptional strikes with full head of Liberty in detail are scarcer and sell for higher sums. This is not a question of *wear,* but simply the quality of the coin as originally struck.

1916–30
Mint Mark is to
Left of Date of Obverse

1916–1917
Type I
No Stars Under Eagle

1917–1930
Type II
3 Stars Under Eagle

DATE	MINTAGE	ABP	G-4 Good	VG-8 V. Good	F-12 Fine	EF-40 Ex. Fine	MS-60 Unc.
☐ 1916	52,000	550.00	970.00	1250.00	1450.00	2100.00	3600.00
☐ 1917	8,792,000	4.00	8.00	10.00	14.00	56.00	320.00
☐ 1917D	1,509,200	6.00	13.00	16.00	23.00	90.00	400.00
☐ 1917S	1,952,000	5.00	12.00	15.00	20.00	80.00	500.00
STARS UNDER EAGLE							
☐ 1917	13,880,000	5.00	11.00	15.00	19.00	42.00	200.00
☐ 1917D	6,224,400	8.00	19.00	26.00	40.00	90.00	210.00
☐ 1917S	5,552,000	8.00	19.00	25.00	34.00	82.00	300.00
☐ 1918	12,240,000	6.00	12.50	16.00	20.00	54.00	300.00
☐ 1918D	7,380,000	8.00	20.00	25.00	35.00	94.00	225.00
☐ 1918S	11,072,000	5.00	12.00	16.00	20.00	51.00	180.00
☐ 1918S over 7		500.00	1000.00	1200.00	1700.00	3800.00	9000.00
☐ 1919	11,324,000	12.00	26.00	31.00	38.00	70.00	175.00
☐ 1919D	1,944,000	24.00	50.00	65.00	92.00	230.00	480.00
☐ 1919S	1,836,000	21.00	46.00	60.00	90.00	210.00	400.00
☐ 1920	27,860,000	5.50	12.00	16.00	18.00	37.00	180.00
☐ 1920D	3,586,400	10.00	24.00	34.00	48.00	110.00	240.00
☐ 1920S	6,380,000	7.00	12.00	19.00	23.00	49.00	180.00
☐ 1921	1,916,000	24.00	52.00	75.00	120.00	240.00	400.00
☐ 1923	9,716,000	5.00	10.00	16.00	19.00	43.00	180.00
☐ 1923S*	1,360,000	42.00	92.00	142.00	200.00	380.00	580.00
☐ 1924	10,920,000	4.50	10.00	14.00	17.00	41.00	175.00

DATE	MINTAGE	ABP	G-4 Good	VG-8 V. Good	F-12 Fine	EF-40 Ex. Fine	MS-60 Unc.
☐ 1924D	3,112,000	10.00	23.00	30.00	40.00	86.00	175.00
☐ 1924S	2,860,000	6.00	14.00	17.00	25.00	46.00	175.00
☐ 1925	12,280,000	1.45	3.00	3.70	7.10	26.00	170.00
☐ 1926	11,316,000	1.45	3.00	3.70	7.10	26.00	170.00
☐ 1926D	1,716,000	1.45	6.00	7.40	13.00	50.00	170.00
☐ 1926S	2,700,000	1.45	3.00	5.00	11.50	60.00	195.00
☐ 1927	11,912,000	1.45	2.90	3.70	7.00	26.00	160.00
☐ 1927D	976,400	3.50	7.90	10.00	17.00	70.00	250.00
☐ 1927S	396,000	4.00	11.50	20.00	50.00	650.00	1525.00
☐ 1928	6,336,000	1.50	2.70	3.70	7.10	26.00	160.00
☐ 1928D	1,627,600	2.20	4.70	7.50	11.00	36.00	160.00
☐ 1928S	2,644,000	1.50	3.00	5.50	9.00	31.00	146.00
☐ 1929	11,140,000	1.50	3.00	3.70	7.00	26.00	135.00
☐ 1929D	1,358,000	1.70	4.50	7.00	12.00	31.00	135.00
☐ 1929S	1,764,000	1.50	3.00	6.00	9.50	30.00	130.00
☐ 1930	5,632,000	1.50	3.00	4.00	8.00	26.00	130.00
☐ 1930S	1,556,000	1.50	3.00	4.00	8.00	29.00	140.00

*Check for altered date

QUARTERS — WASHINGTON, 1932 TO DATE

1932-1967 Mint Mark is on Reverse Below Eagle

1968 on — Mint Mark to Right of Hair Ribbon

DATE	MINTAGE	ABP	G-4 Good	F-12 Fine	EF-40 Ex. Fine	MS-60 Unc.	PRF-65 Proof
☐ 1932	5,404,000	1.50	3.00	4.00	11.00	38.00	
☐ 1932D	436,800	21.00	40.00	60.00	170.00	550.00	
☐ 1932S	408,000	18.00	36.00	45.00	90.00	240.00	
☐ 1934	31,912,052	1.50	4.00	4.00	10.00	50.00	
☐ 1934 Double Die			32.00	50.00	160.00	280.00	
☐ 1934D	3,527,200	1.50	3.00	10.00	18.00	87.00	
☐ 1935	32,484,000	1.50		3.60	8.50	32.00	
☐ 1935D	5,780,000	1.50		6.00	19.00	75.00	
☐ 1935S	5,550,000	1.50		6.00	12.00	80.00	
☐ 1936	41,303,837	1.50		4.00	8.00	50.00	2800.00
☐ 1936D	5,374,000	1.50		8.00	31.00	200.00	
☐ 1936S	3,828,000	1.50		6.00	13.00	74.00	
☐ 1937	19,701,542	1.50		5.00	8.00	46.00	500.00
☐ 1937D	7,189,600	1.50		550.00	11.00	45.00	
☐ 1937S	1,652,000	1.50		10.00	22.00	100.00	
☐ 1938	9,480,045	1.50		5.00	16.00	68.00	400.00

DATE	MINTAGE	ABP	G-4 Good	F-12 Fine	EF-40 Ex. Fine	MS-60 Unc.	PRF-65 Proof
☐ 1938S	2,832,000	1.25		6.00	13.00	55.00	
☐ 1939	33,548,795	1.25		4.00	6.00	20.00	250.00
☐ 1939D	7,092,000	1.25		4.00	9.50	29.00	
☐ 1939S	2,628,000	1.25		6.00	12.00	50.00	
☐ 1940	35,715,246	1.25		4.00	6.10	20.00	250.00
☐ 1940D	2,797,600	1.25		7.00	13.00	60.00	
☐ 1940S	8,244,000	1.25		3.50	6.50	25.00	
☐ 1941	79,047,287	1.25		2.00	4.50	14.00	250.00
☐ 1941D	16,714,800	1.25		3.00	5.50	26.00	
☐ 1941S	16,080,000	1.25		3.00	5.00	25.00	
☐ 1942	102,117,123	1.25		3.00	4.00	12.00	200.00
☐ 1942D	17,487,200	1.25		3.00	4.50	20.00	
☐ 1942S	19,384,000	1.25		3.00	6.00	80.00	
☐ 1943	99,700,000	1.25		3.00	3.70	12.00	
☐ 1943D	16,095,600	1.25		3.00	4.00	21.00	
☐ 1943S	21,700,000	1.25		3.00	5.00	60.00	
☐ 1943S Double Die					EXTREMELY RARE		
☐ 1944	104,956,000	1.25		2.00	4.00	9.00	
☐ 1944D	14,600,000	1.25		2.00	4.00	15.00	
☐ 1944S	12,560,000	1.25		2.00	4.00	16.00	
☐ 1945	74,372,000	1.25		2.00	4.00	8.00	
☐ 1945D	12,341,600	1.25		2.00	4.00	12.00	
☐ 1945S	17,004,001	1.25		2.00	4.00	10.00	
☐ 1946	53,436,000	1.25		2.00	4.00	5.00	
☐ 1946D	9,072,800	1.25		2.00	4.00	8.00	
☐ 1946S	4,204,000	1.25		2.00	4.00	10.00	
☐ 1947	22,556,000	1.25		2.00	4.00	10.00	
☐ 1947D	15,338,400	1.25		2.00	4.00	10.00	
☐ 1947S	5,532,000	1.25		2.00	4.00	10.00	
☐ 1948	35,196,000	1.25		2.00	4.00	8.00	
☐ 1948D	16,768,800	1.25		2.00	4.00	9.00	
☐ 1948S	15,960,000	1.25		2.00	4.00	9.00	
☐ 1949	9,312,000	1.25		2.00	4.00	25.00	
☐ 1949D	10,068,400	1.25		2.00	4.00	12.00	
☐ 1950	24,971,512	1.25		2.00	4.00	7.00	170.00
☐ 1950D	21,075,600	1.25		2.00	4.00	7.00	
☐ 1950S	10,284,004	1.25		2.00	4.00	11.00	
☐ 1951	43,505,602	1.25		2.00	4.00	6.00	80.00
☐ 1951D	35,354,800	1.25		2.00	4.00	7.00	
☐ 1951S	8,948,000	1.25		2.00	4.00	15.00	
☐ 1952	38,862,073	1.25		2.00	4.00	7.00	50.00
☐ 1952D	49,795,200	1.25		2.00	4.00	7.00	
☐ 1952S	13,707,800	1.25		2.00	4.00	8.00	
☐ 1953	18,664,920	1.25		2.00	4.00	7.00	30.00
☐ 1953D	56,112,400	1.25		2.00	4.00	6.00	
☐ 1953S	14,016,000	1.25		2.00	4.00	7.00	
☐ 1954	54,654,503	1.25		2.00	4.00	5.00	16.00
☐ 1954D	46,305,500	1.25		2.00	4.00	5.00	

DATE	MINTAGE	ABP	G-4 Good	F-12 Fine	EF-40 Ex. Fine	MS-60 Unc.	PRF-65 Proof
□ 1954S	11,834,722	1.00		2.00	4.00	5.00	
□ 1955	18,558,381	1.00		2.00	4.00	5.00	12.00
□ 1955D	3,182,400	1.00		2.00	4.00	6.00	
□ 1956	44,813,384	1.00		2.00	4.00	5.00	6.00
□ 1956D	32,334,500	1.00		2.00	4.00	5.00	
□ 1957	47,779,952	1.00		2.00	4.00	5.00	6.00
□ 1957D	77,924,160	1.00		2.00	4.00	5.00	
□ 1958	7,235,652	1.00		2.00	4.00	5.00	7.50
□ 1958D	78,124,900	1.00		2.00	3.00	5.00	
□ 1959	25,533,291	1.00		2.00	3.00	4.00	5.00
□ 1959D	62,054,232	1.00		2.00	3.00	4.00	
□ 1960	30,855,602	1.00		2.00	3.00	4.00	5.00
□ 1960D	63,000,324	1.00		2.00	3.00	4.00	
□ 1961	40,064,244	1.00		2.00	3.00	4.00	5.00
□ 1961D	83,656,928	1.00		2.00	3.00	4.00	
□ 1962	39,374,019	1.00		2.00	3.00	4.00	5.00
□ 1962D	127,554,756	1.00		2.00	3.00	4.00	
□ 1963	77,391,645	1.00		2.00	3.00	4.00	5.00
□ 1963D	135,288,184	1.00		2.00	3.00	4.00	
□ 1964	564,341,347	1.00		2.00	3.00	4.00	5.00
□ 1964D	704,135,528	1.00		2.00	3.00	4.00	
□ 1965	1,819,717,540					.50	
□ 1966	821,101,500					.50	
□ 1967	1,524,031,840					.50	
□ 1968	220,731,500					.50	
□ 1968D	101,534,000					.50	
□ 1968S PROOF ONLY	3,041,500						.90
□ 1969	176,212,000					.40	.90
□ 1969D	114,372,000					.40	.90
□ 1969S PROOF ONLY	2,934,631						.90
□ 1970	136,420,000					.40	
□ 1970D	417,341,364					.40	
□ 1970S PROOF ONLY	2,632,810						.90
□ 1971	109,284,000					.40	
□ 1971D	258,634,428					.40	
□ 1971S PROOF ONLY	3,224,138						.90
□ 1972	215,048,000					.40	
□ 1972D	311,067,732					.40	
□ 1972S	3,267,667						.90
□ 1973	346,924,000					.40	
□ 1973D	232,977,400					.40	
□ 1973S PROOF ONLY	2,796,624						.90
□ 1974	801,456,000					.40	
□ 1974D	363,160,300					.40	
□ 1974S PROOF ONLY	2,612,568						.90
□ 1976 Copper-Nickel Clad	809,780,016					.40	
□ 1976D Copper-Nickel Clad	860,108,836					.40	

DATE	MINTAGE	ABP	G-4 Good	F-12 Fine	EF-40 Ex. Fine	MS-60 Unc.	PRF-65 Proof
☐ 1976S Copper-Nickel Clad Proof	7,055,099						1.25
☐ 1976S Silver Clad						2.40	
☐ 1976 Silver Clad Proof							4.00
☐ 1977	468,556,900					.43	
☐ 1977D	256,524,078					.43	
☐ 1977S PROOF ONLY	2,909,269						.90
☐ 1978	521,452,000					.43	
☐ 1978D	287,373,152					.43	
☐ 1978S PROOF ONLY	3,127,781						1.20
☐ 1979	515,709,000					.43	
☐ 1979D	489,790,020					.43	
☐ 1979S PROOF (I)	3,677,200						1.00
☐ 1979S PROOF (II)							2.00
☐ 1980P	635,832,101					.43	
☐ 1980D	518,327,444					.43	
☐ 1980S PROOF	3,547,130						1.00
☐ 1981P	602,000,000					.38	
☐ 1981D	575,841,732					.38	
☐ 1981S PROOF (I)	4,064,789						1.00
☐ 1981S PROOF (II)							1.50
☐ 1982P	500,000,000					.38	
☐ 1982D	490,665,000						
☐ 1982S PROOF (I)	3,856,941						
☐ 1983P	674,000,000					.38	
☐ 1983D	617,800,000					.38	
☐ 1983S PROOF	3,378,125					.38	
☐ 1984P	675,961,834					.38	
☐ 1984D	550,000,000					.38	
☐ 1984S PROOF	3,164,210						1.20
☐ 1985P	780,201,621					.38	
☐ 1985D	520,888,004					.38	
☐ 1985S PROOF	3,260,112						1.00
☐ 1986P	541,643,221					.35	
☐ 1986D	502,121,106					.35	
☐ 1986S PROOF	3,006,420						1.00
☐ 1987P	572,286,210					.35	
☐ 1987D	642,873,921					.35	
☐ 1987S							1.00
☐ 1988P						.35	
☐ 1988D						.35	
☐ 1988S PROOF							.90
☐ 1989P							.30
☐ 1989D							.30
☐ 1989S PROOF							.80

HALF DOLLARS

EARLY HALF DOLLARS, 1794–1838

As originally conceived, the Half Dollar was to contain precisely—to the grain—half as much metal as the Dollar and was to be struck from metal of the same composition, .8924 silver alloyed with .1076 copper. It weighed 13.48 grams and was slightly larger in diameter than it subsequently became: 32½ mm. Its designer was Robert Scot and its obverse featured a profile portrait of Liberty facing right, the so-called Flowing Hair likeness used on other coins as well, backed by an eagle. Along the edge was stamped its value, as no statement of value appeared within the design, "FIFTY CENTS OR HALF A DOLLAR," the words set apart with small ornamental flourishes. Apparently the initial issue in 1794 was struck from just a single set of dies, but in the following year several dies were employed resulting in a number of minor varieties. This was the final appearance of the Flowing Hair 50¢ piece. The design was replaced in 1796 by the Draped Bust version, to which the shielded eagle reverse was added in 1801. Because of the trading significance of this coin an effort was made to place as many half dollars as possible into circulation during its early years. It was temporarily discontinued in 1804 as a result of speculation along with the silver dollar; but unlike the latter, which did not return for more than 30 years, production of the half dollar was resumed in 1805. In that year more than 200,000 were struck, followed by a striking exceeding 800,000 in 1806. The Capped Bust design was installed on the dollar in 1807, as it was on other coins. Its designer was a German-American named John Reich. The Capped Bust is sometimes referred to as "Turban Head." The word "LIBERTY" appears on the cap or turban band. On either side of the portrait is a series of stars, with the date positioned beneath it. The reverse has a modified shielded eagle (or heraldic eagle) with the motto "E PLURIBUS UNUM" on a banner and "50 C." This coin weighs 13.48 grams and has the same metallic composition as its predecessors. Varieties of the Capped Bust half dollar are so numerous, despite being in use for only about 30 years, that a large collection can be built around this coin. And it is, indeed, an ideal target for specialization, as nearly all specimens fall within the low-to-moderate range of price. Christian Gobrecht redesigned the coin in 1836, retaining the same types but modifying them somewhat. The composition was changed to provide a slightly higher content of silver and a slightly lower content of copper, the ratio now being nine parts silver, one part copper. Its weight was 13.36 grams and the diameter reduced to 30 mm. This design was replaced by Liberty Seated in 1839, which remained in use for more than 50 years.

HALF DOLLARS — FLOWING HAIR, 1794–1795

DATE	MINTAGE	ABP	G-4 Good	F-12 Fine	VF-20 V. Fine
□1794	5,300	650.00	1200.00	2500.00	4100.00
□1795		230.00	450.00	800.00	1350.00
□1795 Recut Date	317,844	280.00	500.00	800.00	1400.00
□1795*		430.00	800.00	1850.00	3000.00

*3 leaves under each wing

HALF DOLLARS — DRAPED BUST, SMALL EAGLE 1796–1797

DATE	MINTAGE	ABP	G-4 Good	F-12 Fine	VF-20 V. Fine
□1796 (15 stars)		5000.00	9800.00	16800.00	25000.00
□1796 (16 stars)		5000.00	9800.00	16800.00	25000.00
□1797	3,918	5000.00	9800.00	16800.00	25000.00

HALF DOLLARS — DRAPED BUST, 1801–1807 EAGLE ON REVERSE

DATE	MINTAGE	ABP	G-4 Good	VF-20 Fine	EF-40 V. Fine	MS-60 Unc.
☐1801	30,289	85.00	180.00	760.00	1200.00	8900.00
☐1802	29,890	90.00	160.00	600.00	1000.00	8100.00
☐1803 Large 3............		45.00	100.00	400.00	600.00	7100.00
☐1803 Small 3............	188,234	70.00	130.00	500.00	800.00	6600.00
☐1805		40.00	90.00	300.00	600.00	6400.00
☐1805 over 4.............	211,722	80.00	170.00	550.00	900.00	7100.00
☐1806		40.00	80.00	250.00	600.00	5500.00
☐1806 over 5.............	839,576	40.00	82.00	250.00	600.00	5500.00
☐1806 inverted (over 6)....		40.00	82.00	380.00	800.00	5000.00
☐1806 Knobbed 6, Lg. Stars		40.00	82.00	280.00	500.00	5000.00
☐1806 Knobbed 6, Stem not through Claw					EXTREMELY RARE	
☐1807	301,076	38.00	75.00	300.00	650.00	5000.00

HALF DOLLARS —TURBAN HEAD OR "CAPPED BUST," 1807–1836

Motto Above Eagle, Lettered Edge, Large Size

DATE	MINTAGE	ABP	G-4 Good	F-12 Fine	EF-40 V. Fine	MS-60 Unc.
☐1807 Sm./Stars		33.00	60.00	160.00	400.00	1500.00
☐1807 Lg./Stars	750,500	44.00	80.00	200.00	400.00	1500.00
☐1807 .50 over .20........		24.00	40.00	81.00	275.00	1300.00
☐1808	1,368,600	22.00	35.00	65.00	125.00	1100.00
☐1808 over 7.............		22.00	35.00	65.00	140.00	1000.00
☐1809	1,405,810	22.00	35.00	50.00	120.00	980.00
☐1810	1,276,276	22.00	35.00	50.00	120.00	980.00
☐1811	1,203,644	22.00	35.00	50.00	120.00	980.00

DATE	MINTAGE	ABP	G-4 Good	F-12 Fine	VF-20 V. Fine	MS-60 Unc.
☐1812	1,628,059	21.00	35.00	60.00	82.00	900.00
☐1812 over 11		23.00	42.00	70.00	110.00	900.00
☐1813	1,241,903	19.00	40.00	55.00	70.00	900.00
☐1814	1,039,075	19.00	40.00	55.00	70.00	1000.00
☐1814 over 13		24.00	38.00	76.00	105.00	1000.00
☐1815 over 12	47,150	340.00	670.00	1400.00	1800.00	5000.00
☐1817	1,215,567	20.00	30.00	40.00	70.00	1000.00
☐1817 over 13		40.00	60.00	210.00	310.00	1600.00
☐1818	1,960,322	17.00	30.00	40.00	70.00	1100.00
☐1818 over 17		17.00	30.00	42.00	72.00	1100.00
☐1819	2,208,000	17.00	30.00	40.00	65.00	1100.00
☐1819 over 18 Large 9		17.00	30.00	40.00	70.00	1050.00
☐1820	751,122	17.00	30.00	70.00	67.00	1100.00
☐1820 over 19		17.00	28.00	60.00	120.00	1000.00
☐1821	1,305,797	17.00	28.00	60.00	110.00	1000.00
☐1822	1,559,573	17.00	28.00	60.00	110.00	1000.00
☐1822 over 21		27.00	40.00	110.00	190.00	1000.00
☐1823	1,694,200	17.00	29.00	40.00	90.00	1000.00
☐1823 Ugly 3		18.00	29.00	40.00	120.00	1000.00
☐1824	3,504,954	16.00	29.00	41.00	70.00	1000.00
☐1824 over 21 & others ...		20.00	29.00	41.00	110.00	1000.00
☐1825	2,943,166	12.00	29.00	40.00	50.00	900.00
☐1826	4,044,180	12.00	29.00	40.00	50.00	900.00
☐1827*	5,493,400	12.00	29.00	40.00	50.00	900.00
☐1827 over 6 curled 2		12.00	29.00	60.00	86.00	900.00
☐1828	3,075,200	12.00	29.00	39.00	50.00	900.00
☐1829	3,712,156	12.00	29.00	39.00	50.00	900.00
☐1829 over 27		12.00	29.00	39.00	50.00	900.00
☐1830**	4,764,800	12.00	29.00	39.00	50.00	900.00
☐1831	5,873,660	12.00	29.00	39.00	50.00	900.00
☐1832***	4,797,000	12.00	29.00	39.00	50.00	900.00
☐1833	5,206,000	12.00	29.00	39.00	50.00	900.00
☐1834	6,412,000	12.00	29.00	39.00	50.00	900.00
☐1835	5,352,006	12.00	29.00	39.00	50.00	900.00
☐1836 ALL KINDS	6,546,200	12.00	29.00	39.00	50.00	900.00

*Square—Based 2. **Small O, in Date, Large O, in Date: Same Price
***Small Letters, Large Letters: Same Price

HALF DOLLARS—TURBAN HEAD OR "CAPPED BUST," 1836–1839
NO MOTTO ABOVE EAGLE, REEDED EDGE, REDUCED SIZE

1836–
1837
"50 cents"

1838–
1839
"HALF DOL."

DATE	MINTAGE	ABP	G-4 Good	F-12 Fine	EF-40 Ex. Fine	MS-60 Unc.	PRF-65 Proof
☐1836*		21.00	40.00	75.00	180.00	1000.00	
☐1836 Reeded Edge		210.00	400.00	700.00	1900.00	4000.00	
☐1837	3,629,820	18.00	36.00	50.00	220.00	1000.00	
☐1838	3,546,000	18.00	36.00	50.00	220.00	1000.00	
☐1838O	Approx. 20	EXTREMELY RARE-Stack's Sale 1975: $50,000.00					
☐1839	3,334,500	18.00	36.00	50.00	220.00	1000.00	
☐1839O	179,000	50.00	105.00	220.00	660.00	3600.00	

*Lettered edge 50 over 00

HALF DOLLAR—LIBERTY SEATED, 1839–1866
WITHOUT MOTTO ABOVE EAGLE

The Seated Liberty half dollar was based on the now-celebrated design of Christian Gobrecht. The goddess sits looking left, holding a shield on which the word "LIBERTY" appears and, in the other hand, a staff. The upper portion of the design is encircled by stars. On the reverse is a shield or heraldic eagle holding arrows and branch. Beneath the eagle are the words "HALF DOL." After some minor modification of both the obverse and reverse design, the numerals used for giving the date were enlarged in 1846 and a major change occurred in 1853. Because the California gold strikes of 1849 had brought great quantities of this metal into circulation, public confidence in silver was gradually eroding. To inspire greater acceptance of silver coinage their composition was revised to include a higher proportion of bullion. The new ratio—not just for half dollars but silver pieces in general—was nine parts silver to one of copper, the one part of copper being necessary to give this durable metal a fair stability. The weight was 12.44 grams and the diameter 30.6 mm. A pair of arrows was placed on the obverse beside the date, as warning that the metal content had changed, and—in the event this was overlooked—sunrays were installed on the reverse, radiating from behind the eagle. These were discontinued in 1856. Beginning in 1866, and probably not coincidentally because the Civil War had recently ended, the motto "IN GOD WE TRUST" was incorporated into the reverse design, on a banner that flies above the eagle's head. When the weight was increased 6/10 of a gram in 1873, resort was again made to arrows at the date, but no sunrays adorned the reverse. The arrows were removed in 1875. The Seated Liberty Half Dollar continued to be struck until 1891, though throughout the 1880s its output was very limited.

Mint Mark is Below Eagle on Reverse

DATE	MINTAGE	ABP	G-4 Good	F-12 Fine	EF-40 Ex. Fine	MS-60 Unc.	PRF-65 Proof
☐1839 no drapery from elbow		20.00	40.00	70.00	600.00	5000.00	
☐1839	3,334,560	9.50	20.00	31.00	99.00	950.00	
☐1840	1,435,008	8.50	20.00	31.00	105.00	950.00	
☐1840O	855,100	10.00	19.00	32.00	120.00	900.00	
☐1841	310,000	20.00	40.00	80.00	250.00	1000.00	
☐1841O	401,000	12.00	24.00	39.00	120.00	1000.00	
☐1842	2,012,764	11.00	19.00	30.00	90.00	1000.00	
☐1842O small date		350.00	740.00	1700.00	4000.00		
☐1842O large date		8.50	18.00	31.00	110.00	1000.00	
☐1843	3,844,000	8.50	18.00	31.00	90.00	900.00	
☐1843O	2,268,000	8.50	18.00	31.00	82.00	900.00	
☐1844	1,766,000	8.50	18.00	30.00	80.00	900.00	
☐1844O	2,005,000	8.50	18.00	30.00	80.00	1100.00	
☐1845	589,000	14.00	22.00	50.00	170.00	800.00	
☐1845O	2,094,000	8.50	16.00	25.00	90.00	800.00	
☐1846	2,110,000	8.50	20.00	25.00	75.00	800.00	
☐1846 over horizontal 6		40.00	70.00	120.00	300.00	1300.00	
☐1846O	2,304,000	8.00	16.00	24.00	70.00	900.00	
☐1847	1,156,000	8.00	16.00	29.00	65.00	900.00	
☐1847 over 6		600.00	1100.00	2800.00	4600.00		
☐1847O	2,584,000	7.00	18.00	28.00	75.00	900.00	
☐1848	580,000	12.00	29.00	50.00	165.00	900.00	
☐1848O	3,180,000	7.00	18.00	29.00	70.00	900.00	
☐1849	1,252,000	7.00	18.00	29.00	72.00	1100.00	
☐1849O	2,310,000	7.00	18.00	29.00	65.00	900.00	
☐1850	227,000	40.00	60.00	110.00	360.00	1400.00	
☐1850O	2,456,000	7.00	17.00	29.00	76.00	1000.00	

DATE	MINTAGE	ABP	G-4 Good	F-12 Fine	EF-40 Ex. Fine	MS-60 Unc.	PRF-65 Proof
□1851	200,750	63.00	80.00	180.00	350.00	1300.00	
□1851O	402,000	16.00	20.00	40.00	100.00	700.00	
□1852	77,130	80.00	110.00	210.00	520.00	1700.00	
□1852O	144,000	29.00	50.00	100.00	300.00	1200.00	
□1853**	3,532,708	10.00	16.00	39.00	250.00	2000.00	
□1853O**	1,328,000	11.00	18.00	44.00	300.00	2400.00	
□1853O NO ARROWS —EXTREMELY RARE				AUCTION SALE 1979: $40000.00			
□1854***	2,982,000	7.00	15.00	30.00	100.00	1000.00	
□1854O***	5,240,000	7.00	15.00	30.00	110.00	1100.00	
□1855***	759,500	12.00	21.00	35.00	150.00	1400.00	10500.00
□1855O	3,688,000	7.00	15.00	30.00	100.00	1300.00	
□1855S***	129,950	160.00	310.00	600.00	2400.00	5400.00	
□1856	938,000	7.00	15.00	28.00	66.00	600.00	6000.00
□1856O	2,658,000	7.00	15.00	28.00	66.00	600.00	
□1856S	211,000	22.00	30.00	60.00	220.00	1500.00	
□1857	1,988,000	7.00	13.00	28.00	66.00	900.00	6500.00
□1857O	818,000	7.50	15.00	30.00	95.00	900.00	
□1857S	158,000	22.00	40.00	50.00	280.00	1000.00	
□1858	4,226,000	7.00	14.00	26.00	66.00	900.00	5000.00
□1858O	7,294,000	7.00	14.00	26.00	65.00	800.00	
□1858S	476,000	9.50	20.00	31.00	130.00	900.00	
□1859	748,000	8.50	16.00	28.00	80.00	800.00	4100.00
□1859O	2,834,000	8.50	15.00	27.00	65.00	900.00	
□1859S	566,000	9.00	20.00	30.00	130.00	900.00	
□1860	303,700	9.00	20.00	30.00	100.00	900.00	3500.00
□1860O	1,290,000	8.00	15.00	28.00	70.00	800.00	
□1860S	472,000	12.00	21.00	39.00	110.00	800.00	
□1861	2,888,400	7.50	15.00	27.00	60.00	800.00	3500.00
□1861O	330,000	7.50	15.00	27.00	60.00	900.00	
□1861S	939,500	8.00	16.00	27.00	70.00	900.00	
□1862	252,350	12.00	24.00	40.00	120.00	800.00	3500.00
□1862S	1,352,000	8.00	16.00	26.00	65.00	800.00	
□1863	503,660	9.00	21.00	29.00	80.00	800.00	3500.00
□1863S	916,000	8.00	15.00	26.00	60.00	800.00	
□1864	379,570	8.75	21.00	30.00	130.00	800.00	3500.00
□1864S	658,000	7.00	18.00	31.00	80.00	800.00	
□1865	511,900	7.00	18.00	30.00	95.00	700.00	3500.00
□1865S	675,000	7.00	18.00	28.00	75.00	750.00	
□1866S†		30.00	50.00	150.00	370.00	4600.00	

**With Arrows and Rays ***With Arrows
†Part of Total Mintage: 1,054,000

HALF DOLLARS — LIBERTY SEATED, 1866–1891 WITH MOTTO ON REVERSE

Arrows at Date

No Arrows at Date

Mint Mark is Below Eagle on Reverse

DATE	MINTAGE	ABP	G-4 Good	F-12 Fine	EF-40 Ex. Fine	MS-60 Unc.	PRF-65 Proof
☐1866	745,625	6.60	13.00	31.00	80.00	600.00	3200.00
☐1866S***		6.60	13.00	31.00	60.00	600.00	
☐1867	424,325	9.00	16.00	36.00	100.00	800.00	3200.00
☐1867S	1,196,000	7.00	15.00	31.00	62.00	800.00	
☐1868	378,000	12.00	20.00	32.00	120.00	900.00	3200.00
☐1868S	1,160,000	8.50	14.00	36.00	70.00	700.00	
☐1869	795,900	7.00	14.00	31.00	65.00	700.00	3200.00
☐1869S	656,000	8.00	14.00	31.00	100.00	750.00	
☐1870	600,900	9.00	14.00	31.00	90.00	700.00	3200.00
☐1870CC	54,617	200.00	400.00	1000.00	3200.00	Unknown in BU	
☐1870S	1,004,000	7.50	14.00	30.00	80.00	500.00	
☐1871	1,165,360	9.00	14.00	32.00	60.00	500.00	3200.00
☐1871CC	139,950	50.00	90.00	160.00	680.00	4000.00	
☐1871S	2,178,000	7.00	15.00	31.00	70.00	600.00	
☐1872	881,550	6.50	19.00	31.00	80.00	780.00	3200.00
☐1872CC	272,000	20.00	43.00	80.00	360.00	2000.00	
☐1872S	580,000	11.50	18.00	40.00	90.00	900.00	
☐1873 w/arrows	1,815,700	9.00	14.00	32.00	200.00	1200.00	5000.00
☐1873 no arrows	801,800	7.50	14.00	32.00	115.00	600.00	4300.00
☐1873CC w/arrows	214,560	25.00	54.00	100.00	410.00	2400.00	
☐1873CC no arrows	122,500	46.00	80.00	210.00	400.00	2900.00	
☐1873 w/arrows	288,000	18.00	41.00	80.00	300.00	1900.00	
☐1873S no arrows	5,000			NONE KNOWN TO EXIST			
☐1874	2,360,300	8.00	20.00	30.00	180.00	900.00	5000.00
☐1874CC	59,000	60.00	110.00	400.00	1100.00	4500.00	
☐1874S	394,000	14.00	29.00	50.00	210.00	1600.00	
☐1875	6,027,500	7.00	13.00	32.00	62.00	610.00	3400.00
☐1875CC	1,008,000	7.00	16.00	36.00	100.00	610.00	
☐1875S	3,200,000	7.00	13.00	32.00	65.00	610.00	
☐1876	8,419,150	7.00	13.00	32.00	65.00	610.00	3400.00
☐1876CC	1,956,000	7.00	16.00	32.00	75.00	600.00	
☐1876S	4,528,000	7.00	13.00	36.00	70.00	500.00	
☐1877	8,304,510	7.00	13.00	32.00	70.00	500.00	3400.00

***Part of Total Mintage: 1,054,000

DATE	MINTAGE	ABP	G-4 Good	F-12 Fine	EF-40 Ex. Fine	MS-60 Unc.	PRF-65 Proof
☐1877CC	1,420,000	7.00	18.00	31.00	72.00	600.00	
☐1877S	5,356,000	7.00	11.00	31.00	66.00	500.00	
☐1878	1,378,400	7.00	11.00	31.00	60.00	500.00	3500.00
☐1878CC	62,000	106.00	210.00	350.00	1000.00	2400.00	
☐1878S	12,000	1200.00	3200.00	5400.00	9000.00	19000.00	
☐1879	5,900	100.00	210.00	210.00	400.00	1000.00	5000.00
☐1880	1,355	97.00	160.00	200.00	400.00	1000.00	5000.00
☐1881	10,975	97.00	160.00	190.00	400.00	1000.00	5000.00
☐1882	5,500	120.00	210.00	200.00	350.00	1000.00	5000.00
☐1883	9,039	92.00	160.00	190.00	350.00	1000.00	5000.00
☐1884	5,275	145.00	200.00	200.00	350.00	1100.00	5000.00
☐1885	6,130	90.00	150.00	210.00	350.00	1100.00	5000.00
☐1886	5,886	100.00	140.00	200.00	350.00	1100.00	5000.00
☐1887	5,710	100.00	150.00	190.00	350.00	1100.00	5000.00
☐1888	12,833	85.00	120.00	180.00	300.00	900.00	5000.00
☐1889	12,711	85.00	120.00	180.00	300.00	900.00	5000.00
☐1890	12,590	85.00	120.00	180.00	300.00	900.00	5000.00
☐1891	200,600	15.00	36.00	60.00	110.00	700.00	5000.00

HALF DOLLARS — LIBERTY HEAD OR BARBER, 1892–1915

These coins, which resemble the Morgan Dollar in portraiture, were prepared from designs by Charles E. Barber and really have no connection with the Morgan Dollar aside from the possibility that Barber may have been inspired by it. The face of Liberty, which faces right, is strong and classical, suggesting the portraiture of Greek coins of ancient time. The weight is somewhat greater than the final version of the Seated Liberty half, 12½ grams, but its composition is the same, 90% silver and an alloy of 10% copper. The reverse has an attractive eagle with shield and wings spread wide; it holds the traditional arrows and branch. The mint mark appears directly beneath the eagle's tail feathers. Without question this was artistically the finest coin of the half dollar series. It was struck at Philadelphia, New Orleans, Denver, and San Francisco. Not a single rarity is to be found among the Barber halves, with the result that it offers splendid opportunities for completion—even if one wishes to include all the mint marks.

Mint Mark is Below Eagle on Reverse

DATE	MINTAGE	ABP	G-4 Good	F-12 Fine	EF-40 Ex. Fine	MS-60 Unc.	PRF-65 Proof
☐ 1892	935,245	5.50	12.00	30.00	167.00	700.00	4000.00
☐ 1892O	390,000	37.00	90.00	160.00	400.00	900.00	4000.00
☐ 1892S	1,029,028	36.00	90.00	160.00	390.00	950.00	4000.00
☐ 1893	1,826,792	4.50	11.00	26.00	175.00	600.00	4000.00
☐ 1893O	1,389,000	7.50	15.00	41.00	230.00	700.00	4000.00
☐ 1893S	740,000	11.00	50.00	122.00	360.00	900.00	4000.00
☐ 1894	1,148,972	3.60	9.50	30.00	200.00	600.00	4000.00
☐ 1894O	2,138,000	3.60	9.00	32.00	215.00	700.00	4000.00
☐ 1894S	4,048,690	3.60	8.00	26.00	190.00	600.00	4000.00
☐ 1895	1,835,218	3.00	9.00	26.00	170.00	600.00	4000.00
☐ 1895O	1,766,000	3.20	9.00	30.00	175.00	700.00	4000.00
☐ 1895S	1,108,086	6.50	15.00	41.00	210.00	600.00	4000.00
☐ 1896	950,762	3.60	9.50	32.00	180.00	600.00	4000.00
☐ 1896O	924,000	5.10	12.00	42.00	280.00	920.00	4000.00
☐ 1896S	1,140,948	18.00	45.00	80.00	310.00	1100.00	4000.00
☐ 1897	2,480,731	3.00	6.00	23.00	130.00	700.00	4000.00
☐ 1897O	632,000	18.00	40.00	90.00	420.00	1200.00	4000.00
☐ 1897S	933,900	31.00	70.00	125.00	430.00	1150.00	4000.00
☐ 1898	2,956,735	3.50	6.00	23.00	170.00	600.00	4000.00
☐ 1898O	874,000	5.00	16.00	40.00	300.00	700.00	4000.00
☐ 1898S	2,358,550	3.00	9.00	26.00	190.00	600.00	4000.00
☐ 1899	5,538,846	3.00	6.00	24.00	160.00	600.00	4000.00
☐ 1899O	1,724,000	3.00	9.00	29.00	180.00	700.00	4000.00
☐ 1899S	1,686,411	3.00	8.00	28.00	160.00	600.00	4000.00
☐ 1900	4,762,912	3.00	6.00	22.00	160.00	600.00	4000.00
☐ 1900O	2,744,000	3.00	6.00	25.00	160.00	700.00	4000.00
☐ 1900S	2,560,322	3.00	6.00	24.00	160.00	600.00	4000.00
☐ 1901	4,268,813	3.00	6.00	21.00	155.00	600.00	4000.00
☐ 1901O	1,124,000	3.00	10.00	29.00	210.00	1200.00	4000.00
☐ 1901S	847,044	3.00	6.00	40.00	350.00	1500.00	4000.00
☐ 1902	4,922,777	3.00	6.00	22.00	130.00	600.60	4000.00
☐ 1902O	2,526,000	3.00	6.00	20.00	150.00	700.00	4000.00
☐ 1902S	1,460,670	3.00	6.00	25.00	180.00	700.00	4000.00
☐ 1903	2,278,755	3.00	6.00	26.00	140.00	600.00	4000.00
☐ 1903O	2,100,000	3.00	6.00	26.00	160.00	600.00	4000.00
☐ 1903S	1,920,772	3.00	6.00	26.00	170.00	600.00	4000.00
☐ 1904	2,992,670	3.00	6.00	21.00	170.00	600.00	4000.00
☐ 1904O	1,117,600	3.20	7.00	30.00	240.00	1200.00	4000.00
☐ 1904S	553,038	4.20	10.00	40.00	280.00	1100.00	4000.00
☐ 1905	662,727	3.20	9.00	30.00	260.00	600.00	4000.00
☐ 1905O	505,000	4.20	9.00	45.00	280.00	700.00	4000.00
☐ 1905S	2,494,000	2.80	7.00	25.00	170.00	700.00	4000.00
☐ 1906	1,638,675	2.80	6.00	21.00	150.00	600.00	4000.00
☐ 1906D	4,028,000	2.80	6.00	20.00	150.00	700.00	4000.00
☐ 1906O	2,446,000	2.80	6.00	20.00	140.00	700.00	4000.00
☐ 1906S	1,740,154	2.80	6.00	25.00	150.00	700.00	4000.00
☐ 1907	2,598,575	2.80	6.00	21.00	130.00	600.00	4000.00
☐ 1907D	3,856,000	2.80	6.00	21.00	130.00	600.00	4000.00

DATE	MINTAGE	ABP	G-4 Good	F-12 Fine	EF-40 Ex. Fine	MS-60 Unc.	PRF-65 Proof
□ 1907O	3,946,600	2.80	6.00	24.00	140.00	700.00	
□ 1907S	1,250,000	2.80	7.00	25.00	160.00	700.00	
□ 1908	1,354,545	2.80	6.00	24.00	140.00	600.00	4000.00
□ 1908D	3,280,000	2.80	6.00	22.00	140.00	700.00	
□ 1908O	5,360,000	2.80	6.00	20.00	135.00	700.00	
□ 1908S	1,644,828	2.80	6.00	23.00	160.00	750.00	
□ 1909	2,368,650	2.80	6.00	23.00	135.00	600.00	4000.00
□ 1909O	925,400	3.30	7.00	25.00	215.00	900.00	
□ 1909S	1,764,000	2.80	6.00	24.00	165.00	700.00	
□ 1910	418,551	2.80	9.00	35.00	230.00	700.00	4100.00
□ 1910S	1,948,000	2.80	6.50	21.00	150.00	600.00	
□ 1911	1,406,543	2.80	6.50	22.00	135.00	600.00	4000.00
□ 1911D	696,080	2.80	7.00	22.00	144.00	700.00	
□ 1911S	1,272,000	2.80	6.50	22.00	160.00	700.00	
□ 1912	1,550,700	2.80	6.50	21.00	135.00	700.00	4000.00
□ 1912D	2,300,800	2.80	6.50	21.00	135.00	600.00	
□ 1912S	1,370,000	2.80	6.50	21.00	145.00	650.00	
□ 1913	188,627	7.00	16.00	40.00	240.00	900.00	4000.00
□ 1913D	534,000	2.80	6.50	26.00	170.00	600.00	
□ 1913S	604,000	2.80	6.50	28.00	170.00	700.00	
□ 1914	124,610	12.00	24.00	70.00	300.00	850.00	4000.00
□ 1914S	992,000	2.85	6.00	21.00	172.00	600.00	
□ 1915	138,450	7.00	17.00	50.00	300.00	850.00	4000.00
□ 1915D	1,170,400	2.80	6.50	20.00	135.00	600.00	
□ 1915S	1,604,000	2.80	6.50	22.00	150.00	650.00	

HALF DOLLARS — LIBERTY WALKING, 1916–1947

This attractive design, introduced in 1916, pictured a full-length representation of Liberty on the obverse, dressed in a diaphanous gown and strolling along a field, her right arm upraised as if in acknowledgment of the splendors of nature. In the distance the sun rises (or sets). The designer was A. Weinman, whose initials may be observed—if one has a coin with virtually no wear—on the reverse. His rendition of the eagle on the coin's reverse, a naturalistic type bearing little resemblance to the previously employed shield or heraldic eagle, is a noteworthy piece of art. Sadly the Liberty Walking half dollar suffered a great deal from rubbing in circulation and much of its delicate linework wore down rapidly, resulting in a shortage of presentable specimens. The collector who wishes to build up a set would be well advised to seek the finest condition obtainable, and be prepared to give a slight premium for coins of the best quality, rather than collect "average" specimens which are, truly, mere shadows of their original selves. The Liberty Walking 50¢ piece was struck at Philadelphia, San Francisco, and Denver. Its composition is 90% silver and 10% copper with a weight of 12½ grams and diameter of 30.6 mm.

Note: The sale of Liberty Walking halves as silver bullion should be approached with care. While the majority of common dates in average condition are of no special numismatic value, this series, though modern, does include scarce dates and mint marks which deserve a better fate than the smelter's pot. The silver in these coins amounts to .36169 ounce, or slightly more than one-third of an ounce.

DATE	MINTAGE	ABP	G-4 Good	F-12 Fine	EF-40 Ex. Fine	MS-60 Unc.	PRF-65
☐ 1916	608,000	9.50	18.00	51.00	200.00	410.00	
☐ 1916D on obverse	1,014,400	5.50	13.00	30.00	155.00	380.00	
☐ 1916S on obverse	508,000	13.00	26.00	100.00	360.00	820.00	2500.00
☐ 1917	12,292,000	3.00	6.00	12.00	35.00	170.00	
☐ 1917D on obverse	765,400	3.20	10.00	31.00	176.00	525.00	
☐ 1917D on reverse	1,940,000	2.60	8.00	24.00	155.00	570.00	
☐ 1917S on obverse	952,000	4.60	14.00	39.00	350.00	1000.00	2500.00
☐ 1917S on reverse	6,554,000	2.50	5.00	15.00	50.00	260.00	
☐ 1918	6,634,000	2.50	5.00	11.00	110.00	380.00	
☐ 1918D	3,853,040	2.50	5.00	10.00	120.00	740.00	
☐ 1918S	10,282,000	2.50	5.00	11.00	50.00	320.00	
☐ 1919	962,000	2.50	10.00	31.00	360.00	1200.00	
☐ 1919D	1,165,000	2.50	9.00	31.00	400.00	2000.00	

Mint Mark is Under "In God We Trust" on 1916 and Early 1917. Later Left of "H" on Reverse

DATE	MINTAGE	ABP	G-4 Good	F-12 Fine	EF-40 Ex. Fine	MS-60 Unc.	PRF-65
☐ 1919S	1,552,000	2.50	8.00	21.00	350.00	1800.00	
☐ 1920	6,372,000	2.50	6.00	11.00	60.00	270.00	
☐ 1920D	1,551,000	2.50	6.00	26.00	245.00	1000.00	
☐ 1920S	4,624,000	2.50	6.00	15.00	130.00	900.00	
☐ 1921	246,000	32.00	50.00	200.00	900.00	2100.00	
☐ 1921D	208,000	40.00	84.00	265.00	1100.00	2300.00	
☐ 1921S	548,000	5.00	16.00	40.00	1200.00	6600.00	
☐ 1923S	2,178,000	2.50	6.00	10.00	140.00	910.00	
☐ 1927S	2,393,000	2.50	5.50	10.00	80.00	740.00	
☐ 1928S	1,940,000	2.50	5.50	10.00	100.00	800.00	
☐ 1929D	1,001,200	2.50	5.50	10.00	70.00	410.00	
☐ 1929S	1,902,000	2.50	5.50	9.00	70.00	380.00	
☐ 1933S	1,786,000	2.50	5.50	9.00	50.00	370.00	
☐ 1934	6,964,000	2.50	4.30	6.00	19.00	89.00	
☐ 1934D	2,361,400	2.50	4.30	6.00	35.00	175.00	
☐ 1934S	3,652,000	2.50	4.30	6.00	26.00	330.00	
☐ 1935	9,162,000	2.50	4.30	6.00	17.00	72.00	
☐ 1935D	3,003,800	2.50	4.30	6.00	35.00	190.00	
☐ 1935S	2,854,000	2.50	4.30	6.00	30.00	210.00	
☐ 1936	12,617,901	2.50	4.30	6.00	17.00	70.00	3800.00

DATE	MINTAGE	ABP	G-4 Good	F-12 Fine	EF-40 Ex. Fine	MS-60 Unc.	PRF-65
□ 1936D	4,252,400	2.50	4.40	5.50	26.00	130.00	
□ 1936S	3,884,000	2.50	4.40	5.50	26.00	140.00	
□ 1937	9,527,728	2.50	4.40	5.50	16.00	70.00	2200.00
□ 1937D	1,760,001	2.50	4.40	5.50	35.00	230.00	
□ 1937S	2,090,000	2.50	4.40	5.50	30.00	170.00	
□ 1938	4,118,152	2.50	4.40	5.50	18.00	115.00	1850.00
□ 1938D	491,600	8.00	24.00	37.00	92.00	430.00	
□ 1939	6,820,808	2.50	4.40	5.10	16.00	100.00	1700.00
□ 1939D	4,267,800	2.50	4.40	5.10	17.50	90.00	
□ 1939S	2,552,000	2.50	4.40	5.10	21.00	135.00	
□ 1940	9,167,279	2.50	4.40	5.10	14.50	62.00	1550.00
□ 1940S	4,550,000	2.50	4.40	5.10	10.00	100.00	
□ 1941	24,207,412	2.50	4.40	5.10	10.00	50.00	1400.00
□ 1941D	11,248,400	2.50	4.40	5.10	10.00	67.00	
□ 1941S	8,098,000	2.50	4.40	5.10	12.00	190.00	
□ 1942	47,839,120	2.50	4.40	5.10	9.50	48.00	1200.00
□ 1942D	10,973,800	2.50	4.40	5.10	9.50	75.00	
□ 1942S	12,708,000	2.50	4.40	5.10	9.50	100.00	
□ 1943	53,190,000	2.50	4.40	5.10	9.50	52.00	
□ 1943D	11,346,000	2.50	4.40	5.10	9.50	76.00	
□ 1943S	13,450,000	2.50	4.40	5.10	9.00	100.00	
□ 1944	28,206,000	2.50	4.40	5.10	9.00	40.00	
□ 1944D	9,769,000	2.50	4.40	5.10	9.00	55.00	
□ 1944S	8,904,000	2.50	4.40	5.10	8.50	74.00	
□ 1945	31,502,000	2.50	4.40	5.10	8.50	48.00	
□ 1945D	9,966,500	2.50	4.40	5.10	8.50	62.00	
□ 1945S	10,156,000	2.50	4.40	5.10	8.50	76.00	
□ 1946	12,118,000	2.50	4.40	5.10	8.50	50.00	
□ 1946D	2,151,000	2.50	4.40	5.10	8.50	55.00	
□ 1946S	3,724,000	2.50	4.40	5.10	8.50	78.00	
□ 1947	4,094,000	2.50	4.40	5.10	8.50	78.00	
□ 1947D	3,900,000	2.50	4.40	5.10	8.50	76.00	

HALF DOLLARS — FRANKLIN OR "LIBERTY BELL," 1948–1963

The likeness of Benjamin Franklin, which had not previously appeared on a U.S. coin, was installed on the half dollar in 1948. That he was not President can be accounted for by mere circumstance. Had the federal government been formed ten or twenty years sooner, before Franklin had advanced into old age, there is little doubt but that he would have attained the office. Like the Roosevelt dime, introduced two years earlier, this coin was designed by John R. Sinnock. On the reverse is a large representation of the Liberty Bell, adapted from the artwork on the 1926 Sesquicentennial medal celebrating the 150th anniversary of our Declaration of Independence. Franklin is shown in profile facing right. The mint mark is atop the Liberty Bell on the reverse, directly below the words "UNITED STATES OF AMERICA." Composition is 90% silver, 10% copper, with a weight of 12½ grams. The diameter is 30.6 mm. It contains .36169 ounce of pure silver, or slightly more than one-third of an ounce.

DATE	MINTAGE	ABP	F-12 Fine	EF-40 Ex. Fine	MS-60 Unc.	PRF-65 Proof
☐ 1948	3,006,814	2.50	4.00	9.00	30.00	
☐ 1948D	4,028,600	2.50	4.00	9.00	25.00	
☐ 1949	5,714,000	2.50	4.00	9.00	120.00	
☐ 1949D	4,120,600	2.50	4.00	10.00	80.00	
☐ 1949S	3,744,000	2.50	8.00	25.00	190.00	
☐ 1950	7,793,509	2.50	4.00	10.00	70.00	700.00
☐ 1950D	8,031,600	2.50	4.00	10.00	40.00	
☐ 1951	16,859,602	2.50	4.00	9.00	21.00	400.00
☐ 1951D	9,475,200	2.50	4.00	6.00	60.00	
☐ 1951S	13,696,000	2.50	4.00	6.00	52.00	
☐ 1952	21,274,074	2.50	4.00	6.00	21.00	250.00
☐ 1952D	25,394,600	2.50	4.00	6.00	21.00	
☐ 1952S	5,526,000	2.50	4.00	6.00	50.00	
☐ 1953	2,796,920	2.50	4.00	7.00	42.00	150.00
☐ 1953D	20,900,400	2.50	4.00	5.50	19.00	
☐ 1953S	4,148,000	2.50	4.00	5.50	30.00	
☐ 1954	13,421,503	2.50	4.00	5.50	15.00	90.00
☐ 1954D	25,445,580	2.50	4.00	5.50	15.00	
☐ 1954S	4,993,400	2.50	4.00	5.50	19.00	
☐ 1955	2,876,381	2.50	5.00	10.00	18.00	90.00
☐ 1956	4,701,384	2.50	4.50	5.25	18.00	60.00
☐ 1957	6,361,952	2.50	4.00	5.25	17.00	50.00
☐ 1957D	19,996,850	2.50	4.00	5.25	14.00	
☐ 1958	4,917,652	2.50	4.00	5.25	13.00	55.00
☐ 1958D	23,962,412	2.50	4.00	5.25	12.00	
☐ 1959	7,349,291	2.50	4.00	5.25	12.00	50.00
☐ 1959D	13,053,750	2.50	4.00	5.25	12.00	
☐ 1960	7,715,602	2.50	4.00	5.25	12.00	40.00
☐ 1960D	18,215,812	2.50	4.00	5.00	12.00	
☐ 1961	11,318,244	2.50	4.00	5.00	12.00	35.00
☐ 1961D	20,276,442	2.50	4.00	5.00	10.00	
☐ 1962	12,932,019	2.50	4.00	5.00	10.00	35.00
☐ 1962D	35,473,281	2.50	4.00	5.00	10.00	
☐ 1963	25,239,645	2.50	4.00	5.00	10.00	35.00
☐ 1963D	67,069,292	2.50	4.00	5.00	10.00	

HALF DOLLARS — JOHN F. KENNEDY, 1964 TO DATE

Following the death of President Kennedy in 1963 there was considerable public sentiment for honoring his memory on coinage. As all coins except the half dollar already carried portraits of Presidents, it was decided to install his likeness on this coin, even though its design had been changed as recently as 1948. The portrait was designed by Gilroy Roberts and Frank Gasparro, the reverse featuring a shield eagle surrounded by stars. As introduced in 1964, the coin was of regular silver composition (90% silver, 10% copper, .36169 ounces of silver by weight) but was altered in 1965 to the clad standard, consisting of a 21% silver/79% copper interior covered with 80% silver/20% copper, total weight of silver being .14792 ounces. Its weight was 11½ grams, down from 12½. In 1971 the silver was removed from its core and a new composition used for the exterior, comprising three parts copper to one of nickel. The silver had been entirely replaced and the weight fell to 11.34 grams. The only alteration in design occurred in 1976 when a figure of Independence Hall in Philadelphia was added to the reverse, supplanting the eagle, as part of the Bicentennial program. On the obverse the date appeared as "1775–1976." In the following year the normal reverse was readopted. A quantity of silverclad pieces were struck in 1976, the first (and last) in this series since 1970. This has been termed a difficult coin on which to find the mint mark. As first issued it may be observed on the reverse, above the "L" and "F" in the world "HALF." In 1968 it was brought to the obverse, beneath the portrait and above the date. Scarcest Kennedy half dollar is the 1970D, not minted for general circulation. The Kennedy half dollar has a diameter of 30.6 mm.

COIN	MINTAGE	ABP	EF-40 Ex. Fine	MS-60 Unc.	PRF-65 Proof
□1964	277,254,766	2.40	3.00	7.00	15.00
□1964D	156,205,446	2.40	3.00	7.00	
CLAD COINAGE					
□1965	65,879,366	.85		2.90	
□1966	108,984,933	.85		2.30	
□1967	295,045,968	.85		2.30	
□1968D	246,951,930	.85		2.30	
□1968S PROOF	3,041,508				4.00
□1969D	129,881,800	.85		2.30	
□1969S PROOF	2,934,631				4.00
□1970D	2,150,000			26.00	
□1970S PROOF	2,632,810				9.00
□1971	155,164,000			1.20	
□1971D	302,097,424			1.20	

COIN	MINTAGE	ABP	EF-40 Ex. Fine	MS-60 Unc.	PRF-65 Proof
☐ 1971S PROOF	3,224,138				2.50
☐ 1972	153,180,000			1.15	
☐ 1972D	141,890,000			1.15	
☐ 1972S PROOF	3,224,138				2.50
☐ 1973	64,964,000			1.15	
☐ 1973D	83,171,400			1.15	
☐ 1973S PROOF	2,769,624				2.75
☐ 1974	201,588,250			.95	
☐ 1974D	79,088,210			.95	
☐ 1974S PROOF	2,617,350				3.00
☐ 1976 Copper-nickel clad	234,318,200			1.00	
☐ 1976D Copper-nickel clad	287,565,290			1.00	
☐ 1976S Copper-nickel clad	7,123,300				2.00
☐ 1976S Silver clad	4,250,000			3.10	
☐ 1976S Silver clad PROOF	3,215,730				7.00
☐ 1977	43,569,000			1.10	
☐ 1977D	31,450,250			1.10	
☐ 1977S PROOF	3,450,895				2.25
☐ 1978	14,350,000			1.40	
☐ 1978D	13,765,799			1.40	
☐ 1978S PROOF	3,127,781				2.75
☐ 1979	68,311,400			1.00	
☐ 1979D	15,815,400			1.00	
☐ 1979S PROOF (I)	3,677,200				2.00
☐ 1979S PROOF (II)					16.00
☐ 1980P	29,500,000			1.00	
☐ 1980D	33,456,450			1.00	
☐ 1980S PROOF	3,555,000				1.75
☐ 1981P	29,544,206			1.00	
☐ 1981D	27,839,525			1.00	
☐ 1981S PROOF (I)	4,063,000				1.75
☐ 1981S PROOF (II)					26.00
☐ 1982P	10,920,700			1.00	
☐ 1982D	13,150,000			1.00	
☐ 1982S PROOF (I)	3,229,000				6.00
☐ 1983P	34,100,000			1.00	
☐ 1983D	32,475,000			1.00	
☐ 1983S PROOF	3,228,621				6.00
☐ 1984P	26,031,084			1.00	
☐ 1984D	26,275,000			1.00	
☐ 1984S PROOF					10.00
☐ 1985P	18,922,112			1.00	
☐ 1985D	19,911,760			1.00	
☐ 1985S PROOF	3,372,220				10.00
☐ 1986P	12,110,530			.90	
☐ 1986D	15,463,220			.90	
☐ 1986S PROOF	3,111,000				10.00
☐ 1987P				3.00	

COIN	MINTAGE	ABP	EF-40 Ex. Fine	MS-60 Unc.	PRF-65 Proof
☐1987D				3.00	
☐1987S PROOF					6.00
☐1988P				.90	
☐1988D				.90	
☐1988S PROOF					5.00
☐1989P				.90	
☐1989D				.90	
☐1989S PROOF					5.00

SILVER DOLLARS

EARLY, 1794–1804; PATTERNS, 1836–1839; REGULAR ISSUE, 1840–1873

The silver dollar, probably the most significant U.S. coin of the 19th century, was authorized on April 2, 1792, and intended as the chief currency piece or standard for other silver coinage. However, striking was not begun until 1794. The word "dollar" is a corruption of Taler or Thaler, a large silver coin widely distributed in Europe and well known to Colonial America. Prior to use of this term in domestic coinage it had become common to refer to Spain's "pieces of eight" as dollars, so it was natural that this crown-like silver piece should likewise be called a dollar. The first design, the Flowing Hair variety, was executed by Robert Scot and may be observed on other coinage of that era. Its reverse was an eagle surrounded by the words "UNITED STATES OF AMERICA." The composition was .8924 silver and .1076 copper, the addition of this roughly one-tenth part of base-metal being needed to provide ruggedness. It weighed 26.96 grams and was the heaviest U.S. silver coin excepting the Trade Dollar of much later vintage. Its diameter varies between 39 and 40 mm. Along the edge is impressed the words "HUNDRED CENTS ONE DOLLAR OR UNIT," interspersed with typographical ornament. There was very limited striking of dollars in the initial year of their appearance, less than 2,000 being turned out. The following year, 1795, witnessed greatly increased production, but because of the surface softness of these coins and the extensive handling to which they were subjected it is not easy finding specimens in the best grades of condition. "Average" examples can be had rather easily. There are two reverse varieties of the 1795 Flowing Hair dollar, one in which three leaves appear beneath the eagle's wings on either side, another with two leaves. Toward the end of 1795 the Flowing Hair obverse was replaced by the Draped Bust, with the so-called "Small Eagle" reverse (the eagle's wings and body in general being scaled smaller than previously). The Draped Bust obverse is found with dates in small or large numerals, and with the legend "UNITED STATES OF AMERICA" in small or large letters on the reverse. There are also differences in the number of stars on the obverse. In 1798 the shield eagle reverse was introduced, still with the Draped Bust portrait. These types were continued until 1803 when the striking of silver dollars was suspended. It was at one time believed that the Mint coined a few dollars in 1804 but it has now been established beyond reasonable doubt that silver dollars dated 1804 were struck in the 1830s for inclusion in proof sets. Apparently the die for an 1804 coin was prepared before any decision was reached to discontinue production and it was stored away at the Mint for those 30 years. In any case the 1804 dollar is an extremely rare piece whose popularity (and price) has not suffered in the least by results of research into its origins. A handful of restrikes were made later, in 1859. There is scarcely any difference in rarity or value between the 1830s proofs and the 1859 restrikes. Of all 1804 silver dollars (both types), 15 exist.

In 1836 Christian Gobrecht prepared designs for a new silver dollar, which at first was struck in limited numbers to test public response. A seated figure of Liberty appeared on the obverse with a flying eagle reverse. The obverse carried no wording whatever. On the reverse were the words "UNITED STATES OF AMERICA" and "ONE DOLLAR," the eagle set within a ground of stars. There are some varieties of this reverse containing no stars. Full-scale output of silver dollars was not resumed until 1840. For this issue, and for many years following, the shield or heraldic eagle was used for the reverse and the face value was abbreviated into "ONE DOL." In 1866 the motto "IN GOD WE TRUST" was added to the reverse, on a banner flowing above the eagle. The mint mark is located below the eagle and above the statement of value. Striking of dollars in this design ceased in 1873.

SILVER DOLLARS — LIBERTY WITH FLOWING HAIR, 1794–1795

DATE	MINTAGE	ABP	G-4 Good	F-12 Fine	VF-20 V. Fine	MS-60 Unc.
□1794	1,758	4000.00	7000.00	16000.00	27000.00	100000.00
□1795*	160,295	490.00	900.00	1450.00	2475.00	30000.00

*Includes both 2 Leaf and 3 Leaf Varieties

SILVER DOLLARS — DRAPED BUST, 1795–1798
SMALL EAGLE ON REVERSE

DATE	MINTAGE	ABP	G-4 Good	F-12 Fine	VF-20 V. Fine	MS-60 Unc.
☐1795	42,738	400.00	780.00	1450.00	2000.00	20000.00
☐1796	72,920	400.00	700.00	1200.00	2000.00	15000.00
☐1797 sm. letters		400.00	700.00	1175.00	2000.00	15000.00
☐1797 lg. letters	7,776	400.00	700.00	1175.00	2000.00	15000.00
☐1797 9 stars left, 7 right, sm. letters		700.00	1400.00	2500.00	4000.00	24000.00
☐1798 (Small eagle)	327,536	700.00	1350.00	2600.00	3500.00	19000.00

SILVER DOLLARS - DRAPED BUST, 1798–1804
LARGE EAGLE ON REVERSE

DATE	MINTAGE	ABP	G-4 Good	F-12 Fine	VF-20 V. Fine	MS-60 Unc.
☐1798**		180.00	360.00	600.00	1200.00	10500.00
☐1799***	423,515	180.00	360.00	600.00	1200.00	10000.00
☐1800***	220,920	180.00	360.00	600.00	1200.00	10000.00
☐1801***	54,454	220.00	450.00	750.00	1300.00	9500.00
☐1802***	41,650	180.00	360.00	800.00	1300.00	9200.00
☐1802 over 1***		180.00	360.00	800.00	1300.00	9500.00
☐1803***	66,064	180.00	360.00	800.00	1300.00	9500.00

☐1804 One of the most valued coins in the world—less than 15 known. In March 1980, THE GARRETT SPECIMEN was sold for $400,000.00. In 1982 another specimen brought $190,000.00. In 1985 the Dr. Jerry Buss specimen was sold for $280,000.00.

**Includes both 13 star and 15 star varieties

***Includes all types

SILVER DOLLARS — LIBERTY SEATED (GOBRECHT), 1836–1839
WITH FLYING EAGLE ON REVERSE

DATE	MINTAGE	ABP	VF-20 V. Fine	EF-40 Ex. Fine	PRF-65 Proof
☐1836	approx. 1,025	820.00	3400.00	4000.00	8500.00
☐1838	approx. 31	7800.00	PROOF ONLY		13500.00
☐1839	approx. 303	5500.00	PROOF ONLY		12000.00

SILVER DOLLARS – LIBERTY SEATED, 1840–1865
NO MOTTO OVER EAGLE

DATE	MINTAGE	ABP	G-4 Good	F-12 Fine	VF-20 V. Fine	MS-60 Unc.	PRF-65 Proof
☐1840	61,005	100.00	200.00	280.00	390.00	1000.00	
☐1841	173,000	93.00	190.00	215.00	340.00	990.00	
☐1842	184,618	86.00	180.00	240.00	360.00	990.00	
☐1843	165,100	86.00	180.00	240.00	360.00	990.00	
☐1844	20,000	100.00	200.00	300.00	410.00	1650.00	
☐1845	24,500	100.00	210.00	290.00	410.00	1650.00	
☐1846	110,600	68.00	110.00	280.00	360.00	1000.00	
☐1846O	59,000	93.00	215.00	270.00	500.00	2900.00	
☐1847	140,750	72.00	150.00	210.00	350.00	1000.00	
☐1848	15,000	110.00	300.00	400.00	500.00	1600.00	
☐1849	62,600	80.00	200.00	250.00	400.00	1000.00	
☐1850	7,500	210.00	400.00	500.00	800.00	3400.00	
☐1850O	40,000	172.00	300.00	400.00	600.00	3100.00	
☐1851	1,300	1600.00	3500.00	4500.00	6000.00	12500.00	
☐1852	1,100	1500.00	3200.00	5000.00	7000.00	11000.00	
☐1853	46,110	98.00	200.00	270.00	400.00	1000.00	

DATE	MINTAGE	ABP	G-4 Good	F-12 Fine	EX-40 Ex. Fine	MS-60 Unc.	PRF-65 Proof
☐1854	33,140	300.00	500.00	1000.00	1200.00	2750.00	
☐1855	26,000	300.00	500.00	980.00	1200.00	2175.00	10000.00
☐1856	63,500	110.00	250.00	400.00	400.00	1800.00	9000.00
☐1857	94,000	110.00	250.00	400.00	400.00	1700.00	10000.00
☐1858 PROOFS ONLY	80						11000.00
☐1859	256,500	120.00	300.00	400.00	500.00	1500.00	7500.00
☐1859O	360,000	70.00	100.00	200.00	210.00	900.00	
☐1859S	20,000	140.00	300.00	300.00	500.00	3500.00	
☐1860	218,930	140.00	300.00	400.00	500.00	1800.00	5000.00
☐1860O	515,000	63.00	100.00	180.00	200.00	1000.00	
☐1861	78,500	160.00	300.00	400.00	600.00	1800.00	5000.00
☐1862	12,090	170.00	300.00	400.00	600.00	2300.00	5000.00
☐1863	27,660	100.00	210.00	300.00	400.00	1800.00	5000.00
☐1864	31,170	92.00	190.00	300.00	410.00	1800.00	5000.00
☐1865	47,000	92.00	190.00	250.00	380.00	1800.00	5000.00
☐1866 No Motto—2 Known —PROOF—$175,000							

SILVER DOLLARS — LIBERTY SEATED, 1866–1873 MOTTO "IN GOD WE TRUST" ADDED

DATE	MINTAGE	ABP	G-4 Good	F-12 Fine	EF-40 Ex. Fine	MS-60 Unc.	PRF-65 Proof
☐1866	49,625	90.00	210.00	250.00	380.00	1400.00	6000.00
☐1867	47,525	90.00	210.00	250.00	380.00	1400.00	6000.00
☐1868	162,700	80.00	150.00	240.00	340.00	1200.00	6000.00
☐1869	424,300	60.00	150.00	230.00	340.00	1200.00	6000.00
☐1870	416,000	60.00	150.00	220.00	310.00	1200.00	6000.00
☐1870CC	12,462	150.00	200.00	300.00	700.00	2400.00	
☐1870S	RARE—$62,500.00: 1973 Sale						
☐1871	1,074,760	52.00	100.00	160.00	300.00	1200.00	6000.00
☐1871CC	1,376	600.00	900.00	1100.00	2500.00	800.00	
☐1872	1,106,450	47.00	105.00	170.00	300.00	1100.00	6000.00
☐1872CC	3,150	400.00	800.00	600.00	1600.00	4500.00	
☐1872S	9,000	100.00	160.00	300.00	700.00	3000.00	
☐1873	193,600	68.00	110.00	200.00	360.00	1200.00	6500.00
☐1873CC	2,300	900.00	2000.00	2200.00	3900.00	11000.00	
☐1873S	700	UNKNOWN IN ANY COLLECTION					

SILVER DOLLARS — TRADE, 1873–1885

In the early 1870s there was mounting pressure to increase the silver dollar's weight, as American commerce with Japan was being hindered by the fact that our silver dollar was somewhat smaller than European crowns. It was decided to strike a special coin, known as the "Trade Dollar," to weigh 27.22 grains and be composed of nine parts silver to one part copper. Much agitation to retain the silver dollar as a domestic circulating coin resulted in the government authorizing this new enlarged version to pass as legal tender (for its $1 face value) in transactions of $5 or less. This caused confusion and dissatisfaction, and in 1878 striking of a separate domestic silver dollar, based upon the pre-Trade Dollar standard, was resumed. For a while they were issued simultaneously until the Trade Dollar died a gradual death, its final year of striking being 1885. The last year in which they were struck in numbers that could be termed sufficient for free circulation was 1878. The Trade Dollar has sometimes been called one of the handsomest U.S. coins of that denomination. True enough, the design is well drawn, but striking of circulating specimens was in such low relief that the slightest handling all but obliterated the more attractive detailing. Only when seen in proof state can the Trade Dollar's beauty be recognized. The designer was William Barber. On the obverse is a seated figure of Liberty, with an eagle reverse. The wording "TRADE DOLLAR" appears at the foot of the reverse. This is the only U.S. coin to proclaim its composition; the reverse is inscribed "420 GRAINS, 900 FINE." Meaning, of course, .900 silver to .100 base metal. Beginning in 1876 the Trade Dollar was no longer legal for domestic use. The Treasury Department (assailed from all sides in those days) left itself open to sharp criticism by not offering to redeem Trade Dollars until 1887, 11 years later. In diameter the Trade Dollar was no larger than the normal issues, 38.1 mm., but somewhat thicker. It was the heaviest U.S. silver coin ever minted. Only recently has it come into what might be termed popularity among collectors. In terms of mintage totals vs. regular dollars it is still rather underpriced.

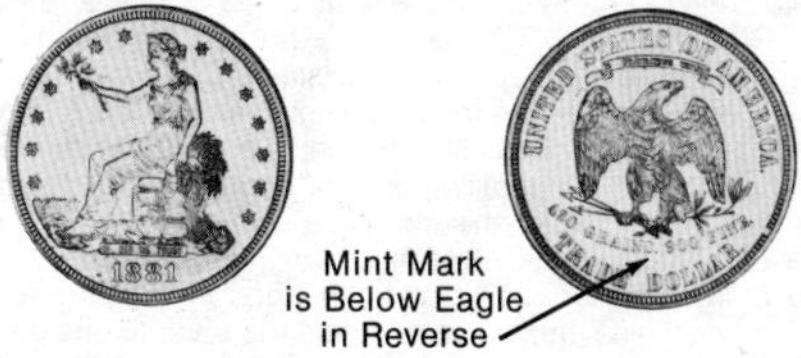

DATE	MINTAGE	ABP	F-12 Fine	EF-40 Ex. Fine	MS-60 Unc.**	PRF-65 Proof
☐1873	397,500	50.00	100.00	210.00	800.00	6000.00
☐1873CC	124,500	60.00	110.00	300.00	1200.00	
☐1873S	703,000	50.00	100.00	280.00	1000.00	
☐1874	987,800	70.00	110.00	280.00	700.00	6000.00

DATE	MINTAGE	ABP	F-12 Fine	EF-40 Ex. Fine	MS-60 Unc.**	PRF-65 Proof
□1874CC	1,373,200	56.00	90.00	210.00	1100.00	
□1874S	2,549,000	50.00	95.00	220.00	700.00	
□1875	218,000	100.00	210.00	300.00	1200.00	6000.00
□1875CC	1,573,700	50.00	90.00	200.00	800.00	
□1875S	4,487,000	45.00	95.00	200.00	700.00	
□1875S over CC		160.00	300.00	600.00	1600.00	
□1876	456,150	50.00	90.00	200.00	700.00	6000.00
□1876CC	509,000	63.00	95.00	210.00	980.00	
□1876S	5,227,000	43.00	75.00	170.00	700.00	
□1877	3,039,710	49.00	80.00	180.00	700.00	6000.00
□1877CC	534,000	66.00	110.00	220.00	1200.00	
□1877S	9,519,000	37.00	76.00	180.00	800.00	
□1878	900	3000.00	PROOFS ONLY			7000.00
□1878CC	97,000	110.00	210.00	870.00	3100.00	
□1878S	4,162,000	34.00	70.00	170.00	800.00	
□1879	1,541	3000.00	PROOFS ONLY			7000.00
□1880	1,987	3000.00	PROOFS ONLY			7000.00
□1881	960	3000.00	PROOFS ONLY			7000.00
□1882	1,097	3000.00	PROOFS ONLY			7000.00
□1883	979	3000.00	PROOFS ONLY			7000.00
□1884	10	20000.00	PROOFS ONLY*			50000.00
□1885	5	PROOFS ONLY—EXTREMELY RARE: $125,000.00				

*KREISBERG AUCTION 1976

**Superbly struck pieces bring proportionately more than prices shown

SILVER DOLLARS — LIBERTY HEAD OR "MORGAN," 1878–1904 AND 1921

For the resumption of the standard silver dollar series a new design was chosen. The work of George T. Morgan, and thereby popularly called Morgan Dollar, it showed a profile head of Liberty backed with an eagle holding arrows and branch. The motto "IN GOD WE TRUST" was installed above the eagle in Old English Gothic lettering. On the obverse appeared the slogan "E PLURIBUS UNUM." For many years the Morgan dollar was the best known and probably most respected silver "crown" in the world. Artistically the work is superb, rendered all the more impressive by the fact that its detailing did not become easily effaced with use. Morgan's goal was to fashion for this country a coin which, if it did not carry the financial power of ancient Greek silver pieces, might be regarded as their equal in design. The Morgan dollar remained unchanged in weight and composition throughout its history. It was comprised of nine parts silver to one part copper and weighed 412.5 grains. The diameter is 38.1 mm. After having been struck in large quantities for two and a half decades, production sometimes exceeding 30 million pieces annually, it was suspended in 1904 because of a shortage of silver. Striking was resumed in 1921, but only briefly, as the new Peace Dollar was introduced that same year. However there were more Morgan dollars coined in 1921—over 80 million—than in any previous year. The mint mark is placed below the eagle on the reverse. The Morgan dollar contains .77344 ounce of silver, or slightly more than three-quarters of an ounce.

Mint Mark is Below Eagle on Reverse

DATE	MINTAGE	ABP	F-12 Fine	EX-40 Ex. Fine	MS-60 Unc.	PRF-65 Proof
☐ 1878 7 Tail Feathers	416,000	9.50	16.00	21.00	70.00	8000.00
☐ 1878 8 Tail Feathers	750,000	9.50	20.00	30.00	80.00	8000.00
☐ 1878 7 over 8 Tail Feathers		9.50	24.00	34.00	87.00	
☐ 1878CC	2,212,000	9.50	30.00	45.00	120.00	
☐ 1878S	9,774,000	9.50	16.00	21.00	80.00	
☐ 1879	14,807,100	9.00	16.00	21.00	60.00	7800.00
☐ 1879CC	756,000	60.00	90.00	270.00	1000.00	
☐ 1879O	2,887,000	9.00	15.00	21.00	66.00	
☐ 1879S	9,110,000	9.00	15.00	30.00	67.00	
☐ 1880	12,601,355	9.00	15.00	21.00	55.00	7800.00
☐ 1880CC	591,000	21.00	40.00	80.00	210.00	
☐ 1880 over 79CC		21.00	50.00	80.00	210.00	
☐ 1880O	5,305,000	8.00	15.00	21.00	70.00	
☐ 1880S	8,900,000	8.00	16.00	22.00	72.00	
☐ 1881	9,163,975	8.00	15.00	20.00	110.00	7800.00
☐ 1881CC	206,000	40.00	70.00	120.00	280.00	
☐ 1881O	5,708,000	8.00	16.00	20.00	65.00	
☐ 1881S	12,760,000	8.00	16.00	20.00	80.00	
☐ 1882	11,101,000	8.00	16.00	20.00	65.00	7800.00
☐ 1882CC	1,133,000	16.00	25.00	45.00	140.00	
☐ 1882O	6,090,000	8.00	14.00	20.00	100.00	
☐ 1882O, O over S		8.00	17.00	21.00	90.00	7800.00
☐ 1882S	9,250,000	8.00	17.00	21.00	60.00	
☐ 1883	12,191,039	8.00	15.00	20.00	50.00	7800.00
☐ 1883CC	1,204,000	14.00	25.00	45.00	110.00	
☐ 1883O	8,725,000	8.00	14.00	20.00	40.00	
☐ 1883S	6,250,000	8.00	19.00	31.00	400.00	
☐ 1884	14,070,875	8.00	14.00	21.00	60.00	7800.00
☐ 1884CC	1,136,000	12.00	30.00	45.00	120.00	
☐ 1884O	9,730,000	8.00	15.00	21.00	45.00	
☐ 1884S	3,200,000	8.00	16.00	39.00	1800.00	
☐ 1885	17,787,767	8.00	14.00	20.00	40.00	7800.00
☐ 1885CC	228,000	60.00	100.00	185.00	290.00	
☐ 1885O	9,185,000	8.00	18.00	21.00	45.00	
☐ 1885S	1,497,000	8.00	18.00	22.00	125.00	

DATE	MINTAGE	ABP	F-12 Fine	EX-40 Ex. Fine	MS-60 Unc.	PRF-65 Proof
☐ 1886	19,963,886	8.50	16.00	20.00	35.00	7800.00
☐ 1886O	10,710,000	8.50	16.00	21.00	360.00	
☐ 1886S	750,000	8.50	20.00	35.00	160.00	
☐ 1887	20,290,710	8.50	15.00	25.00	60.00	7800.00
☐ 1887O	11,550,000	8.50	15.00	21.00	60.00	
☐ 1887S	1,771,000	8.50	16.00	25.00	80.00	
☐ 1888	19,183,833	8.50	15.00	20.00	45.00	7800.00
☐ 1888O	12,150,000	8.50	16.00	21.00	45.00	
☐ 1888S	657,000	11.00	20.00	36.00	140.00	
☐ 1889	21,726,811	8.50	16.00	21.00	40.00	7800.00
☐ 1889CC	350,000	174.00	300.00	600.00	5600.00	
☐ 1889O	11,875,000	8.00	16.00	21.00	90.00	
☐ 1889S	700,000	8.00	25.00	40.00	130.00	
☐ 1890	16,802,590	8.00	15.00	21.00	45.00	7800.00
☐ 1890CC	2,309,041	16.00	24.00	45.00	240.00	
☐ 1890O	10,701,000	8.75	15.00	19.00	65.00	
☐ 1890S	8,230,373	8.75	15.00	19.00	64.00	
☐ 1891	8,694,206	8.75	15.00	19.00	70.00	7800.00
☐ 1891CC	1,618,000	14.00	20.00	46.00	210.00	
☐ 1891O	7,954,529	8.00	16.00	23.00	80.00	
☐ 1891S	5,296,000	8.00	16.00	21.00	70.00	
☐ 1892	1,037,245	8.00	16.00	21.00	150.00	7800.00
☐ 1892CC	1,352,000	20.00	38.00	82.00	380.00	
☐ 1892O	2,744,000	8.00	15.00	24.00	130.00	
☐ 1892S	1,200,000	16.00	60.00	140.00	5600.00	
☐ 1893	378,792	21.00	45.00	90.00	380.00	7900.00
☐ 1893CC	667,000	60.00	100.00	360.00	860.00	
☐ 1893O	300,000	31.00	80.00	210.00	1000.00	
☐ 1893S	100,000	550.00	1100.00	3100.00	18700.00	
☐ 1894	110,972	110.00	200.00	415.00	1000.00	7900.00
☐ 1894O	1,723,000	8.00	19.00	34.00	500.00	
☐ 1894S	1,260,000	12.00	28.00	90.00	370.00	
☐ 1895*	12,880				14000.00	19000.00
☐ 1895O	450,000	31.00	72.00	210.00	2200.00	
☐ 1895S	400,000	40.00	80.00	330.00	1000.00	
☐ 1896	9,976,762	8.00	12.00	21.00	5000.00	7800.00
☐ 1896O	4,900,000	8.00	12.00	22.00	820.00	
☐ 1896S	5,000,000	8.00	28.00	110.00	530.00	
☐ 1897	2,822,731	8.00	12.00	19.00	40.00	7700.00
☐ 1897O	4,004,000	8.00	16.00	19.00	460.00	
☐ 1897S	5,825,000	8.00	16.00	19.00	70.00	
☐ 1898	5,884,725	8.00	12.00	19.00	55.00	7800.00
☐ 1898O	4,440,000	8.00	16.00	19.00	45.00	
☐ 1898S	4,102,000	8.00	14.00	20.00	160.00	
☐ 1899	330,846	16.00	32.00	50.00	110.00	7700.00
☐ 1899O	12,290,000	8.00	14.00	19.00	40.00	
☐ 1899S	2,562,000	8.00	17.00	22.00	160.00	
☐ 1900	8,830,912	8.00	14.00	19.00	40.00	7700.00

DATE	MINTAGE	ABP	F-12 Fine	EX-40 Ex. Fine	MS-60 Unc.	PRF-65 Proof
□1900O	12,590,000	8.00	14.00	21.00	40.00	
□1900S	3,540,000	8.00	12.00	21.00	125.00	
□1901	6,962,813	12.00	25.00	40.00	990.00	7800.00
□1901O	13,320,000	8.00	14.00	22.00	45.00	
□1901S	2,284,000	8.00	12.00	40.00	300.00	
□1902	7,994,777	8.00	12.00	20.00	62.00	7800.00
□1902O	8,636,000	8.00	12.00	20.00	46.00	
□1902S	1,530,000	17.00	38.00	90.00	250.00	
□1903	4,652,755	8.00	16.00	20.00	60.00	7900.00
□1903O	4,450,000	80.00	120.00	210.00	300.00	
□1903S	1,241,000	11.00	42.00	160.00	1875.00	
□1904	2,788,650	8.00	12.00	20.00	90.00	7800.00
□1904O	3,720,000	8.00	12.00	20.00	43.00	
□1904S	2,304,000	18.00	38.00	115.00	910.00	
□1921	44,690,000	8.00	12.00	16.00	41.00	
□1921D	20,345,000	8.00	12.00	16.00	45.00	
□1921S	21,695,000	8.00	12.00	16.00	46.00	

*Check carefully for removed mint mark.

Note: Superbly struck specimens with few bag marks bring substantially more than the prices listed.

SILVER DOLLARS — PEACE, 1921–1935

It was decided, following the Armistice of 1918, to issue a coin commemorating world peace, and to make this a circulating coin rather than a limited issue. As production of silver dollars was being resumed in 1921, this was the logical denomination. This coin, known as the Peace Dollar, was designed by Anthony DeFrancisci, who had some reputation as a designer of medals. Its obverse pictured a profile head of Liberty, quite different in character from those on other coins, and a standing eagle (perched on a mound) on its reverse. The word "Peace" was incorporated into the reverse. As originally engraved, the dies were similar in nature to those of a medal, intended to strike in high relief. The following year modified dies were introduced. Coining of silver dollars was halted in 1935 and never resumed, the subsequent Ike and Anthony dollars being of a different metallic composition. Mint mark appears beneath the word "ONE" in "ONE DOLLAR" on the reverse. The Peace dollar is composed of 90% silver and 10% copper and has a weight of 412½ grains. The diameter is 38.1 mm. and the silver content is .77344 of an ounce.

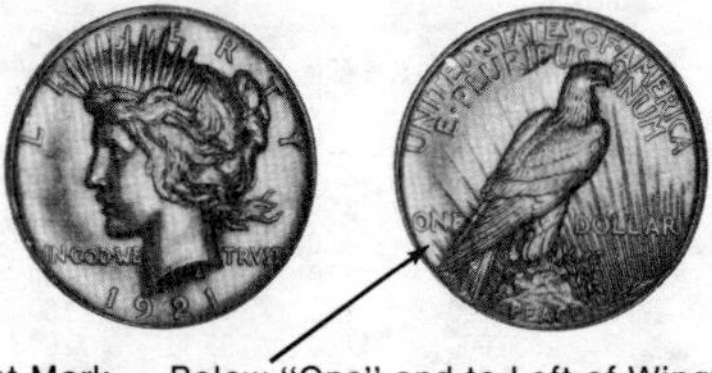

Mint Mark — Below "One" and to Left of Wingtip

DATE	MINTAGE	ABP	F-12 Fine	EX-40 Ex. Fine	MS-60 Unc.
☐ 1921	1,006,473	13.50	28.00	50.00	220.00
☐ 1922	51,737,000	8.00	13.00	17.00	35.00
☐ 1922D	15,063,000	8.00	13.00	17.00	46.00
☐ 1922S	17,475,000	8.00	13.00	17.00	46.00
☐ 1923	30,800,000	8.00	13.00	17.00	30.00
☐ 1923D	6,811,000	8.00	13.00	17.00	45.00
☐ 1923S	19,020,000	8.00	13.00	17.00	45.00
☐ 1924	11,811,000	8.00	13.00	17.00	35.00
☐ 1924S	1,728,000	8.00	16.00	28.00	160.00
☐ 1925	10,198,000	8.00	14.00	17.00	45.00
☐ 1925S	1,610,000	8.00	17.00	24.00	120.00
☐ 1926	1,939,000	8.00	13.00	17.00	55.00
☐ 1926D	2,348,700	8.00	13.00	17.00	75.00
☐ 1926S	6,980,000	8.00	12.00	17.00	55.00
☐ 1927	848,000	12.00	23.00	28.00	120.00
☐ 1927D	1,268,900	8.00	18.00	27.00	220.00
☐ 1927S	866,000	8.00	19.00	30.00	160.00
☐ 1928	360,649	35.00	82.00	140.00	280.00
☐ 1928S	1,632,000	8.00	17.00	26.00	140.00
☐ 1934	954,057	8.00	19.00	25.00	125.00
☐ 1934D	1,569,500	8.00	16.00	25.00	135.00
☐ 1934S	1,011,000	8.00	85.00	170.00	1300.00
☐ 1935	1,576,000	8.00	15.00	20.00	80.00
☐ 1935S	1,964,000	8.00	18.00	26.00	160.00
☐ 1964D	316,000	NONE KNOWN TO EXIST			

Note: In 1964 it was decided to resume striking silver dollars after a nearly 30 year lapse. The Peace design was used and production was at the Denver Mint. Before the coins reached circulation, the "silver controversy" of the year culminated in the Mint's decision to switch to clad coinage. Production of the 1964D silver dollar was halted and the unreleased total of 316,000 was ordered melted. In the intervening years a number of rumors have circulated about specimens which escaped melting, but there is no proven evidence of any in existence. Technically this coin, if it did exist, would be illegal to own and subject to confiscation.

DOLLARS

EISENHOWER, 1971–1978

In 1971, following the death of President Eisenhower, a dollar piece with his likeness on the obverse, backed by an adaptation of the Apollo 11 insignia, was placed into circulation. Our astronauts had landed on the moon just two years earlier and this was commemorated by the reverse. Frank Gasparro, chief engraver of the Mint, was its designer. Due to the greatly increased price of silver bullion it was not possible to mint this coin as a "silver dollar." Its size was equivalent to that of earlier silver dollars but the composition bore little resemblance to the old standard. Two versions were struck, a collector's edition with an 80% silver content and ordinary circulating coins with an outer layer of three parts copper and one part nickel enclosing an interior of pure copper. The former had a weight of 24.68 grams. Both have a 38.1 mm. diameter. In 1976 a special reverse design was applied, featuring a representation of the Liberty Bell superimposed against the moon, in connection with the Bicentennial. The obverse carried a double date, 1776–1976. Some silver-clad specimens were struck, their specifications the same as stated above. In the following year the original reverse was reinstated. The final year of production was 1978.

Mint Mark Below Head of Obverse

Bicentennial 1776-1976 Reverse

DATE	MINTAGE	MS-60 Unc.	PRF-65 Proof
☐ 1971 Copper-nickel clad	47,799,000	2.50	
☐ 1971D Copper-nickel clad	68,587,424	2.50	
☐ 1971S Silver clad	11,133,764	5.00	8.50
☐ 1972 Copper-nickel clad	75,390,000	2.50	
☐ 1972D Copper-nickel clad	92,548,511	2.40	
☐ 1972S Silver clad	4,004,657	10.00	11.50
☐ 1973 Copper-nickel clad	2,000,056	8.00	
☐ 1973D Copper-nickel clad	2,000,000	8.00	
☐ 1973S Copper-nickel clad	2,760,339	2.50	5.00
☐ 1973S Silver clad	1,883,140	24.00	50.00
☐ 1974 Copper-nickel clad	27,366,000	2.10	
☐ 1974D Copper-nickel clad	45,520,175	2.10	

DATE	MINTAGE	MS-60 Unc.	PRF-65 Proof
☐1974S Copper-nickel clad	2,617,350	2.10	4.00
☐1974S Silver clad	3,216,420	8.00	14.00
☐1976 Copper-nickel clad Variety I	4,021,250	2.90	
☐1976 Copper-nickel clad Variety II	113,325,000	2.30	
☐1976D Copper-nickel clad Variety I	21,048,650	2.10	
☐1976D Copper-nickel clad Variety II	82,179,355	2.10	
☐1976S Copper-nickel clad Variety I	2,845,390		4.00
☐1976S Copper-nickel clad Variety II	4,149,675		4.00
☐1976S Silver clad (40%)	4,239,460	8.00	11.00
☐1977 Copper-nickel clad	12,598,220	3.10	
☐1977D Copper-nickel clad	32,985,000	2.40	
☐1977S Copper-nickel clad	3,250,895		4.00
☐1978 Copper-nickel clad	25,702,000	2.40	
☐1978D Copper-nickel clad	33,012,890	2.40	
☐1978S Copper-nickel clad	3,127,781		6.00

DOLLARS—SUSAN B. ANTHONY, 1979 TO DATE

In 1979 the Eisenhower dollar was replaced by one picturing Susan B. Anthony, agitator for female suffrage in the earlier part of this century. The new coin, the target of much controversy, had the distinction of a number of "firsts":

*First U.S. coin to picture a female (excluding mythological and symbolic types).

*First non-gold dollar coin of small size.

*First U.S. coin with non-circular edge.

The Anthony dollar measures 26½ mm., or about the size of a quarter. To avoid its confusion with coins of that denomination, the edge was not made circular but squared out into sections. Its composition is: exterior, three parts copper to one part nickel; interior, pure copper. The weight is 8 1⁄10 grams. On the reverse appears the Apollo 11 insignia used for the Eisenhower dollar. Public dissatisfaction with the coin has placed its future in doubt. The designer was Frank Gasparro.

DATE	MINTAGE	MS-60 Unc.	PRF-65 Proof
☐1979 Copper-nickel clad	360,200,000	1.50	
☐1979D Copper-nickel clad	287,000,000	1.50	
☐1979S Copper-nickel clad Proof	110,000,000	1.50	8.00
☐1979S Copper-nickel clad (II) Proof	3,677,000		87.00
☐1980P	27,600,000	1.50	
☐1980D	41,595,000	1.50	

DATE	MINTAGE	MS-60 Unc.	PRF-65 Proof
☐1980S	20,425,000	2.25	8.00
☐1981P	2,995,000	4.50	
☐1981D	3,237,631	4.50	
☐1981S	3,500,000	4.50	8.00

GOLD DOLLARS, 1849–1889

No gold dollars were struck in the Mint's early years. It was felt (logically enough, based upon conditions that existed then) that silver would serve adequately for this denomination, and that gold should be restricted to coins of a higher face value. However, a series of events occurred, following the California gold strikes of 1849, which rendered gold dollars a necessity. Chief among them was the growing practice of citizens, especially in the West, to trade with bullion rather than coinage. So in 1849 a gold dollar was introduced. Designed by James Longacre, it carried a Liberty head on the obverse and was backed by a simple reverse featuring a wreath and the numeral one in Arabic. A series of stars encircled the obverse portrait. As this coin was, by necessity, of diminutive size, elaborate designing was not possible. The Liberty Gold Dollar weighed 1.672 grams and was composed of 90% gold and 10% copper. It had a diameter of 13 mm. The mint mark appears below the wreath. In 1854 the obverse was given over to an Indian Head and the coin made flatter, its diameter increased to 15 mm. The weight was unaltered. There was a further change in 1856 when a new die was cast for the obverse, showing the Indian Head a bit larger. This was the final variety for the gold dollar, whose last year of coining was 1889. The gold content by weight for all three types was .04837 of an ounce.

GOLD DOLLARS — LIBERTY HEAD WITH CORONET, SMALL SIZE, 1849–1854

DATE	MINTAGE	ABP in F-12	F-12 Fine	EF-40 Ex. Fine	MS-60 Unc.
☐1849	688,600	120.00	180.00	250.00	1100.00
☐1849C Closed Wreath	11,634	180.00	220.00	240.00	1150.00
☐1849C Open Wreath	4 Known			EXTREMELY RARE	
☐1849D	21,588	198.00	300.00	700.00	3000.00
☐1849O	215,000	115.00	185.00	600.00	1400.00
☐1850	481,953	115.00	185.00	275.00	900.00
☐1850C	6,966	200.00	325.00	700.00	3000.00
☐1850D	8,382	220.00	375.00	800.00	3400.00
☐1850O	14,000	140.00	220.00	400.00	1700.00
☐1851	3,317,671	115.00	170.00	240.00	900.00
☐1851C	41,267	115.00	275.00	575.00	2000.00
☐1851D	9,832	200.00	320.00	800.00	2800.00
☐1851O	290,000	115.00	175.00	260.00	1200.00
☐1852	2,045,351	115.00	165.00	260.00	900.00
☐1852C	9,434	145.00	275.00	700.00	2400.00
☐1852D	6,360	200.00	340.00	800.00	3000.00

DATE	MINTAGE	ABP in F-12	F-12 Fine	EF-40 Ex. Fine	MS-60 Unc.
☐1852O	140,000	115.00	175.00	270.00	1200.00
☐1853	4,076,051	115.00	175.00	240.00	950.00
☐1853C	11,515	130.00	250.00	650.00	3000.00
☐1853D	6,583	230.00	300.00	800.00	3400.00
☐1853O	290,000	115.00	175.00	270.00	1200.00
☐1854*	1,639,445	115.00	165.00	250.00	850.00
☐1854D	2,935	350.00	500.00	1200.00	5200.00
☐1854S	14,635	115.00	220.00	510.00	2600.00

*Includes Indian Headdress Dollars of 1854, Type II

GOLD DOLLARS — SMALL INDIAN HEAD, FEATHER HEADDRESS, LARGE SIZE, 1854–1856

Mint Mark Below Wreath on Reverse

DATE	MINTAGE	ABP in F-12	F-12 Fine	EF-40 Ex. Fine	MS-60 Unc.
☐*1854**	1,639,445	120.00	275.00	550.00	5000.00
☐1854C	4				UNKNOWN
☐1855	758,269	120.00	275.00	550.00	5000.00
☐1855C	8,903	300.00	600.00	1180.00	8800.00
☐1855D	1,811	800.00	2000.00	5600.00	16000.00
☐1855O	55,000	210.00	435.00	900.00	7000.00
☐1856S	24,600	210.00	460.00	1000.00	6800.00

*Includes Indian Headdress Dollars of 1854, Type II
**Includes Mintage of Liberty Head of 1854, Type I

GOLD DOLLARS — LARGE LIBERTY HEAD, FEATHER HEADDRESS, LARGE SIZE, 1856–1889

Mint Mark is Below Wreath on Reverse

DATE	MINTAGE	ABP in F-12	F-12 Fine	EF-40 Ex. Fine	MS-60 Unc.	PRF-65 Proof
☐1856 Slant 5	1,762,936	120.00	175.00	260.00	1100.00	
☐1856D	1,460	1800.00	2800.00	5000.00	17000.00	

DATE	MINTAGE	ABP in F-12	F-12 Fine	EF-40 Ex. Fine	MS-60 Unc.	PRF-65 Proof
☐ 1857	774,789	116.00	160.00	240.00	875.00	
☐ 1857C	13,280	170.00	340.00	650.00	2600.00	
☐ 1857D	3,533	200.00	430.00	1100.00	4400.00	
☐ 1857S	10,000	150.00	320.00	410.00	2400.00	
☐ 1858	117,995	120.00	160.00	250.00	875.00	12000.00
☐ 1858D	3,477	210.00	600.00	1400.00	5200.00	
☐ 1858S	10,000	120.00	310.00	450.00	2000.00	
☐ 1859	168,244	120.00	160.00	260.00	1000.00	10000.00
☐ 1859C	5,235	160.00	400.00	810.00	3500.00	
☐ 1859D	4,952	250.00	450.00	1200.00	4200.00	
☐ 1859S	15,000	120.00	310.00	410.00	2500.00	
☐ 1860	36,688	120.00	160.00	240.00	910.00	10000.00
☐ 1860D	1,566	1600.00	2500.00	5100.00	15000.00	
☐ 1860S	13,000	140.00	210.00	430.00	2100.00	
☐ 1861	527,499	120.00	150.00	240.00	1100.00	8000.00
☐ 1861D		3000.00	4100.00	9000.00	25000.00	
☐ 1862	1,326,865	120.00	150.00	210.00	900.00	9000.00
☐ 1863	6,250	200.00	375.00	700.00	4000.00	9000.00
☐ 1864	5,950	200.00	350.00	610.00	3200.00	9000.00
☐ 1865	3,725	200.00	350.00	700.00	3600.00	10000.00
☐ 1866	7,180	150.00	280.00	600.00	2000.00	10000.00
☐ 1867	5,250	150.00	290.00	570.00	2100.00	9000.00
☐ 1868	10,525	150.00	270.00	500.00	1700.00	10000.00
☐ 1869	5,925	150.00	285.00	540.00	1900.00	10000.00
☐ 1870	6,335	150.00	280.00	500.00	1600.00	9000.00
☐ 1870S	3,000	240.00	480.00	1100.00	3700.00	
☐ 1871	3,930	150.00	280.00	550.00	1850.00	10000.00
☐ 1872	3,530	150.00	280.00	550.00	1950.00	10000.00
☐ 1873 open 3	125,125	116.00	185.00	230.00	1100.00	
☐ 1873 closed 3		116.00	290.00	600.00	2100.00	10000.00
☐ 1874	198,820	116.00	160.00	230.00	1000.00	10000.00
☐ 1875	420	1600.00	1900.00	3300.00	8000.00	20000.00
☐ 1876	3,245	120.00	210.00	390.00	1800.00	7000.00
☐ 1877	3,920	150.00	240.00	500.00	1700.00	8000.00
☐ 1878	3,020	150.00	260.00	500.00	1600.00	8000.00
☐ 1879	3,030	110.00	210.00	400.00	1500.00	10000.00
☐ 1880	1,636	110.00	200.00	400.00	1500.00	10000.00
☐ 1881	7,660	100.00	190.00	300.00	1000.00	8000.00
☐ 1882	5,040	100.00	190.00	300.00	1000.00	8000.00
☐ 1883	10,840	100.00	175.00	260.00	1000.00	8000.00
☐ 1884	6,206	100.00	175.00	260.00	1000.00	8000.00
☐ 1885	12,205	100.00	175.00	260.00	1000.00	8000.00
☐ 1886	6,016	100.00	175.00	260.00	1000.00	8000.00
☐ 1887	8,543	100.00	175.00	260.00	1000.00	8000.00
☐ 1888	16,080	100.00	175.00	260.00	1000.00	8000.00
☐ 1889	30,729	100.00	175.00	260.00	1000.00	8000.00

Note: Many gold dollars in the 1880s were hoarded and appear in gem, prooflike condition. Beware of these pieces being sold as proofs.

QUARTER EAGLES—$2.50 GOLD PIECES

The $2.50 gold piece, authorized on April 2, 1792, was known as a "Quarter Eagle" (i.e., the quarter part of an Eagle or $10 gold piece). Striking was not begun until 1796. As early production was extremely limited—in no year were as many as 10,000 struck until 1834—these are scarce and valuable coins. Designed by Robert Scot, the original type featured a capped Liberty on the obverse and shield eagle reverse. The portrait is quite different than that used on silver coinage and in general the engraving may be said to be somewhat superior. No wording other than "LIBERTY" adorns the obverse, with "UNITED STATES OF AMERICA" on the reverse. The composition was .9167 gold to .0833 copper, or more than 9⁄10 gold, with a weight of 4.37 grams and a diameter which varied slightly but normally was about 20 mm. There are two obverse types, one with and one without a circular border of stars. In 1808 the portrait, while retaining the cap, was entirely redesigned. It was shifted around to face left instead of right, the cap was deemphasized, Liberty's features were redrawn in an effort at greater femininity, her hair was made curlier, and the eagle was likewise refurbished. John Reish was the designer. From 1809 to 1820 no quarter eagles were minted. When the series was resumed in 1821 it was with modified obverse and reverse types and the diameter had shrunk to 18½ mm. However, the coin contained fully as much gold as previously and the decreased diameter was compensated for by a slight increase in thickness. The obverse was changed in 1834 to the so-called "Classic Head" type, a more stylish rendition of Liberty, designed by the Mint's chief designer, William Kneass (pronounced Niece). The weight was reduced to 4.18 grams and the composition altered to contain less than 9⁄10 gold: .8992 to .1008 copper. The diameter was 18.2 mm. Christian Gobrecht made some alterations to this design in 1840 but it was not materially changed. However, the gold content was increased to an even .900 and the diameter brought down to 18 mm. Total gold content by weight was .12094. This design remained in use for 67 years, surpassed for longevity only by the Lincoln Penny (1909–present). An interesting variation occurred in 1848, the so-called "California Quarter Eagle." In that year Colonel Mason, the Military Governor of California, shipped about 230 ounces of gold to Secretary of War Marcy in Washington, D.C. Marcy had the bullion melted down and struck into quarter eagles, distinguished by the abbreviation, "CAL.," above the eagle's head on the reverse. This was not an integral part of the design but was stamped separately. As little more than 1,000 specimens were struck, it became a choice collector's item. Purchasers should be on guard against fakes. The Gobrecht Quarter Eagle was discontinued in 1907. Specimens dated after 1900, and some earlier ones, are valued primarily for their bullion content.

QUARTER EAGLES — LIBERTY CAP, 1796–1807

1796
No Stars

1797–1807
With Stars

1796–1807

DATE	MINTAGE	ABP in F-12	F-12 Fine	EF-40 Ex. Fine	MS-60 Unc.
☐1796 No Stars..............	963	6000.00	9200.00	24000.00	46000.00
☐1796 With Stars	432	4500.00	7000.00	16000.00	37000.00
☐1797	427	2900.00	5100.00	11000.00	21000.00
☐1798	1,094	1700.00	3200.00	6700.00	17500.00
☐1802 over 1................	3,033	1600.00	2800.00	6500.00	18000.00
☐1804 14 Star Reverse.......	3,327	1600.00	2800.00	5900.00	15000.00
☐1804 13 Star Reverse.......		2200.00	4200.00	11000.00	24000.00
☐1805	1,781	1600.00	2800.00	5700.00	17000.00
☐1806 over 4................	1,616	1600.00	2800.00	5700.00	17000.00
☐1806 over 5................		2000.00	3700.00	8000.00	18000.00
☐1807	6,812	1500.00	2800.00	5600.00	16500.00

QUARTER EAGLES — BUST TYPE, TURBAN HEAD, 1808–1834

1808
Draped
Bust
Round Cap

1821–1834
Undraped
Liberty
Round Cap

1808–1834
Motto
Over Eagle

DATE	MINTAGE	ABP in F-12	F-12 Fine	EF-40 Ex. Fine	MS-60 Unc.
☐1808	2,710	2100.00	7000.00	18000.00	48000.00
REDUCED SIZE (18.5 mm. dia.)					
☐1821	6,448	1400.00	3200.00	6700.00	16000.00
☐1824 over 21...............	2,600	1600.00	3200.00	6200.00	16000.00
☐1825	4,434	1600.00	3200.00	6200.00	16000.00
☐1826 over 25...............	760	2400.00	4700.00	9100.00	28000.00
☐1827	2,800	1600.00	3200.00	6200.00	14000.00
☐1829	3,403	1400.00	2900.00	5000.00	14000.00
☐1830	4,540	1400.00	2800.00	5200.00	14000.00

DATE	MINTAGE	ABP in F-12	F-12 Fine	EF-40 Ex. Fine	MS-60 Unc.
☐1831	4,520	1400.00	2700.00	6000.00	13000.00
☐1832	4,400	1400.00	2700.00	6000.00	13000.00
☐1833	4,160	1400.00	2700.00	6000.00	13000.00
☐1834 Motto	4,000	2100.00	5500.00	13000.00	30000.00

QUARTER EAGLES — LIBERTY HEAD WITH RIBBONS, 1834–1839
NO MOTTO OVER EAGLE

Mint Mark is Above Date on Obverse

DATE	MINTAGE	ABP in F-12	F-12 Fine	EF-40 Ex. Fine	MS-60 Unc.
☐1834 No Motto	112,234	150.00	230.00	450.00	2000.00
☐1835	131,402	150.00	230.00	450.00	2000.00
☐1836	547,986	150.00	230.00	450.00	2000.00
☐1837	45,080	150.00	230.00	450.00	2000.00
☐1838	47,030	150.00	230.00	450.00	2000.00
☐1838C	7,908	200.00	450.00	1300.00	5300.00
☐1839	27,021	165.00	230.00	460.00	2400.00
☐1839C	18,173	200.00	380.00	1150.00	5500.00
☐1839D	13,674	280.00	450.00	1300.00	6000.00
☐1839O	17,781	180.00	310.00	700.00	4600.00

QUARTER EAGLES — LIBERTY HEAD WITH CORONET, 1840–1907

Mint Mark is Below Eagle on Reverse

DATE	MINTAGE	ABP in F-12	F-12 Fine	EF-40 Ex. Fine	MS-60 Unc.
☐1840	18,859	135.00	235.00	400.00	1500.00
☐1840C	12,838	180.00	340.00	760.00	3300.00
☐1840D	3,532	400.00	700.00	3000.00	8000.00
☐1840O	26,200	127.00	200.00	430.00	1300.00
☐1841	Stack's 1976: $40,000 in Proof				
☐1841C	10,297	140.00	300.00	700.00	2400.00
☐1841D	4,164	300.00	600.00	1800.00	5800.00
☐1842	2,823	170.00	340.00	900.00	3100.00

DATE	MINTAGE	ABP in F-12	F-12 Fine	EF-40 Ex. Fine	MS-60 Unc.
☐ 1842C	6,737	200.00	400.00	900.00	2700.00
☐ 1842D	4,643	260.00	500.00	1200.00	5000.00
☐ 1842O	19,800	130.00	230.00	1000.00	2100.00
☐ 1843	100,546	130.00	190.00	450.00	1050.00
☐ 1843C Small Date	26,096	450.00	975.00	2500.00	6000.00
☐ 1843C Large Date	26,096	136.00	300.00	750.00	2300.00
☐ 1843D	36,209	135.00	320.00	800.00	2700.00
☐ 1843O Small Date	368,002	120.00	210.00	300.00	1090.00
☐ 1843O Large Date	368,002	120.00	210.00	300.00	1200.00
☐ 1844	6,784	120.00	240.00	500.00	2100.00
☐ 1844C	11,622	173.00	310.00	600.00	2600.00
☐ 1844D	17,332	173.00	400.00	900.00	2800.00
☐ 1845	91,051	130.00	190.00	300.00	1150.00
☐ 1845D	19,460	170.00	400.00	900.00	2800.00
☐ 1845O	4,000	210.00	700.00	1500.00	7000.00
☐ 1846	21,598	130.00	190.00	375.00	1200.00
☐ 1846C	4,808	130.00	400.00	1050.00	3000.00
☐ 1846D	19,303	130.00	400.00	900.00	2900.00
☐ 1846O	66,000	130.00	195.00	300.00	1250.00
☐ 1847	29,814	130.00	195.00	275.00	1200.00
☐ 1847C	23,226	130.00	300.00	500.00	2400.00
☐ 1847D	15,784	130.00	400.00	850.00	2700.00
☐ 1847O	124,000	130.00	182.00	320.00	1150.00
☐ 1848	8,886	130.00	300.00	700.00	2400.00
☐ 1848 Cal. above Eagle	1,389	240.00	3500.00	7500.00	25000.00
☐ 1848C	16,788	160.00	390.00	700.00	2700.00
☐ 1848D	13,771	170.00	310.00	900.00	2200.00
☐ 1849	23,294	125.00	200.00	310.00	1100.00
☐ 1849C	10,220	165.00	300.00	750.00	2600.00
☐ 1849D	10,945	170.00	350.00	950.00	2800.00
☐ 1850	252,923	130.00	160.00	270.00	1100.00
☐ 1850C	9,148	170.00	275.00	800.00	2400.00
☐ 1850D	12,148	160.00	350.00	900.00	2700.00
☐ 1850O	84,000	130.00	175.00	300.00	1100.00
☐ 1851	1,372,748	120.00	170.00	270.00	1100.00
☐ 1851C	14,923	150.00	300.00	750.00	2200.00
☐ 1851D	11,264	180.00	330.00	1000.00	2600.00
☐ 1851O	148,000	125.00	160.00	270.00	900.00
☐ 1852	1,159,681	122.00	160.00	270.00	1000.00
☐ 1852C	9,772	160.00	300.00	800.00	3000.00
☐ 1852D	4,078	180.00	400.00	1200.00	3800.00

DATE	MINTAGE	ABP in F-12	F-12 Fine	EF-40 Ex. Fine	MS-60 Unc.	PRF-65 Proof
☐ 1852O	140,000	110.00	180.00	300.00	1100.00	
☐ 1853	1,404,668	110.00	170.00	250.00	1100.00	
☐ 1853D	3,178	180.00	400.00	1300.00	3600.00	
☐ 1854	596,258	100.00	170.00	300.00	1000.00	
☐ 1854C	7,295	150.00	310.00	800.00	2600.00	
☐ 1854D	1,760	800.00	2000.00	4000.00	11000.00	

DATE	MINTAGE	ABP in F-12	F-12 Fine	EF-40 Ex. Fine	MS-60 Unc.	PRF-65 Proof
☐1854O	153,000	120.00	170.00	270.00	1000.00	
☐1854S	246	EXTREMELY RARE—EF-40: $25,000.00				
☐1855	235,480	100.00	180.00	290.00	950.00	
☐1855C	3,677	400.00	600.00	1400.00	4300.00	
☐1855D	1,123	1000.00	2000.00	4100.00	17000.00	
☐1856	384,240	110.00	170.00	280.00	1100.00	
☐1856C	7,913	200.00	350.00	800.00	2800.00	
☐1856D	874	2200.00	3000.00	8100.00	21000.00	
☐1856O	21,100	115.00	180.00	320.00	1200.00	
☐1856S	71,120	115.00	185.00	300.00	1100.00	
☐1857	214,130	115.00	175.00	300.00	1150.00	
☐1857D	2,364	270.00	500.00	1100.00	4200.00	
☐1857O	34,000	115.00	180.00	300.00	1100.00	
☐1857S	68,000	115.00	180.00	310.00	1200.00	
☐1858	47,377	115.00	180.00	275.00	1100.00	18700.00
☐1858C	9,056	160.00	300.00	700.00	2500.00	
☐1859	39,444	115.00	165.00	280.00	1000.00	12000.00
☐1859D	2,244	310.00	500.00	1600.00	4100.00	
☐1859S	15,200	115.00	170.00	330.00	1100.00	
☐1860	22,675	115.00	175.00	280.00	1000.00	12000.00
☐1860C	7,469	150.00	300.00	800.00	2300.00	
☐1860S	35,600	115.00	180.00	310.00	1100.00	
☐1861	1,272,518	115.00	165.00	260.00	800.00	12000.00
☐1861S	24,000	115.00	185.00	310.00	1100.00	
☐1862	112,353	115.00	175.00	275.00	1000.00	12000.00
☐1862S	8,000	115.00	210.00	700.00	1800.00	
☐1863	30 PROOFS ONLY; AUCTION SALE 1978:					$38000.00
☐1863S	10,800	115.00	190.00	510.00	1700.00	
☐1864	2,874	420.00	725.00	2000.00	5000.00	15000.00
☐1865	1,545	420.00	700.00	1800.00	4500.00	15000.00
☐1865S	23,376	115.00	175.00	350.00	1200.00	
☐1866	3,110	115.00	250.00	510.00	1600.00	15000.00
☐1867	3,250	115.00	180.00	400.00	1200.00	14000.00
☐1867S	28,000	115.00	210.00	310.00	1500.00	
☐1868	3,625	115.00	200.00	400.00	1200.00	12000.00
☐1868S	34,000	115.00	160.00	310.00	1200.00	
☐1869	4,343	115.00	190.00	330.00	1100.00	12500.00
☐1869S	29,500	115.00	150.00	310.00	1200.00	
☐1870	4,555	115.00	170.00	360.00	1250.00	12500.00
☐1870S	16,000	115.00	170.00	345.00	1250.00	
☐1871	5,350	115.00	180.00	340.00	1100.00	12500.00
☐1871S	22,000.00	115.00	155.00	290.00	1190.00	
☐1872	3,030	114.00	200.00	420.00	1200.00	10000.00
☐1872S	18,000	111.00	170.00	275.00	950.00	
☐1873	178,025	111.00	150.00	280.00	1000.00	11000.00
☐1873S	27,000	111.00	170.00	270.00	1000.00	
☐1874	3,940	111.00	175.00	310.00	1100.00	11000.00
☐1875	420	1100.00	2050.00	4100.00	9400.00	22000.00

DATE	MINTAGE	ABP in F-12	F-12 Fine	EF-40 Ex. Fine	MS-60 Unc.	PRF-65 Proof
☐ 1875S	11,600	110.00	175.00	320.00	1000.00	
☐ 1876	4,221	110.00	180.00	340.00	1300.00	11000.00
☐ 1876S	5,000	110.00	180.00	350.00	1100.00	
☐ 1877	1,652	220.00	325.00	625.00	1850.00	11000.00
☐ 1877S	35,000	110.00	170.00	250.00	1100.00	
☐ 1878	286,260	110.00	170.00	250.00	1100.00	11000.00
☐ 1878S	55,000	110.00	170.00	250.00	900.00	
☐ 1879	88,900	110.00	170.00	250.00	1000.00	11000.00
☐ 1879S	43,500	110.00	170.00	250.00	1000.00	
☐ 1880	2,996	110.00	180.00	250.00	1200.00	11500.00
☐ 1881	680	400.00	600.00	1680.00		
☐ 1882	4,040	110.00	210.00	310.00	1200.00	11000.00
☐ 1883	1,960	110.00	230.00	400.00	1150.00	11000.00
☐ 1884	1,993	110.00	230.00	400.00	1300.00	11000.00
☐ 1885	887	300.00	500.00	1100.00		
☐ 1886	4,088	110.00	180.00	280.00	1100.00	11000.00
☐ 1887	6,282	110.00	180.00	280.00	1100.00	11000.00
☐ 1888	16,098	110.00	180.00	280.00	1000.00	10000.00
☐ 1889	17,648	110.00	180.00	280.00	900.00	10000.00
☐ 1890	8,813	110.00	180.00	280.00	1100.00	10000.00
☐ 1891	11,040	110.00	180.00	280.00	900.00	10000.00
☐ 1892	2,545	110.00	180.00	350.00	1200.00	10000.00
☐ 1893	30,106	110.00	200.00	230.00	1000.00	10000.00
☐ 1894	4,122	110.00	160.00	245.00	1100.00	10000.00
☐ 1895	6,119	110.00	160.00	245.00	950.00	10000.00
☐ 1896	19,202	110.00	160.00	245.00	950.00	10000.00
☐ 1898	24,165	110.00	160.00	245.00	950.00	10000.00
☐ 1899	27,350	110.00	160.00	245.00	950.00	10000.00
☐ 1900	67,205	110.00	160.00	245.00	950.00	10000.00
☐ 1901	91,323	110.00	160.00	245.00	950.00	10000.00
☐ 1902	133,733	110.00	160.00	245.00	950.00	10000.00
☐ 1903	201,257	110.00	160.00	245.00	950.00	10000.00
☐ 1904	160,960	110.00	160.00	245.00	950.00	10000.00
☐ 1905	217,944	110.00	160.00	245.00	950.00	10000.00
☐ 1906	179,490	110.00	160.00	245.00	950.00	10000.00
☐ 1907	336,448	110.00	160.00	245.00	950.00	10000.00

Note: Specimens dated 1905S are counterfeits, made either by die striking or applying a false mint mark to a genuine 1905.

QUARTER EAGLES — INDIAN HEAD, 1908–1929

The quarter eagle was redesigned in 1908 by Bela Lyon Pratt. Liberty was removed from its obverse and replaced by a portrait of an Indian wearing a war bonnet. A standing eagle adorned the reverse. The coin has no raised edge and the designs plus inscriptions are stamped in incuse, or recessed beneath the surface, rather than being shown in high relief. The composition is .900 gold, .100 copper, with a weight of 4.18 grams. Its diameter is 18 mm. with total gold content by weight remaining at .12094 ounce. Quarter eagles were last struck in 1929, the year of this nation's financial difficulties.

Mint Mark is to Left of Value on Reverse

DATE	MINTAGE	ABP in F-12	F-12 Fine	EF-40 Ex. Fine	MS-60 Unc.	PRF-65 Proof
☐1908	565,057	110.00	170.00	230.00	400.00	12000.00
☐1908	441,899	110.00	170.00	230.00	400.00	12000.00
☐1910	492,682	110.00	170.00	230.00	400.00	12000.00
☐1911	404,191	110.00	170.00	230.00	400.00	12000.00
☐1911D	55,680	300.00	600.00	960.00	3550.00	
☐1912	616,197	110.00	170.00	230.00	400.00	12000.00
☐1913	722,165	110.00	170.00	230.00	400.00	12000.00
☐1914	240,117	110.00	170.00	230.00	400.00	12000.00
☐1914D	448,000	110.00	170.00	230.00	400.00	
☐1915	606,100	110.00	170.00	230.00	400.00	
☐1925D	578,000	110.00	170.00	230.00	400.00	
☐1926	446,000	110.00	170.00	230.00	400.00	
☐1927	388,000	110.00	170.00	230.00	400.00	
☐1928	416,000	110.00	170.00	230.00	400.00	
☐1929	532,000	110.00	170.00	230.00	400.00	

$3.00 GOLD PIECES

LIBERTY HEAD WITH FEATHER HEADDRESS, 1854–1889

Introduction and apparent public acceptance of the gold dollar in 1849 led to speculation on the possible usefulness of gold coinage in other denominations. The $3 gold piece, composed of 9/10 gold with an alloy of 1/10 copper, was introduced in 1854. It carried an Indian Head on the obverse and a wreathed reverse. Its diameter was 20½ mm. and the weight 5.015 grams. Though the $3 gold piece continued to be struck until 1889 it had become obvious as early as pre-Civil War years that no great demand or popularity was enjoyed by this coin. The designer was James Longacre. In 1854 the word "DOLLARS" was set in smaller characters than subsequently. Total gold content by weight was .14512 ounce.

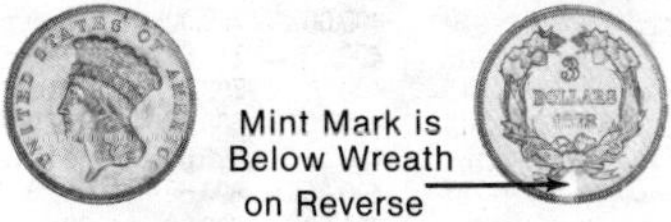

DATE	MINTAGE	ABP in F-12	F-12 Fine	EF-40 Ex. Fine	MS-60 Unc.	PRF-65 Proof
☐1854	136,618	300.00	480.00	900.00	4200.00	
☐1854D	1,120	3600.00	6000.00	12000.00	24000.00	
☐1854O	24,000	300.00	500.00	810.00	5000.00	
☐1855	50,555	300.00	500.00	810.00	3800.00	28000.00
☐1855S	6,000	300.00	600.00	1350.00	7000.00	
☐1856	26,010	300.00	450.00	900.00	4000.00	20000.00
☐1856S*	34,500	400.00	600.00	1150.00	4900.00	
☐1857	20,891	300.00	400.00	900.00	4200.00	18000.00
☐1857S	14,000	400.00	600.00	1200.00	5400.00	
☐1858	2,133	410.00	700.00	1300.00	5400.00	16000.00
☐1859	15,638	360.00	500.00	900.00	4200.00	20000.00
☐1860	7,155	360.00	600.00	1200.00	4100.00	18000.00
☐1860S	7,000	360.00	600.00	1350.00	4100.00	
☐1861	6,072	360.00	600.00	1250.00	4100.00	16000.00
☐1862	5,785	360.00	600.00	1250.00	4100.00	16000.00
☐1863	5,039	360.00	625.00	1250.00	4100.00	16000.00
☐1864	2,680	400.00	600.00	1450.00	5000.00	16000.00
☐1865	1,165	410.00	650.00	1600.00	8000.00	23000.00
☐1866	4,030	360.00	600.00	1200.00	4200.00	19000.00
☐1867	2,650	360.00	600.00	1200.00	4100.00	17000.00
☐1868	4,875	390.00	600.00	1200.00	4100.00	17000.00
☐1869	2,525	390.00	600.00	1200.00	4200.00	18000.00
☐1870	3,535	390.00	600.00	1200.00	4300.00	18000.00
☐1870S	2	One piece was in the Eliasburg Collection. The other piece is in the cornerstone of the San Francisco Mint.				
☐1871	1,330	420.00	700.00	1500.00	5100.00	16000.00
☐1872	2,030	430.00	650.00	1370.00	4000.00	16000.00
☐1873 Open 3	25			PROOF ONLY		42000.00
☐1873 Closed 3 Restrike					9400.00	28000.00
☐1874	41,820	300.00	475.00	810.00	4000.00	20000.00
☐1875 Proofs Only	20					110000.00
☐1876 Proofs Only	†45		Bowers and Ruddy Auction Sale: $30000.00			
☐1877	1,488	400.00	850.00	1500.00	6000.00	22000.00
☐1878	82,324	300.00	500.00	900.00	4000.00	21000.00
☐1879	3,030	400.00	600.00	1200.00	4200.00	18000.00

*Found in Small, Medium and Large "S" Varieties

**Stack's Sale 1976

DATE	MINTAGE	ABP in F-12	F-12 Fine	EF-40 Ex. Fine	MS-60 Unc.	PRF-65 Proof
☐1880	1,036	400.00	700.00	1350.00	4100.00	15000.00
☐1881	550	500.00	900.00	1800.00	7000.00	20000.00
☐1882	1,540	400.00	700.00	1200.00	4100.00	15000.00
☐1883	940	400.00	700.00	1400.00	4600.00	15000.00
☐1884	1,106	400.00	710.00	1350.00	4100.00	14000.00
☐1885	910	400.00	700.00	1350.00	4100.00	14000.00
☐1886	1,142	400.00	600.00	1200.00	4600.00	13000.00
☐1887	6,160	400.00	600.00	1000.00	4000.00	13000.00
☐1888	5,291	400.00	600.00	1000.00	4000.00	13000.00
☐1889	2,429	400.00	600.00	1000.00	4000.00	13000.00

Beware of deceiving counterfeits with the following dates: 1855, 1857, 1878, 1882, and 1888.

"STELLA"—$4.00 GOLD PIECES

LIBERTY HEAD WITH FLOWING OR COILED HAIR, 1879–1880

In 1879 and 1880 proofs were struck, in limited quantities, of a $4 gold coin that never reached circulation. It was called "Stella" and was coined not only in gold but various other metals. The gold specimens are extremely valuable. There are two obverse types, one designed by Barber and the other by Morgan.

Flowing Hair

Coiled Hair

DATE	MINTAGE	ABP in PRF-65	PRF-65 Proof
☐1879 Flowing Hair (PROOFS ONLY)	415	30000.00	60000.00
☐1879 Coiled Hair (PROOFS ONLY)	10	69000.00	120000.00
☐1880 Flowing Hair (PROOFS ONLY)	15	47000.00	82000.00
☐1880 Coiled Hair (PROOFS ONLY)	10	67000.00	120000.00

HALF EAGLES—$5.00 GOLD PIECES, 1795–1908

The Half Eagle or $5 gold piece was authorized on April 2, 1792, and first struck in 1795. It has the distinction of being the first gold coin struck by the U.S. Mint. Production was limited in the early years. Its designer was Robert Scot. The composition was .9167 gold to .0833 copper alloy, yielding a weight of 8.75 grams and a diameter of (generally) 25 mm. A capped portrait of Liberty facing right adorned the obverse, with stars and date appearing below the portrait; on the reverse is a spread-winged eagle holding in its beak a wreath, surrounded by the wording "UNITED STATES OF AMERICA." Some alterations in the number of stars and size of figures in the date will be observed. These should be taken into close account, as they can have a considerable bearing on value. In 1807 John Reich redesigned the Half Eagle. The bust, now "capped and draped," was turned around to face left and the eagle modified. A shortened bust was introduced in 1913. A further modification was made in 1829 but with the same basic design retained. By this time the Quarter Eagle had become an important circulating as well as banking piece, whose significance was to later increase. The year 1834 brought a revised design known as the "Classic Head," the work of William Kneass. The weight of this new coin was 8.36 grams and its composition .8992 gold to .1008 copper, with a diameter of 22½ mm. The slogan "IN GOD WE TRUST," previously used on the reverse, was dropped, probably because of a shortage of space. This was followed by Gobrecht's "Coronet" head in 1839, used until 1908. Its gold content was raised slightly to 9⁄10 and the copper reduced to 1⁄10. Gold content by weight was .24187 ounce. There are small and large date varieties of this coin. In 1866, following the Civil War, "IN GOD WE TRUST" was added to the rather cramped space between the eagle's head and the legend "UNITED STATES OF AMERICA." Composition was as before but the weight was changed to 8.359 grams and the diameter reduced to 21.6 mm. One of the longest lived of coin designs, it remained in use a full 70 years, to be replaced by Pratt's Indian head in 1908.

HALF EAGLES — LIBERTY HEAD, 1795–1807 EAGLE ON REVERSE

Head Right
1795–1807

1795–1798
Small Eagle

1795–1807
Large Eagle

DATE	MINTAGE	ABP in F-12	F-12 Fine	EF-40 Ex. Fine	MS-60 Unc.
☐ 1795 Small Eagle	8,707	3000.00	5600.00	10000.00	26000.00
☐ 1795 Large Eagle		3000.00	5000.00	11500.00	28000.00
☐ 1796 over 95 Small Eagle	3,399	3000.00	5000.00	11000.00	26000.00
☐ 1797 over 95 Large Eagle	6,406	3000.00	6000.00	10000.00	28000.00
☐ 1798 Small Eagle	6 Known			EXTREMELY RARE	
☐ 1798 Large Eagle All Types	24,867	650.00	1310.00	3000.00	10000.00
☐ 1799	7,451	600.00	1100.00	3000.00	9800.00
☐ 1800	37,620	600.00	1100.00	2900.00	9400.00
☐ 1802 over 1	53,176	600.00	1100.00	2900.00	9400.00
☐ 1803 over 2	33,506	600.00	1100.00	2900.00	9400.00
☐ 1804 Small & Large "8"	30,475	600.00	1100.00	2900.00	9400.00
☐ 1805	33,183	600.00	1100.00	2900.00	9400.00
☐ 1806 (Round & Pointed Top 6)	64,093	600.00	1100.00	2900.00	9400.00
☐ 1807 (Head Right)	33,496	600.00	1100.00	2900.00	9400.00

HALF EAGLES — DRAPED BUST, 1807–1812, VALUE 5D ON REVERSE

HEAD LEFT

"Round Cap"

DATE	MINTAGE	ABP in F-12	F-12 Fine	EF-40 Ex. Fine	MS-60 Unc.
☐1807	50,597	700.00	1200.00	2600.00	9600.00
☐1808	55,578	700.00	1200.00	2600.00	9600.00
☐1809/8	33,875	700.00	1200.00	2600.00	9600.00
☐1810	100,287	700.00	1200.00	2600.00	9600.00
☐1811	99,581	700.00	1200.00	2600.00	9600.00
☐1812	58,087	700.00	1200.00	2600.00	9600.00

HALF EAGLES — LIBERTY HEAD, ROUND CAP, 1813–1834 MOTTO OVER EAGLE

DATE	MINTAGE	ABP in F-12	F-12 Fine	EF-40 Ex. Fine	MS-60 Unc.
☐1813	95,428	600.00	1400.00	2800.00	13000.00
☐1814 over 13	15,454	600.00	1600.00	3800.00	13300.00
☐1815	635			EXTREMELY RARE	
☐1818	48,588	600.00	1400.00	2800.00	12600.00
☐1819	51,723			RARE	51000.00
☐1820	263,806	600.00	1400.00	3000.00	13200.00
☐1821	34,641	1700.00	3100.00	8000.00	20000.00
☐1822			Only 3 Known EXTREMELY RARE		
☐1823	14,485	1200.00	2000.00	4400.00	16000.00
☐1824	17,340	2800.00	4200.00	17000.00	30000.00
☐1825 over 21	29,060	1700.00	3000.00	7600.00	20000.00
☐1825 over 24	29,060			EXTREMELY RARE	
☐1826	18,069	1600.00	3000.00	9600.00	22000.00
☐1827	24,913	3800.00	6500.00	18000.00	36000.00
☐1828	28,029				RARE
☐1828 over 27	28,029	4100.00	6500.00	17000.00	36000.00

DATE	MINTAGE	ABP in F-12	F-12 Fine	EF-40 Ex. Fine	MS-60 Unc.
☐1829 Small Date............	57,442				RARE
☐1829 Large Date............			1976 STACK'S AUCTION: $65,000		
☐1830	126,351	1200.00	2300.00	5400.00	16800.00
☐1831	140,594	1200.00	2300.00	5400.00	16800.00
☐1832**	157,487	1800.00	3000.00	10000.00	22000.00
☐1833	193,630	1200.00	2250.00	5700.00	16000.00
☐1834***	50,141	1200.00	2250.00	6000.00	17000.00

**1832 Square Based 2, 13 Stars ***1834 Crosslet 4: Same Price

HALF EAGLES — LIBERTY HEAD WITH RIBBON, 1834–1838 NO MOTTO OVER EAGLE

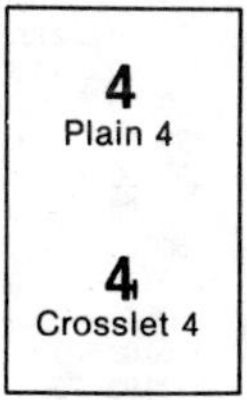

Mint Mark is Above Date on Obverse

DATE	MINTAGE	ABP in F-12	F-12 Fine	EF-40 Ex. Fine	MS-60 Unc.
☐1834 Plain 4*	682,028	160.00	200.00	460.00	2200.00
☐1835	371,534	160.00	200.00	460.00	2100.00
☐1836	553,147	160.00	200.00	460.00	2100.00
☐1837	207,121	160.00	200.00	460.00	2800.00
☐1838	286,588	160.00	200.00	460.00	2100.00
☐1838C......................	12,913	470.00	700.00	2300.00	7000.00
☐1838D......................	20,583	470.00	700.00	2400.00	7500.00

*1834 Crosslet 4 Worth More. MS-60 Unc. $6,000.00

HALF EAGLES — LIBERTY HEAD WITH CORONET, 1839–1908

1839–1908 | 1839–66 No Motto | 1866–1908 With Motto

Mint Mark is Below Eagle on Reverse

DATE	MINTAGE	ABP in F-12	F-12 Fine	EF-40 Ex. Fine	MS-60 Unc.	PRF-65 Proof
□1839	118,143	115.00	200.00	400.00	2100.00	
□1839C	23,467	170.00	400.00	1100.00	3500.00	
□1839D	18,939	140.00	300.00	1100.00	4000.00	
□1840	137,382	115.00	190.00	290.00	2000.00	
□1840C	19,028	170.00	300.00	900.00	3400.00	
□1840D	22,896	125.00	400.00	1100.00	3600.00	
□1840O	30,400	115.00	250.00	600.00	2600.00	
□1841	15,833	115.00	250.00	400.00	2300.00	
□1841C	21,511	120.00	300.00	800.00	3400.00	
□1841D	30,495	120.00	350.00	900.00	3600.00	
□1841O	50		EXTREMELY RARE 2 Known			
□1842	27,578	120.00	190.00	400.00	2200.00	
□1842C (Large Date)	27,480	120.00	250.00	1000.00	2100.00	
□1842D (Small Date)	59,608	140.00	300.00	1100.00	4900.00	
□1842O	16,400	120.00	250.00	900.00	3600.00	
□1843	611,205	120.00	170.00	300.00	1600.00	
□1843C	44,353	160.00	360.00	1000.00	3000.00	
□1843D	98,452	120.00	360.00	1100.00	3800.00	
□1843O	101,075	120.00	210.00	600.00	2400.00	
□1844	340,330	120.00	200.00	400.00	1600.00	
□1844C	23,631	160.00	210.00	1000.00	3500.00	
□1844D	88,982	120.00	340.00	1100.00	4000.00	
□1844O	364,600	120.00	300.00	600.00	2500.00	
□1845	417,099	120.00	190.00	360.00	1600.00	
□1845D	90,629	160.00	250.00	1100.00	4000.00	
□1845O	41,000	120.00	210.00	800.00	3000.00	
□1846	395,942	120.00	165.00	260.00	1600.00	
□1846C	12,995	120.00	400.00	1000.00	3600.00	
□1846D	80,294	120.00	350.00	800.00	3000.00	
□1846O	58,000	120.00	260.00	600.00	3100.00	
□1847	915,981	120.00	160.00	240.00	1600.00	
□1847 Impression of extra 7				VERY RARE		
□1847C	84,151	120.00	300.00	800.00	3100.00	
□1847D	64,405	120.00	300.00	700.00	3200.00	
□1847O	12,000	120.00	310.00	1000.00	3100.00	
□1848	260,775	120.00	170.00	240.00	1600.00	
□1848C	64,472	180.00	400.00	850.00	2800.00	
□1848D	47,465	180.00	400.00	900.00	3200.00	
□1849	133,070	120.00	180.00	240.00	1600.00	
□1849C	64,823	140.00	400.00	800.00	3200.00	
□1849D	39,036	140.00	400.00	900.00	3600.00	
□1850	64,941	110.00	190.00	300.00	1800.00	
□1850C	63,591	140.00	400.00	700.00	3200.00	
□1850D	53,950	140.00	400.00	900.00	4000.00	
□1851	377,505	140.00	180.00	260.00	1600.00	
□1851C	49,176	140.00	350.00	850.00	3100.00	
□1851D	62,710	140.00	400.00	800.00	3200.00	
□1851O	41,000	140.00	270.00	510.00	2800.00	

DATE	MINTAGE	ABP in F-12	F-12 Fine	EF-40 Ex. Fine	MS-60 Unc.	PRF-65 Proof
☐1852	573,901	115.00	170.00	260.00	1600.00	
☐1852C	72,574	140.00	400.00	800.00	3100.00	
☐1852D	91,452	150.00	250.00	850.00	3100.00	
☐1853	305,770	120.00	170.00	260.00	1600.00	
☐1853C	65,571	160.00	300.00	810.00	3100.00	
☐1853D	89,687	140.00	400.00	810.00	3100.00	
☐1854	160,675	120.00	170.00	260.00	1900.00	
☐1854C	39,291	140.00	350.00	810.00	3200.00	
☐1854D	56,413	140.00	400.00	900.00	4000.00	
☐1854O	46,000	140.00	250.00	500.00	2600.00	
☐1854S	268				EXTREMELY RARE	
☐1855	117,098	115.00	170.00	260.00	1600.00	
☐1855C	39,788	160.00	400.00	850.00	3100.00	
☐1855D	22,432	160.00	400.00	900.00	3200.00	
☐1855O	11,100	160.00	400.00	800.00	3100.00	
☐1855S	61,000	120.00	180.00	500.00	2200.00	
☐1856	197,990	115.00	170.00	260.00	1600.00	
☐1856C	28,457	140.00	370.00	900.00	3200.00	
☐1856D	19,786	160.00	380.00	900.00	4000.00	
☐1856O	10,000	160.00	400.00	960.00	4000.00	
☐1856S	105,100	115.00	170.00	300.00	1500.00	
☐1857	98,188	115.00	165.00	260.00	1400.00	
☐1857C	31,360	130.00	400.00	810.00	3200.00	
☐1857D	17,046	250.00	400.00	900.00	3200.00	
☐1857O	13,000	140.00	400.00	800.00	3200.00	
☐1857S	87,000	120.00	170.00	300.00	1800.00	
☐1858	15,136	130.00	200.00	400.00	2100.00	21000.00
☐1858C	38,856	200.00	400.00	900.00	2700.00	
☐1858D	15,362	170.00	400.00	900.00	3300.00	
☐1858S	18,600	140.00	300.00	750.00	2900.00	
☐1859	16,814	130.00	200.00	510.00	2200.00	22000.00
☐1859C	31,487	190.00	400.00	810.00	3100.00	
☐1859D	10,366	200.00	400.00	1000.00	4000.00	
☐1859S	13,220	190.00	200.00	600.00	2400.00	
☐1860	19,825	130.00	210.00	400.00	2100.00	20000.00
☐1860C	14,813	170.00	400.00	900.00	3300.00	
☐1860D	14,635	170.00	400.00	950.00	4000.00	
☐1860S	21,200	150.00	300.00	800.00	2700.00	
☐1861	639,950	115.00	160.00	260.00	1800.00	18000.00
☐1861C	6,879	400.00	900.00	2200.00	8100.00	
☐1861D	1,597	1800.00	3300.00	7200.00	20000.00	
☐1861S	9,500	190.00	300.00	900.00	4400.00	
☐1862	4,465	210.00	350.00	900.00	2500.00	18000.00
☐1862S	9,500	500.00	400.00	1200.00	4900.00	
☐1863	2,472	250.00	500.00	1000.00	3600.00	18000.00
☐1863S	17,000	150.00	300.00	800.00	3800.00	
☐1864	4,220	150.00	300.00	700.00	4200.00	18000.00
☐1864S	3,888	700.00	900.00	2100.00	5500.00	

DATE	MINTAGE	ABP in F-12	F-12 Fine	EF-40 Ex. Fine	MS-60 Unc.	PRF-65 Proof
□ 1865	1,295	200.00	470.00	1400.00	4300.00	20000.00
□ 1865S	27,612	150.00	360.00	1250.00	3000.00	
□ 1866S No Motto	43,020	150.00	360.00	1400.00	3500.00	
□ 1866S With Motto*	43,020	125.00	300.00	1000.00	2500.00	
□ 1866	6,720	170.00	350.00	800.00	2500.00	19000.00
□ 1867	6,920	150.00	310.00	800.00	2500.00	19000.00
□ 1867S	29,000	240.00	375.00	1100.00	3000.00	
□ 1868	5,725	145.00	300.00	850.00	2200.00	19000.00
□ 1868S	52,000	122.00	230.00	850.00	2800.00	
□ 1869	1,785	200.00	350.00	1300.00	2800.00	19000.00
□ 1869S	31,000	130.00	300.00	1000.00	3000.00	
□ 1870	4,035	186.00	320.00	1000.00	2900.00	19000.00
□ 1870CC	7,675	UNKNOWN IN UNC		4200.00		
□ 1870S	17,000	200.00	400.00	1200.00	3400.00	
□ 1871	3,230	195.00	330.00	1150.00	3300.00	20000.00
□ 1871CC	20,770	250.00	450.00	1300.00	3800.00	
□ 1871S	25,000	125.00	230.00	900.00	1600.00	
□ 1872	1,690	200.00	375.00	1200.00	2700.00	17000.00
□ 1872CC	16,980	250.00	450.00	1500.00	4600.00	
□ 1872S	36,400	122.00	270.00	800.00	1500.00	
□ 1873	112,505	122.00	160.00	275.00	700.00	17000.00
□ 1873CC	7,416	250.00	550.00	1500.00	5700.00	
□ 1873S	31,000	155.00	320.00	900.00	3500.00	
□ 1874	3,508	250.00	350.00	900.00	3000.00	21000.00
□ 1874CC	21,198	285.00	390.00	1050.00	3900.00	
□ 1874S	16,000	125.00	360.00	1200.00	2800.00	
□ 1875	220	VERY RARE				†18000.00
□ 1875CC	11,828	270.00	500.00	1400.00	3700.00	
□ 1875S	9,000	125.00	210.00	1300.00	2800.00	
□ 1876	1,477	250.00	450.00	1300.00	3000.00	19000.00
□ 1876CC	6,887	260.00	450.00	1300.00	3000.00	
□ 1876S	4,000	260.00	500.00	2300.00	4500.00	
□ 1877	1,152	240.00	450.00	1200.00	3100.00	20000.00
□ 1877CC	8,680	250.00	475.00	1400.00	2800.00	
□ 1877S	26,700	100.00	160.00	600.00	2200.00	
□ 1878	131,740	100.00	150.00	240.00	400.00	19000.00
□ 1878CC	9,054	410.00	700.00	2500.00	6000.00	
□ 1878S	144,700	100.00	130.00	190.00	500.00	
□ 1879	301,950	100.00	130.00	190.00	450.00	17000.00
□ 1879CC	17,281	140.00	210.00	500.00	1100.00	
□ 1879S	426,200	100.00	140.00	200.00	450.00	
□ 1880	3,166,436	100.00	130.00	185.00	400.00	16000.00
□ 1880CC	51,017	140.00	210.00	500.00	1000.00	
□ 1880S	1,348,900	100.00	135.00	180.00	420.00	
□ 1881	5,708,800	100.00	135.00	180.00	400.00	17000.00
□ 1881CC	13,886	150.00	210.00	550.00	1400.00	

*From 1866 to 1908—All have motto "In God We Trust" over Eagle on reverse

† Only 20 proofs struck in 1875

DATE	MINTAGE	ABP in F-12	F-12 Fine	EF-40 Ex. Fine	MS-60 Unc.	PRF-65 Proof
☐1881S	969,000	100.00	140.00	185.00	400.00	
☐1882	21,514,560	100.00	140.00	185.00	400.00	10000.00
☐1882CC	82,817	110.00	170.00	450.00	1200.00	
☐1882S	969,000	100.00	140.00	180.00	410.00	
☐1883	233,440	100.00	140.00	180.00	460.00	10000.00
☐1883CC	12,958	130.00	200.00	500.00	1200.00	
☐1883S	83,200	100.00	140.00	180.00	500.00	
☐1884	191,048	100.00	140.00	180.00	500.00	10000.00
☐1884CC	16,402	140.00	240.00	600.00	1300.00	
☐1884S	177,000	100.00	140.00	200.00	450.00	
☐1885	601,506	100.00	140.00	190.00	400.00	10000.00
☐1885S	1,211,500	100.00	140.00	190.00	410.00	
☐1886	388,432	100.00	140.00	190.00	410.00	10000.00
☐1886S	3,268,000	100.00	140.00	190.00	400.00	
☐1887	87				RARE	31000.00
☐1887S	1,912,000	100.00	140.00	190.00	410.00	
☐1888	18,296	100.00	140.00	200.00	425.00	10000.00
☐1888S	293,900	100.00	140.00	210.00	500.00	
☐1889	7,565	106.00	150.00	410.00	750.00	10000.00
☐1890	4,328	160.00	200.00	460.00	900.00	10000.00
☐1890CC	53,800	110.00	170.00	440.00	1300.00	
☐1891	61,413	100.00	145.00	212.00	500.00	10000.00
☐1891CC	208,000	115.00	150.00	212.00	750.00	
☐1892	753,572	100.00	140.00	180.00	400.00	10000.00
☐1892CC	82,968	115.00	180.00	500.00	900.00	
☐1892O	10,000	200.00	500.00	1400.00	3400.00	
☐1892S	298,400	100.00	140.00	200.00	520.00	
☐1893	1,528,197	100.00	140.00	180.00	410.00	10000.00
☐1893CC	60,000	110.00	170.00	540.00	1200.00	
☐1893O	110,000	100.00	165.00	325.00	800.00	
☐1893S	224,000	100.00	140.00	180.00	450.00	
☐1894	957,955	110.00	145.00	180.00	410.00	10000.00
☐1894O	16,660	100.00	160.00	370.00	750.00	
☐1894S	55,900	120.00	140.00	270.00	600.00	
☐1895	1,345,936	100.00	140.00	190.00	425.00	10000.00
☐1895S	112,000	100.00	140.00	200.00	500.00	
☐1896	59,063	100.00	140.00	190.00	460.00	10000.00
☐1896S	115,400	100.00	140.00	192.00	520.00	
☐1897	867,883	100.00	130.00	180.00	410.00	10000.00
☐1897S	345,000	100.00	130.00	190.00	450.00	
☐1898	633,495	100.00	130.00	180.00	440.00	10000.00
☐1898S	1,397,400	100.00	130.00	180.00	450.00	
☐1899	1,710,729	100.00	130.00	180.00	400.00	10000.00
☐1899S	1,545,000	100.00	130.00	180.00	440.00	
☐1900	1,405,730	100.00	130.00	180.00	410.00	10000.00
☐1900S	329,000	100.00	130.00	180.00	450.00	
☐1901	616,040	100.00	130.00	180.00	410.00	10000.00

*From 1866 to 1908—all have motto "In God We Trust" over Eagle on reverse

DATE	MINTAGE	ABP in F-12	F-12 Fine	EF-40 Ex. Fine	MS-60 Unc.	PRF-65 Proof
☐ 1901S	3,648,000	100.00	140.00	190.00	425.00	
☐ 1901S 1 over 0					2200.00	
☐ 1902	172,562	100.00	140.00	190.00	410.00	15000.00
☐ 1902S	939,000	100.00	140.00	190.00	410.00	
☐ 1903	227,024	100.00	140.00	190.00	410.00	15000.00
☐ 1903S	1,885,000	100.00	140.00	190.00	410.00	
☐ 1904	392,136	100.00	140.00	190.00	410.00	15000.00
☐ 1904S	97,000	100.00	140.00	190.00	450.00	
☐ 1905	302,308	100.00	140.00	190.00	425.00	15000.00
☐ 1905S	880,700	100.00	140.00	190.00	500.00	
☐ 1906	348,820	100.00	140.00	190.00	410.00	15000.00
☐ 1906D	320,000	100.00	140.00	190.00	410.00	
☐ 1906S	598,000	100.00	140.00	190.00	410.00	
☐ 1907	626,192	100.00	140.00	190.00	410.00	15000.00
☐ 1907D	888,000	100.00	140.00	190.00	410.00	
☐ 1908	421,874	100.00	140.00	190.00	410.00	

*1866 to 1908—All have motto "In God We Trust" over Eagle on reverse

INDIAN HEAD, 1908–1929

Bela Lyon Pratt's Indian Head design replaced the Liberty Head half eagle in 1908. Like the Quarter Eagle these coins are uniquely without raised edges and have designs stamped in incuse or recess rather than raised from the surface. A standing eagle adorns the reverse, with mint mark beneath the wording "E PLURIBUS UNUM." These half eagles contained 90% gold and 10% copper with a weight of 8.359 grains. The diameter is 21.6 mm. and the gold content by weight is .24187 ounce each. Striking of half eagles was suspended during World War I and not resumed until 1929, their final year of production.

Mint Mark is to Left of Value on Reverse

DATE	MINTAGE	ABP in F-12	F-12 Fine	EF-40 Ex. Fine	MS-60 Unc.	PRF-65 Proof
☐ 1908	578,012	100.00	160.00	300.00	1400.00	17000.00
☐ 1908D	148,000	100.00	160.00	300.00	1400.00	17000.00
☐ 1908S	82,000	150.00	200.00	500.00	2400.00	
☐ 1909	627,138	100.00	160.00	300.00	1300.00	17000.00
☐ 1909D	3,423,560	100.00	160.00	300.00	1300.00	
☐ 1909O*	34,200	240.00	300.00	1100.00	6600.00	
☐ 1909S	297,200	100.00	175.00	300.00	1800.00	
☐ 1910	604,250	100.00	175.00	300.00	1400.00	17000.00

DATE	MINTAGE	ABP in F-12	F-12 Fine	EF-40 Ex. Fine	MS-60 Unc.	PRF-65 Proof
□1910D	193,600	100.00	180.00	300.00	1400.00	
□1910S	770,200	100.00	180.00	300.00	2100.00	
□1911	915,139	100.00	180.00	300.00	1500.00	
□1911D	72,500	100.00	240.00	500.00	4700.00	17000.00
□1911S	1,416,000	100.00	180.00	310.00	1600.00	
□1912	790,144	100.00	180.00	300.00	1400.00	
□1912S	392,000	100.00	180.00	300.00	1500.00	
□1913	916,099	100.00	180.00	300.00	1300.00	17000.00
□1913S	408,000	100.00	220.00	300.00	3500.00	
□1914	247,125	100.00	180.00	300.00	1500.00	17000.00
□1914D	247,000	100.00	180.00	300.00	1500.00	
□1914S	263,000	100.00	180.00	300.00	1500.00	
□1915**	588,075	100.00	180.00	300.00	1400.00	17000.00
□1915S	164,000	100.00	180.00	320.00	2600.00	
□1916S	240,000	100.00	180.00	300.00	1500.00	
□1929	662,000	1150.00	1400.00	3600.00	7100.00	

*Some "O" Mint Marks are false. **Coins marked 1915D are not authentic

EAGLES, $10.00 GOLD PIECES, 1795–1907

Gold pieces valued at $10 were released for general circulation in 1795. Despite the large face value and the super-large buying power ($10 in the 1790s was equivalent to about $200 in present-day money), this coin was struck in substantial numbers, chiefly as a banking piece. Though bullion shortages, speculation, and world economic conditions made the Eagle's career far from sedate, it retained great influence throughout most of its history. The first design, conceived by Robert Scot, comprised a capped bust of Liberty facing right with the so-called Small Eagle reverse, depicting an eagle holding a wreath in its beak. The shield or heraldic eagle replaced this type in 1797 and production was stepped up, output reaching more than 37,000 in 1799. The content was .9167 gold to .0833 copper, with a weight of 17½ grams and diameter generally of 33 mm. From 1805 to 1837 no eagles were struck. When production resumed in 1838 the portrait of Liberty had undergone a thorough alteration, at the hands of Christian Gobrecht. This was the Coronet type, with modified shielded eagle on the reverse. It weighed 16.718 grams with a 9-to-1 gold content (alloyed with copper) and diameter of 27 mm. The gold content by weight was .48375 ounces. The slogan "E PLURIBUS UNUM," previously used on the reverse, was dropped. For many years no motto appeared on the reverse until the installation, in 1866, of "IN GOD WE TRUST." The composition and other specifications remained unaltered. No change was made until 1907 when the Indian Head obverse, designed by Augustus Saint-Gaudens, was introduced.

EAGLES — LIBERTY HEAD, SMALL EAGLE, 1795–1797

DATE	MINTAGE	ABP in F-12	F-12 Fine	EF-40 Ex. Fine	MS-60 Unc.
☐ 1795	5,583	2100.00	5000.00	12000.00	32750.00
☐ 1796	4,146	2100.00	5000.00	12000.00	32750.00
☐ 1797 Part of Liberty Head, Small Eagle	3,615	2100.00	5000.00	12000.00	32750.00

EAGLES — LIBERTY HEAD, LARGE EAGLE, 1797–1804

4 Stars Right — 6 Stars Right — Large Eagle

DATE	MINTAGE	ABP in F-12	F-12 Fine	EF-40 Ex. Fine	MS-60 Unc.
☐ 1797 Large Eagle	10,940	1400.00	2750.00	5700.00	18000.00
☐ 1798 over 97 9 Stars Left—4 Right	900	7000.00	11000.00	16000.00	32000.00
☐ 1798 over 97 7 Stars Left—6 Right	842		AUCTION SALE EF-45:		46000.00
☐ 1799	37,449	1350.00	2600.00	4500.00	15000.00
☐ 1800	5,999	1350.00	2600.00	4500.00	15000.00
☐ 1801	44,344	1350.00	2600.00	4500.00	15000.00
☐ 1803	15,017	1350.00	2600.00	4500.00	15000.00
☐ 1804	3,757	1500.00	2850.00	6000.00	19000.00

EAGLES — LIBERTY HEAD WITH CORONET, 1838–1907

1862

1838–1866
No Motto

1866–1907
With Motto

Mint Mark is Below Eagle on Reverse

DATE	MINTAGE	ABP in F-12	F-12 Fine	EF-40 Ex. Fine	MS-60 Unc.	PRF-65 Proof
☐ 1838 Large Letters	7,200	365.00	470.00	1900.00	7500.00	
☐ 1839 Large Letters	25,800	250.00	450.00	1500.00	6300.00	
☐ 1839 Small Letters	12,447	300.00	650.00	2200.00	8900.00	
☐ 1840	47,338	200.00	350.00	550.00	4600.00	
☐ 1841	63,131	200.00	350.00	550.00	4650.00	
☐ 1841O	2,500	370.00	500.00	2500.00	6800.00	
☐ 1842	81,507	210.00	410.00	580.00	4600.00	
☐ 1842O	27,400	210.00	410.00	580.00	4600.00	
☐ 1843	75,462	210.00	410.00	500.00	4600.00	
☐ 1843O	175,162	210.00	360.00	480.00	4300.00	
☐ 1844	6,361	240.00	370.00	1100.00	5700.00	
☐ 1844O	118,700	210.00	350.00	470.00	4900.00	
☐ 1845	26,153	260.00	360.00	500.00	5600.00	
☐ 1845O	47,500	210.00	350.00	500.00	5600.00	
☐ 1846	20,095	285.00	400.00	600.00	6000.00	
☐ 1846O	81,780	210.00	360.00	500.00	5350.00	
☐ 1847	862,258	210.00	250.00	375.00	1600.00	
☐ 1847O	417,099	210.00	410.00	500.00	4600.00	
☐ 1848	145,484	210.00	290.00	375.00	2600.00	
☐ 1848O	35,850	250.00	410.00	1100.00	4700.00	
☐ 1849	653,618	210.00	260.00	375.00	2050.00	
☐ 1849O	23,900	240.00	400.00	1100.00	5300.00	
☐ 1850	291,451	210.00	270.00	350.00	1700.00	
☐ 1850O	57,500	210.00	350.00	500.00	3800.00	
☐ 1851	176,328	210.00	240.00	410.00	1800.00	
☐ 1851O	263,000	210.00	240.00	400.00	1650.00	
☐ 1852	263,106	210.00	320.00	500.00	2800.00	
☐ 1852O	18,000	210.00	320.00	800.00	4100.00	
☐ 1853	201,253	210.00	250.00	400.00	2000.00	
☐ 1853O	51,000	210.00	350.00	500.00	3600.00	
☐ 1854	54,250	210.00	350.00	500.00	3600.00	
☐ 1854O	52,500	210.00	250.00	500.00	3600.00	
☐ 1854S	123,826	210.00	250.00	500.00	2000.00	
☐ 1855	121,701	210.00	250.00	500.00	2000.00	50000.00

DATE	MINTAGE	ABP in F-12	F-12 Fine	EF-40 Ex. Fine	MS-60 Unc.	PRF-65 Proof
□1855O	18,000	250.00	400.00	850.00	4000.00	
□1855S	9,000	240.00	425.00	1800.00	5200.00	
□1856	60,490	210.00	340.00	500.00	3000.00	50000.00
□1856O	14,500	210.00	410.00	700.00	3700.00	
□1856S	26,000	210.00	360.00	625.00	3600.00	
□1857	16,606	210.00	370.00	500.00	3600.00	
□1857O	5,500	370.00	600.00	1800.00	6000.00	
□1857S	26,000	230.00	390.00	700.00	3800.00	
□1858*	2,521	1200.00	2300.00	5700.00		50000.00
□1858O	20,000	230.00	360.00	560.00	3850.00	
□1858S	11,800	250.00	460.00	1200.00	3850.00	
□1859	16,093	210.00	390.00	700.00	3700.00	50000.00
□1859O	2,300	600.00	1400.00	3900.00	8600.00	
□1859S	7,007	390.00	650.00	2600.00	6000.00	
□1860	11,783	210.00	375.00	610.00	3800.00	40000.00
□1860O	11,100	210.00	400.00	720.00	3800.00	
□1860S	5,500	400.00	600.00	2500.00	5000.00	
□1861	113,233	210.00	250.00	380.00	1900.00	38000.00
□1861S	15,500	215.00	370.00	850.00	3500.00	
□1862	10,995	205.00	310.00	600.00	3500.00	34000.00
□1862S	12,500	210.00	460.00	1650.00	3500.00	
□1863	1,248	1300.00	2000.00	5600.00	9000.00	35000.00
□1863S	10,000	230.00	490.00	1600.00	4300.00	
□1864	3,580	370.00	660.00	2100.00	5300.00	29000.00
□1864S	2,500	700.00	1800.00	4300.00	9000.00	
□1865	4,005	285.00	610.00	1800.00	5600.00	32000.00
□1865S	16,700	220.00	470.00	1500.00	4700.00	
□1866 With Motto	3,780	250.00	550.00	1100.00	2000.00	32000.00
□1866S No Motto	8,500	600.00	1000.00	2400.00	6000.00	
□1866S With Motto	11,500	270.00	400.00	1100.00	1900.00	
□1867	3,140	360.00	650.00	1300.00	2100.00	32000.00
□1867S	9,000	380.00	700.00	2400.00	6500.00	
□1868	10,655	215.00	410.00	750.00	1700.00	31000.00
□1868S	13,500	230.00	440.00	1000.00	3300.00	
□1869	1,855	510.00	800.00	2000.00	5200.00	38000.00
□1869S	6,430	370.00	700.00	1200.00	5000.00	
□1870	2,535	310.00	600.00	1000.00	3700.00	32000.00
□1870CC	5,908	700.00	1200.00	4400.00	8500.00	
□1870S	8,000	250.00	425.00	1400.00	4800.00	
□1871	1,780	370.00	600.00	2200.00	6300.00	37000.00
□1871CC	7,185	470.00	700.00	1600.00	4100.00	
□1871S	16,500	270.00	500.00	1300.00	3400.00	
□1872	1,650	700.00	1250.00	3000.00	7500.00	31000.00
□1872CC	5,500	410.00	700.00	2000.00	4000.00	32000.00
□1872S	17,300	200.00	420.00	1150.00	3100.00	
□1873	825	1000.00	1500.00	5600.00	9800.00	40000.00
□1873CC	4,543	475.00	750.00	2500.00	6000.00	

*Check for removed mint mark

DATE	MINTAGE	ABP in F-12	F-12 Fine	EF-40 Ex. Fine	MS-60 Unc.	PRF-65 Proof
☐1873S	12,000	200.00	450.00	1800.00	4000.00	
☐1874	53,160	200.00	310.00	410.00	800.00	29000.00
☐1874CC	16,767	275.00	500.00	1200.00	4000.00	
☐1874S	10,000	200.00	450.00	1200.00	5400.00	
☐1875	120				AUCTION:	$95000.00
☐1875CC	7,715	450.00	750.00	2200.00	4000.00	
☐1876	732	1300.00	2100.00	4000.00	8400.00	23000.00
☐1876CC	4,696	500.00	650.00	3100.00	5000.00	
☐1876S	5,000	320.00	450.00	1400.00	3300.00	
☐1877	817	1200.00	2100.00	4800.00	8000.00	25000.00
☐1877CC	3,332	520.00	860.00	2700.00	5000.00	
☐1877S	17,000	200.00	300.00	800.00	2600.00	
☐1878	73,800	175.00	200.00	310.00	600.00	30000.00
☐1878CC	3,244	750.00	1100.00	2500.00	2500.00	
☐1878S	26,100	160.00	360.00	650.00	2100.00	
☐1879	384,770	160.00	200.00	260.00	600.00	29000.00
☐1879CC	1,762	1875.00	2500.00	4900.00	12500.00	
☐1879O	1,500	1200.00	2100.00	3800.00	8200.00	
☐1879S	224,000	160.00	200.00	270.00	600.00	
☐1880	1,644,876	160.00	200.00	260.00	550.00	30000.00
☐1880CC	11,192	250.00	350.00	750.00	2000.00	
☐1880O	9,500	235.00	260.00	575.00	1750.00	
☐1880S	506,205	160.00	200.00	270.00	600.00	
☐1881	3,877,260	160.00	200.00	250.00	550.00	28000.00
☐1881CC	24,015	160.00	240.00	500.00	1300.00	
☐1881O	8,350	160.00	270.00	600.00	1900.00	
☐1881S	970,000	160.00	200.00	250.00	540.00	
☐1882	2,324,480	160.00	200.00	250.00	530.00	26000.00
☐1882CC	6,764	210.00	410.00	860.00	2200.00	
☐1882O	10,280	180.00	260.00	550.00	1700.00	
☐1882S	132,000	180.00	210.00	260.00	650.00	
☐1883	208,740	180.00	200.00	250.00	520.00	26000.00
☐1883CC	12,000	200.00	370.00	750.00	2000.00	
☐1883O	800	1100.00	2000.00	4500.00		
☐1883S	38,000	175.00	200.00	400.00	1250.00	
☐1884	76,017	175.00	200.00	410.00	1200.00	34000.00
☐1884CC	9,925	200.00	360.00	700.00	1850.00	
☐1884S	124,250	165.00	200.00	250.00	650.00	
☐1885	124,527	165.00	200.00	250.00	640.00	25000.00
☐1885S	228,000	165.00	200.00	210.00	560.00	
☐1886	236,160	165.00	200.00	240.00	630.00	25000.00
☐1886S	826,000	165.00	200.00	200.00	550.00	
☐1887	53,680	165.00	200.00	250.00	550.00	25000.00
☐1887S	817,000	165.00	200.00	250.00	530.00	
☐1888	132,996	165.00	200.00	250.00	630.00	25000.00
☐1880O	21,335	165.00	200.00	350.00	630.00	
☐1888S	648,700	165.00	200.00	275.00	580.00	
☐1889	4,485	200.00	260.00	500.00	950.00	30000.00

DATE	MINTAGE	ABP in F-12	F-12 Fine	EF-40 Ex. Fine	MS-60 Unc.	PRF-65 Proof
□ 1889S	425,400	175.00	210.00	290.00	500.00	
□ 1890	58,043	175.00	210.00	290.00	600.00	24000.00
□ 1890CC	17,500	175.00	210.00	450.00	11000.00	
□ 1891	91,868	175.00	210.00	250.00	500.00	25000.00
□ 1891CC	103,732	175.00	210.00	400.00	850.00	
□ 1892	797,552	175.00	210.00	280.00	550.00	25000.00
□ 1892CC	40,000	175.00	210.00	600.00	1100.00	
□ 1892O	28,688	175.00	210.00	400.00	600.00	
□ 1892S	115,500	175.00	210.00	260.00	500.00	
□ 1893	1,840,895	175.00	210.00	300.00	550.00	25000.00
□ 1893CC	14,000	175.00	300.00	540.00	1100.00	
□ 1893O	17,000	175.00	210.00	400.00	700.00	
□ 1893S	141,350	175.00	210.00	290.00	500.00	
□ 1894	2,470,782	175.00	210.00	290.00	500.00	24000.00
□ 1894O	197,500	175.00	210.00	290.00	500.00	
□ 1894S	25,000	175.00	240.00	500.00	1600.00	
□ 1895	567,826	175.00	210.00	300.00	500.00	24000.00
□ 1895O	98,000	175.00	210.00	300.00	500.00	
□ 1895S	49,000	175.00	300.00	600.00	1500.00	
□ 1896	76,348	175.00	210.00	300.00	500.00	24000.00
□ 1896S	123,750	175.00	210.00	300.00	1500.00	
□ 1897	1,000,159	175.00	210.00	280.00	500.00	24000.00
□ 1897O	42,500	175.00	210.00	280.00	500.00	
□ 1897S	234,750	175.00	210.00	280.00	600.00	
□ 1898	812,197	175.00	210.00	280.00	500.00	24000.00
□ 1898S	473,600	175.00	210.00	280.00	500.00	
□ 1899	1,262,305	175.00	210.00	280.00	500.00	24000.00
□ 1899O	37,047	175.00	210.00	280.00	500.00	
□ 1899S	841,000	175.00	210.00	280.00	500.00	24000.00
□ 1900	293,960	175.00	210.00	280.00	500.00	24000.00
□ 1900S	81,000	175.00	210.00	280.00	500.00	
□ 1901	1,718,825	175.00	210.00	280.00	500.00	24000.00
□ 1901O	72,041	175.00	210.00	280.00	500.00	
□ 1901S	2,812,750	175.00	210.00	280.00	500.00	
□ 1902	82,513	175.00	210.00	280.00	500.00	24000.00
□ 1902S	469,500	175.00	210.00	280.00	500.00	
□ 1903	125,926	175.00	210.00	280.00	500.00	24000.00
□ 1903O	112,771	175.00	210.00	280.00	500.00	
□ 1903S		175.00	210.00	280.00	500.00	
□ 1904	162,038	175.00	210.00	280.00	500.00	24000.00
□ 1904O	108,950	175.00	210.00	280.00	500.00	
□ 1905	201,078	175.00	210.00	280.00	500.00	24000.00
□ 1905S	369,250	175.00	210.00	280.00	500.00	
□ 1906	165,496	175.00	210.00	280.00	500.00	24000.00
□ 1906D	981,000	175.00	210.00	280.00	500.00	
□ 1906O	86,895	175.00	210.00	280.00	500.00	
□ 1906S	457,000	175.00	210.00	280.00	500.00	
□ 1907	1,203,973	175.00	210.00	280.00	500.00	24000.00

DATE	MINTAGE	ABP in F-12	F-12 Fine	EF-40 Ex. Fine	MS-60 Unc.	PRF-65 Proof
☐1907D	1,020,000	175.00	190.00	275.00	500.00	
☐1907S	210,000	175.00	190.00	310.00	510.00	

EAGLES — INDIAN HEAD, 1907–1933

Augustus Saint-Gaudens, a noted sculptor and really the first artist of international repute to design an American coin, strove to inject a touch of creative feeling in coin design. True to the artistic spirit of the times he sacrificed such supposedly old-fashioned qualities as balance to achieve imagination of line and composition. His eagle, on the reverse, is totally stylized, its strength and symmetry purposely over-emphasized. At first the motto "IN GOD WE TRUST" was omitted, owing to President Theodore Roosevelt's opinion that the name of God was not suitable for use on coinage in any context. He was overruled by Congress in 1908 and the motto appeared shortly thereafter. Striking of eagles, which had reached as high as nearly 4½ million pieces in a single year ($45,000,000 face value), was discontinued in 1933. The Saint-Gaudens Eagle contained 90 percent gold and 10 percent copper, with a diameter of 27 mm. and a weight of 16,718 grams. The bullion weight is .48375 of an ounce.

DATE	MINTAGE	ABP in F-12	F-12 Fine	EF-40 Ex. Fine	MS-60 Unc.	PRF-65 Proof
☐1907 W/O Periods	239,406	250.00	350.00	600.00	1600.00	
☐1907 Wire Rim with Periods Before and After U.S.A.	500				11000.00	
☐1907 Rolled Rim, Periods	42				37000.00	
☐1908 No Motto	33,500	250.00	350.00	600.00	2000.00	
☐1908 W/Motto	341,486	250.00	350.00	500.00	1700.00	32000.00
☐1908D No Motto	210,000	250.00	350.00	600.00	1750.00	
☐1908D	386,500	250.00	350.00	600.00	1750.00	
☐1908S	59,850	250.00	400.00	700.00	4000.00	
☐1909	184,863	250.00	350.00	500.00	1500.00	31000.00
☐1909D	121,540	250.00	350.00	500.00	1600.00	
☐1909S	292,350	250.00	350.00	500.00	2000.00	
☐1910	318,704	250.00	350.00	500.00	1500.00	32000.00
☐1910D	2,356,640	250.00	350.00	500.00	1500.00	
☐1910S	811,000	250.00	350.00	500.00	1800.00	
☐1911	505,595	250.00	350.00	500.00	1500.00	33000.00
☐1911D	30,100	400.00	600.00	1000.00	5500.00	
☐1911S	51,000	250.00	350.00	600.00	3000.00	
☐1912	405,083	250.00	350.00	500.00	1400.00	32000.00

DATE	MINTAGE	ABP in F-12	F-12 Fine	EF-40 Ex. Fine	MS-60 Unc.	PRF-65 Proof
☐1912S	300,000	250.00	350.00	500.00	2600.00	
☐1913	442,071	230.00	310.00	500.00	1200.00	30000.00
☐1913S	66,000	300.00	500.00	900.00	9800.00	
☐1914	151,050	250.00	320.00	500.00	1600.00	30000.00
☐1914D	343,500	250.00	320.00	500.00	1400.00	
☐1914S	208,000	250.00	320.00	510.00	2400.00	
☐1915	351,075	250.00	320.00	500.00	1500.00	30000.00
☐1915S	59,000	250.00	320.00	550.00	3100.00	
☐1916S	138,500	250.00	320.00	500.00	1900.00	
☐1920S	126,500	4000.00	6000.00	3600.00	16000.00	
☐1926	1,014,000	250.00	350.00	500.00	1500.00	
☐1930S	96,000	2100.00	3000.00	5200.00	12800.00	
☐1932	1,463,000	255.00	350.00	500.00	1500.00	
☐1933	312,500			19000.00	72000.00	

Note: The rare dates of this series are heavily counterfeited. Be sure that you buy from a reputable dealer.

DOUBLE EAGLES, $20.00 GOLD PIECES

The Double Eagle or $20 gold piece was the largest denomination coin issued for regular use by the U.S. Mint. It was introduced in 1849, as a direct result of the California gold strikes. Discovery of gold at Sutter's Mill had not only made vast new supplies available to the government, but focused increased attention on gold as a medium of exchange. Necessity for a $20 face value coin was further prompted by the fact that the Treasury Department was not yet issuing paper currency.

These coins are known as "Double Eagles," as a result of being twice the size of Eagles or $10 gold pieces. Their composition was exactly the same as the lower denomination gold coins, .900 fine, or nine parts of 24K gold alloyed with one part copper. The Double Eagle contained .96750 of an ounce of pure gold, or just a slight fraction under one full ounce. With the copper content added, the coin's weight was more than an ounce—making it not only our highest denomination coin, but the heaviest physically. However, it was smaller in diameter than the Silver $1, at 34 mm.

The first Double Eagles carried a portrait of Liberty facing left, by James B. Longacre, with a heraldic eagle on the reverse. Two significant changes were made during the use of this design, which was removed in 1907. In 1866 the motto "IN GOD WE TRUST" was added above the eagle, and in 1877 the statement of value (on the reverse) was changed from "TWENTY D." to "TWENTY DOLLARS."

DOUBLE EAGLES — LIBERTY HEAD, 1849–1866

DATE	MINTAGE	ABP in F-12	F-12 Fine	EF-40 Ex. Fine	MS-60 Unc.	PRF-65 Proof
☐1849			Unique—only 1 known in U.S. Mint Collection			
☐1850	1,170,261	400.00	480.00	700.00	2600.00	

Mint Mark is Below Eagle on Reverse

DATE	MINTAGE	ABP in F-12	F-12 Fine	EF-40 Ex. Fine	MS-60 Unc.	PRF-65 Proof
☐1850O	141,000	300.00	450.00	950.00	4000.00	
☐1851	2,087,155	300.00	400.00	900.00	1500.00	
☐1851O	315,000	310.00	500.00	970.00	3400.00	
☐1852	2,053,026	350.00	475.00	850.00	1400.00	
☐1852O	190,000	300.00	500.00	1100.00	3200.00	
☐1853	1,261,326	300.00	475.00	900.00	1400.00	
☐1853O	71,000	300.00	600.00	1200.00	3600.00	
☐1854	757,899	300.00	400.00	900.00	1700.00	
☐1854O	3,250			35000.00	60000.00	
☐1854S	141,469	300.00	400.00	910.00	3000.00	
☐1855	364,666	300.00	400.00	910.00	1600.00	
☐1855O	8,000	1100.00	1900.00	5100.00	11000.00	
☐1855S	879,675	300.00	410.00	600.00	1600.00	
☐1856	329,878	300.00	410.00	600.00	1600.00	
☐1856O	2,250			EXTREMELY RARE		
☐1856S	1,189,750	300.00	410.00	600.00	1600.00	
☐1857	439,375	300.00	410.00	600.00	1600.00	
☐1857O	30,000	450.00	600.00	1800.00	4100.00	
☐1857S	970,500	300.00	450.00	600.00	1400.00	
☐1858	211,714	300.00	450.00	600.00	1600.00	50000.00
☐1858O	35,250	300.00	500.00	1700.00	4200.00	
☐1858S	846,710	300.00	450.00	600.00	1800.00	
☐1859	43,597	300.00	600.00	1600.00	3600.00	50000.00
☐1859S	636,445	300.00	400.00	600.00	3300.00	
☐1859O	9,100	1000.00	1800.00	3600.00	7000.00	
☐1860	577,670	300.00	450.00	700.00	1600.00	40000.00
☐1860O	6,600	2000.00	3100.00	5000.00	8500.00	
☐1860S	544,950	300.00	450.00	600.00	1600.00	
☐1861	2,976,453	300.00	450.00	600.00	1400.00	40000.00
☐1861O	5,000	1000.00	1200.00	2600.00	7400.00	
☐1861S	768,000	300.00	480.00	600.00	1900.00	
☐1862	92,133	300.00	410.00	900.00	3600.00	40000.00
☐1862S	854,173	300.00	480.00	600.00	1600.00	
☐1863	142,790	300.00	430.00	800.00	3600.00	40000.00
☐1863S	966,570	300.00	430.00	700.00	2400.00	
☐1864	204,285	300.00	430.00	900.00	3500.00	40000.00

DATE	MINTAGE	ABP in F-12	F-12 Fine	EF-40 Ex. Fine	MS-60 Unc.	PRF-65 Proof
☐ 1864S	793,660	300.00	450.00	800.00	2500.00	
☐ 1865	351,200	300.00	450.00	800.00	2500.00	38000.00
☐ 1865S	1,042,500	300.00	450.00	600.00	1900.00	
☐ 1866S Part of	842,250	300.00	600.00	1400.00	4900.00	

DOUBLE EAGLES — LIBERTY HEAD, 1866–1876, WITH MOTTO AND "TWENTY D" ON REVERSE

Mint Mark is Below Eagle on Reverse

DATE	MINTAGE	ABP in F-12	F-12 Fine	EF-40 Ex. Fine	MS-60 Unc.	PRF-65 Proof
☐ 1866	698,775	420.00	460.00	600.00	1700.00	38000.00
☐ 1866S	842,250	420.00	460.00	600.00	1650.00	38000.00
☐ 1867S	920,250	420.00	460.00	600.00	1400.00	
☐ 1868	98,600	420.00	460.00	600.00	2400.00	38000.00
☐ 1868S	837,500	420.00	460.00	600.00	1500.00	
☐ 1869	175,155	420.00	460.00	600.00	1500.00	38000.00
☐ 1869S	686,750	420.00	460.00	600.00	1500.00	
☐ 1870	155,185	420.00	460.00	600.00	1500.00	38000.00
☐ 1870CC	3,789		Auction—$21000.00			
☐ 1870S	982,000	420.00	460.00	700.00	1400.00	
☐ 1871	80,150	420.00	460.00	900.00	2400.00	32000.00
☐ 1871CC	14,687	1100.00	1300.00	3200.00	6000.00	
☐ 1871S	928,000	420.00	460.00	600.00	1000.00	
☐ 1872	251,880	420.00	470.00	600.00	920.00	32000.00
☐ 1872CC	29,650	420.00	600.00	1200.00	3100.00	
☐ 1872S	780,000	420.00	460.00	600.00	900.00	
☐ 1873	1,709,825	420.00	460.00	600.00		33000.00
☐ 1873CC	22,410	420.00	700.00	1500.00	3400.00	
☐ 1873S	1,040,600	420.00	450.00	600.00	930.00	
☐ 1874	366,800	420.00	450.00	600.00	900.00	33000.00
☐ 1874CC	115,085	420.00	460.00	800.00	3500.00	
☐ 1874S	1,241,000	420.00	450.00	600.00	900.00	
☐ 1875	295,740	420.00	450.00	750.00	900.00	85000.00
☐ 1875CC	111,151	400.00	470.00	1000.00	2000.00	

DATE	MINTAGE	ABP in F-12	F-12 Fine	EF-40 Ex. Fine	MS-60 Unc.	PRF-65 Proof
☐1875S	1,230,000	400.00	400.00	500.00	800.00	
☐1876	583,905	400.00	400.00	500.00	800.00	35000.00
☐1876CC	138,441	400.00	400.00	800.00	1400.00	
☐1876	1,597,000	400.00	400.00	600.00	800.00	

1861 and 1861-S both with A. C. Paquet Rev.
61-5 rare; 61 ex. rare

DOUBLE EAGLES—LIBERTY, 1877–1907, WITH MOTTO AND "TWENTY DOLLARS" ON REVERSE

Mint Mark is Below Eagle on Reverse

DATE	MINTAGE	ABP in F-12	F-12 Fine	EF-40 Ex. Fine	MS-60 Unc.	PRF-65 Proof
☐1877	397,670	400.00	460.00	500.00	800.00	35000.00
☐1877CC	42,565	400.00	480.00	900.00	2900.00	
☐1877S	1,735,000	400.00	470.00	500.00	800.00	
☐1878	534,645	400.00	470.00	500.00	800.00	35000.00
☐1878CC	13,180	400.00	500.00	1000.00	3000.00	
☐1878S	1,739,000	400.00	490.00	600.00	900.00	
☐1879	207,5630	400.00	490.00	600.00	900.00	34000.00
☐1879CC	10,708	600.00	900.00	1700.00	4000.00	
☐1879O	2,325	800.00	1800.00	3700.00	8500.00	
☐1879S	1,223,800	400.00	460.00	500.00	900.00	
☐1880	51,456	400.00	460.00	500.00	1200.00	33000.00
☐1880S	836,000	400.00	460.00	500.00	900.00	
☐1881	2,260	1000.00	2100.00	6000.00	16500.00	40000.00
☐1881S	727,000	400.00	460.00	500.00	900.00	
☐1882	630	3400.00	6000.00	16000.00	37000.00	46000.00
☐1882CC	39,140	400.00	460.00	900.00	1700.00	
☐1882S	1,125,000	400.00	450.00	600.00	900.00	
☐1883	40	PROOFS ONLY				80000.00
☐1883CC	59,962	400.00	500.00	900.00	1600.00	
☐1883S	1,189,000	400.00	460.00	630.00	900.00	
☐1884	71	PROOFS ONLY				76000.00
☐1884CC	81,139	400.00	460.00	900.00	1600.00	
☐1884S	916,000	400.00	460.00	500.00	900.00	
☐1885	828	2800.00	4100.00	9600.00	28000.00	
☐1885CC	9,450	500.00	800.00	1600.00	4000.00	
☐1885S	683,500	390.00	400.00	500.00	900.00	

DATE	MINTAGE	ABP in F-12	F-12 Fine	EF-40 Ex. Fine	MS-60 Unc.	PRF-65 Proof
□ 1886	1,106	2900.00	6000.00	11000.00	20000.00	38000.00
□ 1887	121	PROOFS ONLY				45000.00
□ 1887S	283,000	390.00	400.00	500.00		
□ 1888	226,266	390.00	400.00	500.00	800.00	35000.00
□ 1888S	859,600	390.00	400.00	500.00	800.00	
□ 1889	44,111	390.00	400.00	700.00	1000.00	30000.00
□ 1889CC	30,945	390.00	500.00	1000.00	1500.00	
□ 1889S	774,700	390.00	400.00	500.00	900.00	
□ 1890	75,995	390.00	400.00	700.00	900.00	30000.00
□ 1890CC	91,209	390.00	400.00	800.00	1300.00	
□ 1890S	802,750	390.00	400.00	600.00	950.00	
□ 1891	1,442	1200.00	1800.00	3600.00	8000.00	30000.00
□ 1891CC	5,000	600.00	1000.00	2800.00	6000.00	
□ 1891S	1,288,125	390.00	400.00	500.00	800.00	
□ 1892	4,523	500.00	800.00	1800.00	4800.00	26000.00
□ 1892CC	27,265	390.00	500.00	1100.00	2400.00	
□ 1892S	930,150	390.00	400.00	500.00	800.00	
□ 1893	344,399	390.00	400.00	500.00	800.00	27000.00
□ 1893CC	18,402	390.00	400.00	1000.00	3000.00	
□ 1893S	996,175	390.00	400.00	500.00	700.00	
□ 1894	1,368,990	390.00	400.00	500.00	700.00	24000.00
□ 1894S	1,048,550	390.00	400.00	500.00	700.00	
□ 1895	1,114,656	390.00	400.00	500.00	700.00	24000.00
□ 1895S	1,143,500	390.00	400.00	500.00	700.00	
□ 1896	792,663	390.00	400.00	500.00	700.00	24000.00
□ 1896S	1,403,925	390.00	400.00	500.00	700.00	
□ 1897	1,383,261	390.00	400.00	500.00	700.00	24000.00
□ 1897S	1,470,250	390.00	400.00	510.00	700.00	
□ 1898	170,470	390.00	400.00	520.00	700.00	24000.00
□ 1898S	2,575,175	390.00	400.00	520.00	700.00	
□ 1899	1,669,384	390.00	400.00	520.00	700.00	24000.00
□ 1899S	2,010,300	390.00	400.00	520.00	700.00	
□ 1900	1,874,584	390.00	400.00	520.00	700.00	24000.00
□ 1900S	2,459,500	390.00	400.00	520.00	700.00	
□ 1901	111,526	390.00	400.00	520.00	700.00	24000.00
□ 1901S	1,596,000	390.00	400.00	520.00	700.00	
□ 1902	31,254	390.00	400.00	700.00	1000.00	24000.00
□ 1902S	1,753,625	390.00	400.00	520.00	700.00	24000.00
□ 1903	287,428	390.00	400.00	520.00	700.00	24000.00
□ 1903S	954,000	390.00	400.00	520.00	700.00	
□ 1904	6,256,797	390.00	400.00	520.00	700.00	24000.00
□ 1904S	5,134,175	390.00	400.00	520.00	700.00	
□ 1905S	59,011	390.00	400.00	600.00	900.00	24000.00
□ 1905S	1,813,000	390.00	400.00	520.00	700.00	
□ 1906	69,690	390.00	400.00	520.00	800.00	24000.00
□ 1906D	620,250	390.00	400.00	520.00	700.00	
□ 1906S	2,065,750	390.00	410.00	600.00	800.00	
□ 1907	1,451,864	390.00	410.00	600.00	800.00	25000.00

DATE	MINTAGE	ABP in F-12	F-12 Fine	EF-40 Ex. Fine	MS-60 Unc.	PRF-65 Proof
☐ 1907D	842,250	390.00	410.00	600.00	800.00	
☐ 1907S	2,165,800	390.00	410.00	600.00	800.00	

DOUBLE EAGLES, $20.00 GOLD PIECES, 1907–1933

The Longacre Liberty design was replaced by the Saint-Gaudens in 1907, featuring a striding figure of Liberty holding a torch on the obverse and an eagle in flight on the reverse. A fact seldom mentioned is that this, of all representations of Liberty on our coins, was the only full-face likeness, the others being profiles or semi-profiles. Composition and weight remained as previously. The motto "IN GOD WE TRUST," at first omitted on request of Theodore Roosevelt, was added by Act of Congress in 1908. Striking of Double Eagles ceased in 1933. This final version of the mighty coin had a 90% gold/10% copper composition, with a weight of 33,436 grams (of which .96750 of an ounce was pure gold—almost a full ounce). Its diameter was 34 mm.

As a speculative item for gold investors, the Double Eagle has enjoyed greater popularity and media publicity in recent months than ever in its history. This should not be surprising, as it contains very nearly an exact ounce of gold and its worth as bullion can be figured easily based upon daily gold quotations.

DOUBLE LIBERTY STANDING "ST. GAUDENS" ROMAN NUMERALS MCMVII

Roman Numeral High Relief, Wire Rim,
Plain Edge, 14 Rays over Capitol.
Three Folds on Liberty's skirt

DATE	MINTAGE	ABP in F-12	F-12 Fine	EF-40 Ex. Fine	MS-60 Unc.	PRF-65 Proof
☐ 1907-MCMVII Ex. High Relief—Lettered Edge				AUCTION: $220000.00		
☐ 1907-MCMVII Ex. High Relief—Plain Edge			VERY RARE: $500000.00			
☐ 1907 Flat Rim*		2500.00	3000.00	6000.00	12000.00	
☐ 1907 Wire Rim*	11,250	2500.00	3000.00	6000.00	12000.00	

*Note: Separate mintage figures were not kept on these varieties.

DOUBLE EAGLES — LIBERTY STANDING "ST. GAUDENS," 1907–1908 DATE IN ARABIC NUMERALS, NO MOTTO ON REVERSE

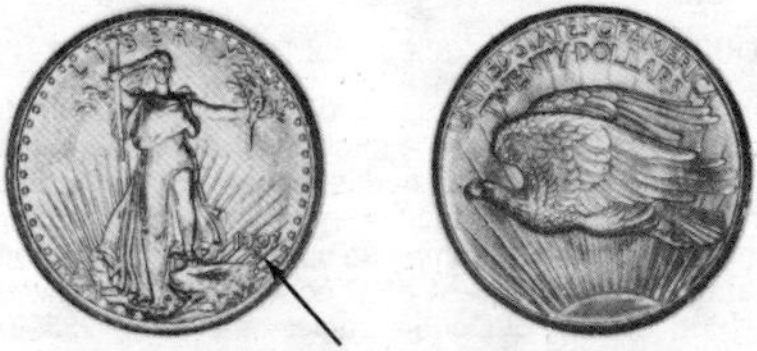

Mint Mark is Below Date on Obverse

DATE	MINTAGE	ABP in F-12	F-12 Fine	EF-40 Ex. Fine	MS-60 Unc.
☐ 1907*	361,667	450.00	500.00	650.00	1000.00
☐ 1908	4,271,551	450.00	500.00	650.00	1000.00
☐ 1908D	66,750	450.00	500.00	650.00	1000.00

*Small Letters on Edge. Large Letter on Edge-Unique.

DOUBLE EAGLES — LIBERTY STANDING "ST. GAUDENS," 1908–1933 WITH MOTTO ON REVERSE

Mint Mark is Below Date on Obverse

DATE	MINTAGE	ABP in F-12	F-12 Fine	EF-40 Ex. Fine	MS-60 Unc.	PRF-65 Proof
☐ 1908	156,359	450.00	500.00	800.00	1200.00	30000.00
☐ 1908D	349,500	450.00	500.00	700.00	1200.00	
☐ 1908S	22,000	450.00	500.00	1000.00	3900.00	
☐ 1909	161,282	450.00	500.00	800.00	1400.00	30000.00
☐ 1909 over 8	161,282	450.00	500.00	700.00	1400.00	
☐ 1909D	52,500	450.00	500.00	700.00	2600.00	
☐ 1909S	2,774,925	450.00	500.00	600.00	1000.00	
☐ 1910	482,167	450.00	500.00	600.00	800.00	
☐ 1910D	429,000	450.00	500.00	600.00	800.00	
☐ 1910S	2,128,250	450.00	500.00	600.00	800.00	

DATE	MINTAGE	ABP in F-12	F-12 Fine	EF-40 Ex. Fine	MS-60 Unc.	PRF-65 Proof
□1911	197,350	450.00	490.00	500.00	800.00	
□1911D	846,500	450.00	490.00	500.00	800.00	
□1911S	775,750	450.00	490.00	500.00	800.00	
□1912	149,824	450.00	490.00	500.00	1100.00	32000.00
□1913	168,838	450.00	490.00	500.00	1000.00	32000.00
□1913D	393,500	450.00	490.00	500.00	900.00	
□1913S	34,000	450.00	490.00	500.00	1400.00	
□1914	95,320	450.00	490.00	500.00	1100.00	32000.00
□1914D	453,000	450.00	490.00	500.00	900.00	
□1914S	1,498,000	450.00	490.00	500.00	900.00	
□1915	152,050	450.00	490.00	500.00	1000.00	32000.00
□1915S	567,500	450.00	490.00	500.00	900.00	
□1916S	796,000	450.00	490.00	500.00	1000.00	
□1920	228,250	450.00	490.00	500.00	1000.00	
□1920S	558,000	2800.00	5000.00	8800.00	19000.00	
□1921	528,500	3200.00	7200.00	12000.00	22000.00	
□1922	1,375,500	450.00	490.00	500.00	900.00	
□1922S	2,658,000	450.00	490.00	700.00	1100.00	
□1923	566,000	450.00	490.00	500.00	900.00	
□1923D	1,702,000	450.00	490.00	700.00	900.00	
□1924	4,323,500	450.00	490.00	500.00	1000.00	
□1924D	3,049,500	450.00	490.00	1000.00	2000.00	
□1924S	2,927,500	450.00	490.00	1100.00	2000.00	
□1925	2,831,750	450.00	490.00	500.00	1000.00	
□1925D	2,938,500	450.00	500.00	1200.00	2000.00	
□1925S	2,776,500	450.00	500.00	1200.00	2700.00	
□1926	816,750	450.00	490.00	500.00	900.00	
□1926D	481,000	450.00	500.00	1100.00	2500.00	
□1926S	2,041,500	450.00	500.00	1100.00	1900.00	
□1927	2,946,750	450.00	490.00	500.00	900.00	
□1927D	180,000				275000.00	
□1927S	3,107,000	1300.00	2400.00	4700.00	11000.00	
□1928	8,816,000	450.00	490.00	500.00	910.00	
□1929	1,779,750	800.00	1600.00	4000.00	8600.00	
□1930S	74,000.00	2100.00	4600.00	9800.00	21000.00	
□1931	2,938,250	1800.00	3500.00	7600.00	16000.00	
□1931D	106,500	1700.00	3300.00	7400.00	17000.00	
□1932	1,101,750	3200.00	5100.00	8800.00	20000.00	
□1933	445,525	NEVER PLACED IN CIRCULATION BECAUSE OF GOLD RECALL LEGISLATION.				

SILVER COMMEMORATIVE COINAGE

Commemorative coinage—that is, coins whose designs present a departure from the normal types for their denomination—was first struck in the ancient world. Roman emperors delighted in issuing coins portraying members of the family or topical events; they served an important propaganda purpose. Commemorative coins must be distinguished from medals, as the former have a stated face value and can be spent as money while the latter serve a decorative function only. During the Mint's first century it coined no commemoratives whatever. Its first was the Columbian half dollar of 1892, issued in connection with the Columbia Exposition. To date the total has reached 158 pieces, of which one is a silver dollar; one a silver quarter; 143 are half dollars (comprising 48 major types); two are $2.50 gold pieces; two are $50 gold pieces; and nine are $1 gold pieces. There is some objection to including the $50 "Quintuple Eagles" as commemorative *coins,* as regular coins of this denomination were never issued. They do, however, bear a statement of face value and were spendable.

Commemorative coins are issued by a special act of Congress and overseen by a committee established for the purpose. Sale of commemoratives is made to the public (and coin dealers) at an advance in price over the face value, this advance being excused on grounds that specimens supplied as choice and uncirculated have, presumably, sufficient collector appeal to be worth more than their stated denomination. While commemoratives have certainly not all advanced in price at a comparable pace, all have shown very healthy increases and proved excellent investments for their original or early purchasers.

A pair of medals is traditionally collected in conjunction with commemorative silver coins and careful note should be taken of them. These are the "Octagonal Norse American Centennial, 1828–1925," designed by Opus Fraser, struck on thick and thin planchets in a total issue of 40,000 (the latter are scarcer); and the "Wilson Dollar," designed by George T. Morgan of Morgan Dollar fame in connection with the opening of the Philippine Mint. The 2 Kroner commemoratives of 1936 issued by Sweden are also frequently collected with our commemoratives, though small in size and quite plentiful, as they relate to the Delaware Tercentenary, or 300th anniversary.

The extent to which commemorative coins have been used as money is not precisely determined but is thought to be very limited. As the original owners paid a premium for these coins it is not likely that many—except in time of dire need—would have cared to exchange them merely at face value. It should not automatically be presumed that specimens in less than uncirculated condition were indeed used as money and passed through many hands. Their substandard preservation could well be the result of injury, ill-advised cleaning or mounting procedures, or wear received from handling in traveling from collection to collection. Nevertheless, discriminating buyers expect commemoratives to be in uncirculated state and anything inferior is worth much less (the discount being sharper than for a circulating coin).

The existence of proofs among the commemorative series has aroused much debate. Commemoratives are occasionally seen as proofs, notably the Columbian and Isabella quarters, but this is no evidence that all or even a majority of commemoratives were available in proof state. It is easy to be confused on this point, as well-struck uncirculated specimens frequently have a proof-like appearance.

SILVER COMMEMORATIVE, 1892–1894 ISABELLA QUARTER DOLLAR

Comparatively little notice was at first taken of this handsome commemorative, because the Columbian Exposition (at which it was issued) had already produced a commemorative and a larger one, in 50¢ denomination. The Isabella Quarter Dollar, originally sold at the exposition for $1, soon became a popular favorite of collectors. Agitation for it was made by the fair's Board of Lady Managers, which may explain why it portrays a female on the obverse—Isabella of Spain, who helped finance Columbus' voyage round the world—and a symbol of "female industry" on its reverse. The coin was designed by C. E. Barber and struck in 1893.

DATE	MINTAGE	ABP in MS-60	MS-60 Unc.	MS-65 Unc.
□1893	24,214	350.00	600.00	4000.00

LAFAYETTE DOLLAR

The celebrated Lafayette Dollar holds a special rank among commemoratives, being the first $1 denomination coin of its sort and the first to portray an American President. On its obverse is a profile bust of General Lafayette (the French officer so instrumental to our efforts in ending colonial domination) over which a profile of Washington is superimposed. The reverse carries a fine equestrian likeness of Lafayette, adapted from a statue put up in Paris as a gift from the American people. This coin was designed by C. E. Barber and struck in 1900. It was sold originally at twice the face value, with proceeds going to the Lafayette Memorial Commission.

DATE	MINTAGE	ABP in MS-60	MS-60 Unc.	MS-65 Unc.
□1900	36,026	450.00	900.00	8000.00

SILVER COMMEMORATIVE HALF DOLLARS

COLUMBIAN
EXPOSITION
HALF DOLLAR

1892–1893

DATE	MINTAGE		ABP in MS-60	MS-60 Unc.	MS-65 Unc.
☐ 1892 Columbian Expo	950,000		42.00	75.00	1500.00
☐ 1893 Columbian Expo	1,550,405		42.00	75.00	1500.00
☐ 1921 Alabama Centennial....	59,038		120.00	300.00	4500.00
☐ 1921 Same w/2 x 2 on Obverse	6,006		200.00	350.00	4700.00
☐ 1936 Albany, N.Y.	17,671		140.00	300.00	1200.00
☐ Arkansas Centennial	Type		60.00	100.00	900.00
☐ 1935 Arkansas Centennial ...	13,012				
☐ 1935D Arkansas Centennial..	5,505	SET	180.00	300.00	3000.00
☐ 1935S Arkansas Centennial..	5,506				
☐ 1936 Arkansas Centennial ...	9,660				
☐ 1936D Arkansas Centennial..	9,660	SET	180.00	310.00	3000.00
☐ 1936S Arkansas Centennial..	9,662				
☐ 1937 Arkansas Centennial ...	5,505				
☐ 1937D Arkansas Centennial..	5,505	SET	190.00	310.00	3000.00
☐ 1937S Arkansas Centennial..	5,506				
☐ 1938 Arkansas Centennial ...	3,156				
☐ 1938D Arkansas Centennial..	3,155	SET	350.00	600.00	5000.00
☐ 1938S Arkansas Centennial..	3,156				
☐ 1939 Arkansas Centennial ...	2,104				
☐ 1939D Arkansas Centennial..	2,104	SET	600.00	1200.00	7000.00
☐ 1939S Arkansas Centennial..	2,105				
☐ 1936 Arkansas (Robinson) ...	25,265		90.00	160.00	800.00
☐ 1937 Battle of Antietam	18,028		210.00	460.00	1200.00
☐ 1936 Battle of Gettysburg....	26,030		165.00	300.00	1000.00
☐ Boone Bi-Centennial	Type		80.00	150.00	600.00
☐ 1934 Boone Bi-Centennial ...	10,007		75.00	140.00	500.00
☐ 1935 Boone Bi-Centennial ...	10,010				
☐ 1935D Boone Bi-Centennial..	5,005	SET	200.00	380.00	1700.00
☐ 1935S Boone Bi-Centennial..	5,005				
☐ 1935 Boone Bi-Cent. Sm. 1934 Rev.	10,008				
☐ 1935D Type of 1934	2,003	SET	600.00	1100.00	3800.00
☐ 1935S Type of 1934	2,004				
☐ 1936 Type of 1934..........	12,012				
☐ 1936D Type of 1934	5,006	SET	200.00	390.00	1800.00

DATE	MINTAGE		ABP in MS-60	MS-60 Unc.	MS-65 Unc.
☐ 1936S Type of 1934	5,005				
☐ 1937 Type of 1934..........	9,810				
☐ 1937D Type of 1934	2,506	SET	400.00	700.00	2000.00
☐ 1937S Type of 1934	2,506				
☐ 1938 Type of 1934..........	2,100				
☐ 1938D Same	2,100	SET	700.00	1350.00	2400.00
☐ 1938S Same	2,100				
☐ 1936 Bridgeport, Conn.	25,015		100.00	180.00	1200.00
☐ 1925S California Diamond Jubilee	86,594		80.00	160.00	1600.00
☐ 1936 Cinc. Music Center.....	Type		90.00	340.00	2600.00
☐ 1936 Cinc. Music Center.....	5,005				
☐ 1936D Cinc. Music Center ...	5,005	SET	500.00	975.00	6000.00
☐ 1936S Cinc. Music Center ...	5,006				
☐ 1936 Cleveland Exposition ...	50,030		65.00	115.00	1100.00
☐ 1936 Columbia, S.C.	Type		125.00	270.00	900.00
☐ 1936 Columbia, S.C.	9,007				
☐ 1936D Columbia, S.C.	8,009	SET	500.00	1000.00	2000.00
☐ 1936S Columbia, S.C.	8,007				
☐ 1935 Conn. Tercentennial....	25,018		110.00	280.00	1300.00
☐ 1936 Delaware Tercentennial	20,993		110.00	280.00	1400.00
☐ 1936 Elgin, Illinois	20,015		110.00	280.00	1250.00
☐ 1925S Fort Vancouver	14,944		250.00	500.00	1800.00
☐ 1922 Grant Memorial........	67,405		80.00	180.00	1200.00
☐ 1922 Same w/Star on Obverse	4,256		500.00	750.00	11000.00
☐ 1928 Hawaii Sesquicentennial	9,958		600.00	900.00	6000.00
☐ 1935 Hudson Sesquicentennial	10,008		350.00	600.00	3400.00
☐ 1918 Illinois Centennial	100,058		80.00	160.00	1400.00
☐ 1946 Iowa Centennial	100,057		50.00	130.00	500.00
☐ 1925 Lexington-Concord	162,013		40.00	70.00	1600.00
☐ 1936 Long Island	81,826		50.00	115.00	1500.00
☐ 1936 Lynchburg, Va.	20,013		120.00	240.00	1100.00
☐ 1920 Maine Centennial	50,028		80.00	160.00	1700.00
☐ 1934 Maryland Tercentennial .	25,015		90.00	150.00	1200.00
☐ 1921 Missouri Centennial	15,428		300.00	500.00	6000.00
☐ 1923 Monroe Doctrine.......	274,077		40.00	80.00	3600.00
☐ 1938 New Rochelle	15,226		270.00	465.00	1100.00
☐ 1936 Norfolk, Va............	16,936		260.00	500.00	800.00
☐ 1936 Oakland Bay Bridge....	71,424		70.00	160.00	1200.00
☐ 1935 Old Spanish Trail	10,008		350.00	700.00	2000.00
☐ Oregon Trail	Type		70.00	135.00	650.00
☐ 1926 Oregon Trail	47,955		70.00	125.00	650.00
☐ 1926S Oregon Trail	83,055		60.00	125.00	650.00
☐ 1928 Oregon Trail	6,028		150.00	300.00	950.00
☐ 1933D Oregon Trail	5,008		170.00	340.00	1200.00
☐ 1934D Oregon Trail	7,006		150.00	220.00	1400.00
☐ 1936 Oregon Trail	10,006		80.00	200.00	800.00

DATE	MINTAGE		ABP in MS-60	MS-60 Unc.	MS-65 Unc.
☐1936S Oregon Trail	5,006		130.00	290.00	800.00
☐1937D Oregon Trail	12,008		80.00	140.00	700.00
☐1938 Oregon Trail	6,006				
☐1938D Oregon Trail	6,005	SET	350.00	600.00	2000.00
☐1938S Oregon Trail	6,006				
☐1939 Oregon Trail	3,004				
☐1939D Oregon Trail	3,004	SET	700.00	1250.00	3400.00
☐1939S Oregon Trail	3,005				
☐1915S Pan Pacific Exposition	27,134		300.00	500.00	4200.00
☐1920 Pilgrim Tercentennial ...	152,112		40.00	72.00	1100.00
☐1921 Pilgrim Tercentennial ...	20,053		110.00	150.00	1700.00
☐Rhode Island	Type		85.00	140.00	1100.00
☐1936 Rhode Island..........	20,013				
☐1936S Rhode Island	15,010	SET	200.00	360.00	3000.00
☐1936S Rhode Island	15,011				
☐1937 Roanoke Island, N.C. ..	29,030		100.00	260.00	1100.00
☐1935S San Diego Exposition .	70,132		60.00	110.00	700.00
☐1936D San Diego Exposition .	30,082		80.00	150.00	700.00
☐1926 Sesquicentennial	141,120		30.00	62.00	4000.00
☐1925 Stone Mountain	1,314,709		29.00	50.00	600.00
☐Texas Centennial	Type		85.00	150.00	570.00
☐1934 Texas Centennial	61,413		70.00	150.00	550.00
☐1935 Texas Centennial	9,996				
☐1935D Texas Centennial.....	10,007	SET	200.00	440.00	1700.00
☐1935S Texas Centennial.....	10,008				
☐1936 Texas Centennial	8,911				
☐1936D Texas Centennial.....	9,039	SET	200.00	490.00	1650.00
☐1936S Texas Centennial.....	9,055				
☐1937 Texas Centennial	6,571				
☐1937D Texas Centennial.....	6,605	SET	200.00	460.00	1700.00
☐1937S Texas Centennial.....	6,637				
☐1938 Texas Centennial	3,780				
☐1938D Texas Centennial.....	3,775	SET	410.00	600.00	2000.00
☐1938S Texas Centennial.....	3,814				
☐1927 Vermont (Bennington) ..	28,162		150.00	240.00	2000.00
☐1924 Huguenot-Walloon	142,080		65.00	130.00	1200.00
☐Washington Carver..........	Type		600.00	18.00	100.00
☐1951 Washington Carver	110,018				
☐1951D Washington Carver ...	10,004	SET	55.00	125.00	1800.00
☐1951S Washington Carver ...	10,004				
☐1952 Washington Carver	2,006,292				
☐1952D Washington Carver ...	8,006	SET	60.00	150.00	2000.00
☐1952S Washington Carver ...	8,006				
☐1953 Washington Carver	8,003				
☐1953D Washington Carver ...	8,003	SET	75.00	180.00	2500.00
☐1953S Washington Carver ...	108,020				
☐1954 Washington Carver	12,006				
☐1954D Washington Carver ...	12,006	SET	50.00	130.00	2400.00
☐1954S Washington Carver ...	122,024				

DATE	MINTAGE		ABP in MS-60	MS-60 Unc.	MS-65 Unc.
☐ B. T. Washington	Type		8.00	15.00	90.00
☐ 1946 B. T. Washington	1,000,546				
☐ 1946D B. T. Washington.....	200,113	SET	20.00	50.00	500.00
☐ 1946S B. T. Washington.....	500,279				
☐ 1947 B. T. Washington	100,017				
☐ 1947D B. T. Washington.....	100,017	SET	30.00	70.00	550.00
☐ 1947S B. T. Washington.....	100,017				
☐ 1948 B. T. Washington	8,005				
☐ 1948D B. T. Washington.....	8,005	SET	60.00	145.00	600.00
☐ 1948S B. T. Washington.....	8,005				
☐ 1949 B. T. Washington	6,004				
☐ 1949D B. T. Washington.....	6,004	SET	90.00	210.00	600.00
☐ 1949S B. T. Washington.....	6,004				
☐ 1950 B. T. Washington	6,004				
☐ 1950D B. T. Washington.....	6,004	SET	80.00	175.00	600.00
☐ 1950S B. T. Washington.....	512,091				
☐ 1951 B. T. Washington	510,082				
☐ 1951D B. T. Washington.....	7,004	SET	50.00	125.00	550.00
☐ 1951S B. T. Washington.....	7,004				
☐ 1936 Wisconsin	25,015		100.00	170.00	1500.00
☐ 1936 York County, Me.	25,015		100.00	160.00	2000.00

GEORGE WASHINGTON 250TH ANNIVERSARY

The U.S. resumed its commemorative coin program with this silver half dollar in 1982, after a lapse of 28 years. The reason for its long suspension was that the value of silver far exceeded the traditional face values of commemorative coins. However, since commemoratives are issued for collectors and not for circulation, it was finally decided that the public would not object to low face values. The year 1982 marked the 250th anniversary (technically, "sesquicentennial," though the term is seldom used) of George Washington's birth. This was considered an appropriate occasion for resumption of the commemorative series. This coin is .900 silver and has the same specifications as earlier silver commemorative half dollars, and likewise the same as circulating half dollars up to 1964. The obverse carries an equestrian portrait of Washington looking left, with a view of Mount Vernon on the reverse. The artistic style was designed to conform, at least generally, to that of the majority of earlier commemorative halves.

DATE	MINTAGE	ABP in MS-60	MS-65 Unc.	PRF-65 Proof
☐ 1982P—NONE ISSUED				
☐ 1982S—PROOFS ONLY		9.00		12.00
☐ 1982D		8.00	13.00	

STATUE OF LIBERTY COMMEMORATIVE

The Statue of Liberty clad half dollar commemorates what our country means to all of those who seek peace and a chance at a new way of life. The obverse shows the Statue of Liberty emblazoned on the horizon of a new day. The reverse depicts a family looking toward the dawning of a new day and a new way of life.

DATE	ABP	MS-65 Unc.	PRF-65 Proof
☐1986D	4.50	7.25	
☐1986S	5.50		8.75

HALF-DOLLAR CLAD COIN

The new edition of the half-dollar clad coin commemorates the Bicentennial of the Congress of the United States of America.

DATE	ABP	MS-65 Unc.	PRF-65 Proof
☐1989D	5.00	6.00	
☐1989S	5.00		7.00

LOS ANGELES XXIII OLYMPIAD

The set of two commemorative silver dollars issued in 1983 and 1984 for the Los Angeles Olympic Games marked the first $1 silver commemoratives in more than 80 years. Enormous publicity and controversy surrounded these coins, concerning their designs, face values, and the method of distributing them to the public. The first coin, dated 1983, pictures a discus thrower on the obverse with a profile bust of an eagle on the reverse. The second, dated 1984, shows the entrance to the Los Angeles Coliseum (site of the 1984 games) on the obverse, and a full-length eagle on the reverse. These coins have the same specifications as the standard U.S. silver dollar, last struck in 1935, and contain approximately three fourths of an ounce of .999 + silver. Debate raged over whether or not they should show a face value and, if so, the amount. It was decided that they should have a $1 face value, in spite of the fact that they contain several times that value in silver. This virtually insured that they—unlike some commemoratives of the past—will never end up in circulation. Yet they are legal tender, and could be passed at $1 if an owner desired.

DATE	MINTAGE	MS-65 Unc.	PRF-65 Proof
☐1983P		30.00	
☐1983S		35.00	30.00
☐1983D		45.00	
☐1984P		25.00	
☐1984S		45.00	30.00
☐1984D		50.00	

STATUE OF LIBERTY SILVER DOLLAR COMMEMORATIVE

The Statue of Liberty Commemorative silver dollar, .900 Fine: This beautiful coin commemorates and celebrates the Statue of Liberty. The obverse portrays a classic likeness of our Lady of Liberty standing on Ellis Island. The reverse shows the Torch of Liberty with the famous inscription inviting all of those who love and look for freedom.

DATE	ABP	MS-60 Unc.	PRF-65 Proof
☐1986P	20.00	32.00	
☐1986S	21.00		35.00

CONSTITUTION SILVER DOLLAR COMMEMORATIVE

The Constitution silver dollar commemorative, .900 Fine: The obverse shows a quill pen and the words "We the People" superimposed over the Constitution document. The reverse depicts a group of "We the People."

DATE	ABP	MS-65 Unc.	PRF-65 Proof
☐1987P	20.00	28.00	
☐1987S	21.00		31.00

ONE DOLLAR SILVER 1988 U.S. OLYMPIC COIN

The Olympiad silver dollar commemorates the United States' participation in the Seoul, Korea, Olympics.

DATE	ABP	MS-65 Unc.	PRF-65 Proof
☐1988P	21.00	24.00	
☐1988S	21.00		30.00

ONE DOLLAR SILVER COIN

The silver dollar Bicentennial coin celebrated Congress' 200th anniversary.

DATE	ABP	MS-65 Unc.	PRF-65 Proof
☐1989P	21.00	24.00	
☐1989S	21.00		30.00

SILVER COMMEMORATIVE MEDALS COLLECTED WITH COMMEMORATIVES

NORTH AMERICAN CENTENNIAL

DATE	MINTAGE	ABP in MS-60	MS-60 Unc.	MS-65 Unc.
□ 1925 (Thin)	40,000	35.00	78.00	180.00
□ 1925 (Thick)	40,000	28.00	65.00	120.00

SO-CALLED WILSON DOLLAR

DATE	MINTAGE	ABP in MS-60	MS-60 Unc.	MS-65 Unc.
□ 1920 Silver	2,200	110.00	250.00	500.00

2 KRONER, SWEDEN

DATE	MINTAGE	ABP in MS-60	MS-60 Unc.	MS-65 Unc.
□ 1936 2 Kroner Delaware Swedish Tercentennial	500,000	15.00	35.00	70.00

GOLD COMMEMORATIVE COINAGE, 1903–1989

The gold commemorative series began not long after the silver, in 1903. Far fewer gold commemoratives were issued, as the large physical size necessary for impressive designing resulted in a coin of very high face value. Experiments were made with $1 gold commemoratives, which some critics called puny, and goliaths of $50 denomination, which were indeed eye-catching but well beyond the budget of most citizens in those days. The value of these pieces in extremely fine condition is about one-third the price for uncirculated—ample proof that most buying activity originates with numismatists rather than bullion speculators.

ONE AND $2.50 GOLD

1903–Jefferson

1903–McKinley

1922–Grant

DATE	MINTAGE	ABP in MS-60	MS-60 Unc.	MS-65 Unc.
□ 1903 Jefferson Dollar	17,500	350.00	750.00	4500.00
□ 1903 McKinley Dollar	17,500	350.00	750.00	4500.00
□ 1904 Lewis & Clark Dollar	10,025	850.00	1250.00	10000.00
□ 1905 Lewis & Clark Dollar	10,041	820.00	1250.00	10000.00
□ 1915S Panama-Pacific Dollar*	15,000	370.00	800.00	4600.00
□ 1915S Panama-Pacific $2.50 Dollar*	6,766	900.00	1850.00	8000.00
□ 1916 McKinley Dollar	10,003	400.00	800.00	4700.00
□ 1917 McKinley Dollar	10,004	400.00	825.00	5000.00
□ 1922 Grant Dollar	5,016	420.00	1200.00	5300.00
□ 1922 Grant Dollar w/star	5,000	500.00	1300.00	5600.00
□ 1926 Philadelphia Sesquicentennial $2.50	46,019	360.00	650.00	4700.00

*Struck to commemorate the opening of the Panama Canal.

ONE DOLLAR GOLD

Panama-Pacific

$2.50 GOLD

Philadelphia

PANAMA-PACIFIC FIFTY DOLLARS

This huge coin, containing nearly 2½ ounces of gold, was not the world's largest gold piece but by far the most substantial coin of that metal struck by the U.S. government. (To give some indication of changes in the market from 1915, the date of issue, until today, \$50 worth of gold today is about ⅙ of an ounce.) It was issued for the Panama-Pacific Exposition and was struck in two varieties, one with round and one with octagonal edge, the former being somewhat scarcer and more valuable. Minerva is pictured on the obverse and the Athenian state symbol, the owl, representative of wisdom, on the reverse. The place of issue was San Francisco and the designer Robert Aitken. This is definitely not a piece for bullion speculators as its value is many times that of the gold content and under no circumstances would a \$50 Panama-Pacific—or any U.S. gold commemorative—be melted down.

ROUND

DATE	MINTAGE	ABP in MS-60	MS-60 Unc.	MS-65 Unc.
☐1915S Round	483	20000.00	30000.00	80000.00

OCTAGONAL

DATE	MINTAGE	ABP in MS-60	MS-60 Unc.	MS-65 Unc.
☐ 1915S Octagonal	645	18000.00	26000.00	65000.00
☐ COMPLETE SET, 50.00 Gold Round and Octagonal, 2.50 & 1.00 Gold and Half Dollar Silver		44000.00	60000.00	110000.00
☐ DOUBLE SET IN ORIGINAL FRAME—Superior Sale, January 1985—$160,000.00				

Note: The double sets were authorized mint issues. They consisted of two specimens of each coin, mounted so that both sides could be seen. The original price in 1915 was $400.

STATUE OF LIBERTY GOLD COMMEMORATIVE

The Statue of Liberty $5 Gold Commemorative: The obverse depicts the head of the Statue of Liberty and the date. The reverse is a version of a flying eagle.

DATE	ABP	MS-65 Unc.	PRF-65 Proof
☐ 1986W	230.00	290.00	250.00

CONSTITUTION GOLD COMMEMORATIVE

The Constitution $5 Gold Commemorative: The obverse depicts a flying eagle with a superimposed quill pen. The reverse again shows the quill pen over which is superimposed "We the People."

DATE	ABP	MS-65 Unc.	PRF-65 Proof
☐ 1987W	100.00	170.00	155.00

FIVE DOLLAR GOLD 1988 U.S. OLYMPIC COIN

The five dollar 1988 gold Olympiad coin celebrates the United States' participation in the Seoul, Korea, Olympics.

DATE	ABP	MS-65 Unc.	PRF-65 Proof
□ 1988W	100.00	150.00	190.00

FIVE DOLLAR GOLD COIN

The five dollar gold commemorative coin celebrates the Congressional Bicentennial.

DATE	ABP	MS-65 Unc.	PRF-65 Proof
□ 1989W	100.00	150.00	190.00

LOS ANGELES XXIII OLYMPIAD $10

This $10 gold commemorative, carrying the date 1984, marked U.S. reentry into commemorative gold—which many forecasters claimed would never occur. Issuance of a gold commemorative under modern circumstances called for a drastic change in approach. Traditionally (prior to the Gold Recall Act of 1933), our gold commemoratives contained slightly less than their face value in gold, just as did our gold circulating coins. With today's much higher gold prices, the Los Angeles XXIII Olympiad $10 gold commemorative contains about twenty times its face value in gold. They were distributed to the public at prices which took this factor into account, as well as including a handling fee (which many persons in the numismatic community charged to be exorbitant). A pair of torch bearers is shown on the obverse, symbolizing the ceremony of "lighting the Olympic flame" to open the games. The American eagle symbol with stars, arrows, and branches is pictured on the reverse. This coin has the same specifications used in striking circulating $10 gold pieces, prior to their discontinuance.

DATE	MINTAGE	ABP	MS-65 Unc.	PRF-65 Proof
☐1984P		700.00		800.00
☐1984D		400.00		550.00
☐1984S		300.00		400.00
☐1984W*		250.00	350.00	400.00

Note: "W" mint mark indicates West Point, New York.

AMERICAN EAGLE GOLD AND SILVER BULLION COINS

The American Eagle bullion coins are minted in $5: weight 52.4 grains, contains 1/10 oz. pure gold; $10: weight 130.9 grains, contains 1/4 oz. pure gold; $25: weight 261.8 grains, contains 1/2 oz. pure gold; $50: weight 523.6 grains, contains 1 oz. pure gold. The obverse design is similar to the St. Gaudens $20 gold piece, 1907–1933 design. The coin date appears in roman numerals. The reverse shows a group of American eagles.

DATE		ABP	MS-65 Unc.	PRF-65 Proof
☐1986	$5.00	50.00	65.00	
☐1986	$10.00	100.00	130.00	
☐1986	$25.00	200.00	300.00	
☐1986	$50.00	400.00	475.00	
☐1986W	$50.00	600.00		700.00
☐1987	$5.00	50.00	65.00	
☐1987	$10.00	90.00	125.00	
☐1987	$25.00	200.00	280.00	
☐1987P	$25.00	300.00		400.00
☐1987	$50.00	400.00	500.00	
☐1987W	$50.00	500.00		600.00
☐1988	$5.00	35.00	50.00	
☐1988P	$5.00	60.00		70.00
☐1988	$10.00	90.00	110.00	
☐1988P	$10.00	110.00		150.00
☐1988	$25.00	190.00	250.00	
☐1988P	$25.00	200.00		250.00
☐1988	$50.00	400.00	475.00	
☐1988W	$50.00	500.00		700.00
☐1989	$50.00	300.00	400.00	
☐1989W	$50.00	400.00		500.00

AMERICAN SILVER DOLLAR EAGLE BULLION COIN

The American Silver Eagle Dollar bullion coin is minted in 99.93 fine silver; weight, 479.9 grains; contains 1 oz. pure silver. The obverse design was taken from the famous Walking Liberty half dollar coin. The reverse shows an American Eagle with breasted shield.

DATE	ABP	MS-65 Unc.	PRF-65 Proof
☐1986P	7.00	14.00	
☐1986S	30.00		35.00
☐1987P	7.00	11.00	
☐1987S	25.00		30.00
☐1988P	7.00	10.00	
☐1988S	31.00		50.00
☐1989P	7.00	10.00	
☐1989S	20.00		35.00

CONFEDERATE COINAGE

Following its secession from the Union in 1861, the Confederate government of Louisiana took control of the federal mint at New Orleans (the only mint operating in southern territory), along with its materials and machinery. Jefferson Davis, President of the C.S.A., appointed C. G. Memminger his Secretary of the Treasury and authorized production of a "Confederate Half Dollar." This was presumably manufactured by taking ordinary half dollars and removing their reverse motif, to which was added a shield with seven stars (one for each state that had joined the C.S.A.), a Liberty cap, a wreath of sugar cane and cotton, and the wording "CONFEDERATE STATES OF AMERICA HALF DOL." No serious effort was made to circulate this coin, only four specimens being struck. Restrikes were later made. J. W. Scott somehow got hold of the original reverse die and, having keen business aptitude, struck off 500 examples for sale to souvenir hunters. He used his own obverse, consisting of wording without portraiture or other design.

1861
HALF DOL.

CONFEDERATE HALF DOLLAR

DATE	MINTAGE	ABP in MS-60	VF-20 V. Fine	MS-60 Unc.	MS-65 Unc.
☐ 1861 Half Dollar (Rare)	4				VERY RARE
☐ 1861 Half Dollar Restrike	500	700.00	900.00	2000.00	3000.00
☐ 1861 Scott Token Obverse, Confederate Reverse	500	150.00	160.00	600.00	1000.00

CONFEDERATE CENT

This was the only Confederate coin intended for general circulation—and it never got that far. Robert Lovett of Philadelphia was commissioned by agents of the C.S.A. to prepare coins in the denomination of 1¢ in 1861. He was to design the coin, engrave their dies, and do the actual striking as well. After producing a certain quantity, of which only 12 have been discovered, Lovett ceased operations and hid both the coins and the dies from which they were struck, fearing, as a resident of the North, arrest by authorities on grounds of complicity with the enemy. Restrikes were subsequently made, in gold, silver, and copper, by John Haseltine. The figures given here for mintages of the restrikes are based on best available information. Haseltine, in his memoirs of the affair, states that the die broke on the 59th coin. There are nevertheless believed to be 72 restrikes in existence. Haseltine made a point of striking no reproductions in nickel for fear they might be taken for originals.

ORIGINAL

RESTRIKE

DATE	MINTAGE		MS-60 Unc.	MS-65 Unc.
□ 1861 Cent (original)	12		9000.00	17000.00
□ 1861 Restrike, Silver	12	PROOF	4000.00	5000.00
□ 1861 Restrike, Copper	55		2000.00	5000.00

U.S. PROOF SETS, 1936 TO DATE

The technical definition of a Proof is a coin made for presentation or collector purposes. Beginning in the second half of the 19th century the Mint struck proofs of many of its coins; some, but not a great number, appeared previously. A proof is not made from a specially manufactured die but rather an ordinary die set aside exclusively for use in proofs. The dies are cleaned and polished more frequently than those used for ordinary circulating coins. When any sign of wear or imperfection appears, the die is scrapped. This is why proofs have a somewhat higher surface relief (bas-relief) than uncirculated specimens, leading to the conclusion—mistakenly—that more deeply engraved dies are employed. After coming from the press, proofs are not touched except with gloves or special tongs made for the purpose, and are inspected for uniformity. Any exhibiting flaws of any nature are rejected. Proofs that pass inspection are housed in holders, so that nothing may interfere with their finish.

Frosted proofs are no longer produced. These have a lustrous shining ground but the design and lettering are non-reflective or frosted. So-called "matte" proofs have a granular finish. These, too, are a thing of the past. Brilliant proofs, those struck from 1936 to date, are mirrorlike over the entire surface, not only the ground but design and lettering. It is well to keep in mind (for beginners) that a coin found in circulation is never a proof, regardless of the brilliance of its lustre or perfection of its condition. It is simply a "proof-like" coin.

Proof sets have been struck by the Mint since 1936, though none were issued in the years 1943–49. Beginning in 1968 they were issued in stiff plastic holders rather than pliable vinyl. Proof sets are now struck only at the San Francisco Mint and all coins carry the "S" mint mark.

DATE	MINTAGE	ABP	MS-65 Proof
□ 1936	3,837	3200.00	5000.00
□ 1937	5,542	2800.00	3600.00
□ 1938	8,045	1100.00	1800.00
□ 1939	8,795	1000.00	1600.00

DATE	MINTAGE	ABP	MS-65 Proof
☐ 1940	11,246	800.00	1400.00
☐ 1941	15,287	900.00	1250.00
☐ 1942 One Nickel		900.00	1250.00
☐ 1942 Two Nickels	21,120	1000.00	1400.00
☐ 1950	51,386	400.00	650.00
☐ 1951	57,500	260.00	390.00
☐ 1952	81,980	160.00	250.00
☐ 1953	128,800	100.00	165.00
☐ 1954	233,300	60.00	85.00
☐ 1955	378,200	52.00	75.00
☐ 1956	699,384	30.00	50.00
☐ 1957	1,247,952	16.00	25.00
☐ 1958	875,652	20.00	33.00
☐ 1959	1,149,291	15.00	22.00
☐ 1960 Small Date		17.00	26.00
☐ 1960 Large Date	1,691,602	15.00	20.00
☐ 1961	3,028,244	13.00	19.00
☐ 1962	3,218,019	12.00	18.00
☐ 1963	3,075,645	12.00	18.00
☐ 1964	3,949,634	12.00	16.00
☐ 1968S	3,041,508	4.50	7.00
☐ 1968S Without "S" 10¢		6000.00	8500.00
☐ 1969S	2,360,000	4.00	7.00
☐ 1970S	2,600,000	8.00	12.00
☐ 1970S Small Date ¢		57.00	80.00
☐ 1970S Without "S" 10¢	2,200	500.00	600.00
☐ 1971S	3,244,138	4.00	5.00
☐ 1971S Without "S" 5¢	1,655	800.00	1000.00
☐ 1972S	3,267,667	3.75	5.00
☐ 1973S	2,769,624	8.00	11.00
☐ 1974S	2,617,350	8.00	11.00
☐ 1975S	2,850,715	6.00	9.00
☐ 1976S (40%-3 pieces)	3,215,730	14.00	17.00
☐ 1976S	4,150,210	7.00	10.00
☐ 1977S	3,251,125	5.00	7.00
☐ 1978S	3,127,781	4.75	8.00
☐ 1979S	3,677,175	8.00	12.00
☐ 1979S TYPE 2		70.00	100.00
☐ 1980S	3,547,130	5.00	7.00
☐ 1981S	4,110,000	6.00	7.00
☐ 1981S TYPE 2		230.00	275.00
☐ 1982S	3,857,479	4.00	7.00
☐ 1983S	3,139,000	8.00	12.00
☐ 1983S Pres.		75.00	95.00
☐ 1984S	2,850,110	16.00	20.00
☐ 1984S Pres.		40.00	60.00
☐ 1985S	3,460,210	16.00	20.00
☐ 1986S	2,391,100	14.00	21.00

DATE	MINTAGE	ABP	MS-65 Proof
□1986S Pres.		40.00	51.00
□1987S	462,200	9.00	11.00
□1987S Pres.		35.00	42.00
□1988S		15.00	20.00
□1988 Pres		40.00	50.00
□1989S		9.00	12.00
□1989S Pres		50.00	65.00

Note: Some mintage totals for Proof Sets represent estimates based upon best available information.

U.S. MINT SETS, 1947–1989

Beginning collectors habitually confuse the terms "proof set" and "mint set." It is important to recognize the distinction between them, especially as the values are quite different. The buyer who thinks he has a bargain on a proof set, when in fact he has bought a mint set, may have paid too much.

Mint sets originated well after the selling of special proof sets had become established. Manufacture of proof sets was suspended during World War II. Following conclusion of the war (1945), the mint chose not to immediately resume proof sets, but instead to sell mint sets as a substitute. They were introduced in 1947, sold well, and continued to be produced after proof sets were reinstated in 1950.

Mint sets contain the same coins as proof sets (one of each denomination, from each mint, for that year), but the coins are not proofs. They are standard "business strikes," just like coins released into general circulation. Naturally they are uncirculated, as the mint takes specimens from its assembly lines that have not gone into circulation. In terms of specific grade, this is really a matter of luck. Some coins in mint sets are flawless and merit a full MS-70 rating. The vast majority are not quite so fine, and would grade between MS-60 and MS-65. In buying a mint set from a dealer, you can be certain that all the coins will be uncirculated, but a condition grade higher than MS-60 should not be anticipated for any of them. In offering mint sets, dealers do not mention condition grade, as it can vary from coin to coin within a set.

To carry the values indicated, sets must be in the original sealed holders in which they were sold. In the years 1965, 1966 and 1967, when no proof sets were struck, mint sets were placed in rigid plastic holders and called "Special Mint Sets," in hopes they would appeal to the regular buyers of proof sets. The standard packaging for mint sets was originally a cardboard holder, which was abandoned in favor of plastic envelopes in 1959.

Mintage figures are not recorded for mint sets, as the coins involved are not specially produced for that purpose.

DATE	ABP	MS-60 Or Better
□1947	560.00	835.00
□1948	160.00	225.00
□1949	550.00	800.00

DATE	ABP	MS-60 Or Better
☐1950*		
☐1951	300.00	400.00
☐1952	200.00	300.00
☐1953	160.00	240.00
☐1954	100.00	140.00
☐1955	60.00	85.00
☐1956	50.00	70.00
☐1957	60.00	85.00
☐1958	60.00	80.00
☐1959	24.00	35.00
☐1960	16.00	22.00
☐1961	14.00	20.00
☐1962	18.00	25.00
☐1963	16.50	23.00
☐1964	11.00	17.00
☐1965 Special Mint Set	5.00	8.00
☐1966 Special Mint Set	5.00	7.00
☐1967 Special Mint Set	8.00	11.00
☐1968	4.00	6.00
☐1969	5.00	7.00
☐1970	14.00	20.00
☐1971	5.00	6.00
☐1972	4.00	5.00
☐1973	7.00	12.00
☐1974	6.00	9.00
☐1975	6.00	7.00
☐1976	6.00	8.00
☐1976S (25¢, 50¢, $1 only—no 1¢, 5¢, 10¢)	10.00	12.00
☐1977	6.00	8.00
☐1978	6.00	8.00
☐1979	4.00	6.50
☐1980	5.00	7.00
☐1981	8.00	12.00
☐1984	12.00	18.00
☐1985	15.00	22.00
☐1986	22.00	36.00
☐1987	6.00	9.00
☐1988	15.00	21.00
☐1989	6.00	9.00

*No mint sets were sold this year, only proof sets. Many mint sets were, however, assembled by dealers and placed in packaging similar to that of the Mint's. In cases where the coins in these privately assembled mint sets are strictly uncirculated, they will have a slight premium value.

SPECIAL REPORT ON BU ROLLS

BU rolls are now among the most talked about and heavily traded of all numismatic items. The total quantity of coins sold in rolls far exceeds all other coin sales combined. They have become the favorite numismatic investment among thousands of investors. To a lesser extent they are also bought by collectors, though sales to collectors have not appreciably increased.

What is a BU roll? The term BU, which has been used in coin collecting for more than two generations, stands for *Brilliant Uncirculated.* Some define it as Best Uncirculated, or Bright Uncirculated. Regardless of the way one interprets it, the important point about a BU coin is that it is uncirculated. Its condition grade is a minimum of MS-60 on the ANA grading scale. It may be higher than MS-60 but in buying rolls advertised only as BU, with no grade specified, do not expect any of the coins to grade higher than MS-60. It is possible to get BU rolls in MS-63 and MS-65 but, of course, the price is higher.

A roll comprises coins of the same denomination and, almost always, the same type. If Indian Head and Lincoln Cents were mixed in the same roll this would be advertised as a "mixed roll." Most BU roll trading occurs in *solid date rolls.* A solid date roll is one in which all the coins are of the same date and same place of manufacture: 1946-D, 1948-S, 1982-P, etc. The number of coins in a roll varies by denomination: Cents, fifty coins; Nickels, forty; Dimes, fifty; Quarters, forty; Half Dollars, twenty. The roll may be wrapped in bank paper or contained in a lucite holder.

All rolls passing through the coin market are "assembled rolls." They were not put together at the Mint but by coin dealers, collectors, and investors. The possibility always exists that a circulated coin might have slipped in, so it is advisable to examine all the coins in a roll.

Because new rolls are constantly being made up and old ones broken, the scarcity factor is difficult to determine. While the vast majority of BU rolls are of twentieth century coins, they are also available for most of the common-date coins of the late nineteenth century as well. Generally they are not available for scarce coins of the nineteenth century, nor even for some scarce dates of the twentieth. If the coin is very common, with a mintage of 100 million or more, there will be literally thousands of BU rolls passing through the market. It may seem paradoxical, but the common coins are often preferred by investors, who feel that their low prices make them an ideal speculation. Some rolls can be had for less than $1, such as late-date Lincolns, and these too are bought by investors. At the other end of the spectrum are rolls bringing $7000 or more, such as the 1941-S Walking Liberty Half Dollar. Rolls, like single coins, come in all price ranges.

It is important to note that the price of a BU roll does not necessarily reflect the value of the same coin when sold singly. You cannot multiply the single coin price to arrive at the roll price. BU rolls find their own value levels in trading, and the price can sometimes be quite far out of line with that of the individual coin. There are various reasons for this, chiefly tied to supply and demand. At any given time there may be a huge surplus of certain BU rolls on the market, or such an extreme shortage that dealers cannot buy them fast enough to fill orders. The availability of any coin in BU rolls may be a very different story than its availability as a single specimen. Also, investors will frequently "bandwagon" a group of coins in BU rolls, all buying the same rolls. They do not buy the single specimens, so the shortage of supply is not reflected in single specimens. This is becoming more pronounced in today's coin market, now that BU rolls have become so popular with investors. Of course, the dealers also influence the prices. When a dealer is buying common to medium-scarce coins for his stock, he prefers to buy in rolls, regardless of whether he intends to sell the coins in rolls or individually. It is more convenient for him and, in many cases, more economical.

The following prices for BU rolls were current at the time of going to press.

Lincoln Cents— 1935 $95.00 • 1935D $200.00 • 1935S $450.00 • 1936D $150.00 • 1936S $150.00 • 1938D $90.00 • 1938S $75.00 • 1940S $40.00 • 1941D $120.00 • 1941S $90.00 • 1943 $35.00 • 1943D $50.00 • 1943S $85.00 • 1944D $13.00 • 1944S $14.00 • 1945 $25.00 • 1945D $18.00 • 1945S $16.00 • 1946 $10.00 • 1946D $800.00 • 1946S $15.00 • 1949 $25.00 • 1949D $25.00 • 1949S $70.00 • 1950 $23.00 • 1950S $24.00 • 1951 $24.00 • 1951S $29.00 • 1952 $20.00 • 1952S $24.00 • 1953S $12.00 • 1954 $17.00 • 1955S $12.00 • 1960 SM DT $80.00 • 1960D SM DT $1.50 • 1970S SM DT $800.00.

Buffalo Nickels— 1934 $3500.00 • 1935 $1500.00 • 1935S $2500.00 • 1936D $1400.00 • 1936S $1600.00 • 1937 $900.00 • 1937D $1000.00 • 1937S $1000.00.

Jefferson Nickels— 1939 $50.00 • 1939D $1600.00 • 1939S $800.00 • 1940D $80.00 • 1940S $80.00 • 1941D $75.00 • 1941S $90.00 • 1942P TY2 $350.00 • 1942S $300.00 • 1943 $140.00 • 1943D $90.00 • 1943S $150.00 • 1944 $160.00 • 1944D $300.00 • 1944S $240.00 • 1945 $170.00 • 1945D $140.00 • 1945S $100.00 • 1950 $40.00 • 1950D $200.00 • 1951S $50.00.

Mercury Dimes— 1934 $1900.00 • 1934D $4000.00 • 1935 $1200 • 1935D $3500.00 • 1935S $1700.00 • 1937 $1000.00 • 1937D $2000.00 • 1939 $900.00 • 1939D $950.00.

Roosevelt Dimes— 1946D $70.00 • 1946S $125.00 • 1947 $80.00 • 1947D $100.00 • 1947S $100.00 • 1948 $275.00 • 1948D $240.00 • 1948S $210.00 • 1949 $650.00 • 1949D $300.00 • 1949S $1100.00 • 1950 $150.00 • 1950D $125.00 • 1950S $650.00 • 1951S $400.00 • 1952S $160.00 • 1953S $40.00 • 1955 $60.00 • 1955D $38.00 • 1955S $40.00 • 1958 $42.00 • 1958D $30.00.

Washington Quarters— 1934 $1400.00 • 1934D $5000.00 • 1935 $1100.00 • 1935D $5000.00 • 1935S $4000.00 • 1936 $1000.00 • 1936S $3650.00 • 1937 $1100.00 • 1937D $1600.00 • 1937S $4900.00 • 1938 $2300.00 • 1938S $2300.00 • 1939 $700.00 • 1939D $1300.00 • 1939S $2400.00 • 1940 $600.00 • 1940D $2400.00 • 1941 $240.00 • 1941D $800.00 • 1941S $700.00 • 1942 $280.00 • 1942D $450.00 • 1942S $3200.00 • 1943 $200.00 • 1943D $600.00 • 1943S $1200.00 • 1944D $350.00 • 1944S $350.00 • 1945 $200.00 • 1945D $300.00 • 1945S $240.00 • 1946 $200.00 • 1946S $190.00.

Walking Liberty Halves— 1937 $1800.00 • 1937D $4500.00 • 1937S $3800.00 • 1938 $2400.00 • 1939 $2400.00 • 1939D $2000.00 • 1939S $3200.00 • 1940 $2100.00 • 1940S $1700.00 • 1941 $1600.00 • 1941D $2800.00 • 1942 $1500.00 • 1942D $3000.00 • 1942S $2800.00.

Franklin Halves— 1948 $600.00 • 1948D $300.00 • 1949 $1200.00 • 1949D $1000.00 • 1949S $2900.00 • 1950 $1200.00 • 1950D $600.00 • 1951 $380.00 • 1951D $900.00 • 1951S $900.00 • 1952 $250.00 • 1952D $250.00 • 1952S $800.00 • 1953 $600.00 • 1953D $300.00 • 1953S $500.00 • 1954 $200.00 • 1954D $150.00 • 1954S $225.00.

Kennedy Halves— 1964 $50.00 • 1964D $50.00 • 1965 $30.00.

COIN INVESTING

Coin investing from a purely speculative point of view—buying coins solely for the purpose of making money on them—is no longer confined to professional dealers. In fact, it is likely that the volume of coins bought for profit by the public exceeds purchases by dealers. Investment groups have sprung up, in which investors band together and contribute sums toward the purchase of expensive rarities that they could not individually afford. They then own "shares" of the coin, shares which, of course, pay no dividends until the coin is sold. There are coin investment clubs and dealers who make a specialty of "investment parcels," sometimes with a guarantee to buy back the coins at full cost or a slight advance after a stated period of time.

This kind of coin investment thrives regardless of gold and silver bullion prices. It concentrates upon coins of established numismatic popularity, in VF or better condition.

It is undeniable that coin investing offers the potential for very satisfactory capital growth, based on past market performances. Frank Pick of Barron's Magazine went so far as to call rare coins "the number one hedge against inflation." The following increases in average retail values of certain coins (not all of them terribly rare by any means) from 1948 to 1989 can be matched by few commodities or other types of investments:

	MS-60 1948 value	MS-60 1991 value
1853 Half Dime w/arrows	1.50	380.00
1880 $3 Gold	50.00	4100.00
1804 Half Cent	16.50	775.00
1901 Quarter	4.00	400.00
1864 2¢ Piece	1.00	560.00

As is clearly evident, these coins are not all extremely old, nor are they all made of precious metal. It should not be assumed that *every* U.S. coin has advanced at this rate, which is certainly not the case. Most, however, have demonstrated healthy price jumps.

There are many questions the potential investor should ask before plunging ahead.

Is coin investing "safe"?

No investment is 100% safe. In numismatics the safer investments are coins that are not valued chiefly for their metallic content. This shouldn't be taken to mean gold and silver coins are bad investments. They can be quite the reverse, provided coins are chosen in which the numismatic value is greater than the metal value. For example: common-date silver dollars are not good speculative investments. Their value is almost entirely in their metal. To gain a worthwhile profit on common-date silver dollars (or any common-date silver coins), silver would need to double its current price. It may do this. But this could take a very long time, during which inflation would probably be rising, and the resulting net gain would be negligible. On the other hand, key-date or key-mark silvers are an attractive investment, as they tend to appreciate at a fairly steady rate regardless of the bullion market's ups and downs. Why? Because of these two important factors:

1. Many investors are buying them.
2. In addition to investors, these coins always have a demand with collectors.

Why have certain coins, whose values inched slowly upward for years, suddenly doubled and tripled in price?

Because of increased investor activity. Coin collectors alone—people buying coins strictly as a hobby with no thought of profit—could never make such sharp impacts on the market. Collectors have an influence and their influence is growing, but investors account for most of the wildly spiraling prices. The more investors, the higher prices will go.

Don't prices come down just as far when investors sell as they were before they bought?

No. It isn't necessary that a coin be scarcer on the market to be more valuable. So long as buying activity is increased, the same coins can keep coming up for sale and still gain in price. Buying activity is the key.

How long must coins be held to show a satisfactory profit?

This depends on what is meant by satisfactory. The question is difficult to answer at any rate because there is no established or reliable growth rate. In a boon year, such as 1979, rare coins in general can double in price in just twelve months. Some even did better. But there have been years, even in the recent past, when the overall rate of increase was less than 20%. It is impossible to forecast what the future holds. This, however, should be taken into account. Just as with any investment, the paper profit on coins is not necessarily the actual profit. For coins to be converted into cash they must be sold and the dealer or agent to whom you sell will not pay the full retail price. When you buy you pay the full retail price but in selling you receive the retail price less the dealer's margin of profit, which is figured into the next sale. Unlike you, the dealer is not interested in holding his coins for years until they appreciate greatly in value. He wants to sell them immediately, as soon as they reach his hands, and would rather have a 20% profit on a coin today than wait a year and sell it for much more. The margin of profit depends on the type of coin and its value. For a popular U.S. key coin worth $1,000 in uncirculated condition, which the dealer knows he will have no trouble selling quickly, you are likely to be paid as much as 80% of the retail value, especially if you sell at a time of strong demand. If the coin is not so popular, or is less than VF in condition, the dealer will probably pay from 60% to 70% of his retail selling price.

You can calculate your potential success as an investor based upon this situation *plus* the rate of inflation. Obviously, future trends taken by the inflation rate are very difficult to predict. Assuming it to be 10% annually over the next five years, this would present the following prospects:

Coin bought for $1,000 in 1986	$1,000
Coin increases to $5,000 by 1991, coin is sold for $5,000 less 20%	$4,000
Inflation has reduced buying power of the dollar by 25%, so your $4,000 becomes.	$1,000
net profit	$3,000

This is a very simplistic example which should not be taken too seriously. It merely shows how to operate the arithmetic.

Assuming one has decided to invest in coins, should he trust his own abilities or rely on the services of a numismatic broker?

While brokers are of invaluable aid to persons uninformed about coins and the coin market, there is no question but that a well-educated investor can do as well, or better, on his own. Often, "investment parcels" made up by so-called brokers (a title that can be used indiscriminately, without license) consist of coins that a broker, in his regular trading as a coin dealer, was unable to sell profitably. The likelihood of their being sound investments is slim. If you need expert advice, a reputable dealer is usually the best source, one to whom you can speak personally. If you purchase good key coins from his stock in uncirculated condition they are likely to prove as good an investment as any broker could supply.

What price range should the investor buy in? If I have $1,000 to spend, should I buy a single $1,000 coin or five for $200? Or ten for $100?

There is no established "best way" in this situation. Generally, a $1,000 coin with a proven record of growth would be a more attractive investment than several coins of lower value. Selection of the coins to buy is more important than their price range. You must confine yourself to VF or Uncirculated only. It is true that many early coins are not available in such high grades of condition but these are not considered prime investment pieces. Be careful that the coins are not overgraded and that you aren't buying above the market. Shop around and compare prices but don't take too long doing this: the price may go up.

Do we advise coin investment? We neither advise nor discourage it. The purpose of this book is to point out the realities of buying and selling coins and provide potential buyers (investors and collectors) with the information they need to make their own decisions.

PRIMARY METALS

COPPER

Copper has the distinction of use in more U.S. coins than any other metal. In fact there has only been one coin in U.S. history—the 1943 cent—which did not contain copper. Copper was used in its pure state for the early Half Cent and Large Cent; alloyed into bronze for the later Small Cent; alloyed with nickel for the 5¢ piece; and, usually in a 1-to-9 ratio, as an alloy metal for all our silver and gold coins from the eighteenth to twentieth centuries. The most notable use of copper for our coins was in the Half Cent and Large Cent. As these coins were entirely unalloyed, they show the true beauty of pure copper, many specimens having toned to remarkable shades of red, yellow, burgundy, violet, orange, and virtually every known color. A brief copper shortage during World War II, when it became a vital material in war production, resulted in the non-copper 1943 cent, as well as a reduction in the copper content of 5¢ pieces for several years. Inflation and the heavy industrial demand for copper made it necessary, in 1982, for the cent's composition to be changed to zinc with a copper coating.

SILVER

From the earliest days of the Mint, silver was regarded as the chief metal for coins in general circulation. It was used in coins having face values from 1¢ to $1, those of higher value being struck in gold. Problems arose during the administration of Thomas Jefferson, when silver bullion carried a higher value abroad than in the U.S. Huge quantities of our silver coins were exported by speculators, for the purpose of melting. This brought about a long suspension of the silver $1. Then in 1965, the rising market price of silver in both the U.S. and Europe prompted its removal from the 10¢ and 25¢. It remained in the 50¢ in reduced quantity, but was later removed from that coin, too. Silver has traded for as much as $50 per ounce on the bullion market (early 1980) and currently is in the neighborhood of $6 to $7.

GOLD

The most glamorous of the metals used in U.S. coinage, gold was employed by the Mint in striking coins of $1, $2.50, $3, $4, $5, $10 and $20 denominations, as well as a commemorative coin with $50 face value. The $10 gold piece, struck for more than 100 years, was called an Eagle, and its subdivisions were similarly named: Quarter Eagle ($2.50) and Half Eagle ($5), with the $20 termed Double Eagle. The standard fineness for all these coins, during most of their years of manufacture, was .900 with an alloying of .100 copper to give stability. Though all gold denominations were available for general circulation, their actual use in circulation became limited after the Civil War, when paper currency was introduced. The Great Depression of this century caused President Roosevelt to halt all striking of gold coins and to "call in" all gold coins for redemption (Gold Recall Act of 1933). Prohibition against private ownership of gold was removed in the presidency of Gerald Ford, resulting in its widespread purchase by investors and others. In January 1980, gold was being traded for as much as $800 per troy ounce. At the time of compiling this edition, the price is approximately $450.

SILVER COIN VALUE CHART
Prices Reflect Melt Value of Individual Coins

Silver Price Per Ounce	Amount of Pure Silver	5.00	10.00	15.00	20.00	25.00	30.00	35.00	40.00	45.00	50.00	55.00	60.00	Change in Value per Dollar
1942-45 5¢ U.S.	.05626 oz.	.28	.56	.85	1.13	1.41	1.69	1.97	2.25	2.54	2.82	3.10	3.38	.056
1965-70 U.S. 50¢ (40%)	.14792 oz.	.74	1.48	2.22	2.96	3.70	4.44	5.18	5.92	6.66	7.40	8.14	8.88	.148
U.S. $1.00 (40%)	.31625 oz.	1.58	3.16	4.75	6.33	7.91	9.49	11.07	12.65	14.24	15.82	17.40	18.98	.316
1964 & Earlier U.S. 10¢	.07234 oz.	.36	.72	1.09	1.45	1.81	2.17	2.54	2.90	3.26	3.62	3.98	4.34	.072
1964 & Earlier U.S. 25¢	.18084 oz.	.90	1.80	2.72	3.62	4.53	5.43	6.33	7.24	8.14	9.05	9.95	10.85	.18
1964 & Earlier U.S. 50¢	.36169 oz.	1.81	3.62	5.43	7.24	9.05	10.85	12.66	14.47	16.28	18.09	19.90	21.71	.362
1935 & Earlier U.S. $1	.77344 oz.	3.87	7.73	11.61	15.47	19.34	23.21	27.07	30.94	34.81	38.68	42.54	46.41	.772

Dealers who purchase silver coins to be melted normally pay 15% to 25% under melt value in order to cover their cost of handling.

GOLD COIN VALUE CHART
Prices Reflect Melt Value of Individual Coins

Gold Price Per Ounce	Amount of Pure Gold	200.00	300.00	400.00	500.00	550.00	600.00	650.00	700.00	800.00	900.00	1000.00	Change in Value per Dollar
U.S. $1.00	.04837 oz.	9.68	14.52	19.35	24.19	26.61	29.03	31.44	33.86	38.70	43.54	48.37	.048
U.S. $2.50	.12094 oz.	24.19	36.29	48.38	60.47	66.52	72.57	78.62	84.66	96.76	108.85	120.94	.121
U.S. $3.00	.14512 oz.	29.03	43.54	58.05	72.56	79.82	87.08	94.33	101.59	116.10	130.61	145.12	.145
U.S. $5.00	.24187 oz.	48.38	72.57	96.75	120.94	133.03	145.13	157.22	169.31	193.50	217.69	241.87	.242
U.S. $10.00	.48375 oz.	96.75	145.13	193.50	241.88	266.07	290.25	314.44	338.63	387.00	435.38	483.75	.484
U.S. $20.00	.96750 oz.	193.50	290.25	387.00	483.75	532.13	580.50	628.88	677.25	774.00	870.75	967.50	.967

Dealers normally purchase U.S. Gold Coins for a premium over melt. As an example, with Gold at $635.00/ounce you could expect a dealer to pay $700.00 for a common dated twenty dollar gold coin in extremely fine or better condition.

WEIGHTS AND MEASURES

WEIGHTS OF U.S. COINS

DENOMINATION	DATE OF ISSUE	WEIGHT GRAINS	WT. TOL. + OR − GRAINS
Half Cent	1793-1795	104.0	
	1796-1857	84.0	
Large Cent	1793-1795	208.0	
	1795-1857	168.0	
Small Cent	1856-1864	72.0	2.0
	1864-	48.0	2.0
	1943	42.5	2.0
Two Cent	1864-1873	96.0	2.0
Three Cent Nic.	1865-1889	30.0	
Three Cent Sil.	1851-1854	12.345	
	1854-1873	11.574	
Half Dime	1794-1837	20.8	
	1837-1853	20.625	
	1853-1873	19.2	
Five Cents	1866-	77.16	3.0
Dime	1796-1837	41.6	
	1837-1853	41.25	1.5
	1853-1873	38.4	1.5
	1873-1964	38.58	1.5
	1965-	35.0	1.5
Twenty Cent	1875-1878	77.162	
Quarter	1796-1838	104.0	
	1838-1853	103.09	3.0
	1853-1873	95.99	3.0
	1873-1964	96.45	3.0
	1965-	87.5	3.0
Half Dollar	1794-1836	208.0	
	1836-1853	206.17	4.0
	1853-1873	192.0	4.0
	1873-1964	192.9	4.0
	1965-1970	177.5	4.0
	1971-	175.0	4.0
	1976S (Sil.)	177.5	4.0
Silver Dollar	1794-1803	416.0	
	1840-1935	412.5	6.0
Clad Dollar	1971-	350.0	8.0
40% Silver	1971-1976	379.5	8.0
Trade Dollar	1873-1885	420.0	
Gold Dollar 1	1849-1854	25.8	0.25
Gold Dollar 2	1854-1856	25.8	0.25
Gold Dollar 3	1865-1889	25.8	0.25
$2½ Gold	1796-1834	67.5	0.25
	1834-1929	64.5	0.25
$3 Gold	1854-1889	77.4	0.25
$5 Gold	1795-1834	135.0	0.25
	1834-1929	129.0	0.25
$10 Gold	1795-1834	270.0	0.50
	1834-1933	258.0	0.50
$20 Gold	1849-1933	516.0	0.50

1 Gram = 15.432 grains

FAST-FIND COIN REFERENCE INDEX

JOIN US!

Application for Membership

Check one: □ Reg. □ Jr. □ Assoc. □ Life □ Club

Check one: □ Mr. □ Mrs. □ Ms. □ Club

Name (please print and use first name)

Street

City

State | Zip Code

Birth Date | Occupation

ANA Bylaws require the publication of each application. If you DO NOT wish your STREET address published, please check this box. □

I herewith make application for membership in the American Numismatic Association, subject to the Bylaws of said Association. I also agree to abide by the Code of Ethics adopted by the Association.

Signature of Applicant | Date

Signature of Proposer (optional) | ANA No.

Signature of Parent or Guardian
(Must sign for Junior applicants)

To charge to your credit card, please complete the following:

Account No. (All Digits) □ MasterCard □ Visa

Exp. Date of Card / MasterCard Interbank No.

DUES

Regular (adult)—*U.S. only*	$ 26*
Regular (adult)—*all other countries*	28*
Club—*any country*	30*
Junior (11-17 years old)	11
Associate (child or spouse of R or LM member living at member's address)	4
Life (adult individual) *Installment, $60 with application,** plus $25 per month for 12 months*	350
Life (club)	$1250

* **Add $6 application fee, first year only**

** Includes $10 bookkeeping fee, deducted from final payment if made within 90 days of application. Life Membership is not effective until full $350 fee is paid.

Nonmember annual subscription—*U.S. only* $28

Subscription—*all other countries* $33

Foreign applications must be accompanied by U.S. funds drawn on a U.S. bank.

Send your application to:

American Numismatic Association
P.O. Box 2366
Colorado Springs, CO 80901

The HOUSE OF COLLECTIBLES Series

☐ Please send me the following price guides—
☐ I would like the most current edition of the books listed below.

THE OFFICIAL PRICE GUIDES TO:

☐ 753-3	**American Folk Art** (ID) 1st Ed.	$14.95
☐ 784-3	**Silver & Silverplate** (ID) 6th Ed.	12.95
☐ 513-1	**Antique Clocks** 3rd Ed.	10.95
☐ 091-1	**Antique & Modern Dolls** (ID) 4th Ed.	12.95
☐ 287-6	**Antique & Modern Firearms** 6th Ed.	11.95
☐ 792-4	**Antique & Modern Teddy Bears** 1st Ed.	10.95
☐ 805-X	**Antiques & Collectibles** (ID) 11th Ed.	12.95
☐ 289-2	**Antique Jewelry** 5th Ed.	11.95
☐ 362-7	**Art Deco** (ID) 1st Ed.	14.95
☐ 447-X	**Arts & Crafts: American Decorative Arts, 1894–1923** (ID) 1st Ed.	12.95
☐ 539-5	**Beer Cans & Collectibles** 4th Ed.	7.95
☐ 521-2	**Bottles Old & New** 10th Ed.	10.95
☐ 532-8	**Carnival Glass** 2nd Ed.	10.95
☐ 295-7	**Collectible Cameras** 2nd Ed.	10.95
☐ 548-4	**Collectibles of the '50s & '60s** 1st Ed.	9.95
☐ 803-3	**Collectible Toys** (ID) 5th Ed.	10.95
☐ 531-X	**Collector Cars** 7th Ed.	12.95
☐ 538-7	**Collector Handguns** 4th Ed.	14.95
☐ 748-7	**Collector Knives** 9th Ed.	12.95
☐ 361-9	**Collector Plates** 5th Ed.	11.95
☐ 296-5	**Collector Prints** 7th Ed.	12.95
☐ 787-8	**Costume Jewelry** (ID) 1st Ed.	10.95
☐ 001-6	**Depression Glass** 2nd Ed.	9.95
☐ 589-1	**Fine Art** 1st Ed.	19.95
☐ 311-2	**Glassware** 3rd Ed.	10.95
☐ 243-4	**Hummel Figurines & Plates** 6th Ed.	10.95
☐ 523-9	**Kitchen Collectibles** 2nd Ed.	10.95
☐ 772-X	**Lunch Box Collectibles** 1st Ed.	9.95
☐ 080-6	**Memorabilia of Elvis Presley and The Beatles** 1st Ed.	10.95
☐ 291-4	**Military Collectibles** 5th Ed.	11.95
☐ 788-6	**Movie Memorabilia** (ID) 1st Ed.	9.95
☐ 525-5	**Music Collectibles** 6th Ed.	11.95
☐ 313-9	**Old Books & Autographs** 7th Ed.	11.95
☐ 298-1	**Oriental Collectibles** 3rd Ed.	11.95
☐ 820-3	**Overstreet Comic Book** 20th Ed.	14.95
☐ 522-0	**Paperbacks & Magazines** 1st Ed.	10.95
☐ 297-3	**Paper Collectibles** 5th Ed.	10.95
☐ 809-2	***Peanuts*®Collectibles** 1st Ed.	9.95
☐ 744-4	**Political Memorabilia** 1st Ed.	10.95
☐ 785-1	**Pottery & Porcelain** (ID) 7th Ed.	12.95
☐ 524-7	**Radio, TV & Movie Memorabilia** 3rd Ed.	11.95
☐ 819-X	**Records** 9th Ed.	16.95
☐ 763-0	**Royal Doulton** 6th Ed.	12.95
☐ 280-9	**Science Fiction & Fantasy Collectibles** 2nd Ed.	10.95
☐ 747-9	**Sewing Collectibles** 1st Ed.	8.95
☐ 358-9	**Star Trek/Star Wars Collectibles** 2nd Ed.	8.95
☐ 808-4	**Watches** 10th Ed.	16.95
☐ 248-5	**Wicker** 3rd Ed.	10.95

THE OFFICIAL:

☐ 760-6	**Directory to U.S. Flea Markets** 2nd Ed.	$5.95
☐ 365-1	**Encyclopedia of Antiques** 1st Ed.	9.95
☐ 369-4	**Guide to Buying and Selling Antiques** 1st Ed.	9.95
☐ 414-3	**Identification Guide to Early American Furniture** 1st Ed.	9.95
☐ 413-5	**Identification Guide to Glassware** 1st Ed.	9.95
☐ 412-7	**Identification Guide to Pottery & Porcelain** 1st Ed.	9.95
☐ 415-1	**Identification Guide to Victorian Furniture** 1st Ed.	9.95

THE OFFICIAL (SMALL SIZE) PRICE GUIDES TO:

☐ 309-0	**Antiques & Flea Markets** 4th Ed.	4.95
☐ 269-8	**Antique Jewelry** 3rd Ed.	4.95
☐ 807-6	**Baseball Cards** 10th Ed.	5.95
☐ 647-2	**Bottles** 3rd Ed.	4.95
☐ 544-1	**Cars & Trucks** 3rd Ed.	5.95
☐ 519-0	**Collectible Americana** 2nd Ed.	4.95
☐ 294-9	**Collectible Records** 3rd Ed.	4.95
☐ 306-6	**Dolls** 4th Ed.	4.95
☐ 800-9	**Football Cards** 9th Ed.	5.95
☐ 540-9	**Glassware** 3rd Ed.	4.95
☐ 801-7	**Hockey & Basketball Cards** 1st Ed.	5.95
☐ 526-3	**Hummels** 4th Ed.	4.95
☐ 279-5	**Military Collectibles** 3rd Ed.	4.95
☐ 799-1	**Overstreet Comic Book Companion** 3rd Ed.	4.95
☐ 278-7	**Pocket Knives** 3rd Ed.	4.95
☐ 527-1	**Scouting Collectibles** 4th Ed.	4.95
☐ 494-1	**Star Trek/Star Wars Collectibles** 3rd Ed.	3.95
☐ 088-1	**Toys** 5th Ed.	4.95

THE OFFICIAL BLACKBOOK PRICE GUIDES OF:

☐ 823-8	**U.S. Coins** 29th Ed.	5.95
☐ 822-X	**U.S. Paper Money** 23rd Ed.	5.95
☐ 821-1	**U.S. Postage Stamps** 13th Ed.	5.95

THE OFFICIAL INVESTORS GUIDE TO BUYING & SELLING:

☐ 534-4	**Gold, Silver & Diamonds** 2nd Ed.	12.95
☐ 535-2	**Gold Coins** 2nd Ed.	12.95
☐ 536-0	**Silver Coins** 2nd Ed.	12.95
☐ 537-9	**Silver Dollars** 2nd Ed.	12.95

THE OFFICIAL NUMISMATIC GUIDE SERIES:

☐ 254-X	**The Official Guide to Detecting Counterfeit Money** 2nd Ed.	7.95
☐ 257-4	**The Official Guide to Mint Errors** 4th Ed.	7.95

SPECIAL INTEREST SERIES:

☐ 506-9	**From Hearth to Cookstove** 3rd Ed.	17.95

		TOTAL

SEE REVERSE SIDE FOR ORDERING INSTRUCTIONS